SALT Implications for Arms Control in the 1970s

SALT Implications for Arms Control in the 1970s

WILLIAM R. KINTNER

and

ROBERT L. PFALTZGRAFF, JR.

Editors

University of Pittsburgh Press

Library of Congress Catalog Card Number 72–77192
ISBN 0–8229–3249–0
Copyright © 1973, University of Pittsburgh Press
All rights reserved
Media Directions Inc., London
Manufactured in the United States of America

Part VI, "The Strategic Arms Limitation Agreements of 1972: Implications for International Security," appeared in slightly different form in *Orbis,* XVI (Summer 1972). Used by permission of the Foreign Policy Research Institute.

Grateful acknowledgment is made to the following for permission to quote material that appears in this book:

The Brookings Institution for a quotation from *Sequel to Bretton Woods: A Proposal to Reform the World Monetary System*. A staff paper by Lawrence B. Krause, © 1971 The Brookings Institution, Washington, D.C., pp. 47–48.

The New York Times Company, for quotations from the *New York Times,* June 24 and September 29, 1971. © 1971 by The New York Times Company. Reprinted by permission.

Seminar, for quotations from S. Gopal, "The Choice," *Seminar,* no. 96 (August 1967).

A FOREIGN POLICY RESEARCH INSTITUTE BOOK

Contents

Tables

Preface

ON MAY 26, 1972, the United States and the Soviet Union signed a treaty for the limitation of antiballistic missiles and an interim agreement on offensive weapons. Whatever the historic significance of these accords themselves in relations among the superpowers, they represent a significant phase of negotiations on strategic arms, which will be a recurring feature in international diplomacy in the 1970s.

This volume is an outgrowth of the Fifth International Arms Control Symposium, held in October 1971, whose focus was the strategic arms limitation talks (SALT) that had been in progress between the United States and the Soviet Union since the autumn of 1969. This fifth Symposium assembled a distinguished group of scholars and practitioners in the field of national security affairs from the United States and abroad. Among the overseas participants were experts from Australia, Britain, Canada, France, Germany, India, Israel, Japan, the Netherlands, and the Soviet Union. The U.S. participants included persons from twenty-one universities and eleven private research organizations. The Fifth International Arms Control Symposium was held in Philadelphia in October 1971 under the joint sponsorship of The Fletcher School of Law and Diplomacy, Tufts University; the University of Pennsylvania; the University of Pittsburgh; Saint Joseph's College; and Beaver College. In addition, many departments of the U.S. government were represented, including the U.S. Senate, the National Security Council, the Department of State, the Arms Control and Disarmament Agency, the Joint Chiefs of Staff, the Air Force, the Department of Defense (International Security Affairs), and the Advanced Research Projects Agency.

Among the topics considered at the conference were the rationale for superpower arms control agreement; the effects of the SALT for international politics in the changing international system of the 1970s; the implications of technological innovation for arms control; the nature of the arms control bargaining process; the SALT, proliferation, and international security; and the implications of success or failure of the SALT for international security.

The Fifth International Symposium was the latest of a series of meetings on arms control convened during the past decade. The first meeting was held in December 1962 in Ann Arbor, Michigan, and was sponsored by the Bendix Corporation and the University of Michigan. In March 1964 seven Philadelphia-area colleges sponsored a Philadelphia Collegiate Disarmament Conference. Both of these symposia provided a *tour d'horizon* of the problems of arms control of the early 1960s. The Third International Arms Control Conference, held in April 1966 in Philadelphia and cosponsored by the Bendix Corporation, Saint Joseph's College, and the University of Pennsylvania, focused on arms control topics that were likely to remain crucial for the remainder of the decade of the sixties and into the 1970s. These included the implications of the Sino-Soviet split, the issue of nuclear weapons proliferation, the impact of East-West arms control negotiations on NATO, and the question of ballistic missile defense. From the papers presented at the Philadelphia Collegiate Disarmament Conference in 1964 a volume entitled *The Prospects for Arms Control,* edited by James E. Dougherty with John F. Lehman, Jr. (New York: MacFadden-Bartell Corporation, 1965), was published. Another volume, *Arms Control for the Late Sixties,* coedited by James E. Dougherty and J. F. Lehman, Jr. (Princeton: D. Van Nostrand Company, Inc., 1967), was an outgrowth of the Third International Arms Control Conference.

The Fourth International Arms Control Symposium, with the strategic arms limitation talks (SALT) as the focus, was held in Philadelphia in October 1969 under the joint sponsorship of Saint Joseph's College, the University of Pennsylvania, and the University of Pittsburgh. Several topics directly related to the then impending negotiations on strategic arms limitation were discussed. These included problems of inspection and verification, communication and bargaining, domestic constraints for both the United States and the Soviet Union, and potential implications of SALT for superpower-ally relationships. From this symposium came a series of papers, many of which were published in journals such as *Arms Control and National Security, War/Peace Report, Asia Survey,* and *Freedom at Issue.*

The Fifth International Arms Control Symposium represented an effort to examine the evolution of the SALT since the beginning of negotiations in November 1969. The present volume contains the papers presented at the symposium, as well as an analysis of the discussion among the participants that followed each panel session.

The volume begins with the keynote speech delivered by W. W. Rostow on the opening night of the conference. The subject of this speech was "The Politics of Arms Control or How to Make Nuclear Weapons Wither Away." In many respects this speech reflects the views on strategic arms limitation that were predominant during the period of the sixties. While this volume was in the process of preparation, the United States and the Soviet Union signed the treaty in Moscow for the limitation of antiballistic missiles and the agreement placing limits on strategic offensive weapons. We, the editors, have prepared as the final chapter of this book our own analysis of the Moscow agreements and have related this analysis to the discussions held during the Fifth International Arms Control Symposium. For the interpretations contained in this concluding chapter, the editors accept sole responsibility.

Many persons contributed to the Fifth International Arms Control Symposium. The editors wish to thank the presidents of the sponsoring institutions: Dr. Edward D. Gates, President, Beaver College; the Very Reverend Terrence Toland, President, Saint Joseph's College; Dr. Burton Hallowell, President, Tufts University; Dr. Martin Meyerson, President, University of Pennsylvania; and Dr. Wesley Posvar, Chancellor, University of Pittsburgh.

The members of the advisory board provided invaluable guidance and assistance in the planning of the symposium. Advisory board members included Professor Joseph Coffey, Associate Dean, Graduate School of Public and International Affairs, University of Pittsburgh; Professor James E. Dougherty, Executive Vice President, Saint Joseph's College; Professor Geoffrey Kemp, The Fletcher School of Law and Diplomacy, Tufts University; Professor Diane A. Pfaltzgraff, Beaver College; Mr. Amrom Katz, Consultant, the RAND Corporation; and the editors of this volume.

To Christopher M. Lehman and Gene Maffey, Symposium Coordinators, and to Donna Brodsky, we owe a special debt of gratitude. They played an indispensable role both in the detailed administration of the symposium and in the logistical planning for bringing together the more than one hundred participants for a three-day period. They received valuable assistance from Gerald West during the symposium.

In the preparation of this volume, the editors wish to thank William D. Rossiter, The Fletcher School of Law and Diplomacy, who was primarily responsible for preparing the summaries of the symposium discussions that are included in this volume and the list of abbreviations and glossary of arms control terms. In completing the symposium discussions, he had help from Christopher M. Lehman, also of The Fletcher School, and Michael Salomon and Charles W. Richardson, Jr., of the University of Pittsburgh. For secretarial assistance, both prior to the symposium and in the preparation of this volume, we are indebted to Barbara Sicherman. Without the administrative assistance provided by the Foreign Policy Research Institute, the successful completion of the detailed planning for the symposium and the publication of this volume would have been difficult.

On behalf of all of those associated with the symposium, the editors acknowledge with appreciation the generous support provided by the William H. Donner Foundation, the Earhart Foundation, the Scaife Family Charitable Trust, and the Thiokol Chemical Corporation.

Finally, the editors express thanks to those who contributed the papers that are included in this volume. Their efforts, together with the expert discussion among the distinguished group of participants, made possible the symposium and this volume, which we hope will contribute to an understanding of the complex problems of arms control as they relate to international security in the changing world of the 1970s.

Introduction: The Politics of Arms Control or How to Make Nuclear Weapons Wither Away

IN PREPARING my statement for this meeting, I dug out of my files a memorandom I delivered to President-elect Kennedy on a cold December morning at his house in Georgetown. It was an account of the Pugwash disarmament talks which had taken place in Moscow between November 27 and December 7, 1960, from which I had recently returned.

The central theme of the formal discussions was set by the Soviet delegation. It was the urgency of a treaty for general and complete disarmament. The American delegation was, of course, less monolithic. Nevertheless, our formal responses centered about the question of how such a treaty might be inspected. Out of the give-and-take came the proposition that the degree of inspection should be related to the degree of disarmament. The Soviet delegation challenged the United States to produce a concrete, phased inspection plan to match the stages of a disarmament sequence.

Private discussions with Soviet officials took a somewhat different form. They were less dogmatic about a complete disarmament treaty; but they urged that we convey to the president-elect the simple message: "The Soviet Union is serious about disarmament; our position is not wholly propaganda."

I spent a good deal of time probing, in informal contacts, why these officials might be serious. I reported to the president-elect that I returned "for the first time . . . prepared to contemplate the possibility that there is a component of seriousness in the Soviet message." I then posed the question: "If the message is serious, why?" Here is how I answered the question:

"The Politics of Arms Control or How to Make Nuclear Weapons Wither Away" was presented by W. W. Rostow as the keynote speech at the Fifth International Arms Control Symposium, Philadelphia, Pa., October 15, 1971.

These arguments were adduced for the Soviet position in the various discussions:

—The Nth power problem, centering evidently on China and Germany.

—The danger of accidental war which, it was argued, would rise with the enlargement of the nuclear club.

—The arms race is a technologically precarious dead-end game for the Soviet Union and the United States, which neither can win.

—Disarmament would free resources for domestic purposes and for use in underdeveloped areas.

(Incidentally, Soviet officials were admirably candid in telling us that we must expect unrelenting competition and struggle in the underdeveloped areas, although Soviet policy did not quite make good the temperate threat spoken at the time: "We shall build twenty Aswan Dams.")

I recall this far-off and not very high level affair and these not very remarkable conclusions for a simple reason. In retrospect, it has been the Nth power problem, as it was then called—the question of non-proliferation—rather than arms control in the more conventional sense that has dominated the last eleven years of U.S.-Soviet nuclear diplomacy. The private discussions in Moscow in 1960 correctly reflected the fact that Moscow's primary interest in disarmament arose from the fear of nuclear proliferation. The question of conserving Soviet resources has also been real, and it was reflected in what we could then learn of Soviet thought. But a good deal of what we have faced in recent times, what we face now, and are likely to face in the future is clarified by starting with the question then evidently paramount in Soviet thought: "How can we prevent the further proliferation of nuclear weapons?"

The problems of bilateral U.S.-Soviet arms control negotiations are, in all conscience, complex enough and the stakes intrinsically important enough to justify examination on their own. But it is not accidental that Moscow finally yielded to President Johnson's unrelenting pressure to enter the SALT "in the nearest future" on July 1, 1968 —the day representatives of some fifty nations signed the Non-Proliferation Treaty. The link between the SALT and the Non-Proliferation Treaty is not strictly legal or formal. But Soviet and American authorities knew that the rhetorical pledge made in the context of the Non-Proliferation Treaty had real political meaning, that is, the pledge of the nuclear weapons powers to work toward effective arms control and disarmament.

It simply did not seem credible in either Moscow or Washington that nations capable of producing nuclear weapons would indefinitely forgo that option in a world where an uncontrolled nuclear arms race proceeded between the United States and the Soviet Union. In short, in the past decade the United States and the USSR have concentrated on that kind of disarmament which has consisted in preventing others from manufacturing nuclear weapons; their entrance to the SALT would serve, in part, to support that enterprise in arms control.

II

Against this background, I shall attempt to answer, from our common experience of the past ten years, the question that the Russians obviously had on their minds at Moscow in 1960 and have on their minds today: How can we prevent the proliferation of nuclear weapons beyond their present amply dangerous limits? The answer lies mainly, of course, in the hands of the powers that now possess nuclear weapons and in the kind of environment they create for the nations that have the capacity to produce nuclear weapons but have not done so. These latter nations will not lightly jump the nuclear weapons barrier, and some of them confront important political inhibitions if they should be tempted to do so. But, in the end, I believe the Non-Proliferation Treaty will only be effective if six conditions are satisfied; and these lie mainly in the hands of the nuclear weapons states.

The first condition we have already mentioned, that is, that the United States and the Soviet Union bring their bilateral nuclear arms race under some kind of rational control. The following passage from the preamble to the Non-Proliferation Treaty will have to be taken more seriously than preambles usually are: "Declaring their intention to achieve at the earliest possible date the cessation of the nuclear arms race."

The second is that no nuclear weapons power revive the technique of nuclear blackmail with which Khrushchev experimented in such lively style from his initial sally in Birmingham in April 1956 to the Cuba missile crisis of October 1962. It is not accidental that President Johnson made the following pledge on the occasion of the explosion of the first Chinese Communist nuclear weapon: "Even if Communist China should eventually develop an effective nuclear capability, that capability would have no effect upon the readiness of the United States to respond to requests from Asian nations for help in dealing with Communist Chinese aggression." Then, on October 18 Johnson, in advocating an NPT, added this: "The nations that do not seek national nuclear weapons can be sure that if they need our strong support against some threat of nuclear blackmail, then they will have it." The negotiating history of the Non-Proliferation Treaty required, further, that the Soviet Union, the United Kingdom, and the United States make commitments much like that incorporated in the American statement to the United Nations Security Council of June 17, 1968: "The United States affirms its intention as a permanent member of the United Nations Security Council to seek immediate Security Council action to provide assistance in accordance with the Charter to any non-nuclear weapons state party to the treaty on the nonproliferation of nuclear weapons that is a victim of active aggression or an object of a threat of aggression in which nuclear weapons are used."

I would hope our diplomacy with Peking would underline the meaning of these commitments, not as a threat but as a reminder of the kind of behavior required of all the nuclear weapons powers if the Non-Proliferation Treaty is to become and remain a reality.

Third, we shall have to demonstrate that the distinguished British politician who ran for office in the 1960s on the assertion that even a small national nuclear capability was "a ticket to the top table" was wrong. Since the end of the Berlin and Cuban missile crises of 1961 and 1962, the nuclear question in Europe has abated. The nuclear status of France and Britain has created less tension in Germany and Italy than in the early years of the decade, although I do not believe we have seen the end of the nuclear problem in Europe. But, clearly, the lack of nationally owned nuclear weapons has not prevented Germany from continuing to rise in economic and diplomatic stature; nor has their possession much mitigated the vicissitudes of Great Britain in recent years or enlarged the stature of France vis-à-vis its European partners.

In Asia, however, things are potentially different. The possibility of normalizing relations with Peking began to emerge late in 1967 as the fever of the Cultural Revolution abated and the political leadership turned, after a decade's erratic stagnation, to neglected problems of economic development. All this constitutes an exciting and hopeful possibility for Asia and all humanity, but the return of the prodigal son should not be at the expense of the other less-aberrant members of the family. Specifically, I believe it unwise to grant Communist China the only permanent Security Council seat for Asia.

The Asia of 1971 is not the Asia of 1945. Japan is now once again a full member of the community of nations, and so is India which did not exist as a state in 1945. At the end of the Second World War it was natural for China to be granted the only permanent Security Council seat for Asia; but more than a quarter century later the third industrial power in the world and the second largest nation in the world—and its largest democracy—equally deserve permanent seats on the Security Council. Three seats from Asia, where two-thirds of humanity lives, do not seem excessive to me.

Moreover, Communist China should not be rewarded with a unique permanent Security Council seat for Asia on the grounds that it has managed the not very remarkable feat of producing some thermonuclear weapons; Japan and India could do so as well in a relatively short time. I believe a world in which such countries would feel impelled to do so would be a substantially more dangerous and unstable world than the one in which we now live. Therefore, we all should be exceedingly careful not to grant—or appear to grant—Peking any peculiar political stature in the world community because it chose to go it alone in nuclear matters. If we do, its unique nuclear status in Asia may prove quite transitory.

The fourth condition is a point driven home hard in the course of negotiating the Non-Proliferation Treaty, namely, that nonnuclear weapons states suffer no technological disadvantage thereby. A great deal of work on this point was done in the 1960s. It became interwoven with regional pride and anxiety about industrial espionage when the question of IAEA inspection of EURATOM was raised. Even though that matter is not yet finally settled, I would guess that loyalty to the commitments made in the 1960s by the nuclear weapons states could keep a sense of technological deprivation from becoming a major pressure for nuclear weapons manufacture. But they are commitments that should not be forgotten.

The fifth is a point thus far raised only with respect to Israel, but it could become more general with the passage of time. It is concerned with the pressure to move toward the manufacture of nuclear weapons within a nation systematically harassed by guerrilla aggression across its frontiers. At present the Israeli case appears unique because it alone, among the states now thus harassed, commands the capacity to produce nuclear weapons. But with the passage of time and the forward march of stages of growth, more nations that have been or may be a target of guerrilla aggression across international frontiers will develop a technical base capable of nuclear weapons manufacture. Nations thus harassed, for example, South Korea, Taiwan, and Venezuela—if left unsupported by the international community—are unlikely to accept defeat passively if they develop a capacity to strike back, even if a nuclear riposte promises no more than to pull down the pillars of the temple around them.

I believe that one of the great weaknesses of the international community in the 1960s has been its unwillingness to develop a united front against the technique of aggression called euphemistically "Wars of National Liberation." Continued callousness on this point will, I believe, increasingly have potential nuclear implications, as it already does in the case of Israel.

Finally, there is the question of American reliability. Perhaps only those who have followed intimately the calculus made in Bonn and Jerusalem, Tokyo and New Delhi—and elsewhere—understand how closely the NPT and its future viability hinge on the reliability of the United States as an ally. Inherently there is a simple but profound nationalist difficulty with the NPT. Nations are being asked consciously to deny themselves weapons that they could quite easily produce. And they are being asked to do so at a time when London, Paris, and Peking appear to attach great political value and prestige to those weapons. Nevertheless, there is a rational case for signing the NPT, even in narrow nationalist terms. It is that the deterrent power of the American military establishment-in-being—nuclear and nonnuclear taken together—is vastly greater than any nuclear and nonnuclear military deterrent that could soon be developed in, say, Germany, India, or Japan. And if the decision were made to produce nuclear weapons, the nations concerned would face an extremely awkward and even dangerous interval—an interval when ties with the United States would be weakened but before an alternative deterrent force could be built. For Germany and Japan there would, in addition, be extremely heavy diplomatic pressure from abroad; for India, the danger that Pakistan might invite Chinese Communist nuclear power into the subcontinent.

Nevertheless, the argument for nonproliferation in the non-Communist world has depended in a fundamental way on the reliability of American commitments. Primarily to cover the possibility of American unreliability, the following language was written into the NPT:

Each Party shall in exercising its national sovereignty have the right to withdraw from the Treaty if it decides that extraordinary events, related to the subject matter of this Treaty, have jeopardized the supreme interests of its country. It shall give notice of such withdrawal to all other Parties to the Treaty and to the United Nations Security Council three months in advance. Such notice shall include a statement of the extraordinary events it regards as having jeopardized its supreme interests.

The diplomatic record suggests that the continuity of the American commitment in critical parts of the world will be required if the "supreme national interest" clause of the NPT is not to be raised. (In what I found to be far and away the most interesting passage in Chou En-lai's interview with James Reston of August 9, 1971, Chou did not deny the importance of the American security pact with Japan in keeping Japan from producing nuclear weapons: he simply underlined the extent to which Japan's military capacity was increasing within the framework of the treaty with the United States.)

III

My argument is, then, that the effort of the nuclear weapons states to restrict the size of their club, in a world of rapidly diffusing economic and technological strength, has created a set of imperatives that, I believe, will have to be honored if the Non-Proliferation Treaty is to work over substantial periods of time. These imperatives require not only that Moscow and Washington create a framework of nuclear limitation and stability, but also that nuclear blackmail be forsworn or dealt with by those who committed themselves to deal with it before the Security Council in 1968; that those who command small national nuclear capabilities not be accorded on that account special international political status, that the economic advantages of nuclear technology be made universally available, that the technique of guerrilla warfare conducted across international frontiers be forsworn or dealt with by the international community, and that the security commitments of the United States remain reliable.

In a curious way, the understandable impulse of the nuclear weapons states to limit their number must bring us much closer to stable peace in the world if that impulse is to be fulfilled. The forces that led five nations to produce nuclear weapons were, in various combinations, fear, pride, or ambition of the narrowest and most nationalistic kind. Certainly three—and possibly four—of them were moved, in part, by images of dignity if not grandeur, which the Chinese Communists articulated with force at the peak of the polemical exchange with Moscow in August–September 1963, harking back to the critical days of 1958–59 when the break actually occurred over the nuclear issue:

The Soviet leaders say, how can the Chinese be qualified to manufacture nuclear weapons when they eat watery soup out of a common bowl and do not even have pants to wear?

The Soviet leaders are perhaps too hasty in deriding China for its backwardness. They may or may not have judged right. But in any case, even if we Chinese people are unable to produce an atom bomb for a hundred years, we will neither crawl to the baton of the Soviet leaders nor kneel before the nuclear blackmail of the US imperialists.

The moral . . . is that different people have different aspirations, and it is improper to measure the stature of great men by the yardstick of small men.

But the truth is that it does not take, in Chinese terms, a very "great man" to produce nuclear weapons, and the number of those capable of doing so will clearly expand with the passage of time.

From the beginning, it was clear that there was something humbling about nuclear weapons. In my inaugural lecture at Oxford University in November 1946 I stated: "The great cheapening which has come about in the cost of inflicting human and physical destruction has thrown in doubt whether, in a future war, the total amount of resources commanded on either side will in fact be relevant. . . . In a happier day students of history may be entertained by the irony of America's final acts in a victorious war, which compromised perhaps fatally the two great props of American military security—distance and a preponderance of economic resources."

And, of course, my insight at the time was by no means unique.

IV

What good are nuclear weapons, then, in a world of diffusing economic and technological potential, if the danger and instabilities of further nuclear proliferation are to be avoided? That was the question Khrushchev was trying to answer between the launching of the first Sputnik on October 4, 1957, and the end of the Cuban missile crisis on October 28, 1962. The answer that emerged from his experiments was: "Not much." Rationally, nuclear weapons can deter someone else from launching a first strike. But that is about all. And that answer is not likely to change if civilized life on the planet is to persist. It did not take much time for men on both sides to draw the lesson. By Tuesday, October 30, 1962, a high-ranking Soviet scientist, visiting me at the Policy Planning Council, suggested that the recent crisis might not be in vain if it would lead to heightened efforts to produce a disarmament agreement; and that same evening a high-ranking Soviet diplomat was chatting in the same vein at dinner, underlining the need to get on with the test-ban treaty.

Speaking toward the close of the 1960 Pugwash conference in Moscow, I departed from my text to deal with a point raised by a participant from a small country who expressed a certain uneasiness that the meeting was assuming the form of a Soviet-American dialogue. I said:

I can understand his uneasiness. Since 1945 the smaller nations have vacillated between two views. When the Soviet Union and the United States were far apart and tension was high, they sought to push us closer together. When we appeared to be close together and talking intimately, they exhibited worry that we might be making agreements at their expense.

I believe this perspective on Soviet-American relations is not accurate. As a historian, I am convinced that the central historical fact of our time is this: power is being rapidly diffused away from Moscow and Washington. What we are seeing in the world is an equivalent of the process which occurred after 1815. In 1815 Great Britain was the only country in the world which had absorbed the tricks of then modern technology. It alone had experienced an industrial revolution. In the century after 1815, the industrial revolution took hold in Belgium, France, Germany, Russia, Japan, and North America.

Now the industrial revolution is taking hold in the areas which were skipped during the century after 1815—that is to say the industrial revolution is taking hold in China and Eastern Europe; and it is occurring—or it will soon occur—in the whole southern half of the globe.

The inevitable result is that industrial potential, military power, and influence on the world scene is being diffused and will continue to be diffused.

Faced with this fact, there are three choices open to the Soviet Union and the United States. We can stumble into a war and destroy a large part of what man has built on the face of the earth and a large part of the world's population. We can continue the cold war until the diffusion of power removes the capacity to decide from Moscow and Washington. Or, working constructively together, we can create the terms on which power will become diffused.

This is the limit of the historical powers of the Soviet Union and the United States. I would hope that we would choose the third path. This is the historical responsibility we owe to our peoples.

Clearly, I failed to persuade my Soviet colleagues on that occasion, but I believe more men in Moscow would now accept the point than did eleven years ago. And before we achieve anything like stable peace in the world, the men in Peking as well as Moscow will have to accept its implications.

As we struggle to define nuclear sufficiency in a world of multiplying holes in Soviet soil and MIRVs, of new developments in ABMs and ASW, I would suggest that the SALT—which I regard as perhaps the most important negotiations ever undertaken by men—must be put into a larger context. A world where technically capable nations will be content not to produce nuclear weapons will be, if I am right, a world that has gone a long way toward stable peace. That kind of world has been the goal of most of our efforts and struggles since 1945.

And so I would hope that when Gerard Smith (head of the U.S. Delegation to the SALT from 1969 to 1972) and his Soviet colleagues sit down to dinner some night, one of their toasts will be, "To the withering away of nuclear weapons," and that this objective, with all six of its ramifications, will increasingly suffuse the policies of Peking as well as Moscow, Paris, London, and Washington. For if the world is going to be worth living in, that is what ought to happen to nuclear weapons—in a mutually safe and even-handed way, of course.

PART I

ROBERT L. PFALTZGRAFF, JR.

The Rationale for
Superpower Arms Control

IN THE PAST DECADE the United States and the Soviet Union have been engaged in a series of arms control negotiations, some of which have produced agreement. Each superpower has developed its own rationale for participating in such negotiations and in reaching an agreement with its principal adversary. It is not easy to determine with precision the rationale for superpower arms control in a pluralistic international system, especially one in which the goals, value systems, political systems, and strategies of the principal actors are so widely at variance as in the contemporary world.

The rationale for arms control as set forth by the United States differs in many fundamental respects from that of the Soviet Union. Many variables determine the rationale of a superpower for arms control. These include not only foreign policy goals but also the structure of the political system and the nature of the bureaucratic and decision-making process, the level of economic development and technological-industrial capabilities, the level of armaments, and the strategies deemed essential by a superpower for its security. The rationale for arms control for an anti–status quo power is likely to differ from that of a status quo power. The anti–status quo power, far more than the status quo power, is likely to seek to use arms control negotiations either to promote or to ratify change in the international system. For the status quo power, in contrast, the rationale for arms control may be to forestall the emergence of a changed configuration of strategic power that might favor the anti–status quo power.

Even two superpowers that are essentially status quo in foreign policy orientation may have differing rationales for arms control; for national approaches to arms control, like other elements of foreign policy, are based on a variety of factors, including fundamentally different security requirements because of geographic location, population density, commitments to allies, and approaches to military strategy. The purpose of this paper is to set forth a series of rationales for superpower arms control that take account of differences in superpower goals, value

3

systems, political systems, levels of economic development, levels of armaments, and strategies. In addition, a series of propositions is developed about the determinants of the rationale for superpower arms control based on one or a combination of these variables. Several rationales for superpower arms control based on strategic, political, and economic considerations will be developed and examined.

The Strategic Rationale for Superpower Arms Control

For more than a decade the most general and probably the most important strategic rationale for superpower arms control has been its potential for enhancing the stability of the strategic balance by providing a deterrent at a lower level of armaments.[1] "Stability" is a term—like "balance of power"—that is fraught with ambiguity. A stabilized strategic balance is one in which neither side fears that the other has gained, or is easily capable of acquiring, a first-strike capability that would destroy the retaliatory force of the other. This kind of strategic balance, moreover, is one in which the side that strikes first would lose, rather than gain, in relative military strength vis-à-vis its opponent.[2] As long as both superpowers retain a credible second-strike capability, a condition of strategic stability is present. Under such stability a first-strike nuclear attack based on a rational decision is precluded, since both sides would possess the capacity to inflict an unacceptable level of damage on the other. The existence of such a deterrent relationship may not ensure a politically stable relationship between the superpowers, however, since other factors contribute to the development of a condition of deterrence. These include, for example, the political will of a government; the morale of a people and its leadership; and even sheer chance, which may influence both the foreign policy decisions and perceptions of an adversary. Nevertheless, if the superpowers seek to preserve or to obtain strategic stability as defined above, both have an incentive to enter arms control negotiations. Under such conditions, limitations in existing offensive and defensive capabilities and on R&D programs can serve to promote strategic stability.

Technological considerations furnish an important component of the strategic rationale for superpower arms control. The dimensions of this rationale may be stated succinctly as follows: (1) to reduce the prospect that the other superpower will register major technological breakthroughs; (2) to gain some control over the other superpower's rate of technological innovation and (3) to influence the evolution of the other superpower's R&D program. Under certain circumstances, a superpower may use arms control negotiations to slow its adversary's rate of technological innovation either to gain some form of strategic-political advantage or reduce the uncertainty that new weapons systems may introduce into the strategic equation. Such uncertainty may be reduced by efforts either to curb respective superpower R&D programs or to delay or prevent the actual deployment of destabilizing weapons systems. The prospect for utilizing arms control negotiations for this purpose is enhanced under the following conditions: (1) if they are employed against a superpower desiring to slow its weapons development and deployment and to achieve an arms control agreement for this purpose; (2) if they are used against a superpower within which domestic opinion, during a period of prolonged arms control negotiations, can be mobilized against a continuation of high levels of armaments.

A formal agreement may be designed to limit explicitly either certain qualitative improvements in weapons systems or innovations that could destabilize a deterrent relationship. There has been a body of thought that views the prospects for arms control to be ever more limited by the development of successive generations of increasingly complex technologically advanced weapons systems. Although technological change enhances the prospects for arms control under certain circumstances (e.g., the development of technologies for monitoring violations of an arms control agreement), there is nevertheless an important technological rationale for arms control as a device for curbing potentially destabilizing technological innovation. Although technology has made possible the existence of a deterrent relationship unprecedented in international politics, with important implications for international stability, technology has made it both necessary and possible to place restraints on superpower armaments.

In the SALT, the contention has been made that future technological developments, as well as the deployment of large numbers of weapons from existing technologies (e.g., MIRV by the United States or SS-9 by the Soviet Union) would have a destabilizing effect on the strategic balance. Strategic analysts, both within and outside the U.S. government, have argued that the large-scale development by either side of new offensive or defensive systems not only would have potentially destabilizing effects on the strategic balance, but also would make more complicated and difficult the negotiation of an arms control agreement.[3] This concern about the emerging U.S.-Soviet strategic relationship was voiced by President Nixon in his foreign affairs report of February 25, 1971:

> By any standard, we believe the number of Soviet strategic forces now exceeds the level needed for deterrence. Even more important than the growth in numbers has been the change in the nature of the forces the USSR chose to develop and deploy. These forces include systems—particularly the SS-9 ICBM with large multiple warheads—which, if further improved and deployed in sufficient numbers, could be uniquely suitable for a first strike against our land-based deterrent forces. The design and growth of these forces leads inescapably to profound questions concerning the threats we will face in the future, and the adequacy of our current strategic forces to meet the requirements of our security.[4]

The extent to which such a development actually undermines a stable strategic deterrent relationship depends, of course, on many technical factors, such as Soviet guidance system accuracy and the vulnerability of the U.S. retaliatory capability as well as politico-psychological factors, including the willingness to launch a retaliatory strike with countercity forces after a large part of the U.S. counterforce capability had been destroyed.

Arms control negotiations, as distinct from an arms control agreement, have in themselves an important technological rationale. Negotiations, especially those which are prolonged, as in the case of most arms control talks, provide the setting for the development of a continuing strategic dialogue between the superpowers. Such discussions may make possible on both sides a greater understanding of the political, military, and technical problems facing the two superpowers. The result may be a needed input by each superpower into the other's process of national security policy formulation. Under such circumstances it becomes possible for both superpowers to make decisions on R&D, on the deployment of strategic systems, and on the development of strategic and tactical doctrine on a more rational basis. If the absence of adequate information about an opponent leads to overcompensation in weapons planning, then arms control discussions may promote a more restrained approach to armaments on both sides.[5]

Inherent in this analysis, however, is the assumption that (1) both powers strive for strategic stability as defined earlier in this chapter and (2) both powers are prepared, therefore, to utilize information obtained in an arms control dialogue to achieve stability. If, however, this assumption is inoperative, the prospect arises that one power or the other will make use of arms control negotiations to exploit whatever advantage may be conferred by (1) engaging in prolonged negotiations that slow the weapons development process in the other superpower;

and (2) making use of information gained in such a dialogue to enhance one's own potential strategic advantage.

Strategically such a development may be destabilizing, depending on its effect upon the deterrent relationship outlined above in our definition of stability. Under such circumstances, the rationale for superpower arms control negotiations may be specifically to enhance the position of one superpower at the expense of the other. Whatever the connection with the SALT, since the beginning of the negotiations in Helsinki and Vienna, the Soviet Union has greatly augmented its strategic offensive capabilities. Although such a development may be strategically destabilizing, the extent to which it is *politically* destabilizing depends on the respective foreign policy goals of the superpowers as well as the risks that one superpower or the other is prepared to take in order to exploit its strategic position vis-à-vis the opposing superpower. Presumably, a status quo superpower that enjoys a margin of strategic superiority (however defined) has a politically stabilizing effect on international politics unless such superiority leads the opposing superpower to increase its capabilities in order to achieve for itself a comfortable margin of strategic superiority. An anti–status quo power that has achieved a position of superiority may seek to utilize its strategic position to extract political advantage deemed detrimental to the other superpower or to lesser states that can no longer rely on the extended deterrent of the other superpower for their security.

A rationale for arms control can be found in the general desire of both superpowers to reduce the danger of war by accident or miscalculation. This rationale, acknowledged by most strategic analysts to form an important consideration in the calculations of both superpowers, transcends differences between them in the variables that influence their respective rationales for arms control. Although there are conditions in which uncertainty and the possibility of miscalculation may enhance the deterrent relationship by inducing greater caution in the policies of each superpower, both superpowers have placed considerable value on arms control measures, formal or tacit, bilateral and unilateral, designed to minimize the prospects for miscalculation or accidental war. It follows that a rationale for superpower arms control lies in the potential for limiting the damage to one or both sides in case of irrational or accidental war—hence the interest of both superpowers in the SALT in the conclusion of the accord, signed on September 30, 1971, to improve direct communications links between Washington and Moscow for use in emergency situations. Each party consented, according to Article I of the agreement, to "maintain and to improve, as it deems necessary, its existing organizational and technical arrangements to guard against the accidental or unauthorized use of nuclear weapons under its control." [6]

The Structure of the International System: Implications for Superpower Arms Control Rationales

Both in a bipolar world, such as has existed for much of the past generation, and in the emerging world of limited multipolarity of the 1970s, each superpower has retained close links with allies. Both have seen in arms control a means to separate superpower status and superpower relationships from those between a superpower and lesser powers. The United States and the Soviet Union have developed arms control strategies designed to prevent the other superpower from disseminating nuclear capabilities among its allies. Both superpowers, for distinctive reasons, have refrained from such dissemination. These may be summarized as follows: (1) to prevent the acquisition of atomic weapons by powers that might be politically unstable and internationally irresponsible, and thus increase the risk of accidental war; and (2) to avert the prospect that conflict among smaller nuclear powers would escalate into nuclear conflict between the superpowers. [7]

In the emerging multipolar international system of the 1970s, however, the possibility of using superpower arms control agreements to prevent third parties from gaining a retaliatory capability against a superpower (e.g., China against the Soviet Union) will be reduced. In a world of limited multipolarity, the prospects for the development of additional nuclear powers will be enhanced. We can anticipate that during the next decade the nuclear capability of China will be greatly strengthened. There exists the possibility that Britain and France will achieve some form of nuclear collaboration that could form the nucleus of a more broadly based European force. [8] Both India and Japan are likely to hold open the option of developing a nuclear capability, and Israel has tested a missile, the Jericho, which has a three-hundred-mile range and which is apparently designed to carry a nuclear warhead. [9] In the multipolar world of the future, additional powers will possess at least a nascent second-strike capability. The configuration of international politics is such that these powers are likely to pose a greater risk to the Soviet Union than to the United States because of the greater potential for conflicting national interests between these powers (notably China) and the Soviet Union. In such a period the rationale against the proliferation of nuclear capabilities would be of greater significance to the Soviet Union than to the United States.

Yet if the logic of strategic stability as outlined earlier is extended to a multipolar world, the implication is to introduce an element of deterrence into relationships among states possessing such capabilities, and in some cases (e.g., Europe and Japan) to furnish at least a partial substitute for the deterrent protection once extended by the United States. In such a multipolar context, the rationale for arms control negotiations lies in the preservation of a deterrent relationship at relatively lower levels of armaments, not least because of the more limited industrial, technological, and military resources of potential and emergent power centers. Under such circumstances, the rationale of the Soviet Union for arms control is in the limitation to the greatest extent possible of the opportunities for the emergence of such centers of strategic nuclear power. For such emergent powers, the rationale for arms control rests on the need to retard or prevent technological breakthroughs by the superpowers, and especially the Soviet Union, designed to reduce the deterrent capability of emergent nuclear forces. Such rationales, by no means fully compatible, can be expected to influence the arms control strategies of both sides in strategic arms control negotiations in a multipolar world.

In the past decade both superpowers have striven to control, if not prevent, the emergence of additional nuclear power centers. In the emerging limited multipolar system of the 1970s this rationale for superpower arms control depends upon the assumptions about the conditions for international stability or instability as they may work to the advantage or disadvantage of one superpower or the other. To what extent is a tripolar or a pentapolar international system likely to contribute to, or detract from, international stability as defined earlier in this chapter?

The superpower rationale for arms control rests, above all, on the extent to which the emergence of new centers of strategic power poses a greater or lesser danger to one superpower or the other. The logic of this condition, it has been suggested above, is to lead the superpower most directly affected to press for arms control negotiations and agreements designed to limit the development of such capabilities in third countries. In contrast, the other superpower may develop a rationale that at least condones, if it does not actually support, the proliferation of strategic capabilities targeted against its opponent superpower. Thus, with the end of bipolarity, antiproliferation becomes no longer a principle that is universal in application but rather a policy to be applied only in specified situations.

Under such circumstances, a multilateral framework for arms control negotiations replaces the bilateralism that thus far has characterized the SALT. In keeping with this theoretical framework, an effort to broaden the negotiations for strategic arms control was characteristic of Soviet diplomacy in 1971. Undoubtedly for reasons such as these the Soviets proposed five-power arms control negotiations designed to prevent the emergence of strategic nuclear multipolarity. The effect of the multilateralization of strategic arms control negotiations is severalfold. First, multilateralization may reduce the opportunities inherent in a strictly bilateral framework for lesser powers to conclude that superpowers have engaged in collusion and have negotiated agreements that either do not take sufficient account of their mutual interests or work specifically to their detriment. This problem has contributed to allied dissatisfaction with the United States in NATO during the past decade. The United States, in the SALT, has made a major effort to keep allies, especially in Europe, informed of the SALT. Nevertheless, the extent to which European interests have been accommodated in the SALT remains uncertain.

The effect of the emergence of additional centers of power is to increase the complexity of arms control negotiations and to make even more difficult the development of agreements because of the additional interests that must be satisfied. If the rationale for superpower arms control agreement differs among powers, the accommodation of rationales becomes more difficult if a bipolar context is replaced by one of several powers, with their different rationales. The difficulties are intensified in an international system of great diversity, especially one in which the forces working for international consensus are minimal.

In a multipolar system, the rationale for superpower arms control among the several centers of strength rests on a mutually perceived need to assure deterrence at the lowest possible level of armaments. This rationale, in turn, may result from a recognition that the possibility of any one power attaining a position of clear-cut strategic superiority that could be utilized to extract *political* gains from another power is less likely than in a world of nuclear bipolarity. In a multipolar world other centers of power might combine to achieve at least parity with any power seeking superiority, unless such a super-power registers technological breakthroughs that are destabilizing in nature. In this respect at least, a multipolar international system resembles a classical balance-of-power model.[10] Barring such technological breakthroughs, the prospect for a first strike by one nuclear power against another would be diminished to the extent that such a strike, while inflicting heavy damage, would render the attacking power vulnerable to the other nuclear powers. This condition could only be avoided by the development in the attacking power of a wide margin, both qualitatively and quantitatively, of strategic superiority, as well as an all-horizons offensive (and perhaps defensive) capability.

This rationale rests, however, upon at least two assumptions. First, it is assumed that in a limited multipolar world each power possesses a largely invulnerable second-strike capability and thus there exists a condition of mutual deterrence. Second, it may be assumed that, in some respects like a classic balance-of-power model, all of the other nuclear powers, would not wish to eliminate any one of their number because of its essential role in a multipolar deterrent relationship. The foregoing analysis rests also on the assumption that nuclear powers will utilize their capabilities on behalf of other states, but this assumption is by no means certain either in the present context of bipolarity or in the emerging multipolarity of the 1970s. Even if some doubt exists about the conditions under which such capabilities would be used in behalf of other states, there may be sufficient uncertainty to induce an element of caution in the calculations of a potential attacker.

The quest of superpowers for strategic stability between themselves has potential implications for relations between superpowers and lesser powers and between lesser powers themselves. This quest is potentially destabilizing if the superpowers do not take sufficient account of the interests of lesser powers. For example, an arms control agreement may limit the capacity of a superpower to maintain the linkage between its strategic deterrent and the defense of allies. Ratification, through an arms control agreement, of a form of "parity" between the United States and the Soviet Union may serve to reduce the linkage between the U.S. strategic deterrent and the defense of Western Europe and Japan, although the extent of such reduction depends on the kind of agreement that emerges from arms control negotiations such as the SALT and the effect of the SALT on the interests of allies.

Especially in a bipolar context, an arms control agreement that emphasizes limitations on superpower defensive capabilities such as ABM, in the absence of qualitative or quantitative limitations on offensive strategic capabilities, may enhance the potential of one superpower or the other for a first-strike capability with important gains of a politico-psychological and a possibly destabilized world environment. Under such circumstances, the linkage between superpower deterrents and the defense of allies is reduced and the incentive increased for the strengthening or the building of indigenous forces in states once protected by the superpower. Hence, the decision of a lesser state to acquire advanced strategic capabilities and thus to reinforce tendencies toward multipolarity may be influenced by the nature of the superpower arms control agreement.

Such a decision may also be influenced by the extent to which interests deemed vital to a lesser power are sacrificed by superpowers. A recurrent fear of West European governments has been the prospect that the United States might reach an agreement with the Soviet Union that did not take sufficient account of important European interests. The superpowers might engage in collusion designed to preserve a margin of military strength that was superior to that of other states. Especially in the 1960s, the Chinese leadership criticized the Soviet Union for its alleged willingness to enter negotiations on arms control and other issues with the United States while failing to take sufficient account of the interests of China and other Communist states.

The result may be a tendency toward the acquisition of advanced strategic systems by states formerly protected by superpowers. The extension of nuclear capabilities to lesser states may be stabilizing or destabilizing, depending on several considerations. These include, first, the nature of the threat posed to a superpower by the lesser state. What incentive does the superpower have to eliminate such a nascent capability? This depends not only on the nature of the threat posed by the lesser power to the superpower, but also on the extent to which the defense of the lesser power has been decoupled from the defense of the superpower that had provided a strategic umbrella. According to this logic, the rapid decoupling of lesser power defense from a superpower deterrent as a result of the SALT in an emergent multipolar world is potentially destabilizing so long as the lesser power does not possess at least a modest second-strike capability. Second, the regional context may influence greatly the extent to which this proliferation may be stabilizing or destabilizing. Although certain strategic analysts have argued that the proliferation of nuclear capabilities to all states would be stabilizing, such an assumption rests upon the *deterrent* effect of such weapons. If there are states that would not be deterred from using such weapons if they thought the possibility of a successful first strike was present, then the spread of such weapons in certain instances would be destabilizing. Without necessarily embracing the argument either in support of or against proliferation under any circumstances, it is possible to conceive of states or combinations of states whose possession of nuclear weapons might be stabilizing, destabilizing, or both at a regional level and potentially at the level of superpower interaction.

The Political Rationale for Arms Control Agreements

Paramount in the consideration of the desirability of arms control agreements is the political rationale. It is axiomatic to state that the political rationale governs the decision of a state to enter arms control negotiations or to conclude an arms control agreement. Nations seek arms control to the extent that it accords with their political objectives, be they to preserve an existing military balance or to change the military balance in order to attain some political objective.

Both in official and public discussions of arms control and in the literature of arms control, there is the implicit assumption that arms control negotiations and agreements in themselves are desirable because of an alleged causal nexus between arms races and conflict. Arms races are said to have within them a logic that leads to international strife. If conflict is to be mitigated or eliminated, it is essential to remove the means by which war is waged. Such a view of armaments and conflict, of course, is simplistic, even though much of the popular rationale for arms control is based largely upon its faulty analysis of the causes of conflict and the conditions for peace.

But the political rationale for arms control rests also on the assumption that among the national actors, arms control negotiations and an agreement in one sector (1) are conducive to the initiation and conduct of negotiations and the conclusion of agreements in other sectors of armaments, and (2) create a more favorable political climate for the conduct of negotiations and the conclusion of agreements in still other fields.

This political rationale in the arms control field may be described as the doctrine of "ramification" or "spillover," to adopt terminology that has been widely used in theoretical works in political science on the conditions for economic and political integration at the international level.[11] Implicit in this rationale for arms control is the assumption that among the national actors arms control negotiations and agreements provide a learning process that creates a propensity for further negotiations and agreement. Such exercises furnish a learning experience that contributes to the building of mutual trust and confidence. This is deemed to be a desirable end in itself. The arms control agreements that may result from such a process are themselves useful as foundations for further arms control negotiations and agreements and thereby for the mitigation of tension between superpowers.

The rationale for superpower arms control agreement may lie in the "linkage" that one power perceives in an accord for the reduction of armaments and the possibility of resolving other divisive political issues. This expectation may be based either on a belief that the psychological climate for the settlement of such issues is improved by such an agreement or on the expectation that certain trade-offs exist. In return for an arms control agreement at one level of armaments, a superpower may be prepared to enter negotiations at another level. Thus, a power such as the United States may see in the SALT a means of increasing Soviet cooperation in Vietnam or the Middle East.

The "spillover" rationale for superpower arms control is especially appealing to a status quo power whose political goals lie in the lowering of the military capabilities of both superpowers. It forms not only a rationale but also a strategy that a power desirous of attaining arms control may seek to employ. Implicit is the assumption that by themselves the process of negotiation and the achievement of agreements will contribute to the reorientation of the political behavior of an opponent to a more collaborative outlook. Thus the further assumption is that arms control provides a basis for reorienting the international behavior of states.

The political rationale for superpower arms control negotiations and agreements can lie in the potential that they afford for the disruption of relationships between a superpower and its allies. The potential for such disruption is greater in an alliance system whose members possess considerable latitude in their relations with each other than in an alliance system whose members are bound by coercion. The problems of superpower agreements for relations with lesser powers have been examined earlier in this chapter, within the context of international stability. However, to the extent that superpower arms control agreements contribute to the disruption of an opponent superpower's alliance relationships, they may serve the interests of one superpower and provide a political rationale for such negotiations.

The Economic Rationale for Superpower Arms Control

To a considerable extent, the rationale for superpower arms control rests on economic considerations, The economic rationale is based on the assumption that through arms control agreements the superpowers can reduce their budgetary allocations for weapons systems. Both the United States and the Soviet Union, it has been suggested, have an economic rationale for the control and reduction of strategic armaments. For the United States the economic rationale stems from the need to re-order priorities to provide greater resources for the solution of pressing domestic problems. For the Soviet Union the need to devote additional resources to investment in capital goods, to satisfy consumer needs, and to provide for technological innovation in the nondefense sectors of the economy provides a rationale for strategic agreements.[12] Such funds as are saved will then become available for other projects. Even if the savings are marginal in nature, an economic system in which resources are scarce can benefit even from miniscule reductions in armaments ex-penditures.

The validity of this contention, which is by no means self-evident, is dependent on two assumptions: (1) that savings from armaments re-duction will be placed into domestic works rather than be cut from national budgets in the form of tax reductions; (2) that armaments ex-penditures result in R&D that does not produce technological spinoff into nondefense sectors and that, in any event, programs other than arma-ments efforts would result in even greater technological spinoff.

The extent to which reductions in armaments will lead to reductions in military budgets is dependent on the form that an arms control agree-ment takes. As Hedley Bull has observed: "Soldiers and weapons are expensive; but so also are systems of arms control . . . since, by and large, the greater the degree of disarmament, the more elaborate is the system of inspection required to control it; no arms control system is likely to be cheap." [13] If elaborate schemes of arms control are likely to be expensive, they are also likely to be difficult to negotiate because of the general unwillingness of superpowers to agree to elaborate procedures for inspection and verification. Therefore, in the present context of international politics, any arms control agreement to which the superpowers are inclined to agree in the various phases of the SALT can be expected to have self-enforcing characteristics or to require rela-tively simple techniques for assuring compliance.

Historically, major savings from reductions in armaments have sel-dom found their way into governmental budgets designed to satisfy pressing domestic needs. It is by no means certain, contrary to the con-tention of those who argue for a "reordering of national priorities," that savings from armaments realized from SALT will find their way on a one-to-one basis into projects for rebuilding cities and in other ways renewing the environment and improving the "quality of life." Nor is the economic rationale for superpower arms control set forth by leaders of less-developed countries any more soundly based. It is by no means inevitable, or even likely, that savings from arms control by the superpowers will produce additional resources for economic modernization in less-developed countries. In fact, such a diversion of resources, especially in the present context of international relations, is even more remote than the prospect for the utilization of such funds on a one-to-one basis for domestic reconstruction in the developed states themselves.

Although many of the major technological advances of the past generation have resulted from large-scale governmental investment in defense-related R&D, such an argument cannot be offered in support of the continuation of an arms race. Just as governmental policies can be devised to channel resources into important domestic problems, a national R&D program to ensure that a nation remains in the forefront of technological innovation can be formulated.

Yet the prospects for achieving such programs outside of weapons development and procurement depend vitally upon two important considerations: (1) the nature of the domestic consensus in support of them, and (2) the capacity of a political system to call upon its population to bear the necessary burdens. Historically, the consensus in support of such programs has been lacking in advanced political systems, and especially in the United States, while the political structure and the value systems of such countries, in contrast to the Soviet Union, have not permitted the coercion necessary to extract major sacrifices except during periods of acute international tension.

The economic rationale for superpower arms control extends to yet another consideration. Asymmetries in the levels of economic and technological development of the superpowers may make advantageous the conclusion of an arms control agreement in order to avoid an escalation in the armaments race. If one superpower is superior in industrial and technological resources, the other may have an incentive to seek an arms control agreement in order to avoid an escalation that it could hardly hope to match. In part the rationale for Anglo-American agreement to naval parity at the Washington Disarmament Conference of 1921–22 rested on the British recognition that, in the absence of an agreement, the United States, with its superior resources, might outstrip Britain in advanced naval armaments. It has been suggested that the Soviet rationale for the SALT rests in part on the likelihood that a continuation of the arms race might place the Soviet Union in a progressively worse position in comparison with the United States. According to one analysis: "The next few years in weapons developments will place heavy demands on highly advanced scientific and technological capabilities—resources in which the United States seems more generously endowed than the Soviet Union." [14] Moreover, a U.S. rationale for arms control lies in the opposition of some domestic groups to new expenditures for large-scale weapons systems.

Conclusion

The foregoing analysis of the rationales for superpower arms control presents several implications both for the negotiating process and for the shape of arms control agreements, the SALT in particular. First and foremost, arms control negotiations and agreements, if they are to serve the interests of all parties, must be based on a recognition of the differing and, in some cases, conflicting arms control rationales of nations.

Although it is impossible to draw together in summary fashion all of the inferences for arms control that flow from this analysis, several major conclusions emerge:

1. If the basic strategic rationale lies in the preservation of credible deterrence at a lower level of effort for both sides, such a deterrent relationship has important implications for the force structure of both superpowers, which should be reflected in the SALT. Under such circumstances, strategic stability may be enhanced by a force configuration in which the attacker suffers a greater diminution of offensive strategic capabilities than the attacked (measured in strategic weapons remaining after a first strike). The power whose offensive force is primarily countercity will suffer a loss in relative strategic strength unless the counterforce capabilities of its opponent are limited, especially if the power possessing counterforce capabilities seeks major changes in the international status quo and is prepared to exploit the possession of such capabilities for *political* gain against an opponent. The power whose offensive capabilities are primarily counterforce will suffer a loss in relative strategic strength unless the defensive capabilities of its opponent are limited. In order to obtain a roughly equal degree of stability for both sides, the arms control agreement should provide for limitations on both offensive and defensive weaponry.

2. Technological rationales provide an important consideration in arms control. Negotiations and agreements for arms control may enhance the prospects for diminishing the development of potentially destabilizing technologies, especially between two powers that are essen-

tially status quo in their foreign policy orientation. Such negotiations and agreements, however, may have a destabilizing impact upon the international strategic environment if one of the two superpowers, in its foreign policy, is oriented toward basic change and seeks, through arms control negotiations, to enhance its own technological potential while restricting that of its adversary.

3. Arms control agreements have implications for international politics beyond the relationship between the superpowers. The relationships within alliances, the extent to which the nuclear deterrence of one power can be extended to protect another, and the different intentions of status quo and anti-status quo foreign policies must be considered. Negotiations and agreements that are stabilizing for the superpowers may be destabilizing for lesser powers. An arms control agreement that ratifies a relationship of "parity" between superpowers may serve to reduce the links between a superpower and its allies.

4. There is an important relationship between the structure of the international system and the rationale for arms control. The movement of an international system from a bipolar to multipolar structure has several implications for arms control rationales. In particular, additional centers of advanced strategic power may be created. If such centers develop a second-strike capability against a superpower, the condition of strategic deterrence may be extended for superpower relations to relations between superpowers and lesser powers as well as between such powers themselves. Moreover, in a multipolar world, the obstacles facing a superpower that seeks basic change in international politics may be increased by the existence of additional centers of strategic power.

The rationale for arms control, it has been suggested, depends on a multiplicity of factors related to the values, goals, strategies, structures, technological levels, and capabilities of the respective superpowers, and also to the nature of the international system itself. Although certain of these factors remain relatively constant, others are subject to change, even over a relatively short period of time. The perennial problem of statecraft and of arms control is to ascertain the nature of converging or parallel rationales for superpower arms control as well as the divergent rationales that influence the decisions of superpowers either to enter or to abstain from arms control negotiations or agreements. Such an exercise is essential to the development of arms control accords that enhance the national security of the superpowers and lesser states, while minimizing the prospects that a state will make use of such negotiations or agreements to obtain a strategically or politically destabilizing advantage over other states.

NOTES

1. For an analysis of deterrence and its potential contribution to stability, see André Beaufre, *Deterrence and Strategy* (New York: Praeger, 1966), esp. pp. 23–103.

2. For an analysis of the nature of such strategic stability, see Harold Brown, "Security through Limitations," *Foreign Affairs,* 47 (April 1969), pp. 422–32.

3. See, for example, William C. Foster, "Strategic Weapons: Prospects for Arms Control," *Foreign Affairs,* 47 (April 1969), pp. 413–21: "If either or both sides were to deploy new advanced weapons systems, however, the new uncertainties added to the equation would make the negotiation of an agreement more complicated and difficult. The deployment of extensive ballistic missile defenses by either side, for example, would raise apprehensions on the other side as to the adequacy of its offensive forces to penetrate such defenses so as to maintain deterrence.

Another example: Although the fixed land-based missiles now deployed are relatively easy to detect, if mobile land-based missiles were deployed, an agreement fixing their number would be difficult to verify even with highly intrusive inspections, such as the Soviets have always rejected" p. 415.

4. *U.S. Foreign Policy for the 1970s: Building for Peace,* A Report to the Congress by President Richard Nixon (February 25, 1971), p. 168.

5. For an examination of this problem, see Jerome H. Kahan, "Strategies for SALT," *World Politics,* XXIII (January 1971), p. 171.

6. For the text of this agreement, see the *New York Times* (October 1, 1971), p. 14.

7. See Adrian Fisher, "Global Dimensions," in *Nuclear Proliferation: Prospects for Control,* ed. Bennett Boskey and Mason Willrich (New York: Dunellen, 1970), pp. 3–4.

8. For analyses of this prospect, see Ian Smart, "Future Conditional: The Prospect for Anglo-French Nuclear Cooperation," *Adelphi Papers,* no. 78 (London: Institute for Strategic Studies, 1971); Andrew J. Pierre, "Nuclear Diplomacy: Britain, France and America," *Foreign Affairs,* 49 (January 1971), pp. 283–302; Robert L. Pfaltzgraff, Jr., "NATO and European Security: Prospects for the 1970s," *Orbis,* XV (Spring 1971), pp. 154–78.

9. The *New York Times* (October 5, 1971), p. 1.

10. See, for example, Edward V. Gulick, *Europe's Classical Balance of Power* (Ithaca: Cornell University Press, 1955); Morton A. Kaplan, *System and Process in International Politics* (New York: John Wiley & Sons, 1962).

11. The literature of political integration that contains this rationale is voluminous. See, for example, David Mitrany, *A Working Peace System* (Chicago: Quadrangle Books, 1966), pp. 54–99; Ernst B. Haas, *Beyond the Nation-State*

(Stanford: Stanford University Press, 1964), pp. 3–86. For a review and analysis of such literature see James E. Dougherty and Robert L. Pfaltzgraff, Jr., *Contending Theories of International Relations* (Philadelphia: J. B. Lippincott, 1971), pp. 279–311.

12. For a summary of this and other possible Soviet rationales for strategic armaments limitation, see Thomas W. Wolfe, "Soviet Approaches to SALT," *Problems of Communism,* XIX (September–October 1970), pp. 1–2.

13. Hedley Bull, *The Control of the Arms Race* (New York: Praeger, 1961), p. 19.

14. Roman Kolkowicz, Matthew P. Gallagher, Benjamin S. Lambeth with Walter C. Clemens, Jr., and Peter W. Cohn, *The Soviet Union and Arms Control: A Superpower Dilemma* (Baltimore: The Johns Hopkins Press, 1970), p. 3.

THOMAS W. WOLFE

Soviet Interests in SALT

The Background Setting for Soviet Policy in the Seventies

THE WHOLE PATTERN of international politics is changing; in a fundamental sense, we seem today to be in transition from a postwar period of bipolar confrontation and rather unsubtle ideological cold war to a more diverse and complex pattern of international alignments. In this situation, the familiar lines of rivalry between the two superpowers of the nuclear age are being replaced by as yet unclarified conditions of global competition. To put it another way, the period of attempted postwar containment of the Soviet Union has come to an end, but the rules of engagement under which the Soviet Union and the United States will look after their overlapping global interests in an increasingly multipolar world environment are still in the process of being defined. The SALT, in a basic sense, is a part of this process of redefining the overall power relationship.

With respect to the Soviet Union itself, one may note that there has been a broad trend over time toward globalism in Soviet foreign policy, accompanied by a tendency to generate a military posture to support a widening range of Soviet interests abroad. During the first half of its history, despite an ideology professing universalist goals, the Soviet Union under Stalin pursued a foreign policy of essentially continental scope, and its military posture remained largely oriented in a regional or peripheral direction. The Khrushchev era, by contrast, marked the beginning of the Soviet Union's transformation into a global power, in both a political and military sense, and this process has continued at an accelerated pace under the Brezhnev-Kosygin regime—by now, perhaps, more aptly termed the Brezhnev regime.

A related phenomenon to be noted is what might be called the great power dynamism exhibited by the Soviet state at this juncture of its history. Although it may be argued that the ideological and revolutionary fervor of the Soviet elite is running down, whatever the lip service paid to the Marxist-Leninist verities, it is clearly evident at the same time that an energy and enthusiasm for playing the role of a great power in world affairs is not wanting in the Soviet case. Indeed, the dynamic and rather markedly self-righteous quality that animates

21

the Soviet world outlook and behavior appears not yet to have peaked.[1] This stands, of course, in some contrast with the present mood in the United States, which may have had its fling at trying to police the peace and set the world's affairs in order during the past quarter century.

To the extent that having more of the physical instruments of policy helps to broaden one's options, the men who will be making the Soviet Union's foreign and military policies in the next five to ten years will be able to choose from a richer menu of alternatives than their predecessors. Although it does not necessarily follow that the Soviet leaders will display the will, capacity, and wisdom to make the most of their opportunities, it would seem at first glance that if they do only reasonably well in managing their nation's role in world affairs, we can expect to see a steady expansion of Soviet political and military influence in the decade ahead.

But here one must enter a few important reservations, centering mainly on internal trends that are not easily squared with the image of the Soviet Union as a rising force in global affairs in the 1970s. From the Soviet viewpoint, the internal situation today is marked by what must seem to be some rather disturbing contradictions. In brief, it has become increasingly evident that, while Soviet military technology and the defense production sectors of the economy have managed to compete quite successfully with the West, the Soviet Union is encountering many difficulties in adapting the civilian sectors of its industrial system to the scientific and technical revolution of the modern era. Soviet authorities themselves have expressed repeated concern that the gap in assimilation of new technologies between the USSR and the advanced industrial states of the non-Communist world may widen unless appropriate remedies are found. Thus far, however, the economic-technical reforms applied in the civilian sector over the past few years have not yielded satisfactory results, and to judge from treatment of the reform question at the recent Twenty-fourth Party Congress, a new search for solutions is necessary.

Combined with flagging ideological élan, especially among Soviet youth, and the emergence of some embryonic political dissent that apparently has infected at least a small segment of the scientific intelligentsia, any conspicuous failure of the economic system to meet the domestic needs of a modern advanced society could put the Soviet leadership—which itself faces problems of generational turnover and probable political infighting in the next few years—in the awkward position of having to reconcile a troublesome internal situation with Soviet aspirations for a weightier global role.

There are also constraining external factors that will tend to influence the conduct of Soviet foreign policy and that may limit the leadership's freedom of action abroad. Two such factors, in particular, merit mention. One, long operative in the Soviet case, is awareness of the destructiveness of nuclear conflict, and hence the need to avoid confrontations that might escalate into a nuclear showdown. Another grows out of the deep-seated differences between the Soviet Union and China. In a military sense, the Chinese problem means that an increasing share of Soviet military resources must be tied down in the Far East, with planning obliged to take into account a two-front threat—at the Soviet front door in Europe and at its back door in Asia. Politically, Moscow's stakes in the containment of China not only bespeak the need to cultivate a climate of détente in Europe, but also give incentives for seeking the cooperation of Asian states such as India and Japan. The prospect of some sort of rapprochement between China and the United States adds a further complicating dimension to Soviet relations with both of these powers.

How the various internal and external trends at work may affect Soviet policy in the course of the next decade is by no means clear. Broadly speaking, one possibility is that the attention of the Soviet leadership may turn increasingly inward, tending more toward preoccupation with domestic problems than toward the pursuit of active and potentially destabilizing policies abroad. In essence, the leadership may come to feel that the best hope for restoring economic momentum and getting on with the modernization of Soviet society lies in retrenchment in the military sphere and cultivation of the "quiet life" on the international scene.

But the grounds for expecting quite a different thrust in Soviet policy are also present. Economic problems at home and the waning attraction of orthodox Marxist-Leninist prescriptions both for the Soviet people and as a model for the outside world happen to coincide with the Soviet Union's emergence, for the first time in its history, as a global military power. Moreover, the rise of Soviet power comes at a juncture when the Soviet Union's principal postwar rival appears unsure of itself and disposed to cut back its own global commitments. These congruent circumstances may well persuade the Kremlin leadership to rely increasingly upon more or less classical modes of power politics to extend Soviet influence abroad and to underwrite the negotiation of a new set of international arrangements commensurate with Soviet great-power interests. At the least, the asymmetry between the expansion of Soviet military power and the Soviet system's declining appeal as an example of modern societal growth and progress may tend to push the leadership in this outward direction during the next decade.

Against this background, let us turn next to some of the more specific considerations that bear on Soviet interests in the SALT, beginning with economic factors.

Economic Considerations

There has been a distinct division of opinion in the West on the extent to which economic constraints may impinge upon Soviet military policy and account for Moscow's interest in strategic arms negotiations with the United States. According to one widely held view, both immediate and long-term economic problems have had a compelling influence in leading the Kremlin to seek a genuine halt via SALT in the strategic arms competition. The central argument of this school has been that Soviet needs for growth investment, for meeting rising consumer demands, and for technological innovation in the nondefense sectors of the Soviet economy would make it difficult for the USSR to stand the pace of a major new round of strategic arms procurement, especially since this would place a heavy strain on the kinds of advanced technical and economic resources in which the United States retains a lead.

The increasing emphasis in the latter sixties on working out new methodologies to insure optimum use of resources for military purposes,[2] the apparent increase of defense expenditure during this period at a greater rate than growth of the Soviet GNP,[3] the necessity of downward revisions of economic goals for the eighth Five-Year Plan (1966–70)[4] and the long delay in drawing up the next Plan (1971–75), as well as Brezhnev's caustic criticism of Soviet economic performance at the close of 1969 when the SALT were begun—all these have been taken to suggest that the Soviet economy was hurting from the strategic buildup and other expanded military programs of the sixties, and that the Soviet leadership would therefore welcome the chance afforded by SALT to stabilize the strategic competition.

By contrast, another school of thought has held that economic constraints can no longer be regarded as a severe brake upon Soviet capacity and willingness to compete strategically with the United States, and that therefore the prime motivations behind Soviet participation in

SALT must lie elsewhere. As evidence of Soviet ability to compete, supporters of this view could note that the Soviet economy proved capable of sustaining the strategic buildup of the sixties while at the same time registering a respectable rate of growth.[5] As for Soviet willingness to raise the strategic ante, those arguing this case could cite estimates that Soviet expenditures for strategic arms ran twice as high in 1968–69 as those of the United States,[6] even though these were years in which a cutback of strategic programs might have helped to arrest a decline in Soviet economic growth rates.

A corollary factor that might have enhanced the confidence of the Soviet leaders that their economy could stand the strain of further strategic competition was, in this view, the predicament of the United States itself, which—beset with domestic economic and social problems, the cost of the Vietnam War, and a rising tide of antimilitary and anti-arms-race sentiment at home—appeared likely to be a less formidable strategic competitor than formerly.[7]

With respect to these two differing assessments of the effect of economic considerations upon the Soviet attitude toward SALT, it is fair to say that the first enjoyed the greater weight—or, at least, vogue—during the early stages of the talks, when the 1968–69 slowdown in Soviet economic performance was the object of wide publicity. Then came the 1970 upturn in the Soviet economy,[8] after which the thesis that immediate economic pressures had driven the Soviets into SALT lost some of its edge. However, the question of long-term economic problems as a central driving force behind Soviet interest in SALT remains under contention, much of which relates to the implications of the new ninth Five-Year Plan, finally unveiled in February 1971 after thirty months' delay and approved in draft form at the Twenty-fourth Party Congress in April. Although this is not the place for a full-dress examination of the 1971–75 Plan, a brief résumé of some of its features may serve the train of our discussion.

Perhaps the most conspicuous feature of the ninth Five-Year Plan is its pledge to give the Soviet consumer a better break by projecting a higher rate of growth in consumer goods (Group B) output for the next five years than in the traditionally favored category of producer goods (Group A).[9] The prominence given this reversal of priorities appears largely a matter of cosmetic effect, however, when the actual share of consumer and producer goods in total output is considered. As Brezhnev noted while delivering his report at the Twenty-fourth Party Congress (in a passage deleted, incidentally, in the subsequent published text of his speech), producer goods accounted in 1970 for 76 percent of total production, consumer goods for 24 percent. In the new Plan, this absolute share for consumer goods goes up only to about 30 percent, leaving in a predominant position traditional heavy industry, defense industry, and other growth-modernization industries such as chemicals, electric power, machine-building, electronics, automation equipment, and computers.

Another salient aspect of the 1971–75 Plan as disclosed up to this writing is the paucity of detail as to allocation of new investment. Total planned investment is set to increase 36–40 percent over the period, well below the 47 percent originally projected and no greater than the 40 percent actually achieved during the 1966–70 Plan. But apart from some figures relating to agriculture and light and food industries, no figures were given for projected investment in specific sectors and branches of the economy, suggesting that competing claims for allocation priorities remained unresolved.[10] In this connection, it might be presumed that there was some indecision or controversy over investment parameters for defense versus civilian sectors of the economy. Comment by Brezhnev at the Twenty-fourth Party Congress seemed to straddle the issue. On the one hand, for example, he expressed the view that the ultimate purpose of developing heavy industry was to improve the material lot of the people, and he rebuked "some comrades" for "subjective" failure to understand the need in today's changed times for increasing the production of consumer goods.[11] On the other hand, he gave reassurance that the "future development of defense industry" and heavy industry would be continued as needed to maintain the country's defense potential at "the required level," depending on the international situation and the outcome of talks on disarmament, such as those on strategic arms limitation.

Overall economic growth for the new Plan period is somewhat less ambitious than past targets, with national income planned to increase at an annual rate of 6–7 percent, slightly below the average rate of 7.1 percent claimed for 1966–70.[12] But even the more modest overall goals and fulfillment of various specific output categories are heavily dependent, as emphasized by Brezhnev and others at the Twenty-fourth Congress, on higher productivity through introduction of new technology, better management, labor discipline, and so on, rather than on massive new infusions of capital and labor, upon which the Soviet economy once relied. At the same time, neither the new Plan nor Soviet commentary on it indicates that the leadership is any longer prepared to seek improved productivity through the kinds of economic reform espoused by Kosygin during the past few years, but now being largely ignored. In this connection, if the Plan's projected rise of labor productivity at a rate of 6.7 percent annually should not be achieved, and if the declining rate of growth of the labor force (down from about 2 percent per year in the fifties to less than 1.5 percent in the late sixties) should continue in the seventies, a manpower shortage could threaten fulfillment of the planned production objectives.

Without dwelling further on details of the 1971–75 Plan, let us return here to the question of what it may imply with regard to the Soviet interest in the SALT. If the Plan's consumer coloration is regarded as more than skin deep, and if it is felt that the Soviet economy is experiencing difficulties serious enough to keep it from meeting an expanded menu of consumer commitments, then two broad remedial possibilities appear. One would be systemic, far-reaching reform of the economy itself; the other, a reordering of priorities within essentially the same old centralized command economy. Since the 1971–75 Plan indicates no readiness to embrace systemic reform, this route would appear closed. What about the other?

As some would see it, the Soviet leaders have decided—or may be in the process of deciding—to reorder their priorities rather drastically. In a sense, this view would imply, Khrushchev's successors are returning essentially to his pre-Cuban crisis pattern of priorities—preparing to concentrate on the modernization of their technologically lagging civilian economy at the expense of any large new commitment of resources to defense. Not only may they look to halting the strategic competition, in this view, but the criticality of an expanding labor force to attainment of economic growth goals may lead them to resume a substantial demobilization of military manpower along the lines of Khrushchev's troop reduction programs. A move toward further conversion of defense industry production to civilian needs and the transfer of defense industry research and development (R&D) and management expertise to civilian sectors of the economy are among other possibilities seen to be foreshadowed by Brezhnev's exegesis on the 1971–75 Plan.[13] Brezhnev's own apparent personal ascendancy over the rest of the collective leadership is also considered a development that may give him the power to overcome internal bureaucratic resistance to change in the old order of priorities. Needless to say, if this general interpretation of the direction in which the Soviet leadership intends to move is correct, then a strong and continuing economic incentive to conclude a strategic arms limitation agreement with the United States would obviously exist.

A quite contrary interpretation can of course also be advanced, resting primarily upon the proposition that the growing resources at the disposal of the Soviet leaders today make it possible for them to deal with their economic problems without recourse to fundamental systemic change or a drastic reordering of priorities, either of which would probably encounter internal bureaucratic resistance that even an ascendant Brezhnev, if so inclined, would find difficult to circumvent. In this view, the promises to consumers—which may have been beefed up in the 1971–75 Plan at the last moment to appease workers' discontent of the kind manifested in Poland in late 1970—are still sufficiently modest to be met without disturbing the Plan's preferential treatment for those sectors of the economy supporting military-industrial growth. But in the event that planned commitments should overextend the available resources, the more likely result, according to this view, is that military-industrial priorities would be satisfied first, as in the past—leaving consumers, agriculture, and other residual claimants again shortchanged. The implication here, obviously, is that the new Five-Year Plan imposes no economic imperatives upon the Soviet leadership to bow out of the strategic arms race via the SALT.

As usual, to fall back on that trite but true device of analysis, time alone will tell us which of the foregoing appraisals is the sounder. My own judgment—and biases—tell me that the latter comes somewhat closer to the mark. Although I do subscribe to the view that economic pressures have helped both to bring the Soviet Union to the SALT and to keep them there through more than two years of negotiations, it also seems to me, as I have stated elsewhere,[14] that economic considerations have not been the prime determinant of Soviet strategic policy in the past, nor are they likely to be in the future.

The Soviet leaders have asserted from time to time that their economy can stand the strain of further arms competition and that they will not let themselves be "intimidated" by those who think otherwise. In this instance, we should perhaps take them at their word. Thus, it seems reasonable to suppose that, though they may be quite reluctant to allow any large increases in the military share of available resources, the Soviet leaders are prepared to devote at least as large a proportion of the national income to military purposes as was the case during the strategic buildup of the sixties [15]—*provided that* they consider such a level of military preparation necessary to support Soviet interests. This proviso, of course, is the key point, for it shifts the prime determinants of decision to other than economic grounds.

Institutional and Bureaucratic Considerations

In order properly to understand the influence of institutional and bureaucratic factors upon Soviet policy toward the SALT, one would have to know a lot more about the structure and process of policy-making in the Soviet system than is the case. However, let us make a stab at the subject here, beginning with a few remarks on the two most frequently used analytical models of the Soviet policy-making process.[16]

The first—one might call it the unitary command model—has a lineage that goes back to the totalitarianism of the Stalin period. It rests on the basic assumption that an authoritarian leadership with highly centralized machinery of planning and control at its disposal is in a position to make up its mind according to its own calculation of preferred policy alternatives, and to dictate its decisions to all subordinate echelons of party and state for implementation. Viewed in terms of this model, the Soviet policymaking process is seen as the work of a fully informed unitary leadership that is always the master and never the captive of the overlapping bureaucracies over which it presides,[17] and that, within the parameters of opportunity and constraint confronting any government, will make rational policy choices best suited to serve its perceived interests.

In recent years, a new paradigm or model has come to be favored by some Western scholars looking to the concepts of comparative systems analysis and the theory of complex organizations for better ways to interpret the processes of change, diversification, and interest-group politics at work within the formal structure of Soviet institutions. The basic assumption upon which this second or bureaucratic model rests is that no single centralized leadership entity—even in a highly authoritarian or totalitarian system—has the time or information at its disposal to make all of the important decisions for the system. Since the top leadership cannot master all the details and complexities of the issues with which it deals, it must depend on inputs of information and technical judgment flowing upward from subordinate organizations. These organizations in turn operate according to the "laws" and habits of bureaucracies in general: They have their own axes to grind, constituencies to please, traditional claims on the budget, commitments to programs already laid down; they tend to apply old routines to new problems, to pursue such interests as self-preservation and growth along with their assigned tasks, and so on. As centers of partial power in the system, the various bureaucracies have a claim to be heard; the way they marshal their arguments and the skill of their advocacy can help to shape the issues as they are presented to the top leadership, so that in a sense the policy options open to it are already somewhat circumscribed before they become a matter of decision.

Besides emphasizing the effect of bureaucratic phenomena upon Soviet policy-making, this model views the top leadership itself as a far-from-homogeneous group prepared to speak with a single voice on the issues that come before it. Rather, the ruling oligarchy is presumed to have many differing alignments of interest and ties with various competing pressure groups; it is seen to engage in internal political maneuvering and to strike committee compromises that may tend to water down its decisions or even rob them of logical consistency upon occasion.

Both of the foregoing models would seem to have rather different implications for the Soviet approach to SALT. If the first case applies, for example, one should expect the top Soviet leadership to have gone into the SALT with its "single" mind made up—that is to say, without differing essentially as to what Soviet objectives should be. Moreover, the leadership should have faced no real impediments from within the Soviet bureaucratic structure to working out any agreements it might see fit with the United States. On the other hand, if the second case applies, there may have been not only competing policy preferences within the top leadership itself, but bureaucratic phenomena, and the influence of pressure groups within the system may have made it difficult to arrive at a coordinated position on agreements with the United States.

Which of these cases more closely approximates Soviet reality is open to argument. I am inclined, with certain reservations,[18] toward the second, both on the basis of some evidence—to be taken up later in this chapter [19]—that formulation of a SALT position has been a discordant issue within the Soviet establishment and on more general grounds relating to the role and relative influence of various interest groups on Soviet policy. Let me pursue the latter question further at this point.

For both doctrinal and practical reasons, Soviet leaders have customarily denied the existence of interest groups in the Soviet Union. Doctrinally, it runs against the Marxist-Leninist grain for the Soviet leaders to admit that rival interests may arise within a supposedly classless society.[20] In practical terms, they have sought to suppress the emergence of autonomous groups of any kind that might develop a life of their own and challenge the leadership monopoly of the party. Nevertheless, a kind of creeping pluralism seems to have spread within the system, and the leaders themselves appear to have tacitly recognized this not only by acting as arbiters among various institutional and interest groups, but also by occasionally championing the cause of one group at the expense of another.[21]

Several broad groups that have interests of one kind or another in SALT are discussed briefly here. They include the foreign affairs intelligentsia, the scientific intelligentsia, the military, and that portion of the R&D and industrial establishment best described perhaps as the "military-industrial complex." Each of these in turn embraces a variety of subgroups.

THE FOREIGN AFFAIRS INTELLIGENTSIA

As treated here, this group is understood to exclude the political chieftains who preside over Soviet affairs at the Politburo level; rather, it is made up primarily of those elements of party-government officialdom professionally concerned with foreign policy and related matters and lodged bureaucratically in such places as the Ministry of Foreign Affairs, the apparatus of the Party Secretariat and Central Committee, the intelligence services, and various schools for diplomatic training.[22] This group also includes specialists to be found in certain academic institutes that conduct research in foreign policy and arms control fields, such as the recently founded Institute of the U.S.A. and the older Institute of World Economics and International Relations, both of which come under the aegis of the USSR Academy of Sciences.

The extent to which the foreign affairs intelligentsia may influence policy, as distinct from the part it plays in running the day-to-day business of Soviet diplomacy, is difficult to ascertain. In the past, under both Stalin and Khrushchev, the professional voice of the Ministry of Foreign Affairs apparently carried little policy weight, as epitomized by Khrushchev's remark that "Gromyko only says what we tell him to. . . . If he doesn't we'll fire him and get someone who does."[23] Under the present regime, neither Brezhnev nor Kosygin has stepped into Khrushchev's shoes as the pre-eminent spokesman of Soviet foreign policy, and the fact that Gromyko is no longer treated disparagingly suggests that his stature and that of the professionals who support him have grown.[24]

With respect to the SALT, no one viewpoint can be attributed to a group as diverse as the foreign affairs intelligentsia. However, one might suppose that its general orientation lies in the direction of keeping the negotiations going and exploring the opportunities they present for diplomatic gains. The merging of foreign policy interests, such as Soviet-U.S. relations, with defense considerations is probably of concern to this group, but its competence in the defense field and its direct influence upon military policy decisions would appear to be rather limited. The apparent compartmentalization between the diplomatic and defense personnel in the Soviet SALT delegation, for example, seems to suggest that the integration of foreign and defense policy issues occurs at the upper reaches of the governing apparatus, possibly through ad hoc bodies set up for the purpose, rather than at routine working levels of the bureaucracy.[25]

The policy role of the academic specialists within the foreign affairs intelligentsia merits some additional comment. In recent years, a number of these men have made scholarly visits to the United States, and at least one of them—G. A. Arbatov, director of the Institute of the U.S.A.—has been reputed to have the ear of Kosygin and other highly placed leaders. Since the published material of Arbatov's institute has tended to reflect a more sophisticated analysis of the factors shaping American foreign policy than the "primitive sloganeering" of other Soviet media,[26] the question arises: How may Soviet policy be affected by the addition of this new analytical source to the previously existing information-gathering and analysis networks serving the Soviet leadership? The question is not easily answered, for it immediately raises others: How much access to the political summit do the academic specialists really enjoy, and is their advice treated as a serious input to decision-making? Perhaps, as one observer has put it, the most to be expected from the analytical contributions of the new breed of Soviet researchers is some dilution of the "ideological self-deception" to which the Soviet leadership may be prone.[27]

The Scientific Intelligentsia

From the early days of the Soviet state, the scientific intelligentsia has been treated as a relatively favored group because of the need for its expertise to modernize the society and create the scientific-technological base for Soviet military-industrial power. At the same time, however, successive Soviet regimes have sought to prevent the scientific elite from jelling into a cohesive institutional force that might challenge the decision-making prerogatives of the political leadership.

Thus, while senior Soviet scientists have been invited periodically to high policy councils as individual consultants on problems in their own fields of competence, they have been neither expected nor entitled to argue a case or to voice political judgments.[28] Similarly, despite its high prestige and importance as a national resource, the Soviet Academy of Sciences has been hedged around with restrictions designed to keep it from serving as a significant vehicle for policy-lobbying by the scientific community.[29] Another factor that has tended to discourage potential lobbying by the scientific intelligentsia is the rather large proportion of this group whose activities are wholly or in part associated with the defense sector of the Soviet research and development establishment.[30]

Scientists working in this sector have access to better research facilities and conditions than their counterparts in the civilian sector of the economy, but a side effect of these advantages is the constraint imposed upon expression of any disagreement with official policy.

Despite the various conditions that have acted to muffle potential dissent from Soviet scientists and to insulate them from the policy-making process, developments of the past few years suggest that trouble may be brewing for the Brezhnev-Kosygin regime within the scientific intelligentsia. The clandestine Sakharov "manifesto" of 1968 [31] and subsequent petitions by this eminent physicist and a few other Soviet scientists may be symptomatic of more widespread restiveness among the scientific elite, posing for the regime the delicate problem of how to deal with critics whose professed aim is to improve the Soviet system from within.

As far as SALT is concerned, Sakharov may already have had some influence on the Soviet position. His manifesto made a strong case against ABM defenses; indeed, in terms of traditional Soviet strategic policy and doctrine favoring such defenses, his argument amounted to heresy. It is notable that, although no public debate over the merits of ABM ensued in the Soviet Union, the Soviet side of SALT reportedly shifted later to a position that "concentrated on the need to curb rival anti-missile systems" [32]—a shift that may have been at least indirectly attributable to the man who is sometimes known as the father of the Soviet hydrogen bomb.

Whether or not the regime in fact was responsive to Sakharov's lobbying against ABM, there are some indications that its SALT position may be under general question within the Soviet scientific community. As pointed out recently by two American analysts, the regime has made very little use of scientists as propaganda spokesmen on matters relating to SALT.[33] This is in distinct contrast with the substantial propaganda role Soviet scientists had been called upon to play in the past on other disarmament issues, suggesting perhaps that a critical attitude among the scientific elite toward the regime's approach to the SALT may have counseled against repeating the past practice.

It must be emphasized, of course, that signs of latent dissatisfaction among Soviet scientists do not necessarily mean that the Brezhnev-Kosygin regime has a scientific revolt on its hands. The dissidents may represent only a bold minority, and the bulk of the scientific intelligentsia may have a vested interest in maintaining a status quo that gives high priority to defense-related research and development activity. Indeed, many scientists may side with other groups inclined to argue against tampering with the country's security by diverting Soviet technology from the very field in which it has competed most successfully with the West. If this conception of the national interest were to be widely held within the scientific elite, one might expect its members to favor a policy in the SALT designed to steer clear of agreements of the kind that could have the effect of terminating Soviet efforts to overtake the United States in areas of military technology where the USSR still lags behind, such as MIRV, certain fields of electronics, and data handling.

The Military

Like each previous Soviet regime, the present leadership has faced the problem of staking out the "permissible" limits of military influence on Soviet policy. In part, this problem arises because the military establishment, with its innate tendencies toward professional autonomy, is potentially the most powerful group in the society. True, the military establishment is not without its fair share of divergent internal alignments—among the services, between the professional officer corps and political officers, between a new class of military technicians and traditional line officers, and so on. However, these differing interest alignments tend to be overshadowed by strong binding elements of discipline, duty, and patriotism that give the Soviet military community a greater cohesiveness and sense of purpose than most other segments of the society, with the exception of the party *apparat* itself.

In general, without dwelling on the details of political-military relations under the Brezhnev-Kosygin regime, it can be said that the "permissible" sphere of military influence has grown, though I do not subscribe to the view advanced by an occasional newspaper columnist that there has been a major shift of political power to the marshals.[34] So far as the formal indices of power-standing are concerned, no military men have been taken into the Politburo—where Marshal Zhukov was the only professional soldier admitted in recent times—and the proportion of symbolic military representation on lesser party bodies such as the Central Committee and Central Auditing Commission has remained about the same under the Brezhnev-Kosygin regime as before.[35]

However, despite the unchanged formal footing of the military leaders at the summit of the Soviet policy-making structure, they have acquired greater prestige and influence under the present regime. The reasons for this are complex and cannot be explored here,[36] but the effect has been, by all accounts, to give the Ministry of Defense, headed by Marshal Grechko, and the General Staff, under Marshal Zakharov, both enlarged professional scope in managing the Soviet defense effort and greater opportunity for bringing military advice and expertise to bear in the policy councils of the regime.[37]

The internal channels of communication and the organizational arrangements through which the professional military voice reaches the top leadership are not well understood, but they apparently include the Higher Military Council, a policy-recommending body that brings together leading political and military officials,[38] and, as some analysts have suggested, a committee or commission of military and industrial officials to deal with defense production issues.[39] A high-level supervisory function over military R&D and procurement also rests with D. F. Ustinov, a member of the Party Secretariat, but the agency through which he exercises this function is not known. In addition to military access to the top leadership through intermediary bodies, direct consultation between the Politburo and military leaders has been a customary practice in the past and presumably continues.[40] An indication that military authorities may have been seeking additional institutional arrangements to provide a top-level link between themselves and the political leadership came to the surface in 1967, when the military press dwelt briefly on the need for peacetime creation of a single "supreme military-political organ." [41] However, this theme was soon dropped, with no hint as to whether such an organ had been set up.

Coming now to the question of military influence on Soviet SALT policy, one finds the military leadership in the somewhat ambivalent position of having to support the negotiations while also being concerned lest the talks lead to agreements that might adversely affect the Soviet military posture. This is not, of course, an unfamiliar dilemma for the Soviet military, nor one peculiar to the Soviet side of the arms control negotiating table.

Precisely how hard the Soviet military leaders have dragged their feet with respect to SALT is difficult to gauge, but that they have done so seems hardly disputable. There was clearly reluctance on the part of the military toward entering the talks at all,[42] and since the talks began in late 1969 the subject has been studiously avoided in the public statements of virtually every prominent figure in the Soviet military hierarchy.[43]

Although Soviet military leaders have shied away from discussion of the effects of SALT upon the Soviet military posture, they obviously have a close interest in this question. Some measure of the attention given the negotiations may be found in the composition of the Soviet delegation itself, one-third of which, in the phase 1 talks, was made up of military men.[44] The two most prominent military delegates were Colonel General N. V. Ogarkov, a first deputy chief of the General Staff, and Colonel General N. N. Alekseyev, formerly of the General Staff and now a Deputy Minister of Defense. Both of these men hold important posts having to do with weapons research and selection; they can be presumed to serve not only as informed advisers on these matters to the chairman of the Soviet delegation, Deputy Foreign Minister V. S. Semyonov, but also as watchdogs of the corporate interests of the Soviet military. Whether any of the military men on the delegation were institutional representatives of the Strategic Rocket Forces and the ABM component of the PVO (Air Defense) (the two military entities most immediately concerned with strategic arms) cannot be ascertained from the publicly available information, but presumably these institutions are represented. The defense industry sector appears to have a representative in the person of P. S. Pleshakov, deputy minister of radio industry.

Unfortunately, the confidential nature of the SALT proceedings permits little insight into the negotiating role of the Soviet military representatives or the influence they have had on substantive issues. Some indications of this influence can be obtained, however, in a few instances. One example is the FBS (Forward-based Systems) issue. The Soviet military press in the spring of 1970 zeroed in on the theme that so-called "tactical" aircraft based in the NATO area were "intended mainly to accomplish strategic tasks through direct nuclear strikes against targets in the Soviet Union." [45] Subsequently, it became known through comment in both the American and Soviet press that the Soviet Union had begun at about the same time to insist in SALT that forward-based U.S. tactical aircraft must be included in any limitation on strategic offensive weapons, on the grounds that such aircraft gave the United States "unilateral military advantages." [46] The inference is that urging from Soviet military quarters may have led to adoption of a stiff position on the FBS issue, even though this tended to muddy negotiations on intercontinental delivery systems.

To sum up, so far as one can judge, the Soviet marshals probably are not in a position to call the tune in the SALT. However, they may be able to exert a generally conservative influence on the negotiations, as a result of which the political leadership may tend to avoid proposals that might seem to give away military advantage for the sake of improving the negotiating climate.

The Soviet "Military-Industrial Complex"

Soviet commentators habitually deny that there is any counterpart in the USSR to what is known in the United States as the "military-industrial complex." [47] However, the institutional anatomy of such a complex is certainly visible in the Soviet Union, even though its inner workings are seldom open to scrutiny. It has two major segments: the producers of arms, or what Soviet sources customarily refer to as the "defense industry sector" of the economy; and the users, that is, the military establishment itself. These two bureaucracies and their numerous subgroups, which are knit together in a basic supplier-customer relationship and whose activities are overseen by various coordinating and controlling agencies at the upper levels of the party-government hierarchy, constitute the visible anatomy of the Soviet military-industrial complex.

A detailed description of this complex is not feasible here,[48] but a few words on the makeup of its industrial side may be worthwhile in order to assess its influence. Eight all-union ministries comprise the core of the "defense industry sector," which is responsible for the production of most military goods in the USSR, although several other industrial ministries also contribute to military production.[49] Conversely, some plants in the defense industries also manufacture a variety of products for the civilian economy, an effort which, as noted previously,[50] is currently receiving increased attention.

The defense industry bureaucracy has at least two notable features that bear on its potential as an interest group. The first is its continuity, both organizationally and in terms of key personnel. Since the late thirties, when a separate cluster of defense industries and their supporting R&D institutions was established,[51] these industries have tended to keep their centralized or "vertical" organizational structure intact throughout various industrial shakeups, including the economic decentralization of the 1957–65 period. As a result, though growth and change have occurred in the defense sector,[52] basic enterprise groupings and lines of ministerial authority have remained relatively more stable than in other economic sectors. As for personnel, essentially the same set of major executives has administered the defense-related industries for many years; the collective experience of the eight incumbent ministers (named in note 49), for example, totals more than two hundred years, so one may assume that these are men who know their way around within the Soviet bureaucratic world and who know how to manipulate it to serve their institutional interests.

A second pertinent feature of the defense industry sector is its symbiotic relationship with the military establishment. In the Soviet Union, not only production of military goods but the bulk of military R&D is carried out in institutions under the jurisdiction of the defense-related industrial ministries.[53] At the upper levels of the military establishment and the defense industries, the close link between military requirements and their fulfillment by the R&D and production programs of the defense industry sector apparently has led to a mutual interest in preserving arrangements that have enabled the Soviet Union to compete successfully against the West in the field of military technology.

But this community of interest has operated at sublevels of the interlocking military-industrial bureaucracies as well. An intricate network of ties has emerged between weapons design-production groups in industry and their immediate customers in the military establishment. One result is the formation of what might be called informal subgroup "alliances" devoted to promoting particular weapons categories—for example, between working elements of the Ministry of General Machine Building, which is believed to be responsible for design and production of strategic ballistic missiles,[54] and military representatives of the Strategic Rocket Forces.

How the various weapons procurement subgroups may be able to influence the Soviet SALT position is a highly speculative question. The groups concerned with offensive and defensive strategic systems have the most at stake in SALT, and may conceivably find their interests undercut by nonstrategic alliance groups hoping to capture more defense resources for their purposes. Some mediation of these competing claims presumably occurs within the General Staff and other Ministry of Defense agencies, but other regulatory bodies, involving such key figures as D. F. Ustinov, probably enter the picture before final judgments are made, lest the military agencies become both judges and advocates of their own projects. Finally, however, while the various alliance groups within the military-industrial complex may compete for priority among themselves, and perhaps seek their own power-wielding champions at higher rungs of the organizational ladder, they can also be expected to find common cause in resisting outside efforts to divert military-industrial resources to the civilian sector.

Strategic Considerations

The linkage between the Soviet-U.S. strategic competition and Soviet interest in SALT is a complex but obviously central question, to which the remainder of this chapter will be devoted. If in a broad sense the United States was the more reactive party in the Soviet-U.S. strategic competition of the fifties, responding vigorously first to Korea and then to successive "bomber gap" and "missile gap" alarms, the situation changed notably after the Cuban missile crisis of 1962. Thereafter, it was the Soviet Union that embarked upon a massive buildup of its strategic forces, while the United States, having achieved its own self-imposed strategic force ceilings by the mid-sixties, tended to rest on its strategic oars, as it were, during the last half of the decade, except for largely prudential R&D activity.

There appears to be no doubt that the embarrassment suffered by the Soviet Union in the Cuban showdown and the "never again" reaction of the Soviet leadership contributed significantly to the Soviet strategic buildup under the Brezhnev-Kosygin regime. However, the widespread impression that the buildup was solely a reaction to Cuba and almost wholly the handiwork of Khrushchev's successors does seem open to question, for the foundations of the buildup had in fact been largely laid by R&D programs and initial missile deployments carried out under Khrushchev. At the time of Khrushchev's ouster in the fall of 1964, the Soviet inventory of operational ICBMs had reached about two hundred launchers, mostly the second-generation SS-7, and initial steps for the deployment of the third-generation SS-9 and SS-11 had been taken.

During the early shakedown period of the Brezhnev-Kosygin regime, the strategic programs set in motion under Khrushchev went on without interruption, but there were signs—such as the "stand-pat" military budget for 1965, announced in December 1964—that new defense-resource decisions were being held in abeyance while a general review of defense policy took place. This reappraisal apparently generated some controversy over resource priorities, as suggested by the renewal in 1965 of doctrinal criticism by military writers of Khrushchev's "one-sided" deterrence philosophy, on the grounds that adherence to such thinking ignored the possibility that deterrence might fail and could lead to questioning the need for large defense outlays.[55] The process of reappraisal may have lasted well into 1965, or perhaps up to the Twenty-third Party Congress in April 1966, when Kosygin indicated that, in the light of a worsening international situation attributed to American "aggression" in Vietnam and elsewhere, the case for larger defense expenditures carried the day.[56]

Although the traditional ground, air, and naval forces all seem to have gotten an increased share of the larger military budgets approved by the new regime from 1966 on, the strategic forces in which we are interested here obviously received priority support. The buildup effort that had begun with the construction of SS-9 and SS-11 silos was stepped up sharply, and in 1966 both of these new systems reached operational status. By the fall of 1969, the Soviet ICBM force reached an operational strength of 1,060 launchers—giving the Soviet Union a slightly larger land-based ICBM force than the United States for the first time since the earliest days of the missile age. Meanwhile, the USSR had also begun to modernize and expand its missile-launching submarine force with the introduction in 1968 of the Y-Class nuclear-powered submarine, equipped with sixteen ballistic missile launch tubes.

From the latter part of 1969 to the present, during the first two years of the SALT negotiations, the strategic programs of the Brezhnev-Kosygin regime have appeared to be aimed at bringing about further quantitative and qualitative changes in the Soviet strategic posture. On the quantitative side, the total land-based ICBM force was increased to about fifteen hundred operational launchers, of which around nine hundred were SS-11s and about a third of that number were SS-9s.[57] The remainder consisted of some two hundred SS-7s and 8s and a small number of SS-13s, solid-fuel ICBMs introduced in 1969 but deployed only at a desultory rate thereafter. The SLBM force also grew, thanks to a Y-Class construction program of about eight boats per year, bringing the number of submarine-launched ballistic missiles to about four hundred by October 1971.

On the qualitative side, there were several significant developments. It became known in 1969 that a version of the SS-11 capable of being fired at either peripheral or intercontinental targets was being installed at IR/MRBM launch complexes in the southwestern USSR, a move that promised to give the Soviets a flexible, dual-purpose delivery system against targets in either Europe or the United States.[58] Testing of a new, more accurate warhead for the SS-11 also began in 1969. In the case of the SS-9, Soviet activity included programs for orbital and depressed trajectory versions of this system and another program for development of an MRV capability.[59] The latter program involved numerous test firings from August 1968 through the fall of 1970. This modification program may have been meant to lay the basis for MIRV development also, but up to mid-1971 no positive progress toward a true MIRV capability had been demonstrated.[60]

Another qualitative step in the strategic delivery field was the development and testing of a new long-range ballistic missile, ostensibly for submarine launching, while the appearance in 1969 of a new prototype medium bomber of advanced variable-wing design marked an unexpected Soviet development in the strategic aircraft field.[61] Finally, efforts to improve the qualitative aspects of the Soviet strategic posture were underscored by the initiation in late 1970 of a program for construction of new large silos at launch complexes associated with both the SS-9 and the SS-11.[62] By mid-1971 some eighty of these silos were reported under construction,[63] although how many more are to be built and their intended purpose remain unknown at this writing. Soviet sources have said only that they represent "modernization." [64] At a minimum, the new silos seem meant to improve the survivability of a portion of the existing Soviet missile force; they might also be intended to house an as-yet-untested follow-on missile system.

On the face of it, the sustained buildup of Soviet strategic forces throughout the latter sixties and early seventies would seem to suggest that no serious dissent over strategic policy had arisen within the Brezhnev-Kosygin regime. Moreover, though the regime's military commitments from about 1966 to 1967 on clearly indicated a substantial diversion of resources to support both a costly strategic buildup and new programs to improve the capabilities of other forces, its military policies appear to have been less abrasive internally than those of the Khrushchev era. Despite a seeming climate of consensus, however, it would probably be wrong to conclude that debate over alternative strategic policy courses subsided altogether. Indeed, there were from time to time signs to the contrary.

One such indication was the delay of about eighteen months in the initial Soviet decision to enter the SALT, which suggested that formulation of a position on strategic arms negotiations was a discordant issue within the Brezhnev-Kosygin regime. Although American eagerness to discuss limitation of strategic forces was in a sense a tribute to the political efficacy of the Soviet strategic buildup, the Soviet military in particular displayed a thinly veiled distaste for entering talks to curb further competition. This showed up in a series of patently skeptical articles by military writers in late 1968 and 1969. Among other things, the articles hinted that it was "illusory" to seek Soviet security via arms agreements; they reiterated the familiar theme that Soviet military policy should aim at the attainment of superiority; and they cited Lenin's advice about the inevitability of war between the rival systems as a better guideline for Soviet military preparations than banking on the possibility of preventing war.[65] These views stood in contrast with subsequent commentary from other Soviet quarters that neither side could realistically hope to gain advantage from a "new spiral in the arms race." [66]

A related indication of divergent viewpoints on strategic policy was the continued disputation over the issues of mutual destructiveness of nuclear war and the possibility of victory in such a war. One side of the dialogue was carried by writers who argued that nuclear war could mean only "suicide for both sides" and that consequently Soviet military strategy should concentrate on prevention of war, or deterrence,[67] a viewpoint that was challenged implicitly and explicitly in military literature asserting that Soviet forces should be prepared to win a nuclear war if one occurred.[68] Other issues bearing on Soviet strategic policy also were vented from time to time while the buildup of strategic forces was under way in the sixties. These included the relative importance to be accorded strategic nuclear forces and those for conventional and limited military conflict, the likelihood of a successful surprise attack and its implications, priority for investment between economic growth and further force buildup, and the need to apply some criteria of cost effectiveness in weapons decisions.

Unfortunately, the discourse on such matters has shed little direct light on what probably has been the central issue of strategic policy facing the Soviet leadership since the buildup began, namely: What kind of strategic relationship should be sought vis-à-vis the United States: parity or superiority?

A final answer is not yet in as to the Soviet leadership's stand on this issue. However, a number of pertinent strategic considerations may be noted. Whatever divergent preferences may have existed among the Soviet leaders when the strategic buildup began, all elements of the leadership appear to have agreed in the post-Cuba climate that nothing less than Soviet-American strategic equality would be tolerable any longer. Thus any potential differences between parity and superiority advocates could be submerged for the time being while the military-industrial bureaucracy attended to the business of catching up. By 1967, though parity had not yet been attained, it was at least in sight, the more so because by that time the U.S. standstill at a force ceiling of 1,054 ICBMs had been confirmed.

At the same time, the United States, as perceived from Moscow, probably presented a somewhat confusing strategic stance. On the one hand, there was the undeniable fact that the United States had halted further strategic deployments even in the face of the Soviet buildup. Along with deepening American involvement in Vietnam and overtures to discuss strategic arms limitations, this implied a weariness to continue strategic arms competition with the USSR. On the other hand, U.S. defense officials still spoke of enjoying a margin of strategic superiority of three or four to one, and the United States had taken a series of R&D steps in the strategic field that could be interpreted as measures to keep this margin from eroding. For example, authorization to develop Minuteman III and Poseidon, as well as Sprint and Spartan ABMs in 1965, had been followed in 1967 by decisions to produce MM III and Poseidon, and to develop a Sentinel thin area ABM defense system, later converted, in 1969, to the Safeguard missile-site defense concept. Subsequent disclosure in early 1970 of plans for expansion of the Safeguard concept and the beginning in mid-1970 of a MIRV retrofit program for Minuteman and Poseidon may have sharpened Soviet suspicion that the United States was preparing to bolster its own strategic posture, despite a professed desire to curb the strategic arms race.

From the Soviet viewpoint, therefore, it could be asked: Was the United States in the latter sixties merely employing delaying tactics to hold down its strategic budget until the Vietnam conflict was settled, after which it would embark on a new round of strategic competition based on such new systems as MIRV-equipped Minuteman III and Poseidon? [69] If so, then would it not have been wise for the Soviet Union to press on with its own strategic buildup—even beyond parity, while the opportunity was available? Without necessarily having to link their case to a specific objective, such as attainment of a first-strike capability (the feasibility of which was likely to have remained a contentious issue), advocates of a policy of going beyond parity could argue that further accretion of strategic power would represent an important general asset—providing increased room for political maneuvering, greater leverage in crisis situations, more options for dealing with unforeseen contingencies, and so on. Given the Soviet Union's post-Cuba experience, even those elements of the Soviet leadership disposed to question the utility of superiority and to worry about the cost of the arms race may have found such an argument persuasive. [70] Meanwhile, the SALT forum might also be usefully employed to explore American intentions and possibly to reach agreements that would block or slow down the adoption of new U.S. strategic programs. In effect, what is suggested here is that the Soviet leadership may have found it expedient to stick with a policy of strengthening the Soviet strategic posture to the extent that opportunity would permit, rather than making an explicit choice between halting the buildup at parity or striving for superiority. Although one has no way of knowing whether the matter was thus framed in Soviet policy councils, some such approach would square with the fact that the strategic buildup continued beyond a logical "leveling off" point at the end of the sixties, while at the same time the Soviet Union pursued negotiations with the United States in an apparently serious effort to reach agreement on strategic arms limitations.

What then can be said about the future decisions facing the Soviet leadership with respect to the SALT? One set of decisions seems to center on whether to allow Soviet strategic programs to lose their momentum before knowing for sure what the outcome of the strategic arms limitation talks will be. Obviously, if the talks should founder without agreement, an uninterrupted Soviet buildup could yield important advantage. But even if the prospect of some sort of agreement looks reasonably good, there are still some prickly decisions to be made. For example, should the Soviet Union now accept a freeze of the existing strategic balance, or should it try to keep the door open for improving the Soviet position? Insofar as a strategic balance could be measured toward the end of 1971, both pros and cons were involved from the Soviet viewpoint. The Soviet Union is far ahead of the United States in numbers of land-based ICBMs, and enjoys an advantage in throw weight and megatonnage and in deployed ABM defenses. It is still inferior, however, in total numbers of deliverable warheads, SLBMs, and intercontinental bombers and in MIRV technology and deployment. There is thus a strong likelihood of internal pressure, particularly from the Soviet military, not to curtail Soviet strategic programs until at least some of these deficiencies are remedied.

On the other hand, should the Soviet Union push too hard for advantage by further buildup and selective improvement of its strategic forces, the effect might be counterproductive. Instead of continuing to display a willingness to pay a substantial price for agreement on strategic curbs—the kind of reaction engendered by its past concern over the Soviet buildup, especially the SS-9 program—the United States might conceivably respond by stepping up the strategic competition. The fine line between driving a hard bargain with the United States and stimulating undesirable U.S. response is thus a consideration to be taken into account by the Soviet leadership.

A second area of strategic decision has to do with the kinds of agreements that might be reached in SALT. The Soviet Union had already proposed while the talks were in progress that negotiation on strategic delivery forces be set aside in favor of concentrating on defensive systems, although high-level intervention resulted in a compromise on this issue in May 1971 to keep the talks from bogging down.[71] It is apparent from this proposal that the Soviet side had not yet firmed up its own position on strategic delivery forces, and that it may have been seeking to buy time for construction of new launcher silos and other measures to upgrade these forces before coming to grips with an agreement.

But assuming that both offensive and defensive systems will remain on the negotiating agenda, another issue requiring decision is that of qualitative versus quantitative limitations. The former seem likely to involve inspection too intrusive for Soviet taste, if not for the United States as well, and may also tend to foreclose Soviet efforts to catch up in such lagging areas of technology as MIRV. On the other hand, if any agreements are to be confined to numerical ceilings on strategic systems, the effect may be to convert the strategic competition from a "numbers" into a "quality" race—a situation that would put a high premium upon technological capability. Since the Soviet Union has done well in numbers competition, but somewhat less so in certain areas of technology, its leaders are now faced with assessing Soviet prospects if the strategic race should be driven into exotic forms of technological competition. On this point, expert opinion differs. Some Western observers hold that the U.S. technological edge is such that the Soviet leaders would be very chary of engaging in a spiraling quality race. As others see it, the Soviet Union, operating as a strategic equal from an expanding scientific-technological base, stands a good chance of wresting the lead in military technology from the United States in the decade of the seventies, which should make the Kremlin leadership confident that it could cope with a shift in the strategic competition from numbers to quality.

Although the prospects appear somewhat remote, it is possible that the SALT talks may lead to an agreement that would effectively restrict both numerical and qualitative competition—in short, one that would stabilize strategic forces within the framework of overall power competition between the Soviet Union and the United States. In this event, the major military policy decisions facing the Soviet leadership would probably shift to such questions as how far to go in rechanneling Soviet resources toward further improvement of glob- ally mobile naval and general-purpose forces and toward bolstering the Soviet military posture against China. At the same time, an agreement stabilizing the strategic balance could also have side effects that would impose new decisions upon the Soviet leadership with respect to commitment of Soviet military power abroad. For example, a Soviet Union recognized as the strategic equal of the United States and possessing an improved capacity to intervene in local situations might find itself under greater pressure to come to the help of clients in other continents, where previously Moscow was excused from be-coming directly engaged because it obviously lacked the wherewithal to do so.

But by far the most knotty decisions facing the Soviet leadership —and the American side as well—will doubtless arise should the SALT fail to produce any agreement. Then the critical question will be: Where do we go from here? How this question may be answered remains one of the larger uncertainties of the seventies. So far as the Soviet Union is concerned, the decisions would seem to involve some very tough choices.

Having just sunk a big investment in fixed ICBM forces to over-take the United States, the Soviets would face a period when MIRV plus improved accuracy could render their fixed forces much more vulnerable than was assumed when these forces were planned in the sixties. Even though the new silo program may have been intended as insurance against failure of the strategic arms limitation talks, its extension on a scale sufficient to improve the survivability of a significant proportion of the ICBM force would be an expensive and lengthy process, and in the light of potential delivery accuracies, the force might still remain quite vulnerable.

Where then, under circumstances of a renewed round of strategic competition, should Soviet emphasis be placed? What new mix of fixed or mobile land-based missiles and underseas and airborne de-livery systems would best answer the requirements of the seventies? What role for active defense? How much and what kind of effort to expend on ASW systems? Adding to the perplexity of decisions on such matters, the Soviets could no longer design their strategic forces to overtake a known and relatively static U.S. strategic force posture, but would have to plan against a future U.S. force with perhaps greatly changed characteristics, not to mention other strategic forces that might be fielded by such opponents as China.

Needless to say, it would be imprudent to assume that the problems involved will discourage the Soviet Union from renewing strategic com-petition if future strategic arms limitations talks should collapse. The Soviet strategic position, after all, is relatively much stronger today than it has ever been, and it is quite possible that the United States may prove a less formidable competitor than previously. Moreover, though the difficulties ahead may be numerous, the range of options available to the Soviet Union has also grown. It does appear warranted to conclude, however, that deciding "where to go from here" in the event that SALT comes to naught will confront the Soviet leadership with many more complicated and contentious questions than was the case when the decision was reached earlier, in the sixties, to catch up with the United States.

NOTES

1. In this connection, one may advert to the rather somber reminder offered recently by Peter Wiles: "An imperialist power must feel a great historic righteousness about what it does, and citizens of its core nationality must share much of this feeling." These words appeared in an article entitled "The Declining Self-Confidence of the Superpowers," *International Affairs* (London), 47, no. 2 (April 1971), p. 289. Despite use of the plural in the title, Wiles's article made it plain that the description tends to fit one of the superpowers more than the other.

2. See David Holloway, "Technology, Management and the Soviet Military Establishment," *Adelphi Papers,* Institute for Strategic Studies, no. 76 (London, April 1971), pp. 4–9.

3. According to some Western experts, Soviet GNP grew at an annual rate of 5.7 percent in 1965–67, while defense expenditure increased at a rate of 7.9 percent. See Stanley H. Cohn, "Economic Burden of Soviet Defense Outlays" in *Soviet Economy and National Security* (Washington, D.C.: Congress of the United States, Joint Economic Committee, November–December 1969); John P. Hardt, *Economic Insights on Current Soviet Policy and Strategy* (McLean, Va.: Research Analysis Corporation, December 1969), p. 38.

4. The Brezhnev-Kosygin regime was twice obliged to lower key economic targets for 1970, the terminal year of the eighth Five-Year Plan. See Thomas W. Wolfe, *Impact of Economic and Technological Issues on the Soviet Approach to SALT,* P-4368 (Washington, D.C.: The RAND Corporation, June 1970), p. 8.

5. Industrial output, according to Soviet data, increased at an average annual rate of 8.4 percent during the 1966–70 period. See *Pravda* (February 14, 1971).

6. As stated in speeches by U. S. Secretary of Defense Melvin R. Laird on February 25 and August 26, 1969, Soviet strategic-force expenditures were at an annual rate of about $18 billion, more than double the U.S. level.

7. In this connection, themes that began to receive emphasis in Soviet journals in the late sixties and early seventies included the inability of the American economy to provide "guns and butter simultaneously" and the rise of politically significant domestic opposition, even within U.S. "ruling circles," to the government's arms policies. See, for example: G. A. Arbatov, "Complex Problems, Difficult Solutions," *Izvestiia* (January 11, 1969), and his lead article in *S Sh S*—*Ekonomika, Politika, Ideologiia* [U.S.A.—economics, politics, ideology], no. 1 (January 1970), pp. 21–34; A. Melnikov, "Intelligentsia of the USA: Numbers, Composition, Social Differentiation," *Mirovaia Ekonomika i Mezhdunarodnie Otnosheniia* [World economics and international relations] (January 1970), p. 111; V. Kulish and S. Fedorenko, "The Discussion in the U.S.A. over Strategic Arms," *Mirovaia Ekonomika* (March 1970), pp. 43–46.

8. The rise in overall Soviet output in 1970, the final year of the eighth Five-Year Plan, halted the declining trend of the two preceding years and helped to improve fulfillment of the revised goals of the 1966–70 Plan. Although a bumper

year in agriculture accounted in large part for the 1970 recovery, published statistics also showed an increase in several key economic indices. For example, compared with 1969, the industrial growth rate rose from 7 to 8.3 percent and labor productivity from 4.4 to more than 7 percent. See Report of N. K. Baibakov, Chairman of the USSR State Planning Committee, *Pravda* (February 4, 1971).

9. Group B output is scheduled to grow 44–49 percent, compared with 41–45 percent for Group A. The data here are drawn from the Draft Directives for the ninth Five-Year Plan, published in *Pravda* (February 14, 1971), and from the reports by Brezhnev and Kosygin at the Twenty-fourth Party Congress, *Pravda* (March 31 and April 7, 1971).

10. A compromise formula on allocation of resources was expected to be reached before submission of the Plan's final draft to the Supreme Soviet in September 1971. At this writing, however, it has not been learned how the matter was resolved.

11. Brezhnev also made the unprecedented "revelation" that 42 percent of the production capacity of the defense industries was already being devoted to output of civilian goods.

12. Soviet spokesmen, however, emphasized the far larger absolute national income that would accrue under the 1971–75 Plan, even though the rate of growth would slow somewhat. Kosygin, for example, noted that national income under the new Plan was to average 325 billion rubles annually, compared with a 233 billion average under the previous Plan. This, he said, would provide the "material foundation" for implementing the tasks of the new Plan. See *Pravda* (April 7, 1971).

13. In his Twenty-fourth Party Congress report, Brezhnev made a special point of the need for civilian enterprises to profit from the know-how and efficiency of defense industry (a point that Khrushchev in his time had also made). Brezhnev did not, however, indicate that he was thinking of direct transfer of defense R&D and industrial facilities and personnel to the civilian sector.

14. "Soviet Approaches to SALT," *Problems of Communism,* 19 (September–October 1970), p. 3.

15. What the share of Soviet income allocated to military purposes actually amounts to is, needless to say, a vexatious question, clouded by Soviet secrecy and numerous other problems of measuring the real costs of defense in resource terms. According to figures given by Kosygin at the Twenty-fourth Party Congress, the 80 billion rubles budgeted for defense during the 1966–70 Plan absorbed about 25 percent of the "accumulation" portion of national income (that portion available for growth purposes, as distinct from consumption). How much Soviet military spending might be increased without putting an "intolerable" brake on economic growth rates is another complicated question. Some Western observers, including this writer, have hazarded a guess that an annual military increase of about 4 percent within a GNP growth rate of 5 to 6 percent —roughly the parameters obtained in the latter half of the sixties—would continue to be tolerable. In any case, neither of these two questions immediately affects the point made above—that the Soviet leaders are probably prepared to bear at least as great a military outlay as before should their interests so require.

16. For a more detailed discussion, see Thomas W. Wolfe, *Policymaking in*

the Soviet Union: A Statement with Supplementary Comments P–4131 (Washington, D.C.: The RAND Corporation, June 1969).

17. Although the tendency of bureaucracies to look out for their own interests is recognized by this model, it is assumed that in the Soviet case the political leaders from Stalin onward have successfully managed to ensure compliance from their administrative bureaucracies and to prevent the formation of lower-level power centers in the system.

18. My reservations toward the "pure" bureaucratic model in the Soviet case stem from two points. First, the power of bureaucracies lies more in their ability to obstruct innovation than to take initiatives, and since the Soviet system has shown a capacity for policy initiatives from the central leadership, the latter presumably has found ways to impose its will upon the system's administrative machinery. Second, the dual character of Soviet bureaucracy—a government machine to administer the country's affairs and a party apparatus to give directions and check on performance, with all these divided functions coalescing in a small coterie of leaders at the top—tends to smudge the features of the pure bureaucratic model. As one observer has put it, the Soviet administrative system tends to work precisely because it violates many of the principles of a classical bureaucracy. See Jerry F. Hough, *The Soviet Prefects: The Local Party Organs in Industrial Decision-Making* (Cambridge, Mass.: Harvard University Press, 1969), p. 3.

19. See pp. 41 and 42.

20. Although the Soviet system does not sanction the politics of "social bargaining," the existence of differing "social groups" that share a particular "community of goals and interests" is sometimes recognized. See G. V. Osipov, ed., *Sotsiologiia v SSSR* [Sociology in the USSR], vol. II (Moscow: Izdatel'stvo "Mysl'," 1966), p. 487.

21. Or, conversely, some leaders have courted particular groups to strengthen their own hand in elite politics, a case in point being the support of the military solicited by Khrushchev in 1957 to help repel the challenge of the so-called "antiparty group."

22. For a good description of the Soviet foreign policy elites, see Jan F. Triska and David D. Finley, *Soviet Foreign Policy* (New York: The Macmillan Company, 1968), pp. 75–106.

23. Averell Harriman, "My Alarming Interview with Khrushchev," *Life* (July 13, 1959), p. 33. A discussion of the generally subordinate policy role of the Foreign Ministry under Stalin may be found in Robert M. Slusser, "The Role of the Foreign Ministry" in Ivo J. Lederer, ed., *Russian Foreign Policy* (New Haven: Yale University Press, 1962), pp. 211–39.

24. An index of Gromyko's improved stature is provided by comparing the frequency with which he participated in top-level diplomatic talks with important foreign leaders under the Khrushchev and Brezhnev-Kosygin regimes. During the 1961–63 period, his participation was slightly below 60 percent. In the first two years of the successor regime, the figure went above 85 percent. This comparison is drawn from an unpublished dissertation by Jon D. Glassman, "Soviet Foreign Policy Decision-Making" (Columbia University, 1968), p. 135.

25. For what it is worth, a member of the Institute of World Economics and International Relations stated in a recent interview that ad hoc bodies are fre-

quently convened to recommend resolution of knotty issues involving foreign policy and defense interests. The Soviet scholar in question also implied that an important mediating role in ironing out such issues before they reach the Politburo's agenda is played by the professional staff of the Central Committee.

26. For an analysis of the published output of Arbatov's institute during a six-month period in 1970, see Merle Fainsod, "Through Soviet Eyes," *Problems of Communism,* 19 (November–December 1970), pp. 59–64.

27. Zbigniew Brzezinski, "Know Thy Enemy," *Newsweek* (August 30, 1971), p. 40.

28. *Cf.* Alexander Dallin et al., *The Soviet Union, Arms Control, and Disarmament* (New York: Columbia University, School of International Affairs, 1964), p. 62.

29. The creation of various bodies for the control of scientific activity, such as the State Committee for the Coordination of Scientific Research and its successors, while aimed toward improvement of the national research effort, also has had the effect of reducing the autonomy and potential policy leverage of the Academy of Sciences.

30. Reliable figures are not available on the number of Soviet scientific professional personnel associated with defense R&D. The total number of scientific professionals given by both Soviet and Western sources is, however, in fairly close agreement. For example, the figure of 660,000 for 1966 is given by Nikolai D. Tiamshanskii, *Ekonomika i organizatsiia nauchno-issledovatel'skikh rabot v mashinostroenii* [Economics and organization of scientific-research work in machine building] (Leningrad, 1967), p. 6. This compares with a figure of 670,000 for 1966 in E. Zaleski et al., *Science Policy in the USSR* (Paris: OECD, 1969), p. 137. If Western estimates that 60–75 percent of the total R&D expenditures in the USSR are in the defense sector can be roughly correlated with personnel involved, then the number of scientific professionals associated with defense R&D might be on the order of 400,000 to 500,000.

31. Andrei Sakharov, *Progress, Coexistence, and Intellectual Freedom* (New York: W. W. Norton, 1968). This document has been circulated clandestinely via *samizdat* in the Soviet Union, but has not been published there.

32. Chalmers M. Roberts, "Third Round of SALT Winds Up in Helsinki," *Washington Post* (December 19, 1970).

33. Matthew P. Gallagher and Karl F. Spielmann, Jr., *The Public Understanding of SALT in the Soviet Union: A Study of Soviet Propaganda Policy and the Awareness Levels of Selected Population Groups,* vol. 1 (Arlington, Va.: Institute for Defense Analyses, March 1971), p. 26.

34. See Thomas W. Wolfe, "Are the Generals Taking Over?," *Problems of Communism,* 18 (July–October 1969), pp. 106–10.

35. In fact, the military representation on the Central Committee (full and candidate members) declined slightly at the two Party Congresses held under the Brezhnev-Kosygin regime, to about 8.5 percent from the 10 percent elected at the Twenty-second Party Congress in 1961. On the other hand, the actual number of military men made full members of the Central Committee (i.e., with voting rights) increased from fourteen at the Twenty-second Party Congress to twenty at the Twenty-fourth Party Congress.

36. Several categories of reasons might be briefly mentioned: (1) Internal elite politics. The Brezhnev-Kosygin regime owed some debt to the military for "co-

operating" in Khrushchev's ouster. No single collective leader had, initially at least, the personal prestige to flout professional military opinion as Khrushchev had done. (2) Greater dependence on the instrumental role of the military in support of Soviet policy interests, cases in point being the Czechoslovak intervention, the border crises with China, and the expansion of the Soviet presence in the Middle East and Mediterranean. (3) The "successes" scored by the military, notably the well-executed handling of the military phase of the Czechoslovak episode and the effect of the strategic buildup in boosting the USSR to full strategic equality with the United States. (4) Finally, the increasing complexity and cost of maintaining modern military power, calling for encouragement of innovation and efficiency in the management of military affairs, and thus putting a higher premium on professional expertise.

37. For an informed analysis of some of the trends that have enlarged the professional role of the Soviet military, see the study by David Holloway cited in note 2 of this chapter. Marshal M. V. Zakharov, the aging Chief of the General Staff, was replaced by a younger man, General V. G. Kulikov, in late 1971.

38. The current status of the Higher Military Council (*Vysshii Voennyi Sovet*) is somewhat obscure. Khrushchev chaired this body in his time, but both Brezhnev and Kosygin have been mentioned as succeeding to the role. For background discussion of this institution, see Thomas W. Wolfe, *The Soviet Military Scene: Institutional and Defense Policy Considerations*, RM-4913-PR (Washington, D.C.: RAND Corporation, June 1966), pp. 11–12. See also Roman Kolkowicz, *The Soviet Military and the Communist Party* (Princeton: Princeton University Press, 1967), pp. 58–77, 124–43.

39. See Holloway, "Technology, Management and the Soviet Military Establishment," p. 6; Andrew Sheren, "Structure and Organization of Defense-Related Industries," in *Economic Performance and the Military Burden in the Soviet Union* (Washington, D.C.: Congress of the United States, Joint Economic Committee, 1970), p. 124.

40. Both Khrushchev and the late Marshal R. Ya. Malinovskii, Minister of Defense under Khrushchev, gave public accounts of this practice in the early sixties. See N. S. Khrushchev, *O vneshnei politike Sovetskogo Soiuza: 1960* [The foreign policy of the Soviet Union: 1960], vol. I (Moscow, 1961), p. 34; *Krasnaia zvezda* (April 17, 1964).

41. See Major General V. Zemskov, "For the Theoretical Seminar: An Important Factor for Victory in War," *Krasnaia zvezda* (January 5, 1967).

42. See pp. 41 and 42 in this chapter. See also Gallagher and Spielmann, *Public Understanding of SALT*, pp. 20–25.

43. A conspicuous example was the report delivered by Marshal Grechko at the Twenty-fourth Party Congress, in which he repeatedly accused "U.S. ruling circles" of such nefarious activities as "stepping up preparations for war against the Soviet Union" without once paying even lip service to the strategic arms negotiations. See *Pravda* (April 3, 1971).

44. The original Soviet SALT delegation numbered twenty-four (six delegates and eighteen advisers), of whom eight were military officers (two delegates, six advisers). This compared with a U.S. delegation of twenty-four, of whom five were military officers (one delegate, four advisers). The U.S. delegation also included five civilians currently or formerly associated with the Defense Depart-

ment. How many of the Soviet civilians were in a comparable category is not known. Some changes have occurred in both delegations in the course of the negotiations, but the military-civilian ratio has remained about the same.

45. Colonel V. Aleksandrov, "For Carrying Out an Aggressive Policy: Attack Aviation of the U.S.A.," *Krasnaia zvezda* (May 13, 1970). See also Gallagher and Spielmann, *Public Understanding of SALT*, p. 24.

46. See Hedrick Smith, "After the Helsinki Arms Talks, New Complications," *New York Times* (December 24, 1970); V. Shestov, "What Is Behind the Propaganda Screen?," *Pravda* (February 3, 1971).

47. Soviet assertions that the USSR has no military-industrial complex rest on the fiction that the absence of the profit motive in the Soviet system makes such a complex impossible by definition. See, for example, Colonel General K. Skorobogatkin, "In the Interests of Aggression and Profits," *Krasnaia zvezda* (December 28, 1969).

48. For useful treatment of the subject, see: Sheren, "Structure and Organization of Defense-Related Industries"; William T. Lee, "Soviet Military Industrial Complex," *Armed Forces Management* (May 1970), pp. 25–35; Richard Armstrong, "Military-Industrial Complex—Russian Style," *Fortune* (August 1, 1969), pp. 85–126. See also the *Journal of International Affairs*, 26, no. 1 (1972), for a special issue devoted to the "military-industrial complex" of the United States and the Soviet Union.

49. Sheren, "Structure and Organization of Defense-Related Industries," p. 123, identifies the eight industrial ministries of the defense sector as follows (given in parentheses are abbreviations of the Russian designations of the ministries and the name of the responsible minister): Defense Industry (MOP—S. A. Zverev); Aviation Industry (MAP—P. V. Dementev); Shipbuilding Industry (MSP—B. E. Butoma); Electronics Industry (MEP—A. I. Shokin); Radio Industry (MR—V. P. Kalmykov); General Machine Building (MOM—S. A. Afanasev); Medium Machine Building (MSM—E. P. Slavskii); Machine Building (MM—V. V. Bakhirev). In addition to the ministries listed, others that contribute to military production include the Ministries of Instrument Manufacturing, Tractor and Agricultural Machinery Building, Chemical Industry, and Automobile Industry.

50. See note 13 in this chapter. Following Brezhnev's call at the Twenty-fourth Party Congress for increased defense industry support of the civilian economy, Soviet officials announced plans for greater output of civilian goods by the defense sector. This included oil-drilling equipment, tractors, machine tools, transport equipment, automation devices, and optical instruments. See S. A. Zverev, "The Potentialities of the Sector," *Izvestiia* (July 7, 1971).

51. A Soviet account of the creation of a separate defense industry complex in the 1937–38 period may be found in an article of reminiscences by Marshal M. V. Zakharov, "On the Eve of World War II: May 1938–September 1939," *Novaia i Noveishaia Istoriia* [New and newest history], no. 5 (September-October 1970), pp. 3–27.

52. Sheren, "Structure and Organization of Defense-Related Industries," p. 26.

53. Scientific research institutes (NII), general design bureaus (OKB), and some plant facilities for experimental production comprise the R&D network within the defense industry sector, with cross ties at all levels with military representatives of the Ministry of Defense. See Sheren, "Structure and Organization of Defense-Related Industries," pp. 30, 35.

54. Ibid., p. 130. Similar alliances might be expected between subgroups in the Air Forces and the Ministry of Aviation Industry, the Ground Forces and the Ministry of Defense Industry, and so on. The Ministry of Defense Industry, incidentally, is the oldest of the various defense industries, and has traditionally been the chief producer of conventional ground weapons.

55. For a fuller discussion of this question, see Thomas W. Wolfe, *Soviet Power and Europe: 1945–1970,* Baltimore: The Johns Hopkins Press, 1970), pp. 428–31.

56. *Pravda* (April 6, 1966).

57. The SS-9 program evidently was suspended before completion, as indicated by cessation of construction on eighteen launch silos in 1970. See Michael Getler, "Russians Building New Missile Silos as Limit Is Sought," *Washington Post* (August 9, 1971); William Beecher, "Experts See Nuclear Arsenals in Balance," *New York Times* (May 21, 1971); *The Military Balance 1971–72* (London: Institute for Strategic Studies, September 1971), p. 5.

58. William Beecher, "U.S. Satellites Detect Soviet ICBMs in Medium-Range Missile Complexes," *New York Times* (February 11, 1970). With respect to SALT, one might point out that deployment of the SS-11 at medium-range complexes could be interpreted as an effort to secrete a "reserve" force of ICBMs exempt from a numbers limitation agreement. A less sinister interpretation is that Soviet strategic planners simply ignored the destabilizing implications of a deployment undertaken for other reasons—such as availability of SS-11s to replace aging medium-range missile systems.

59. See Wolfe, *Soviet Power and Europe,* pp. 435–36.

60. Michael Getler, "Russian Missile Faulted," *Washington Post* (June 17, 1971).

61. This aircraft was given the NATO designation "Backfire." See Tad Szulc, "Soviet Said to Fly Big New Bomber; Policy Shift Seen," *New York Times* (September 5, 1971).

62. William Beecher, "U.S. Expects Soviet Union to Test Large New Missiles Soon," *New York Times* (May 19, 1971).

63. Getler, in *Washington Post* (August 8, 1971).

64. See William Beecher, "Pentagon Says the Soviet May Have 2 New ICBMs," *New York Times* (May 27, 1971).

65. For a sampling of such articles, see: Colonel E. Rybkin, "Critique of Bourgeois Conceptions of War and Peace," *Kommunist vooruzhennykh sil* (September 1968), pp. 89–90; Lt. Col. V. Bondarenko, "The Contemporary Revolution in Military Affairs and the Combat Readiness of the Armed Forces," *Kommunist vooruzhennykh sil* (December 1968), pp. 24–29; Major General K. S. Bochkarev, "V. I. Lenin and the Building of the Armed Forces of the USSR," *Morskoi sbornik* (February 1969), pp. 4–5; A. Galitsan, "For a Leninist Line," *Voenno-istoricheskii zhurnal* (March 1969), pp. 12–13.

66. See, for example, "Observer" article, "A Serious Problem," *Pravda* (March 7, 1970), and unsigned article, "Between Helsinki and Vienna," *U.S.A.: Economics, Politics, Ideology,* no. 1 (Moscow, January 1970), pp. 60–64.

67. A. I. Krylov, "October and the Strategy of Peace," *Voprosy Filosofii* [Problems of philosophy], no. 3 (March 1968), pp. 5, 11–13.

68. See citations in note 65 of this chapter.

69. In this connection, charges have been made by well-informed Soviet military writers such as V. V. Larionov that the United States would "try to divert

to the development of new types of strategic weapons the capital released . . . in the seventies through 'Vietnamization' of the war" in Vietnam. See his article, "The Strategic Debates," *U.S.A.: Economics, Politics, Ideology,* no. 3 (Moscow, March 1970), pp. 20–31. Other Soviet writers have accused the United States of practicing deception in order to "misinform" the Soviet Union and "improve its own strategic position." G. A. Trofimenko, "Some Aspects of U.S. Military and Political Strategy," *U.S.A.: Economics, Politics, Ideology,* no. 10 (October 1970), p. 19.

70. Note should be taken of the dissimilar context out of which Soviet and American views on strategic superiority had evolved. The United States—historically the possessor of strategic superiority—became disabused of the value of strategic superiority during the late sixties while the Soviets were cutting down the U.S. margin. There was doubtless a disposition in some Soviet circles to share the Western world's currently fashionable low regard for the political utility of strategic power in particular and other forms of military power in general. But the Soviet Union's own experience since Cuba seemed to point in a different direction: The strategic buildup had "sobered" the American "imperialists," led them to concede that containment of the Soviet Union was a bankrupt strategy, and impelled them to seek settlement of long-standing issues through negotiation instead of confrontation; as for conventional military power, it had brought gratifying results when used to restore Soviet hegemony in Eastern Europe, in contrast to the unhappy plight of the United States in Southeast Asia. It would not be surprising, given the rather different lessons to be drawn from Soviet experience, if the Soviet leadership tended by the early seventies to reconsider some of the familiar arguments about the burden of the arms race and the dubious advantages of superiority.

71. The compromise, announced simultaneously in Moscow and by President Nixon in Washington on May 20, pledged that the negotiators would concentrate in 1971 on "working out an agreement for the limitation of the deployment of anti-ballistic missile systems," but that they would also take up "certain measures with respect to the limitation of offensive strategic weapons."

J . I . C O F F E Y

American Interests
in the Limitation
of Strategic Armaments

Introduction

THE MERE TITLE of this chapter is enough to inspire humility, since strategic, military-technical, political, psychological, economic, and bureaucratic factors will all influence American interests in the limitation of strategic armaments. Each of these factors is both comprehensive and complex, so that one could write a book on almost any one of them—as indeed I have.[1] Moreover, it is difficult to assess their intensity and their direction; for instance, polls that test public opinion concerning the values attached to particular weapons systems are not very frequent, the questions asked are often unsophisticated, these questions are not always repeated, and they may be posed to different audiences.

Even if one can estimate accurately the nature of various factors, their effects cannot always be determined. First of all, they influence American policies in diverse and frequently contradictory ways; thus pressures to allocate more resources to domestic programs may induce some officials to sponsor cuts in defense expenditures but may spur others to demonstrate, by their support for particular weapons systems, American "will" and toughness. Second, it is almost impossible, without persuading decision-makers to undergo narcohypnosis, to ascertain which factors, in which order of importance, influenced individual choices with respect to the limitation—or the buildup—of strategic armaments. Third, the decision-makers themselves may not be aware of certain influences—such as the extent to which infighting among

The author wishes to acknowledge the assistance and the contributions of Captain Stanley Mozden, USA, Major Louis E. Skender, USA, and Major Charles W. Richardson, Jr., USA—all of whom are enrolled in the Graduate School of Public and International Affairs of the University of Pittsburgh. If I have erred, it is despite them, not because of them!

the armed services affected military recommendations concerning given arms control measures.

Furthermore, choices among these measures are affected by factors other than those listed initially. For one thing, positions and offers may be influenced by their negotiability (or by their estimated impact on the negotiations) as well as by domestic pressures. For another, the ways in which decisions are reached may increase or diminish the weight to be given to particular factors and color the outcomes; thus, the lengthy article by Samuel C. Orr in the *National Journal* suggests a concentration within the National Security Council mechanisms on strategic analyses which may not allow for subtle insights into the political consequences of particular measures.[2]

In view of all these complexities, it is impossible to speak with assurance about the effect of American interests on specific measures for the limitation of strategic armaments, yet this is the crucial question. As one way of answering it, I propose to:

1. discuss briefly some of the factors in our changing world that should affect U.S. interests in strategic arms limitations and U.S. positions at the SALT,

2. outline the kinds of measures that are reportedly under consideration in these talks, to include limiting strategic offensive forces, freezing qualitative improvements in weaponry, constraining strategic defensive systems, and restricting the deployment of new weapons.

3. speculate about conceivable interactions among the factors influencing U.S. proposals and shaping the decisions reached—or not reached, and

4. suggest possible implications for the outcome of the SALT and for the acceptability of any agreement to limit strategic armaments —on the assumption, since proven correct, that there will be such an agreement.

Arms Control in a Changing World

Strategic Forces and Strategic Concepts

For the past twenty years the United States has maintained strategic nuclear forces superior in size, in delivery capabilities, and in flexibility of response to those of the Soviet Union; indeed, the rapid buildup of land- and sea-based missiles under the Kennedy Administration resulted, by the middle of the 1960s, in long-range strategic strike forces four or five times as large as those of the USSR. Partly because of domestic pressures and partly because of a belief that strategic superiority was essential to deterrence, the Johnson Administration remained committed to the maintenance of that superiority, in one form or another. It also began, in 1967, to deploy the Sentinel ABM system, which could protect both military installations and centers of population against "light" attacks and which could serve as the nucleus of thicker and more extensive ballistic missile defenses. Thus the United States as late as 1967 not only had a considerable strategic advantage over the Soviet Union but seemed determined to keep it.

Three separate developments began, however, to erode that advantage and to affect that determination. The first of these was the initiation by the USSR of programs for the enlargement and improvement of its strategic nuclear forces which drastically altered the situation. As President Nixon put it: "From 1950 to 1966 we [Americans] possessed an overwhelming superiority in strategic weapons. From 1967 to 1969, we retained a significant superiority. Today, the Soviet Union possesses a powerful and sophisticated strategic force approaching our own." [3] By the end of the decade, if not before, the USSR (as well as the U.S.) had developed strategic strike forces so powerful, so varied, and so secure that they could destroy an opponent as an organized society, even after absorbing an all-out counterforce attack (see table 1).

This in itself would have been bad enough; however, two other developments threatened to undermine further the American position. One was the discovery that exoatmospheric nuclear explosions could damage—and possibly destroy—incoming reentry vehicles over considerable distances, thereby significantly enhancing the effectiveness of ballistic missile defenses, such as those which the Soviet Union had begun to install around Moscow in the late 1960s; if these defenses were thickened and extended, U.S. retaliatory strikes might well be degraded. Another was the perfection of multiple independently targeted re-entry vehicles (MIRVs), which enhanced the counterforce capabilities of existing missiles. By putting three or more MIRVs on each of its large ICBMs, the Soviet Union could conceivably threaten the land-based components of American strategic strike forces. And even though the United States (which led in the development of MIRVs) could multiply its retaliatory capabilities and increase its ability to penetrate missile defenses, it seemed quite likely that the strategic balance would further worsen, as far as the United States was concerned.

Table 1

UNITED STATES AND SOVIET INTERCONTINENTAL
STRATEGIC STRIKE FORCES, 1970

Type	U.S.	USSR
ICBMs		
Small (SS-11, Minuteman)	(1,000)	(940)
Medium (SS-8, Titan II)	(54)	(220)
Large (SS-9)	—	(280)
Subtotal	1,054	1,440
SLBMs	656	350[a]
Bombers	550	145
Total	2,260	1,935
Number of warheads carried (approximate)	5,300[b]	2,225[b]
Deliverable megatonnage (approximate)	5,600	9,700

Sources: The overall figures for 1970 are derived from the *Statement of Secretary of Defense Melvin R. Laird Before the House Armed Services Committee on the FY 1972–1976 Defense Program and the 1972 Defense Budget,* mimeographed (March 9, 1971), pp. 45–47 and table 2, p. 165 (hereafter cited as *Laird Statement,* 1971), The breakout of Soviet ICBMs comes from the *Washington Post* (March 10, 1971), p. 1, and the information concerning the U.S. deployment of MIRVs on fifty Minuteman III missiles (which is reflected in the warhead totals) from the *Pittsburgh Press* (April 1, 1971), p. 16. The calculations of force loadings and deliverable megatonnage were based on information given in *The Military Balance, 1970–1971* (London: The Institute for Strategic Studies, 1970), table 2, pp. 107–8, except that: (1) all U.S. heavy bombers were assumed to carry four 1.1-MT bombs and two 1-MT air-to-surface missiles (ASMs) and (2) all Soviet heavy bombers were assumed to carry two 1-MT bombs and one 1-MT ASM. This slightly overstates the capability of both bomber forces to carry ASMs.

a. Including those SLBMs carried by Soviet nonnuclear submarines. In addition, the Soviets currently have some 350 SLCMs (submarine-launched cruise missiles), which could be employed against targets in the United States.

b. The *Laird Statement,* 1971, table 2, p. 165, arrives at different totals by counting only four weapons per American bomber and one per Soviet plane. In addition, Mr. Laird may have made an arithmetical error, since the total number of Soviet warheads cannot be less than 1,935, a figure which is consistent with the projections for mid-1971.

Under these circumstances, the Nixon Administration had essentially three options. One was to expand American strategic strike forces and/or strengthen strategic defenses in an effort to retain (or regain) superiority. However, given the technical skills, the industrial base, and the economic resources available to the Soviet Union, this could be difficult if not impossible.[4] It could also be extremely costly; as former Secretary of Defense Robert S. McNamara said, *"In all probability all we* [Americans] *would accomplish* [by deploying ballistic missile defenses designed to degrade an attack by the Soviets] *would be to increase greatly both their expenditures and ours without any gain in real security to either side."* [5] Furthermore, an attempt to achieve superiority could also have adverse political effects. As President Nixon put it, even "sharp increases in U.S. strategic nuclear forces might not have any significant political or military benefit. Many believe that the Soviets would seek to offset our actions, at least in part, and that Soviet political positions would harden, tensions would increase and the prospect for reaching agreements to limit strategic arms might be irreparably damaged." [6]

A second option open to the Nixon Administration was that of adopting force postures that would preclude the Soviet Union from achieving superiority without necessarily attempting to maintain it for the United States. To some extent this was done, under the concept of "strategic sufficiency." The administration shifted from a missile defense aimed primarily at protecting American cities to one ostensibly intended to safeguard American missile sites and air bases; it also began to build superhard missile silos, to install MIRVs, and to design a new and more secure Undersea Long-range Missile System (ULMS), all of which would tend to preserve U.S. strategic retaliatory capabilities vis-à-vis the Soviet Union. The administration was not, however, prepared to adopt a doctrine of firing on warning, or even one of launching its missiles after the first salvo from the USSR, either of which would have reduced the need to build up strategic nuclear forces. Neither was it willing to see a diminution in its capacity to inflict damage upon the Soviet Union; in fact, its concern about the impact of stronger Soviet forces on the stability of strategic deterrence and on crisis behavior induced it to increase substantially the level of damage that was deemed "unacceptable" to the USSR. [7]

A third option open to the administration was to try to head off threats and maintain strategic stability through some understanding, formal or tacit, on the limitation of strategic armaments. Such limitations might preclude technological developments that could cast doubt on the maintenance of the deterrent, induce new and continuing efforts to keep up with an opponent, and create greater uncertainty about that opponent's capabilities and intentions—such as the Soviet motives for building so many SS-9 ICBMs or the American ones for developing MIRVs. They could choke off a competition in armaments that would absorb resources, talents, and energies better employed in supplying rising domestic demands. And they could ameliorate the tensions and hostilities between the United States and the Soviet Union, thereby making a nuclear exchange less likely. As President Nixon himself stated, "Through negotiation we can move toward the control of armaments in a manner that will bring a greater measure of security than we can obtain from arms alone." [8]

Although this "greater measure of security" might seem worth almost any price, there are some which the Nixon Administration is apparently unwilling to pay. One would be to concede to the Soviets an actual advantage in the ability to inflict damage, since this could conceivably embolden them to take greater risks or tempt them to strike first. Another would be to accept a posture in which the safety of the retaliatory forces depended largely on the degree of warning they received, or one in which the United States would be "limited to the indiscriminate mass slaughter of enemy civilians as the sole possible response to challenges." [9] Thus, although the United States has apparently abandoned the "counterforce strategy" formulated in 1962 by Mr. McNamara, it has by no means given up the idea of preserving flexibility of response nor the goal of maintaining secure retaliatory forces.

At present, the Nixon Administration also seems unwilling to give up the goal of maintaining mixed forces (bombers, ICBMs, and SLBMs), each component of which is capable of inflicting a high level of damage in a retaliatory strike. [10] Given the larger number of Soviet ICBMs, the possibility that some or all of these can be equipped with MIRVs, and the potential improvements in warhead accuracy, the safety of land-based forces may increasingly rest on ballistic missile defenses. [11] Thus insistence on a mixed force will affect not only arrangements for the limitation of strategic offensive forces but also those for the imposition of constraints on strategic defensive elements.

Inasmuch as the Nixon Administration has apparently concluded that strategic defenses "could not preclude a catastrophic level of U.S. fatalities from a deliberate all-out Soviet attack," [12] it presumably would not be unwilling to accept some restrictions on ABMs. However, the Safeguard system purportedly has two objectives: that of minimizing casualties from a Chinese attack as well as that of securing deterrent forces against a Soviet strike. Although even the two-site deployment of phase 1 would give some protection to U.S. missile silos, it probably could not defend populated areas against Chinese ICBMs; hence, severe constraints on ballistic missile defenses would force the United States to cancel a project to which it seemingly attaches considerable importance. [13]

In sum, even though the Nixon Administration has given up the attempt to maintain superiority and the effort to reduce drastically damage from a nuclear exchange with the Soviet Union, it still supports objectives and concepts which may rule out certain arrangements for the limitation of strategic armaments. Perhaps more importantly, it apparently has certain views about the nature of deterrence and about the political and psychological implications of strategic weapons that may circumscribe even more closely the area of agreement with the Soviet Union.

THE INTERNATIONAL ENVIRONMENT

As the strategic balance has changed in recent years, so too has the international environment. For one thing, all the major powers seem increasingly preoccupied with domestic concerns and more inclined to worry about economic interests than about political ones. For another, the barriers between the countries of Eastern Europe and those in the West seem to be melting slightly, thus enabling more— and more meaningful—interactions, of which Chancellor Willy Brandt's *Ostpolitik* is a good example. For a third, there is a diminution of concern about the likelihood of a "hot" war and a growing antipathy to the cold one. For a fourth, there are greater pressures from the underdeveloped countries for a larger share of the world's goods, and increasing unhappiness with the proportion of the world's resources that the major powers devote to armaments. In short, there are forces making for change, of which these are but a few, imperfect examples.

In spite of continuing tensions and unresolved problems, there seems to be an air of cautious optimism about East-West relations. This derives in part from an apparent recognition of the new realities and an adjustment that reflects the limits of U.S. power, but it also stems from a willingness to use that power for negotiation rather than for confrontation. Four years ago it would have been hard to envision an American withdrawal from Vietnam, much less diplomatic initiatives toward the People's Republic of China and efforts to work out mutual and balanced force reductions in Europe; today, people take these for granted.

These changes do not, of course, derive solely from alterations in American outlooks. The Soviet Union, like the United States, seems genuinely interested in reducing tensions and in resolving at least some of the issues on which the two countries are at odds. Agreements concluded in 1971 on guaranteed access to West Berlin, on banning bacteriological weapons, and on consultation prior to retaliation for the accidental launch of a nuclear weapon tend to confirm Averell Harriman's judgment that "there are real opportunities now for agreement in important areas" [14]—a judgment which has been borne out at least in part by the recent Moscow Summit meeting.

Furthermore, it is at least possible to envision an American understanding with the People's Republic of China. As indicated in the communiqué issued at the close of President Nixon's visit to Peking, progress toward normalization of relations between China and the United States is in the interest of all countries.[15] This statement may reflect not only the desire of the United States for more stable relations in Asia but also decreased concern about the threat of Chinese Communist aggression—if indeed previous rhetoric about this threat reflected concern or simply an attempt to obtain congressional approval of weapons programs. At any event, the Nixon Administration is apparently coming around to the opinion expressed by many Sinologists that Peking's policy is "to avoid any military initiative that might lead to a direct confrontation with U.S. forces, conventional or nuclear." [16]

If the American aim is to reduce tensions and to improve relations with the Soviet Union and China, then arms control can help, both directly and indirectly. For one thing, it can preclude programs which (as evidenced by the American reaction to the Soviet deployment of SS-9 ICBMs and the Soviet criticism of the American decision to install ballistic missile defenses) arouse suspicion, increase hostility, and heighten the danger of misperceptions that could lead to war. For another thing, it can ameliorate worries about the intentions of the adversary in building up strategic nuclear forces, and about the effect on his willingness to run risks, to exert pressures, and even to take steps that could lead to a clash of arms. For a third, it can make such clashes less likely, as by putting an end to the naval practice of playing "chicken" on the high seas.

Equally importantly, arms limitations can assist in promoting "an era of negotiation" by creating a better climate for the settlement of other issues; while it is true that such settlements also promote arms control, there is no sense worrying about whether the chicken or the egg comes first. Finally, arms control can help reassure allies both about actual threats to their security arising from the continued buildup of strategic nuclear forces and about those less solid but more important threats that derive from their perceptions of the intent behind such programs.

This does not mean that strategic arms limitations convey only benefits. Some among the allies may worry about the symbolic meaning of U.S.-Soviet negotiations and about the possibility that agreements may be concluded in which their interests are neither safeguarded nor reflected. Others may be concerned lest strategic arms limitations affect the ability (and reflect the lack of will) of the United States to respond to military threats against them—as by counterforce strikes against Soviet MRBMs and IRBMs targeted on Western Europe. Others may fear lest arms control further diminish the credibility of the American deterrent, give greater freedom of action to the Soviets, and lead to increased threats and pressures of a political—if not a military—nature. And while these fears and concerns are fed by other aspects of U.S. behavior—such as the Nixon Doctrine and the Mansfield Resolution concerning the withdrawal of forces from NATO—the impact of these is sharpened by efforts to come to terms on the limitation of strategic armaments.

These worries about Communist behavior are not limited to the allies. There are those in the United States who argue that if this country does not have nuclear superiority, the Soviet Union may be freer to encourage and support "wars of national liberation," to practice nuclear blackmail, and even to engage in limited aggression; as Senator Henry M. Jackson once said, "International peace and stability depend not on a parity of power but on a preponderance of power in the peace-keepers over the peace-upsetters." [17] Indeed, there are widespread fears lest the Soviet Union (and China) become more bellicose and more aggressive in the future. These fears are fed not only by the experiences and the perceptions of the cold war but by the growth of Soviet "globally mobile power," which gives the USSR greater leverage in crises and confrontations and which, together with the erosion of the US strategic advantage, could weaken the ability and the willingness of the United States to oppose Communist pressures.[18]

These fears and concerns reflect the fact that the United States and the Soviet Union are still engaged in a competition for power and influence, which could again lead to confrontations between them. This motivates both sides to build weapons—or counters to weapons—which could improve the prospects of a "favorable" outcome to a nuclear exchange, should this ever occur. It leads them to place a premium on achieving (or precluding) advantages that could have a psychological impact in a crisis or could contribute to the outcome of bargaining over an issue. And it induces them to shape their forces in ways which enable each to claim "superiority"—the United States in deliverable warheads and the Soviet Union in deliverable megatonnage.

On balance, worries about the credibility of the deterrent are probably not great enough to offset the impetus toward placing limitations on strategic armaments—largely because these will only register what is already extant, that is, strategic parity between the United States and the Soviet Union. These worries may, however, have significant implications for the nature of any arms control measures. They argue against cutbacks in American strategic strike forces, which conceivably might make a nuclear attack less fearful than it now seems and hence, in the eyes of both adversaries and allies, less of a deterrent than it now is. They render less palatable drastic constraints on strategic defenses, since these defenses may enhance the credibility of the deterrent against third powers, if not against the Soviet Union. They incline the United States to reject arms control measures which do not provide a high degree of assurance that they will be implemented; whatever one may think about the desirability of precluding Soviet MIRVs, it is understandable that negotiators who doubt the intentions of the other party should be unwilling to take chances with a ban on test flights. And they lead to a tendency to hedge against strategic arms limitations, both by increasing assured destruction forces and by exempting tactical nuclear forces, which also play a part in deterring aggression. Thus political and psychological concerns, as well as strategic doctrines, tend to restrict the kinds of agreements likely to be reached in the current negotiations.[19]

THE DOMESTIC ENVIRONMENT

These worries about Soviet behavior both reflect and reinforce anti-Communist sentiments among many elements of the population. Businessmen who deem controlled economies anathema, labor organizers who oppose Communist efforts to infiltrate American trade unions, members of conservative groups to whom socialism is abhorrent, and political leaders who are worried about revolutionary movements in the United States may all view the world through ideologically tinted glasses—as may their counterparts in the Soviet Union. Their fears, hatreds, and worries about domestic communism may lead them to espouse foreign policies aiming at containment and based on strength, and to oppose any moves toward *détente* with the Soviet Union.[20] And they may lead to judgments such as that of President Eisenhower that "we face a hostile ideology—global in scope, atheistic in character, ruthless in purpose and insidious in method . . . [so that] a vital element in keeping the peace is our military establishment." [21]

In 1960, when President Eisenhower made this statement, there was strong support for his view among both elites and the public at large, and a predominant belief that the maintenance of peace was dependent on American strategic and scientific superiority.[22] These views still hold among some segments of the population; in general, the less the level of educational attainment, the lower the economic group, and the older the age of an individual, the more he is apt to be distrustful of the Russians and to place emphasis on perceived American power. To illustrate the difference among age groups, 85 percent of nearly fifteen hundred lawyers, journalists, businessmen, and professionals surveyed by the Council on Foreign Relations felt that agreements to limit strategic armaments should be contingent upon the United States "maintaining its nuclear deterrent"; [23] in contrast, 22 percent of the college students polled in 1971 favored unilateral disarmament, which was not even mentioned by the older elites.[24] And among officers of the Navy queried about their willingness to use force in a *Pueblo*-type incident, only half as many junior officers as senior ones responded affirmatively.[25] Whether or not one deems these views naïve, one must recognize that there has been a shift in attitudes toward the Soviet Union, toward the use of force, and with respect to arms control.[26]

Admittedly, older elements among the population, whose views tend to be different, still hold power and influence. Even among the present generation of leaders, however, there are many who have questioned the defense policy of the United States and have urged new initiatives aimed at curbing the arms race; for instance, all of the leading contenders for the Democratic nomination for President were advocates of strategic arms limitations—and quite a few even went so far as to propose unilateral reductions in American forces and programs. Nor is this sentiment limited to only one of the two major parties; a Gallup poll of May 1971 indicated that if President Nixon were not to run again, 30 percent of the registered Republicans would favor potential candidates who emphasized arms control, such as Congressman Paul N. McCloskey and Senator Charles H. Percy.[27] In 1967, President Johnson moved to cut off challenges from the right by undertaking to build the Sentinel antiballistic missile system; President Nixon would find such a response less feasible.

That this shift in attitudes reflects more than sensitivity to political opportunities is indicated by the fact that new groups who are for the most part favorable to arms control have entered into the debate on military policy. Various elements among Blacks, Chicanos, and other minority groups have indicated dissatisfaction with the priority accorded expenditures for armaments. Labor leaders have charged that "our society today is a sick society—and its basic illness can be traced to the war in Vietnam and to our share in the nuclear arms race." [28] Prominent businessmen such as Sol Linowitz, former Chairman of the Board, the Xerox Corporation; David Rockefeller, Chairman of the Board, Chase Manhattan Bank; and James Roche, then Chairman of the Board, General Motors Corporation, have joined in calling for limitations on strategic armaments.[29] Groups of scientists and former government officials have organized into lobbying, educational, and publicity organizations to oppose new weapons programs and to support measures for the control of armaments. And virtually everyone concerned with health care, urban redevelopment, water purification, or any one of the host of other problems confronting the United States has tended to argue for a reallocation of resources now earmarked for various weapons systems; as former Secretary of the Interior Stewart Udall argued, domestic programs have suffered because of "the overpowering priorities we have given to real and supposed defense needs." [30]

These sentiments are increasingly manifest in Congress, with newer members tending to be most opposed to various military requests. Partly because of this and partly because more expertise is now available to Congress, questions that were almost unvoiced five years ago are being raised about the rationales for new weapons systems and about the reasons for believing that antiballistic missiles are useful bargaining instruments in negotiations. Nor are these questions being asked solely by the "liberal" members of Congress; even such a longtime advocate of military preparedness as Senator John C. Stennis, Chairman of the Senate Armed Services Committee, refused to go along with the administration's request for an expansion of the Safeguard system pending the outcome of the current SALT.[31]

To some extent these shifts of sentiment in Congress reflect the changes in its composition (however slowly these may come about), to some extent dismay over the increases in the costs of weapons systems during the past decade, but to some extent they also reflect a sensitivity to the concerns of their constituents. According to a Gallup poll of March 1971, 49 percent of the American people believed defense spending to be too high and only 11 percent thought it too low. More importantly, 59 percent of the college-educated and nearly 55 percent of the middle-income groups contended that defense spending was too high; [32] in short, those elites on whom Congressmen depend most and to whose wishes they respond most readily are potentially in favor of arms control. Many among these middle-class elements may be influenced by the belief that defense spending has directly contributed to, or been primarily responsible for, the current U.S. inflationary spiral; at any rate, spokesmen for groups as varied as the United States Chamber of Commerce and the International Longshoremen's and Warehousemen's Union have expressed this belief.[33] When to concerns about the level of defense spending, inflation, and the underfunding of domestic programs one adds the increasing opposition to taxes, it is probable that the average citizen would support arms control agreements that promised to curb defense costs and certain that he would require strong evidence of an imminent threat before he would accept sizable increases in defense expenditures.

This potential support for arms control is most likely to crystallize around measures which promise to head off new weapons programs. Although strategic nuclear forces account for only 10 percent to 20 percent of defense costs,[34] new weapons loom large—psychologically as well as economically (see table 2). For example, the cost of the Safeguard antiballistic missile system has risen from an initial figure of $4.5 billion to a current one of $14.8 billion and the estimated cost of 240 new B-1 bombers ranges from $15 billion to $75 billion, depending on who does the estimating and what ancillary expenditures (such as those for new tankers) are included. According to one such estimator, unless an agreement comes out of the SALT, the cost of U.S. strategic nuclear forces will rise to at least $30 billion a year [35]—almost double what they now are.

This does not mean that all roads lead to strategic arms limitations. For one thing, previous cuts in defense spending and in the armed services have thrown more than a million men onto the labor market, and further cuts might add to this number. For another, most Congressmen are solicitous of the bases and the installations in their districts, and the executive branch in turn is solicitous of these Congressmen. For a third, industry has been hard hit by cutbacks in space programs and in expenditures for new strategic weapons, with the result that there are sizable pockets of unemployment in California, Texas, New York, and Massachusetts—all states with some significance in American political life. Thus both their self-interest and their perspectives of the world may lead many industrial leaders to argue

Table 2
ESTIMATED COSTS OF NEW STRATEGIC WEAPONS

	Estimated Costs in Billions of Dollars	
	By DoD	By Others
Air Force		
B-1 Bomber	$11.1[a]	$15.0–$75.0[a]
Minuteman II and III	8.9	—
Replacement for KC-135 Tanker	—[b]	15.9[b]
Navy		
Poseidon	6.9	—
ULMS	—[c]	8.0– 30.0
Army		
Safeguard (4 sites)	8.2	16.0[d]
Safeguard (12 sites)	14.8	—
Hardsite	5.0	15.0[d]

Sources: Department of Defense (DoD) estimates for Poseidon and Minuteman are from *Hearings [on the] Military Budget and National Economic Priorities,* part 2, p. 576; those for Safeguard are from *Hearings [on the] Fiscal Year 1972 Authorization for Military Procurement . . . ,* 92 Cong., 1 Sess., part 2, pp. 1488–89; those for Hardsite are from the *Hearings, FY 1972,* part 2, p. 1518. In all cases, they include the costs of nuclear weapons produced by the Atomic Energy Commission.

a. "The Air Force B-1 Intercontinental Bomber," mimeographed (no date), page 31. The lower unofficial estimate is in *Hearings, FY 1972,* part 2, p. 1741, the higher in the *New York Times* (June 7, 1971), p. 33.

b. DoD maintains that no replacement for the KC-135 tanker is currently envisioned. Bruce Holloway, Commanding General of the Strategic Air Command, estimated that it could cost $26 million per tanker to replace the KC-135, and that the Air Force will need more than the 613 now operational (*Hearings, FY 1972,* part 2, p. 1690).

c. DoD has not provided program costs for ULMS. Dr. George W. Rathjens, Jr., estimated that the cost would be in excess of $8 billion (*Hearings [on] Changing National Priorities,* 91 Cong., 1 Sess., part 1, p. 198), and others have spoken of costs running as high as $30 billion (*New York Times,* March 4, 1972, p. 11).

d. Dr. Herbert York estimated that the cost of a four-site Safeguard might be doubled, and that the cost of Hardsite defenses for the same four sites could run to $15 billion, for a combined systems cost of approximately $30 billion (*Hearings, FY 1972,* part 2, pp. 1609–10).

for sizable strategic nuclear forces and many political leaders to support them in these arguments.

So too would large elements of the armed services, albeit for somewhat different reasons. Their advocacy of powerful—if not superior—strategic forces stems partly from their mission, which centers on the use of force to achieve national objectives. It derives partly from their continuing involvement in the assessment of threats and in the determination of countermeasures. It arises in part out of their long and active involvement in the cold war, coupled with their lesser immersion in the changing currents of American life. And it reflects their belief that in a war of any kind the military should be given the tools and the resources needed to achieve "victory."

However, this advocacy may also reflect the fact that strategic arms limitations could preclude or reduce cherished weapons systems programs, with consequent effects on the money the services receive, the prestige they have, and the influence they can exercise both inside and outside the Pentagon. For instance, any curb on antiballistic missiles could directly affect a program that the Army has long supported, while qualitative restrictions could bar the Undersea Long-range Missile System, which is on the drawing boards of Navy architects. Moreover, several of the services may find it in their interest to oppose a particular measure; thus the Air Force might also be expected to oppose limitations on ABMs, which would leave its land-based ICBMs vulnerable to Soviet counterforce strikes and perhaps lead to greater emphasis upon sea-based deterrents.

Conversely, the various services may see merit to particular arms control measures: constraints on MIRVs could improve the position of the Air Force—if not that of the Navy. Furthermore, curbs on expenditures for new strategic weapons systems could help meet the increasing costs of manning and equipping general-purpose forces, which theoretically should play a larger role under conditions of strategic parity. So far the military has sought both new strategic weapons *and* more modern tactical ones; for instance, the Navy is pushing ahead with ULMS while simultaneously asking $5 billion a year for ship construction. In today's world, it is unlikely that the budget will allow for both. And while the services may tend, as Alain C. Enthoven and K. Wayne Smith have pointed out, to "keep the prestige items and cut back the unglamorous support items essential to readiness," [36] it is perhaps questionable whether they would show the same willingness to give up tanks, fighter planes, or frigates in favor of missiles.

The coolness of the military toward arms control is probably matched within the Department of State, where only Secretary Rogers has, to my knowledge, spoken approvingly of the SALT. Many foreign service officers undoubtedly favor maintaining strategic power and keeping strong conventional forces on the grounds that these are reassuring to allies, persuasive to neutrals, useful in coping with Soviet or Chinese pressures, and helpful in maintaining political stability. Although there may be those in the State Department who would favor a less militarized U.S. presence in the world or who would argue that reductions in armaments could be beneficial internationally as well as domestically, their voices seem to be muted.

So are other voices within the executive branch, although for different reasons. The Arms Control and Disarmament Agency (which presumably supports strategic arms limitations) has deliberately—and wisely—chosen to make its case within the government rather than outside it. Departments such as Health, Education, and Welfare or Housing and Urban Development might also welcome curbs on strategic armaments, since these could free resources to meet their own needs; [37] however, they do not shape positions on arms control and have not, so far, used their power bases within Congress and among the people to drum up support for strategic arms limitations.

All this leaves the White House in a rather difficult position. On the one hand, it must satisfy the Department of Defense, which is by far the most powerful of all the bureaus, which probably has the greatest influence both in the Congress and among important elites, and whose high officials and ranking officers are recognized (if not always accepted) authorities on military matters—which means that no President seeking approval of any arms control agreement can afford to go strongly against the recommendations of the Joint Chiefs of Staff and/or the Secretary of Defense. On the other hand, the President must also consider the views not just of other agencies of the government but of important elements among Congress and the public at large, which increasingly oppose new weapons programs, question the utility of large defense expenditures, and seek a redefinition of the national purpose and a redirection of the national effort. It is therefore possible that the White House, caught between the rising costs of defense, pressures for increased domestic expenditures, and sentiment for tax cuts, might also welcome (on this count at least) measures that could avert large new outlays for strategic nuclear forces.

This does not mean that "all systems are go" for arms control. Some research conducted into attitudes concerning the utilities of strategic weapons systems suggests a dichotomy between political and psychological concerns (which cause authors and interviewees to look on nuclear weapons as good) and socio-economic concerns, which tend to generate contrary evaluations.[38] Since those making the final decisions on strategic arms limitations are likely to be concerned primarily about their consequences for deterrence, crisis behavior, and allied solidarity, they may well be willing to pay the economic and social costs associated with high levels of defense expenditures.

It does, however, suggest that when one looks at the domestic scene, more factors favor strategic arms limitations than not—despite the opposition of powerful elements in the executive and legislative branches, the coolness of businessmen and workers in the aerospace industry, and the existence of all kinds of perceptions and misperceptions that make difficult any significant accommodation with the Soviet Union.

Factors Affecting Specific Measures for the Limitation of Armaments

The preceding discussion of factors affecting American interests in arms control might suggest favorable prospects for agreement on measures to limit strategic armaments—as indeed seems to be the case.[39] However, generalized attitudes sometimes change when particular implementing measures are proposed, so that a Congressman may be for "economy in government" but against cuts in farm price supports. Moreover, the nature of agreements will be affected by factors other than those already discussed, including the negotiability of proposals and the ability to verify their implementation. For both these reasons, it would seem necessary to assess the overall acceptability of specific measures to limit strategic armaments, as well as the specific factors affecting overall interest in arms control.

It would seem equally necessary to place some limitations on this assessment, which could otherwise become unmanageable. Accordingly, primary attention will be paid to the four types of measures reportedly discussed during the SALT, to wit:

1. limiting strategic offensive forces,
2. freezing qualitative improvements in existing weapons systems,
3. constraining strategic defenses, and
4. restricting new weapons.[40]

LIMITING STRATEGIC OFFENSIVE FORCES

In any consideration of measures to limit strategic offensive forces there are four major issues. One is how you define strategic offensive forces, that is, what do you count? A second is whether you stabilize forces at the present level, increase them to some agreed future level, or reduce them. A third is whether you impose limitations by type or on an overall basis, that is, do you limit separately bombers, land-based missiles, and submarine-launched ballistic missiles

(SLBMs), or allow a country to shift from one system to another at its discretion? And a fourth is whether these limitations, however defined, shall be based on equality or upon some accepted differences in the force postures of the two powers.

Ideally, restrictions on strategic offensive forces should aim at affecting their reciprocal ability to inflict damage in a retaliatory strike; however, this capability is dependent on so many variables, ranging from the reliability of missiles to the effectiveness of defensive systems, as to be largely undeterminable—and certainly nonnegotiable. It would be simpler to calculate the effects of limitations on deliverable megatonnage or deliverable warheads—at least as long as one did not try to determine those that *could* be delivered; however, even here one would have to rely upon estimates of warhead yield and/or the capabilities of various missiles to carry MIRVs, so that even if both sides accepted the same formula, difficulties in its application would remain. This essentially means that limitations must be imposed on numbers of missiles and bombers, despite the admitted differences in the characteristics of these weapons, in the distribution of populations, and in defensive systems that make launch vehicles a very crude and potentially misleading indicator of strategic power.[41]

From the viewpoint of the United States, there would be many advantages to retaining an edge in strategic delivery capabilities, in that this could help offset asymmetries in population distribution (which means that two hundred 1-MT warheads delivered on the United States will kill as many people as will twelve hundred similar warheads delivered on the Soviet Union) and could facilitate counterforce strikes not only against Soviet intercontinental delivery vehicles but also against the MRBMs and IRBMs targeted against the countries of Western Europe. Moreover, American "superiority" in delivery vehicles would hedge against the sudden deployment of extensive ballistic missile defenses, the accelerated production of SS-9 ICBMs, greater-than-expected improvements in Soviet missile accuracy, and other technical innovations. Furthermore, larger numbers of weapons would have significant political and psychological advantages in the eyes of both allies and adversaries. Thus, from both strategic and military-technical perspectives, superiority would undoubtedly seem advantageous.

Furthermore, U.S. superiority in launch vehicles would satisfy the armed services by enabling them to keep at least the current levels of strategic offensive forces and to maintain intact the three components of those forces: bombers, ICBMs, and SLBMs. It also would silence those concerned about the attrition of the American lead over the Soviet Union and preserve rapport with important interest groups and elites who either view numerical superiority as militarily meaningful or see some advantages to themselves in the effort required to support forces of the level and type needed to maintain it. Moreover, if the Soviet Union stopped building bombers and missiles, the cost to the United States of maintaining stronger forces would not be high, except as modernization were needed or new weapons such as SRAMs (short-range attack missiles) or MIRVs were introduced, so that even those elements opposed to larger defense expenditures would probably be satisfied with arrangements that would ratify existing American advantages. Thus, in terms of U.S. interests, superiority would seem to be desired by many and acceptable to most.

Superiority in numbers of launch vehicles could be maintained in a number of ways: by asking the Soviet Union to accept an inferior posture; by counting all Soviet missiles and bombers, not just those of intercontinental range; by imposing limitations by type of weapon, which would preserve an edge at least for the time needed by the Soviets to build up their bomber and missile-submarine forces. All these, however, presume Soviet acquiescence, and the Soviets have consistently maintained that they will settle for nothing less than "equality" with the United States.[42] Moreover, they are unwilling to count all elements of their Long-range Air Force and Strategic Rocket Force, since this would require them, under the principle of equality, to destroy over one thousand missiles and/or bombers; in fact, when this was suggested, the Soviets countered by defining as "strategic" only those launch vehicles capable of attacking an adversary's homeland, a definition that could have excluded their medium bombers, MRBMs, and IRBMs but included American fighter-bombers and carrier-based aircraft in Western Europe. Nor were the Soviets prepared to accept "equality" in each type of weapon, which would have required them either to cut back on their current ICBM force or to allow the United States to build another four-hundred-odd missiles, in either case reducing their own ability to eliminate through counterforce strikes the land-based components of U.S. strategic power.

Given both the Soviet reactions mentioned above and the ongoing Soviet programs for the improvement of ICBM and SLBM forces, two outcomes seem possible: one that would freeze types of weapons more or less at present levels and one that would permit shifts from one category to another. The first would be simpler and easier to verify; however, it would tend to perpetuate the present ratios among

Table 3

HYPOTHETICAL U.S. AND SOVIET FORCE POSTURES
UNDER ARMS CONTROL, CIRCA 1976

Type	Limitations by Classes of Weapons		Overall Limitations on Weapons	
	U.S.[a]	Soviet[b]	U.S.[e]	Soviet[d]
ICBMs				
Small (Minuteman II & III, SS-11, etc.)	(1,000)	(1,050)	550	880
Medium (Titan II, SS-8, etc.)	(54)	(129)	—	—
Large (SS-9)	—	(300)	54	300
Total	1,054	1,479		
SLBMs				
Polaris A-3 or SSN-6	(160)	(656)	(160)	(880)
Poseidon	(496)	—	(496)	—
Total	656	656	656	880
Bottom-based or ship-borne missiles	—	—	480	—
Bombers	565	140	460	140
Total launchers	2,275	2,275	2,200	2,200
Total warheads (approximate)	13,200	3,200[e]	12,900	3,100[e]
Deliverable megatonnage (approximate)	5,000	7,300	4,700	6,700
Ballistic missile interceptors	100–300	100–300	100–300	100–300

Sources: Information concerning the size and composition of U.S. strategic strike forces in 1975–76 is from the statement by Admiral Thomas H. Moorer, USN, Chairman, Joint Chiefs of Staff, before the Senate Armed Services Committee on February 15, 1972 mimeographed, pp. 9, 12, and 13. The postulated size of the Soviet missile-submarine fleet falls within the limits set in Admiral Moorer's statement, p. 11. The force loadings are the same as those for 1970, except that: (1) The two 1-MT air-to-surface missiles carried by U.S. B-52 G/H bombers have been replaced by twelve short-range attack missiles (SRAMs) of 200 KT each, and six SRAMs have been added to U.S. FB-111 bombers. See *Aviation Week and Space Technology,* 91, no. 32 (December 1969), pp. 47–48. (2) Instead of one 25-MT warhead, the Soviet SS-9 was assumed to have three 5-MT warheads, as estimated by Mr. Laird in U.S. Congress, House, Subcommittees of the Committee on Appropriations, *Hearings [on the] SAFEGUARD Antiballistic Missile System,* 91 Cong., 1 Sess., 1969, pp. 8–10.

a. Assumes that U.S. launch vehicles are frozen at 1971 levels, but that programs for installing MIRVs on Minuteman III and Poseidon and for building SRAMs are continued.

b. Assumes that Soviet SS-13, SS-11, and SS-9 ICBMs are frozen at mid-1972 levels, that Soviet SLBMs are built to a level equaling those of the United States, and that the USSR keeps an excess of land-based missiles pending expansion of its bomber force, which cannot be completed by 1976.

c. Assumes that the United States, as a hedge against improved warheads for the Soviet SS-11 ICBM, puts Minuteman IIs on the bottoms of the Great Lakes, or on barges which could traverse either inland or coastal waterways, pending the development of ULMS, the first unit of which will not be operational before 1978.

d. Assumes that the USSR destroys all large missiles except SS-9s, installs types of forces and would leave some of these open to attack—particularly if the Soviet Union continued to expand its missile-submarine fleet, as it maintains it should be allowed to do.[43] Although an overall freeze would in the short run benefit the USSR (which could, since it has a comparatively small bomber fleet, build more land- and sea-based missiles), in the longer run it would enable the United States to deploy better-balanced and less vulnerable forces than would be possible if no transfers from one category to another were permitted (see tables 3 and 4). However, this type of arrangement would be more expensive to implement than one that placed restrictions on each type of weapon, at least for the United States. Furthermore, it would probably cause infighting among the services, especially if ballistic missile defenses were constrained, with the Navy seeking to put all strategic forces at sea and the Air Force attempting to maintain its bomber and missile components.

Moreover, unless MIRVs are more accurate than we admit, either alternative would reduce the ability of the United States to limit damage from a nuclear exchange, partly because fewer of its land-based weapons could escape counterforce strikes by superior Soviet missile forces and partly because more of those weapons surviving would be needed to cope with missiles directed against the United States and thus could not be spared to attack those targeted against the allies. Neither alternative would satisfy those who are worried either about the actual capabilities of various weapons or about their symbolic value; for instance, acceptance of anything like current force levels would leave the USSR ahead in deliverable megatonnage, in the size of missile forces, and in the number of large ICBMs, all of which may have a considerable impact on both attitudes and behavior.

One way out of this dilemma would be to seek reductions in strategic strike forces that would partially offset these disadvantages. The United States, for instance, is already planning to cut back by 20 percent its force of long-range bombers; if it could induce the USSR to phase out simultaneously its two-hundred-odd obsolescent SS-7 and SS-8 ICBMs, this could preclude a further tipping of the "megaton-

---

MIRVs only on these missiles, and builds as many SLBMs as it can without unduly cutting into its deployment of SS-11 and SS-13 ICBMs.

e. If the Soviets continue to install MRVs (Multiple Reentry Vehicles) on their SS-11 ICBMs, a process which, according to Mr. Laird, they have already begun, they could muster some 5,000 warheads, with a consequent drop in megatonnage. This course of action would, however, diminish the utility of these weapons against hard targets, such as U.S. missile silos.

Table 4

PROJECTED U.S. AND SOVIET FORCE POSTURES
UNDER ARMS CONTROL, CIRCA 1977

Type	If Current Land-based Missiles Are Kept		If Option of Shifting to SLBMs Is Exercised	
	U.S.	Soviet	U.S.[a]	Soviet
ICBMs				
Small (Minuteman II & III, SS-11, etc.)	1,000	1,095[b]	1,000	1,095[b]
Medium (Titan II, SS-8, etc.)	54	210	—	—
Large (SS-9)	—	313[c]	—	313[c]
Total	1,054	1,618	1,000	1,408
SLBMs				
Polaris A-3 or SSN-6	160	740	160	950
Poseidon	496	—	550	—
Total	656	740	710	
Bombers	450	140	450	140
Total launchers	2,160	2,498	2,160	2,498
Total warheads (approximate)	12,800	2,700[d]	13,300	2,700[d]
Deliverable megatonnage (approximate)	4,500	11,000	4,200	10,200
Ballistic missile interceptors	100–200[e]	200	100–200[e]	200

Sources: (1) The basic information on the sizes of U.S. and Soviet forces and on the options open to each came from the statements by Dr. Henry A. Kissinger, Assistant to the President for National Security Affairs, and Ambassador Gerard C. Smith, Director, Arms Control and Disarmament Agency, at their News Conference on the Treaty and the Interim Agreement, May 26, 1972, Weekly Compilation of Presidential Documents, vol. 8, no. 23 (Washington: Office of the Federal Register, 5 June 1972), pp. 929–32, and from the news conference of Dr. Henry A. Kissinger, Assistant to the President for National Security Affairs, May 27, 1972, ibid., pp. 932–37. (2) The breakout of U.S. forces is from the statement by Admiral Moorer in table 3; that of Soviet forces is from the Washington Post, 14 June 1972. (3) The force loadings are those given in The Military Balance, 1971–1972, table 2, pp. 57–58, except for the FB-111s and B-52 G/H bombers, for which see table 3.

a. The United States could not exercise this option before 1978, the date when the first Trident missile-submarine is due to become operational.

b. Includes approximately 100 VRBMs (Variable-range Ballistic Missiles) which have replaced a somewhat larger number of Soviet MRBMs/IRBMs.

c. The SS-9, which has been credited with a single warhead of 25 MT, accounts for almost 75 percent of Soviet deliverable megatonnage. If this or another large missile which the USSR has been testing were MIRVed, megatonnage would go down and the number of warheads (as well as Soviet counter-force capabilities) would go up. See, however, note d below.

d. Assumes that the Soviets do not install MRVs, the program for which has apparently been cancelled, and do not deploy MIRVs.

e. There is some question whether the Congress will approve the administration's request for an ABM complex centered in Washington.

nage balance." Additionally, an arrangement whereby the United States scrapped the ten submarines now carrying Polaris A-3 SLBMs in return for a freeze on Soviet construction (thereby leaving the two fleets roughly equal in size) might ease concerns that the USSR is attempting to achieve a first-strike capability by building up its sea-based forces.[44]

Neither of these steps would markedly affect the strategic balance between the United States and the Soviet Union; as indicated by table 3, each would have more than enough launch vehicles remaining to destroy the other, even in a retaliatory attack. Such reductions could, however, register an improvement in U.S.-Soviet relations, significantly decrease the costs of maintaining and operating strategic nuclear forces, and provide a desired impetus to cutbacks in other strategic armaments. Moreover, it is probable that both technical developments and economic pressures will lead the United States and the Soviet Union to make cuts of this nature anyway, so that the question is not one of inspiring them to carry out reductions but rather of asking them not to compensate for these by equivalent gains in newer weapons or by extensive improvements in older ones.

This does not mean that cutbacks in strategic launch vehicles are just around the corner; for one thing, the Soviets are apparently bent on achieving "equality" through increases in their own forces rather than through decreases in American ones. Even if this were not the case, there would probably be opposition to such cutbacks among elements in the United States concerned with the symbols of power or worried about the resultant improvement in the status of China. Furthermore, the Navy might not be happy about reductions in its operating forces, especially since the trade-off of Polaris boats against more and better Soviet missile-submarines would mainly enhance the security of Air Force bombers and ICBMs. And even those who were less fearful, or less service-oriented, might deem it better to stop before backing up, in order to make sure that any arms control agreement was working properly.

FREEZING QUALITATIVE IMPROVEMENTS

Even if the number of Soviet ICBMs and SLBMs was frozen at present levels, increases in the range, the accuracy, and the payload of these weapons could threaten the land-based components of the U.S. deterrent—and hence, in the eyes of some, strategic stability. Such improvements are likely to provoke counteractions in either offensive or defensive weapons programs; for instance, improved missile accuracy could induce a shift from fixed to mobile ICBMs or the deployment of terminal ballistic missile defenses, such as the Hard-site system now under consideration in the United States. Unless any arms control agreement is all-encompassing, it is likely to shift the nature of the arms race, rather than to stop it, as evidenced by the interwar period.[45] A qualitative race is not likely to be less expensive than a quantitative one; in fact, it may be more costly. And it probably will increase fears and heighten tensions, thereby vitiating one of the objectives of arms control. Thus there are good reasons for seeking to freeze qualitative improvements.

There are equally good reasons for not attempting this, at least *in toto*. One reason is that qualitative improvements are both extensive and continuous, since weapons systems are, at least in theory, upgraded throughout their life cycle and are presumably replaced only by better ones. Another is that freedom to make qualitative improvements could assuage concerns about cheating by the other side and might seem even to those not so concerned to be a prudent hedge against potential technological innovations. A third is that the prevention of some qualitative improvements would require extensive and intrusive inspections; for instance, precluding the installation of new guidance packages in missiles or the placement of better electronic jammers in bombers would be virtually impossible. Prohibiting a country from introducing a new launch vehicle in place of an old one would probably be unacceptable; neither the United States nor the Soviet Union would agree to replicate the missile-submarines built ten years ago, even if this were technically feasible. Finally, the interests of the American military, those of the aerospace industry, the attitudes of some elites, and the opinions of some segments of the public all would be against these kinds of limitations, since great importance is attached to maintaining technological superiority.

This suggests that attention be focused on those kinds of improvements which are extremely threatening. For example, larger missiles, with heavier payloads, could be more devastating against civilian targets, for which fewer would be needed; could free additional weapons for counterforce attacks; could (by virtue of their high-yield warheads) make such attacks more effective; could make possible the installation of MIRVs on vehicles that might not now be able to carry them (thereby presumably benefiting the Soviet Union); and could carry more and better penetration aids—only the last of which would necessarily be beneficial to the United States. More accurate warheads

(even if they do not achieve the thirty-yard circular error probable *
(CEP) predicted by one analyst [46]) could knock out even super-
hardened silos and could make even the smallest MIRV a meaningful counterforce weapon.

In order to head off such developments, the United States has suggested that both sides forgo shifting to larger delivery vehicles, and
specifically that the Soviet Union not build more of the powerful
SS-9s, with their 25-MT warheads. If the USSR agreed to this, its
near-term ability to destroy U.S. missile silos would be reduced, since
it is the combination of an increase in the number of SS-9s and of
MIRVs for these high-thrust rockets that makes them a potential
threat. And while the Soviet Union could in time improve the accuracy of its ICBMs, and thus acquire in another way more meaningful
counterforce capabilities, this might be viewed as less threatening
than the recent growth of the SS-9 force. Moreover, limitations on
the accuracy of reentry vehicles, if these could be worked out, could
further postpone the day when the Soviets would be able to knock
out any sizable portion of U.S. land-based missiles.

These kinds of qualitative limitations would not markedly affect
American weapons programs or strategic concepts, although restrictions
on missile accuracy could rule out those precise attacks with small
warheads that some see as a useful option during the first phase of
a nuclear exchange.[47] Nor would such limitations threaten service
interests or arouse political concern, since the issue is too technical
to have much meaning for those who are worried about the political
and psychological connotations of strategic arms limitations. Furthermore, those seeking to reduce defense expenditures would probably
acquiesce, since both the further construction of SS-9s and any sharp
increases in the accuracy of Soviet missiles would undoubtedly induce
costly offsetting measures, such as the deployment of mobile ICBMs
or the procurement of ULMS. The problems do not arise from
domestic opposition to such restrictions but from their negotiability,
since the USSR is unlikely to halt the deployment of SS-9s without
some compensatory measure by the United States, such as acquiescence in the further growth of the Soviet submarine fleet. And in the
case of limitations on missile accuracy, there is the further difficulty
of monitoring test firings with sufficient precision to obtain reliable
data and insure against unauthorized improvements. At the moment,

---

* The circular error probable is the radius of a circle around a target within
which half of the attacking missiles will fall.

therefore, only the crudest and simplest of qualitative controls seems likely.

CONSTRAINING STRATEGIC DEFENSES

The same can be said with respect to the imposition of constraints on strategic defenses. For one thing, most defensive systems are extremely complex, the number of elements involved is very large, and some of these (such as fighter-interceptors and frigates) have too many uses for restrictions to be readily enforceable or easily verifiable. For another, the unknowns with respect to the capabilities of these systems are so numerous that it would be hard to determine the consequences of any given limitation. And for a third, although restrictions on shore-based sonar and other detection devices could limit the effectiveness of antisubmarine warfare forces and air defense units, such restrictions are likely to be asymmetrical in their impact on Soviet and American capabilities and hence unacceptable.

Moreover, constraints on defensive systems encounter opposition on other grounds. For one thing, they would tend to cut deeply into service programs; for instance, the Army and the Air Force together spend about 4.4 billion annually on air defenses and the Navy at least half that much on antisubmarine warfare. For another, constraints would tend to inhibit or choke off new weapons development, thereby affecting elements both inside and outside the Department of Defense. And for a third, they might, if extended to antiballistic missile systems, leave the land-based components of U.S. strategic retaliatory forces somewhat more vulnerable than is now the case and American cities exposed to even small-scale attacks.

Furthermore, there is a mixed feeling about defenses among both elites and the general public. Some strategists have tended to welcome defenses, either because of their utility in safeguarding land-based weapons systems or because they promise to make reductions in offensive forces more palatable to both sides.[48] Moreover, there is a strong psychological support for the concept of defenses, which seem *ipso facto* to be more reassuring and less provocative than offensive weapons. Additionally, defensive systems (with the exception of ABMs) have not received much attention nor encountered much opposition.

On the other hand, defenses can be costly, especially when one counts in the procurement of new weapons such as the Airborne Warning and Control System (AWACS), the F-15 fighter plane, and the P-3C patrol aircraft. Moreover, existing defenses are not very effective and may well become less so; for example, the increased speed and greater quietness of Soviet missile submarines, together with the longer-range missiles they now carry, will make them much less vulnerable than their predecessors to U.S. ASW forces. Finally, unless and until ABMs are deployed, key components of existing defensive systems are open to precursor attacks which could significantly degrade their already limited capabilities.

Despite this, the difficulty of negotiating restrictions on air defenses and antisubmarine warfare forces, coupled with the intensity of opposition to any meaningful constraints, suggests that both the administration and Congress are more likely to deal with individual weapons on a case-by-case basis than to seek systems restrictions through arms control. This is not true of ballistic missile defenses, which are new, costly, relatively simple to control, and more likely to promote interactions than other defensive systems. The total abolition of BMD (ballistic missile defenses) would insure that the retaliatory forces of each side could reach their targets; however, it would also leave the land-based components of those forces vulnerable to attacks by ICBMs—or, in the case of the United States, by Soviet missile submarines, which can approach closely enough to reduce the warning time available to bombers. "Light" ballistic missile defenses, such as the proposed Safeguard system, would, of course, provide considerable security to offensive forces (as well as afford some protection against a small-scale or unsophisticated nuclear attack on cities); however, the Soviets apparently balked at such extensive defenses, even on a mutual basis. This means that the United States either has to accept a total ban or look to partial deployments, around missile silos, as the Americans suggested, or around national capitals, as the Soviets proposed.

Unfortunately, partial deployments could also present severe problems. For one thing, Soviet strategic rockets—and especially their MRBMs/IRBMs—are generally closer to concentrations of population than are those in the United States, so that defenses designed to protect weapon sites could reduce Soviet fatalities relative to those that would be suffered by the United States. This in itself would not affect the strategic balance, as even a Soviet system comparable to Safeguard could not markedly degrade U.S. retaliatory strikes; however, once the radars for such a system were built, the USSR could quickly enhance its effectiveness by deploying additional interceptors, thereby gaining a psychological advantage if not a military one. Furthermore, there is always the possibility that the Soviets might upgrade their far-flung air defense system, which relies heavily on surface-to-air missiles, so that it could cope with incoming warheads.[49] Thus, if the United States is to feel secure, it will have to work out agreements that limit the positioning of radars as well as the deployment of interceptors.

The United States may also have to negotiate agreements which would satisfy diverse and potentially conflicting elements at home. Some elites would favor ballistic missile defenses as a contribution to deterrence, even though there is increasing acceptance of the fact that ABMs cannot significantly reduce damage from a Soviet strike and decreasing support for the argument that they are essential to blunt a Chinese one. However, other elites strongly oppose BMD, on the ground that this could encourage countermeasures by the Soviet Union that would intensify the arms race. And finally, some of the allies might not like agreements on ballistic missile defenses that would enable the Soviets to deploy a system capable of degrading strikes by NATO tactical nuclear forces or by British and French strategic ones; in fact, West German Defense Minister Helmut Schmidt has already indicated that under such circumstances the allies themselves would want ABM.[50]

On balance, the military would probably favor the completion of the Safeguard system and would be unhappy with a ban on ballistic missile defenses—which would mean the abolition of an important Army program and could enhance the potential danger to several Air Force weapons systems. They would probably accept some constraints on ballistic missile defenses, especially if this enabled them to allocate resources to other programs of importance to them. And they would probably be more willing to do this if the option were kept open for Hardsite and other improvements in terminal defenses—although whether the Soviets would feel the same way is questionable.

Some elements of the aerospace industry would, like the military, oppose a ban on ABMs and favor at least a partial deployment; however, others—who may stand to benefit from a different allocation of defense funds—would be at least neutral. Other interest groups would prefer to see constraints on ballistic missile defenses that could avoid both the direct expenditure of $12 billion for Safeguard and the indirect expenditures which are likely to result from efforts to offset any substantial Soviet deployment. Congress, which approved the Safeguard program by only one vote, is not likely to look favorably upon a full system, and might more readily accept one limited to three or four sites. The best guess is, therefore, that whatever the strategic value of ballistic missile defenses, the preponderance of U.S. interests is against a full twelve-site system and that the administration will have to settle for something less, both in terms of domestic factors and in terms of negotiability. As of February 18, 1972, the United States was reportedly discussing much more limited deployments of 150–200 interceptors in each country, rather than the 300 or so mentioned in previous proposals.[51]

RESTRICTING NEW WEAPONS

As evidenced by the history of ABMs, new weapons will probably have a major political and psychological impact; are likely to pose—or to seem to pose—serious threats to the strategic balance; are likely to provoke responses by the other side; and thus can intensify the arms race, with all its attendant costs. For these reasons, most of those who are worried about the priorities afforded defense expenditures and many of those whose political interests lie in reducing tensions may be against new weapons. This probably includes many among the allies, who may feel less reassured by new American weapons than threatened by new Soviet ones. Moreover, there should be strong potential support among at least the Air Force for this, since new weapons are more likely to be seaborne than land-based, whether fixed or mobile.

When it comes to specific weapons, however, the picture changes. The only major new weapon on both sides is the MIRV, which many in the United States view as a hedge against the threat of new Soviet developments, such as high-thrust ICBMs, more accurate warheads, ABMs, and their own MIRVs. Moreover, MIRVs represent a multiplication of the present deterrent, which both reinforces the utility of some weapons systems, such as submarine-launched missiles, and preserves the overall ability of the United States to inflict high levels of damage. Thus, despite the fact that the installation of MIRVs by the Soviet Union would constitute a threat to the United States, that they make the kill ratio more favorable to the attacker (thereby increasing the likelihood of a preemptive strike in a time of crisis), and that offsetting measures as well as implementing programs are extremely expensive, MIRVs have had considerable support.

The concerns that MIRVs could cause argue for banning them entirely, especially if ABMs are also banned or severely constrained; in fact, the United States has indicated that if ballistic missile defenses were restricted, it would be willing to scrap its program and to dismantle the MIRVs already installed.[52] This would, however, leave it with the potential of installing proven—if low-accuracy—MIRVs clandestinely, and the Soviets with a similar potential for installing multiple re-entry vehicles (MRVs), which do not yet have an independent targeting capability but could readily be given one. To some extent, increases in the accuracy of American MIRVs, and independent targeting capabilities for Soviet MRVs, could be slowed down by limiting the testing of such weapons; however, assurance would not be absolute and, barring on-site inspection (which the Americans have insisted be authorized under any agreement that would preclude MIRVs and which the Soviets have rejected as too intrusive), each side would have to proceed on the basis that the other had workable MIRVs and program its forces accordingly.

This does not mean that failure to control MIRVs will automatically result in the United States or the Soviet Union gaining an advantage; the forces on both sides are too powerful, too diverse, and too widely deployed for this to happen. It does, however, suggest that the two countries may either have to accept the resultant degradation in their land-based forces (relying on MIRVs to maintain their capacity for assured destruction), build a "hard-point" missile defensive system (perhaps utilizing smaller radars and short-range interceptors), or make their ICBMs mobile, thereby handicapping targeting for a first strike.

Although neither of these latter steps would necessarily be incompatible with arrangements to limit strategic armaments, they would make agreement more difficult and implementation more complex. Moreover, they would be comparatively costly, so that the U.S. defense budget would have to bear not only the expenses of Minuteman III and Poseidon, but also, as a by-product of MIRVs, the charges for superhardening missile silos, building terminal ABMs, or launching ULMS. Politically there is likely to be little support for MIRVs, since the issue of installing or banning them is technically complicated and symbolically not very significant. (In fact, most experts outside government have deplored the installation of MIRVs as likely to intensify the arms race by forcing the Soviets to take exactly the kinds of countermeasures described earlier.) Nor does it necessarily follow that the services are solidly in favor of MIRVs; as one former Pentagon analyst said: "Actually, the Air Force should be leading the opposition to MIRVs, in its own interest. MIRVs are the biggest long-range threat to our land-based weapons." [53]

Why, then, is there little progress toward a ban on these weapons? One reason, already suggested, is that they do represent a hedge against uncertainties and a means of maintaining the ability to inflict heavy damage on the Soviet Union. Another reason is that it would be difficult to rule them out without very intrusive and probably unacceptable inspection, and although restrictions on missile testing would slow their development, it could not preclude it entirely. A third is that concerns about the certainty of verification, reinforced by fears and worries about Soviet "cheating," may enable the proponents of MIRVs to resist pressures for limitations. A more significant one, however, may be that the USSR is not interested; in fact, according to newspaper accounts, it (like the United States) has given up all efforts to curb these weapons.[54]

The Prospects for the SALT

This brief analysis of the arms control measures discussed during the Strategic Arms Limitation Talks suggests that each offers advantages and suffers from disadvantages. Which combination of measures is chosen depends on one's priorities. If the purpose is to save money, then immediate reductions in numbers of weapons, by type; a freeze on obvious and significant qualitative improvements; a ban on ballistic missile defenses; and restrictions on the deployment of new weapons would seem warranted, since these would both preclude costly new programs and maintain the strategic balance more or less at present levels. However, despite the pressures for cutbacks in U.S. defense expenditures, it seems unlikely that the government would have to accept such stringent limitations on strategic weapons, which are likely to be opposed by influential elements throughout the country. Moreover, this combination would make it impossible to protect centers of population against attacks by smaller nuclear powers, which continues to be an American objective, if not a Soviet one. Perhaps more importantly, each side could, in the absence of very intrusive inspection, install MIRVs clandestinely, thereby increasing its ability to inflict damage and, as missile accuracy increased or maneuverable re-entry vehicles were introduced, its ability to launch counterforce strikes. Such developments could, over the long run, arouse concern about the vulnerability of land-based weapons systems and generate pressures for a shift to seaborne missiles, for the construction of ballistic missile defenses, or for both. Thus it is unlikely that this particular combination of measures could be either agreed upon or, if it were adopted, long maintained.

If one's primary objective is to reduce damage from a nuclear war, then restrictions should be placed on numbers of weapons, by type; on qualitative improvements; and on innovations such as MIRV, but not on ballistic missile defenses. The subsequent expansion and improvement of ABM systems could (assuming they were effective) enable the United States and the Soviet Union to knock down increasingly higher percentages of each other's incoming missiles, thereby appreciably reducing losses from a nuclear exchange without necessarily lessening the deterrent effect of a potential exchange. And it is conceivable that the resultant sense of security would encourage the United States and the Soviet Union to agree on cutbacks in their strategic strike forces—although this sense of security would depend in part on the effectiveness of controls over MIRVs. Whether either side would accept so radical a transformation of the strategic environment may be questionable; whether, even if it did, it would opt for so complex and costly a way of achieving this transformation is perhaps even more questionable.

If, instead, one's aim is to preserve the present strategic balance rather than to establish a new one, other combinations of measures might seem more rewarding. For example, overall limitations on strategic strike forces, rather than limitations on each type of launch vehicle, would enable each side to shift from fixed weapon systems to mobile ones, or from land-based systems to seaborne ones, thereby both maintaining relatively secure retaliatory forces and minimizing the possibility that the other could gain any advantage from striking first. If this measure were combined with one controlling the numbers of high-thrust missiles that each side could have, this would inhibit improvements in first-strike capabilities resulting from the installation of multimegaton maneuverable warheads, or from very large-yield single ones, as well as reduce the damage that a force of any given size could inflict. Furthermore, authorization for the deployment of "light" missile defenses would protect both sides against attacks by third powers as well as against improvements in the accuracy and maneuverability of re-entry vehicles that might threaten land-based weapons systems.

Unfortunately, this combination of measures (which is basically the one initially advanced by the United States during the talks on the limitation of strategic armaments) [55] poses several difficulties. One is that as long as the MIRVs are left uncontrolled and maneuverable warheads are not precluded, limited ballistic missile defenses might not be very effective, and effective ones might not be very limited. Another is that this set of proposals would require far more substantial adjustments in the Soviet force posture than in the American one, which is essentially that projected for 1976, and far greater concessions from the Soviet Union than from the United States. And still another is that it could prove very costly, which might trouble the United States Congress, if not the executive branch.

If one's objective is to devise arrangements that would be negotiable abroad and acceptable at home, then one should probably look to measures that are simple rather than complex, partial rather than comprehensive, cheap rather than costly, and aimed more at limiting further increases in strategic nuclear forces than at reducing those now on hand. One such measure will almost certainly be the imposition of restrictions on antiballistic missiles; in fact, the major question at issue is whether each country will be authorized to deploy two hundred to three hundred antimissile missiles around weapons sites, as the United States proposes, or one hundred around its capital city, as the Soviets have suggested.[56] The American proposal apparently stems from the fact that three batteries of interceptors have already been authorized, that these could help protect U.S. air bases and missile silos against any Soviet counterforce attack, and that this in turn could remove any Soviet temptation to launch a first strike during a crisis in an effort to alter the strategic balance. (Left unsaid is that American officials may doubt whether the United States Senate, which approved the Safeguard ABM program by only one vote, would agree to deploy antimissile missiles around Washington, as called for in the Soviet scheme.) For their part, the Russians are understandably reluctant to scrap the embryonic missile defenses around Moscow, unconvinced of the utility of defending weapons sites, and unwilling to permit the Americans to have more interceptors than they themselves have; hence, they have not been enthusiastic about either the primary U.S. proposal or an alternative one, which would equate the ninety-six Soviet interceptors being placed around Moscow with the three hundred that the United States hopes to build in Missouri, Montana, and North Dakota. Since, however, President Nixon and Soviet Premier Alexei Kosygin undertook in 1971 to reach agreement as soon as possible on measures to limit antiballistic missiles, some kind of compromise will probably be worked out.

Inasmuch as the two leaders have also made a commitment to "agree on certain measures with respect to the limitation of offensive strategic weapons," [57] one can reasonably expect some results in this area—but not extensive ones. Although the Soviets have seemingly been willing, as part of the Nixon-Kosygin agreement, to shelve their demand that certain U.S. tactical nuclear delivery vehicles be counted under any agreement for the limitation of strategic weapons systems,[58] they have not given up their insistence on "equality." Since their forces of intercontinental range are still smaller than comparable American forces, they probably will oppose the two-year freeze on the construction of missile silos and missile-submarines that the United States reportedly has proposed.[59] This does not mean that they will necessarily shun an agreement based on parity in numbers of launch vehicles, which would enable them to build up their fleet of modern missile-submarines to a level approaching that of the United States. Nor does it mean that they will continue to deploy large ICBMs such as the SS-9, to whose limitation the United States attaches so much importance; in fact, as of late 1971 the number of SS-9s had remained virtually constant for over a year. It does, however, suggest that any agreement will at best set a limit to further increases in Soviet strategic strike forces, rather than reduce them—or even hold them to current levels.

As for constraints on new weapons, the Soviets simply do not seem interested. They have continued to test the Fractional Orbital Bombardment System (FOBS), a large missile fired on a depressed trajectory that gives shorter warning of attack; they have begun to install VRBMs (variable-range ballistic missiles) capable of striking at targets either in Europe or in America; they have continued their development of multiple warheads; and they have exerted little or no pressure for a ban on MIRVs. Since the United States not only has continued with its own program for the installation of MIRVs but has reportedly dropped its earlier suggestion that these be precluded,[60] the prospects for banning them are indeed dim. And since both sides are continuing their programs to replace obsolescent weapons by newer and presumably more effective ones, controls over qualitative improvements seem ruled out, at least for the present. Thus the shape emerging from the long-drawn-out negotiations in Helsinki and Vienna was that of an agreement which would restrict the deployment of ABMs, stop the buildup of Soviet strategic strike forces at a level approximating that of American ones, perhaps put a ceiling on the number of high-thrust ICBMs deployed, and do precious little else.

Such an outcome is not likely to please everyone; however, it is not likely to displease everyone either. Those concerned with the credibility of the deterrent can take comfort from the limitations placed on Soviet SS-9s and the retention of an embryonic American ABM system, even though these may be purchased at the cost of accepting "equality" in strategic delivery vehicles. Even if MIRVs are left uncontrolled, those interested in curbing the arms race will have achieved a partial victory, as will those anxious to hold down defense expenditures. Aside from a reduction in the Safeguard system (a reduction which was probably inevitable in any event), the armed services will have lost nothing, and will—if approval is forthcoming—be able to continue both their current programs for the modernization of existing weapons and their cherished proposals for the development of new ones. Accordingly, while one may expect extensive and perhaps bitter debate in Congress, and attacks and counterattacks in the press, the prospects for approval of such an agreement are undoubtedly good.

The significant question may be not the shape or the likelihood of an initial agreement to limit strategic armaments but what happens subsequently. In the long run, a number of developments could jeopardize the American objective of reducing the danger of war through strategic arms limitations, of achieving a new commitment to stability, and of influencing Soviet attitudes toward other issues.[61] For example, the strategic balance could be threatened by MIRVs if these are not banned, by improvements in the accuracy and thrust of missiles if these are not somehow proscribed or offset, and by lasers or other exotic defensive weapons if these are not ruled out. Moreover, since both the United States and the Soviet Union have allies and interests that are threatened by the other (or by third parties), some way must be found to alleviate those threats, lest the arms race be fueled anew. Finally, the deployment of new weapons tends to arouse fears and concerns that could make more difficult the improvement of relations between the two superpowers and could conceivably enhance the danger of war.

If, therefore, arms control is to do what the United States—and presumably the Soviet Union—want it to do, it must inevitably involve weapons not yet encompassed (such as MIRVs and spaceborne interceptors), programs not yet constrained (such as those for the upgrading of missile-submarines), and forces not yet covered, such as the Soviet MRBMs and IRBMs and the American Forward Based Aircraft in Western Europe. At some stage, also, French and British nuclear forces must be at least weighed in the scale, if not specifically covered by arms control agreements. And last—but certainly not least—efforts must be made to induce the People's Republic of China to limit its strategic strike forces, lest their continued growth not only lead the United States and the Soviet Union to abrogate their own agreements on the limitation of strategic armaments but also once again arouse fears and exacerbate tensions which now seem to be diminishing slightly.

At the moment such suggestions seem unrealistic if not visionary. However, arms control can have a dynamism of its own, just as can an arms race, and judicious agreements can increase the momentum, at least to a point well beyond where we now are. Prudence requires that the United States follow the advice of former President Johnson and "assure that no nation can ever find it credible to launch a nuclear attack or to use its nuclear power as a credible threat against us or our allies." However, it also behooves us to heed his further counsel to do this by slowing down the arms race, as a prelude to the larger-scale understanding toward which both the United States and the Soviet Union have been groping during the past decade.[62]

NOTES

1. J. I. Coffey, *Strategic Power and National Security* (Pittsburgh: University of Pittsburgh Press, 1971).

2. Samuel C. Orr, "Defense Report/National Security Council Network Gives White House Tight Rein Over SALT Strategy," reprinted in the *Congressional Record* (May 19, 1971), pp. E4,642 ff.

3. "Foreign Policy for the 1970's: A New Strategy for Peace," the *New York Times* (February 19, 1970), p. 17M.

4. For a further discussion of the difficulties of achieving meaningful strategic advantages see Coffey, *Strategic Power and National Security,* pp. 21–45.

5. *Statement of Secretary of Defense Robert S. McNamara before a Joint Session of the Senate Armed Services Committee and the Senate Sub-Committee on Department of Defense Appropriations on the Fiscal Year 1968–72 Defense Program and 1968 Defense Budget,* mimeographed (January 23, 1967), p. 53. The emphasis is his.

6. "Foreign Policy for the 1970's," p. 24M.

7. This is at least a reasonable inference from Secretary of Defense Melvin R. Laird's testimony that if the Soviets could kill 100 million people and the Americans only 50 million, he would not want "that great a disparity," even though the 50 million figure falls within the range earlier prescribed by Mr. McNamara. See the exchange between Mr. Laird and Senator Clifford P. Case in U.S. Congress, Senate Committee on Foreign Relations, Subcommittee on Arms Control, International Law and Organization, *Hearings [on] ABM, MIRV, SALT and the Nuclear Arms Race,* 91 Cong., 2 Sess. (1970), p. 311. The formal criterion is "to prevent the Soviets from gaining the ability to cause considerably greater destruction than the United States could inflict in any type of a nuclear exchange" (Ibid., p. 308).

8. The President's Message to the Congress, transmitting the Ninth Annual Report of the U.S. Arms Control and Disarmament Agency, February 26, 1970 (Washington, D.C.: GPO, 1970), no page number.

9. *United States Foreign Policy for the 1970s: Building for Peace,* A Report by President Richard Nixon to the Congress, February 25, 1971 (New York: Harper & Row, 1971), p. 138.

10. Ibid., p. 141.

11. Although the United States has reportedly built a synchronous orbital satellite that could give thirty minutes' warning of any Soviet ICBM launch, this warning would not, under present concepts, benefit ICBMs in fixed sites; and only if this (or another) satellite could give similar warning of SLBM

launches would it significantly enhance the security of the bomber fleet, which, despite improved procedures, requires a minimum of seven minutes to launch all planes on alert status.

12. *Statement of the President [on Ballistic Missile Defenses]*, mimeographed (March 14, 1969), p. 1.

13. For a description of the Safeguard system and the rationales for its deployment, see the testimony by Secretary of Defense Laird in U.S. Congress, House of Representatives, Subcommittees of the Committee on Appropriations, *Hearings [on the] Safeguard Antiballistic Missile System*, 91 Cong., 2 Sess. (1969), pp. 5–40.

14. "We Must Talk with Moscow," the *New York Times* (February 23, 1971), p. 35.

15. "Text of U.S.–Chinese Communiqué," the *(New York Times* February 28, 1972), p. 16.

16. Alice L. Hsieh, *Communist China's Military Policies, Doctrine and Strategy*, Publication 3–960 (Santa Monica, Calif.: The RAND Corporation, 1968), p. 21. In his briefing for key members of Congress in June 1972, Dr. Kissinger stated that the "likelihood of our being involved in any conflict with the People's Republic of China was considerably less than it was at the time the Safeguard [ABM] program was submitted . . ." and that therefore limitations on ABMs could be accepted (*Congressional Record,* Senate, June 19, 1972, p. S9604).

17. Henry M. Jackson, "National Security: Basic Tasks" (Address to the Hoover Institution on War, Revolution and Peace, Conference on 50 Years of Communism in Russia, October 11, 1967), reprinted in U.S. Congress, House Subcommittee on Military Applications of The Joint Committee on Atomic Energy, *Hearings [on the] Scope, Magnitude and Implications of the United States Antiballistic Missile Program,* 90 Cong., 2 Sess. (1969), p. 49 (hereafter cited as *Hearings [on the] . . . United States Antiballistic Missile Program*).

18. These concerns have domestic as well as international implications and sometimes cut both ways: One argument for strategic arms limitations is that these could save resources that could be better applied to building up the United States Navy.

19. For a more detailed discussion of these concerns, an evaluation of their validity, and an assessment of their implications for arms control, see Coffey, *Strategic Power and National Security,* esp. pp. 46–104, 160–68.

20. In this connection, see the evaluation by Leslie H. Gelb of the effect of domestic anticommunism on U.S. policy in "Vietnam: The System Worked," *Foreign Policy,* no. 3 (Summer 1971), esp. pp. 143–44, 166–67.

21. "Farewell Address" quoted in U.S. Congress, Joint Economic Committee, *Hearings [on] The Military Budget and National Economic Priorities,* 90 Cong., 2 Sess., part 2 (1969), p. 470.

22. Michael J. Driver, Technical Report #4.2, *American Mass Opinion & International Assurance,* p. 22, *Studies in Social and Psychological Aspects of Verification, Inspection and International Assurance,* ACDA/E-104 (December 1968).

23. Rolland Bushner, ed., *The Middle East and U.S.-Soviet Relations* (New York: Council on Foreign Relations, 1971), p. 8.

24. "Opinion on Campus," *National Review,* 23, no. 23 (June 15, 1971), p. 638.

25. James A. Barber, Jr., "Is There a Generation Gap in the Naval Officer Corps?" *Naval War College Review,* 22, no. 9 (May 1970), p. 31.

26. In 1963, nearly 80 percent of the college students surveyed gave unqualified support to war, if the choice was surrender or a nuclear exchange with the Soviet Union; by 1971 this had dropped to 37 percent. "Opinion on Campus," *National Review,* 15, no. 13 (October 1, 1963), pp. 282–83; ibid., 23, no. 23 (June 15, 1971), p. 638.

27. *Gallup Opinion Index,* Report no. 72 (June 1971), p. 9.

28. Leonard Woodcock, President of the United Automobile Workers, in U.S. Congress, Joint Economic Committee, Subcommittee on Economy in Government, *Hearings [on] Changing National Priorities,* 91 Cong., 2 Sess., part 2 (1970), p. 374.

29. U.S. Congress, Senate Committee on Armed Services, *Hearings [on the] Fiscal Year 1972 Authorization for Military Procurement, Research and Development, Construction and Real Estate Acquisition for the SAFEGUARD ABM, and Reserve Strengths,* 92 Cong., 1 Sess., part 2 (1971), p. 1,741 (hereafter cited as *Hearings [on the] Fiscal Year 1972 Authorization for Military Procurement . . .*).

30. *Hearings [on] The Military Budget and National Economic Priorities,* part 1, p. 257.

31. The *New York Times* (September 30, 1971), p. 1. The Senate Armed Services Committee approved full-scale deployment at only two of the four ABM sites the administration had requested.

32. *Gallup Opinion Index,* Report no. 71 (May 1971), p. 23.

33. U.S. Congress, Joint Economic Committee, *The 1971 Economic Report of the President,* 92 Cong., 1 Sess., part 3 (1971), pp. 669, 776–77.

34. The 10 percent is the average direct cost for Fiscal Years 1968 through 1972, as given in the *Statement of Secretary of Defense Melvin R. Laird before the House Armed Services Committee on the Fiscal Year 1972–1976 Defense Program and the 1972 Defense Budget,* mimeographed (March 9, 1971), table 1, p. 163. The 20 percent includes indirect costs obtained by eliminating all charges for Airlift and Sealift, Guard and Reserve Forces, and Support of Other Nations, and then allocating costs for Intelligence and Communications, Research and Development, and other support activities in proportion to the expenditures for Strategic Nuclear Forces. Even though not all program packages relate to Strategic Nuclear Forces in the same way, this is believed to be reasonable, especially since about 50 percent of DoD's research effort is strategically oriented. *Hearings [on] Changing National Priorities,* part 1, p. 244.

35. George W. Rathjens, in *Hearings [on] Changing National Priorities,* part 1, p. 194.

36. Alain C. Enthoven and K. Wayne Smith, *How Much is Enough? Shaping the Defense Program, 1961–1969* (New York: Harper & Row, 1971) p. 336.

37. One estimate is that the federal government will, by FY 1974, need an additional $35 billion annually just to meet automatic increases in Federal civilian expenditures, and at least another $35 billion to cover the projected needs of *existing* domestic programs. Joseph A. Califano, Jr., former Special Assistant to the President, in U.S. Congress, Joint Economic Committee, Subcommittee on Economy in Government, *Hearings [on] The Military Budget and National Eco-*

nomic Priorities, 91 Cong., 1 Sess., part 1 (1969), p. 275. See also the testimony of Dr. Charles L. Schultze, former Director of the Bureau of the Budget in the *Hearings,* pp. 46–47.

38. J. I. Coffey and Jerome H. Laulicht, *The Implications for Arms Control of Perceptions of Strategic Weapons Systems,* prepared for the U.S. Arms Control and Disarmament Agency by the Research Office of Sociology, University of Pittsburgh, November 30, 1971), ACDA/E-163, vol. II, pp. 15–23.

39. Report of a meeting between Secretary of State William P. Rogers and Soviet Foreign Secretary Andrei Gromyko, the *New York Times* (October 1, 1971), p. 14.

40. The *Washington Post* (May 21, 1970), p. 1. For further details, see the *New York Times* (July 28, 1970), p. 2; (July 23, 1971), p. 4, and (September 24, 1971), p. 1.

41. For a more detailed discussion of the difficulties of measuring the capabilities of strategic forces, see Coffey, *Strategic Power and National Security,* pp. 22–24.

42. For illustrations of the Soviet opposition to "one-sided" agreements and insistence upon "equal security," see the Report of General Secretary Leonid I. Brezhnev to the 24th Congress of the Communist Party of the Soviet Union, March 30, 1971, *Pravda* (March 31, 1971), pp. 2–10, translated and reprinted in *The Current Digest of the Soviet Press,* XXIII (April 20, 1971), p. 12, and the replies of Premier Alexei N. Kosygin to questions asked by the newspaper *Asahi, Pravda* (January 3, 1971), p. 1, in *The Current Digest,* XXIII (February 2, 1971), p. 11.

43. The *Washington Post* (September 25, 1971), p. 1.

44. See, for example, Captain James A. Winnefield, U.S. Navy, and Carl H. Builder, "ASW—Now or Never," United States Naval Institute *Proceedings,* 97, no. 9/823 (September 1971), pp. 18–25.

45. See, in this connection, Hedley Bull's piece, *Strategic Arms Limitation: The Precedent of the Washington and London Naval Treaties,* An Occasional Paper of the Center for Policy Study (Chicago: University of Chicago, 1971), esp. pp. 37–40.

46. D. C. Hoag, "Ballistic-missile Guidance" in *Impact of New Technologies on the Arms Race,* eds. B. T. Feld *et al.,* A Pugwash Monograph (Cambridge, Massachusetts: The M.I.T. Press, 1971), p. 100.

47. Richard L. Garwin, *Superpower Postures in SALT: An American View,* An Occasional Paper of the Center for Policy Study (Chicago: University of Chicago, 1971), pp. 17–18.

48. Donald G. Brennan, "The Case for Missile Defense," *Foreign Affairs,* 47 (April 1969), pp. 432–38.

49. See the testimony to this effect of Dr. John S. Foster, Jr., Director of Defense Research and Engineering in U.S. Congress, House of Representatives, Committee on Foreign Affairs, Sub-Committee on National Security Policy and Scientific Developments, *Hearings [on the] Diplomatic and Strategic Impact of Multiple Warhead Missiles,* 91 Cong., 1 Sess. (1969), p. 248.

50. Interview with West German Defense Minister Helmut Schmidt in *Die Welt* (February 16, 1970), p. 7, quoted in Lother Ruehl, "The Impact of Strategic Arms Control Upon European Security and Defense Systems," paper pre-

sented at the Joint Conference on Strategic Arms and U.S.-West European Relations, Talloires, France, mimeographed (June 17–19, 1970), p. 6.

51. The *New York Times* (February 18, 1972), p. 10. The agreed figure was 200 interceptors.

52. See the testimony to this effect of Dr. John S. Foster, Jr., Director of Defense Research and Engineering, reported in the *New York Times* (June 5, 1970), p. 10.

53. Orr, "Defense Report/National Security Council Network Gives White House Tight Rein over SALT Strategy," *Congressional Record,* p. E4,651.

54. The *Washington Post* (February 4, 1971), p. 8.

55. The *Washington Post* (May 21, 1970), p. 14.

56. The *New York Times* (September 24, 1971), p. 1.

57. Statement of President Richard M. Nixon, the *New York Times* (May 21, 1971), p. 2.

58. For the Soviet demand and the reasons therefor, see "What Is Hidden Behind the Propaganda Screen?" by V. Shestov in *Pravda* (February 4, 1971), pp. 4–5, translated and reprinted in *The Current Digest of the Soviet Press,* XXIII (March 2, 1971), esp. p. 8.

59. The *New York Times* (July 23, 1970), p. 1. See also ibid. (January 12, 1972), p. 1.

60. Ibid. (July 23, 1970), p. 1.

61. *United States Foreign Policy for the 1970s: Building for Peace,* pp. 152–53.

62. State of the Union Message, January 10, 1967, the *New York Times* (January 11, 1967), p. 16.

The Rationale for Superpower Arms Control Agreements: Conflicting Interpretations

THE OPENING SESSION of the symposium set forth a series of alternative rationales for superpower arms control. An effort was made to relate arms control rationales to major foreign policy goals, domestic political systems, and the structure of the international system. In addition to establishing a theoretical framework, this session provided a discussion of contrasting U.S. and Soviet strategic arms control rationales.

The topics discussed can be categorized as follows:

1. the transformation of the international system and the SALT,
2. the uncertainty factor and the SALT,
3. alternative explanations of the dynamics of the Soviet-American strategic relationship,
4. constraints on the superpowers and the SALT, and
5. areas and issues requiring further study.

The bulk of attention was given to alternative explanations of the dynamics of the Soviet-American strategic relationship.

The Transformation of the International System and the SALT

The transformation of the international system from bipolarity to some form of "emerging multipolarity" both affects and is affected by superpower negotiations (SALT) and possible agreements concerning nuclear weapons. First, multipolarity accompanied by the attempts of superpowers to limit their competition in the field of strategic weaponry increases the likelihood that proliferation will occur in the future. As strategic parity is codified in an agreement from the SALT, extended nuclear guarantees by the superpowers will become less credible. Hence

In addition to those presenting papers Samuel T. Cohen and William E. Griffith participated in the discussion. Presiding over the session was Lincoln P. Bloomfield.

potential Nth countries might seek a nuclear capability in order to provide for their own security.

Second, in a system of emerging multipolarity, arms control negotiations will inevitably become more complex because of the necessity of including more parties in the negotiations. Any agreements now being forged should take into consideration the need to include other parties in the negotiations at some future date.

Third, the problems of U.S.-Soviet strategic asymmetries so evident in the SALT will be exacerbated in a multipolar world and will require multilateral negotiations. An understanding of the strategic calculus of each party in a negotiation process will be more difficult, and hence the need for extensive efforts to achieve some form of mutuality of interests between the various parties will increase. The task of solving the current problem of asymmetry between the superpowers foreshadows difficulties in strategic arms control negotiations within an emerging multipolar system.

The triangular relationship among the United States, the Soviet Union, and China is developing into a situation of multipolarity in which there is not a balance of power in the classical sense. For instance, it would be possible that the United States could deal fairly well with Moscow and Peking, but the last two could not find common ground with each other. In such a context (which closely reflects the present situation), it would be likely that the United States and the Soviet Union could use arms control negotiations to reassure each other that neither is trying to play up to the Chinese for unilateral advantage. This same situation might apply to negotiations between either of the two superpowers and the Chinese. In such a situation, the party left out of the bilateral negotiations would exhibit a great deal of suspicion concerning such negotiations. This problem would become more acute if the triangular relationship were to become transformed into one characterized by increased multilateral interactions with other nuclear powers.

There was widespread agreement that a transformation of the system is taking place and that its implications are important for an understanding of strategic arms limitation negotiations.

The Uncertainty Factor and the SALT

The problem of uncertainty in analyzing ongoing negotiations and predicting future developments was underscored several times during the session. Statements by former Secretary of Defense Robert McNamara and former SAC Commander Thomas S. Power were cited to illustrate the hazards of prophecy. In 1965, Mr. McNamara had said that by the early 1970s the United States could expect to retain a significant lead over the Soviet Union in numbers of ICBMs and SLBMs and a very substantial lead in effectiveness of delivery systems. General Power, on the other hand, had stated in 1964 that in his opinion the Soviet Union could and would strive for vast superiority in missile numbers that, when coupled with dramatic advances in missile accuracy, would provide a high mathematical probability of destroying most or all of the U.S. hardened ICBMs before they could be launched in retaliation. General Power proved to be correct but, it was asserted, not because of any great predictive acumen. From McNamara's mistake and Power's "lucky guess," it was suggested that predictions about the intentions of adversaries are likely to be either wrong or right for the wrong reasons.

Another uncertainty relates to the problem of establishing whether an actual dialogue is taking place, or has ever taken place, between the superpowers. To illustrate this point, it was contended that during the test ban discussion from 1957 to 1963 there was no real dialogue. There was, on the contrary, a great U.S. monologue. The Soviets were willing to sit still and listen, but there was very little indication of Soviet comprehension of the U.S. viewpoint and practically no indication that there was ever a "meeting of the minds" on the subject matter. When an agreement did occur, it was hailed as a significant event in efforts at arms control. Pious statements as to the possibility of now being able to look forward to a more promising future—one which would intensify efforts to reach further substantive limitations on the arms race—came forth in profusion. What really resulted was far less than the expectations espoused by various analysts.

This example indicates that although an inclination to negotiate now exists, the milieu in which the SALT have taken place is far different from that envisaged by the euphoric statements uttered at the time of the signing of the Nuclear Test Ban Treaty in 1963. The overall strategic balance has been drastically altered by both sides pursuing separate courses in their respective strategic postures. The Test Ban Treaty certainly did not inhibit the Soviet strategic missile buildup or the qualitative improvements in the U.S. strategic force. Thus, what resulted from the Test Ban Treaty was not a dampening of the arms race but a limited prohibition on certain kinds of nuclear weapons testing. Once again, predictions proved to be excessively expansive.

The discussants pointed out several additional areas of uncertainty. First, a great degree of uncertainty was seen to surround what the actual form of a strategic arms control agreement might be. It was considered unlikely that any qualitative limitations on weapons would occur given the present American lead in MIRV technology, which the Soviets are unlikely to accept as a permanent condition. An agreement was seen as likely to be restricted to quantitative limitations on land-based ICBMs and ABM deployment. Although an agreement will probably produce minimal results, it might contribute to optimism about the future, as did the Nuclear Test Ban Treaty in 1963.

Second, uncertainty exists over the possible effects of either success or failure in the SALT. It was posited that if no agreement is reached and the arms race is continued, the likely result, as far as the United States is concerned, would be heightened apprehension among allies, the alienation of neutrals, and a possible return to a cold war relationship with the Soviet Union. Several other participants, however, did not believe that failure to reach an agreement, in and of itself, would have a great effect on the present global situation.

Participants found it difficult to predict the impact of a possible agreement. Both sides would be likely to continue to develop new armaments; however, they would divert and reshape their efforts according to the nature of the agreement. The consequences that would arise from these readjustments were not easily foreseeable. The most optimistic view was that arms control might have a dynamism of its own similar to that of the arms race, and that an initial agreement might possibly lead to more substantive developments.

In sum, the problem of uncertainty in relation to a great many issues was cited as central to evaluating and understanding the implications of strategic arms limitation negotiations.

Alternative Explanations of the Dynamics of the Soviet-American Strategic Relationship

Consideration was given during this discussion to two alternative ways of viewing the strategic relationship between the United States and the Soviet Union. The first viewpoint focused on the concept of "imperial will" and the belief that the Soviet Union currently is exhibiting such a will, whereas the United States is gradually losing its international dynamism. The contrasting styles in which each superpower engages in international politics were mentioned as indicative of this asymmetry of will.

The concept of imperial will was immediately challenged. It was pointed out that if the Soviet imperial will were operative, one might expect a series of crises, probes, a possible revival of the cold war, and various other Soviet challenges to the West. But on the contrary, the SALT exist, an agreement on Berlin has been reached, the Hot Line concept has been improved, and a movement toward a viable *détente* is taking place. Can these developments, it was asked, be reconciled to the thesis of Soviet imperial will? Were not the advocates of such a thesis playing the favorite Western game of projecting onto the Soviet Union what they felt would be the U.S. reaction if it were in a position similar to that of the Soviets?

These questions led to a refining of the concept of imperial will. One participant observed that Moscow had lately been trying to give the impression that it was negotiating from a position of strength. Russian interest in an entire series of negotiations was seen to stem from two considerations: (1) a desire to validate the situation of de facto strategic parity by means of a formal agreement and (2) a determination to resolve the outstanding issues from World War II in a manner legitimizing Soviet predominance in Eastern Europe. In this context the Soviet Union's goal in these negotiations is to ratify its status as an imperial power by winning international recognition of its new authority.

At this juncture the point was made that the Soviet imperial will reflects a certain degree of Soviet self-righteousness about its mission in the world. This provides evidence of a striking contrast to the situation in the United States, where significant numbers of elites are engaged in a period of soul-searching and self-recrimination.

Several other qualifying remarks on the thesis of imperial will were made. First, the technological gap between the United States and the Soviet Union at highly sophisticated levels provides an alternative explanation for the current strategic Soviet buildup. Second, the Soviet dispute with China can be seen as a prime motivating factor in the buildup, especially given the historical Soviet nightmare of encirclement, which heightens Moscow's perception of its security needs. Nevertheless, although these additional pressures can help explain current Soviet dynamism, the imperial-will thesis was seen by other discussants as valid, not only in regard to the self-confidence of Soviet ruling elites, but also as a reflection of Soviet perceptions that the imperial will of American elites was shattered by the experiences of the 1960s. This has led to a Soviet perception that the United States is in decline, while they themselves have not yet reached a peak.

Even with the above qualifications, several participants were not satisfied with the thesis of imperial will as an explanation of Soviet behavior. The belief was expressed that the Soviet Union might be exhibiting a decrease in imperial will. Its relative "toleration" of dissent within Russia, its "paper bear" approach to the Sino-Soviet border clashes, and its willingness to continue to devote more attention to consumer demands suggest a lack of political militancy. These factors would seem to indicate a certain lack of will to seek aggrandizement at the expense of a "weakened" United States.

An alternative to the imperial-will thesis emphasized "strategic interaction" as the determining factor in the Soviet-American relationship. This thesis emphasizes the existence of a marked U.S. superiority in strategic weaponry during the early and mid-1960s. From the Soviet viewpoint, especially after the Cuban missile crisis, tremendous international political and military pressures required a major response to an obvious situation of marked strategic inferiority. Thus, the Soviet strategic buildup might be explained as a result of a long-standing inferiority complex rather than a result of Soviet imperial will.

This thesis of strategic interaction was challenged as being unable to explain why the Soviet Union had exceeded the point of general equality with the United States in its strategic buildup. If one were to accept the interaction thesis, namely, that the Soviet strategic buildup was a result of the American strategic buildup which occurred as a result of the missile-gap illusion, then the action-reaction syndrome should be carried back even further to the bomber gap–missile gap reaction of the mid-1950s. The participants were cautioned to be careful in selecting chronologies to explain the phenomenon of the Soviet strategic buildup in the 1960s; for if one looks closely at the genesis of the buildup, all the current Soviet systems were initiated before Khrushchev was ousted. Thus, the research and development stage must have been started before the American buildup in the early 1960s. This perspective breaks the interaction pattern. The question was raised: Why didn't the United States respond in kind to the extensive Soviet strategic buildup during the late 1960s?

Given these problems surrounding the thesis of strategic interaction, another explanation of the current Soviet buildup might be that the Soviets are now encouraged to push ahead because of the American standstill in the deployment of land-based ICBMs. This view, of course, is more in accord with the imperial-will thesis.

Objections were raised to the assertion that the United States did not react strongly to Soviet strategic increases during the late 1960s or even in the early 1970s. The development of MIRV and the continuing pressure to deploy an extensive ABM system in the United States were cited as but two examples of an American response.

This discussion of the relative merits of the imperial-will thesis versus that of the strategic interaction was ended with the remark that there are several alternative ways to view the interaction process. The issue was seen as being so complicated that no one approach could offer a fully reliable explanation. The variables change in importance over time, making causal explanations difficult.

Constraints on the Superpowers and the SALT

The three papers presented during this session of the symposium examined the various pressures exerted on the superpowers to engage in the SALT. Robert Pfaltzgraff suggested that a basic rationale might be the desire of both superpowers to preserve credible deterrence at a lower level of effort. If this assessment is correct, then a strategic arms control agreement should reflect a willingness to scale down both offensive and defensive systems.

Joseph I. Coffey pointed out in his paper that a wide range of elite opinion in the United States was now favorable to extensive efforts to slow down the arms race. He suggested that many U.S. government officials appear to have become convinced that the rapid growth of Soviet strategic forces has rendered improbable the idea that a meaningful strategic superiority can be retained by the United States. Hence, a feeling has been developing that some attempt at codifying parity should be made.

It was also suggested that countervailing pressures have impeded any efforts toward reaching an accommodation with the Soviets that would be construed as an acceptance of superpower equality. Those in the United States who still maintain a Manichean view of the East-West struggle remain opposed to any agreement with the Soviet Union. Pressures against arms control agreements with the Soviets until they discontinue their strategic buildup have also been exerted by those who, while having no objection in principle to agreements with the Russians, nevertheless feel that the strategic equation is not currently favorable to the United States. Under such conditions an agreement would be detrimental to the United States.

Several comments on U.S. interests in the SALT gave great emphasis to economic considerations. It was noted that the main economic rationale in the United States concerns the need to reorder priorities and to place greater emphasis on domestic problems than on defense expenditures. However, several participants stated that an agreement at the SALT would result in no significant reallocation of money from defense to domestic programs. It was emphasized that arms control was likely to be a very expensive proposition. Moreover, qualitative improvements, because of their higher degree of sophistication, would probably prove very costly.

The discussion of the various constraints on U.S. policy led participants to a general consensus that the United States is amenable to agreement to limit strategic arms. A few persons suggested that the United States might be too anxious for an agreement and might sacrifice more than it should in the SALT.

In discussing Soviet motivations at the SALT, Thomas Wolfe asserted that it would be erroneous to view the Soviet Union as a monolithic state where decisions can be made without consideration of their implications for domestic interest groups' perceptions. His comments and several from the audience stressed that foreign policy elites, bureaucracies, and members of the academic intelligentsia must be taken into consideration by the Soviet leadership in the process of decision-making. But it was also noted that the Soviet leadership is able to make decisions without the extensive pressures with which American leaders must contend.

In a discussion of the current Soviet position, Thomas Wolfe noted that the Soviet Union is becoming a global power with extensive interests and influence underwritten by a vast military capability. The growth of Soviet interests reflects a dynamic impetus, an imperial will, that, unlike the United States, has not yet crested. It was viewed as likely that this dynamism will continue to characterize Soviet policy as both the physical and political instruments of influence are diversified to provide the Soviet leadership with more options in the pursuit of its goals.

Soviet economic considerations were mentioned as being susceptible to analysis from two points of view. The first emphasizes that long-range economic problems could compel the Soviet Union to seek an end to the strategic arms competition via SALT. The need for growth investments and technological innovations in the nondefense sector of the economy, added to rising consumer demands, could militate against extensive outlays in the future for increased strategic armaments. Thus, in this view strategic stabilization at present or near-term levels would be acceptable to the Soviet leadership.

Another point of view contended that the Soviet Union has achieved a sufficient industrial and economic capacity to enable it to continue to expand its strategic weaponry and still meet the demands of the consumer and nonmilitary sectors of the economy. Consequently, the Soviet leaders may see an opportunity to gain a marginal strategic superiority over the United States, which is currently in the process of reevaluation and readjustment following the experience in Vietnam and the domestic strife of the 1960s. Soviet leaders may also anticipate certain political advantages as a result of its possessing vast strategic capabilities.

Areas and Issues Requiring Further Study

Throughout the discussion during this session, reference was made to areas of insufficient knowledge, suggesting the need for future studies:

1. A gap was seen to exist in relating strategic theory to current realities. The old concepts of mutually assured destruction and second-strike capability were seen by some participants as now outdated. An extensive rethinking of strategic theory was thus thought to be necessary.

2. The political uses of nuclear weapons have not been sufficiently explored. It was stated that the more "theological" literature on arms control has not seriously considered this issue.

3. It was emphasized that the need exists to study the implications of strategic parity for levels of conventional armament.

4. Further thought should be given to the timing variable in the action-reaction syndrome of the superpower strategic relationship.

5. There is an immediate need to develop theories about the effect of technological innovation on strategic stabilization.

PART II

Technological Change and the Strategic Arms Race

IN THE SECOND SESSION the symposium departed from the format of the other sessions. In place of papers, a group of discussants was assembled to examine several issues:

1. the strategic framework and technological considerations,
2. offensive weapons systems and the SALT,
3. defensive weapons systems and the SALT,
4. strategic oceanic systems and alternative strategic force configurations,
5. technological innovation and the SALT,
6. lead-time problems, research and development, and budgetary considerations, and
7. the nature and effect of a strategic arms limitation agreement and technological considerations.

The Strategic Framework and Technological Considerations

Benson Adams began the session by outlining the general strategic framework within which technological considerations should be viewed. He stressed three points: (1) strategy, as the study of war, is essentially an eclectic discipline and requires a broad sampling of many fields of study; (2) it is erroneous to view deterrence and strategy as synonymous, for the latter term is applicable to a much broader field than just deterrence theory and practice; and (3) strategy is a dynamic process.

Given these assumptions about strategy, a basic question in the nuclear age is: Do nuclear weapons have political utility? If the answer is no, then one does not need a great number of nuclear weapons— only a sufficient number to deter a would-be aggressor from attack. Possession of some form of assured destruction capability would be

The discussants included Benson Adams, Harold Agnew, Donald G. Brennan, John B. Craven, Richard B. Foster, George Rathjens, and General Robert Richardson III. William Beecher presided over the session.

sufficient. Benson Adams pointed out that mutual deterrence under these conditions requires that both sides be interested in the maintenance of the status quo. If this is not the case, then the situation tends toward dangerous instability.

However, if the answer to the question posed above is yes, then one must ask: How do nuclear weapons acquire political utility? Several possibilities exist: (1) such weapons could be used as psychological tools over time to influence an opponent's or an ally's foreign policy; (2) they could be used to erode a nation's will to resist political and military pressures; and (3) they could be employed to weaken the confidence of an opponent's allies in the reliability of their alliance. If nuclear weapons do have political utility and if the Russians are more willing to use them for political purposes than the United States, the Russians may take part in short-term arms control negotiations while continuing a maximum buildup of their strategic arsenal for use in the future. This may be the current reality of the situation.

Benson Adams then suggested that a dialectic exists between offensive and defensive weaponry. This approach interprets the strategic arms race in ways different from the one-sided U.S. emphasis on concepts such as *mutual assured destruction* (MAD) *capability* or *sufficiency*. Thus, it might not be appropriate to look at security from the viewpoint of an "offense"-dominated mutual deterrence strategy because of the existence of this dialectical relationship between offensive and defensive weaponry.

Support from the audience was given to the view that it is impossible to decouple technological considerations from political and strategic constraints. It was suggested that discussions about the linkage between nuclear weaponry and political utility tend toward extremes. It might be more beneficial to explore the possibility of middle choices. Two questions were posed: (1) Can a nation gain a diplomatic advantage because it has a numerical edge in offensive nuclear weapons? (2) Is there utility in having certain kinds and numbers of weapons so that if deterrence fails a nation has a war-fighting or damage-limiting capability? There was no effort during this session to answer these questions definitively.

Several persons commented on the current U.S. strategy of mutual assured destruction. It was noted, somewhat ironically, that the shorthand acronym of such a strategy—MAD—casts doubt on its soundness. Such a strategy poses two specific problems. First, war could occur and MAD would insure that such a military conflict would be an unlimited disaster. A change from MAD to a less destructive strategy would not necessarily increase the likelihood of nuclear war because the results of such a conflict would still be extremely unfavorable to either side. However, a strategy emphasizing strategic defense rather than strategic offense could mitigate the effects of conflict.

A second problem of the MAD strategy concerns its immorality in the sense that potentially less disastrous alternative strategies have not been fully explored. It seems immoral to opt for a strategy that would make it likely that millions of essentially innocent people would be exterminated in a war when an alternative strategy might diminish the likelihood of such sweeping destruction.

It was suggested that a strategy of MAD was not necessarily a permanent feature of the international system and that perhaps one of the goals of future negotiations between the superpowers would be to work toward a systematic framework that would lessen the dangers inherent in MAD.

Offensive Weapons Systems and the SALT

George Rathjens's remarks concerning the implications of MIRV (multiple independently targeted re-entry vehicle) technology for the SALT led to a discussion of offensive systems. The problem was discussed under four general categories: (1) MIRV—the state of the art; (2) the development of MIRV as a counterforce weapon and the implications of such a development for the military balance; (3) prospects for further advances in MIRV technology; and (4) the effect of MIRV on a strategic arms limitation agreement.

At the present time, according to Rathjens, the MIRV capability of the U.S. is sufficient to penetrate any existing Ballistic Missile Defense (BMD) system, but accuracy has not yet been advanced to the point where MIRV could be considered a credible counterforce weapon. The United States leads the Soviet Union in MIRV technology and system development, whereas the Soviet Union has an advantage in potential deliverable payload.

In discussing MIRV as a potential counterforce weapon, the panel suggested that the basic technological problem is the accuracy variable. MIRV's potential to become a counterforce weapon in the future has several implications. First, the short-term developmental prospects of MIRV were perceived to hold little danger for the stability of the strategic deterrent relationship between the superpowers. It was seen as highly unlikely that MIRV, in the near future, would lead to a credible first-strike capability for either superpower. However, persons in both the Soviet Union and the United States could perceive (erroneously, in the technological sense, as far as Rathjens was concerned) MIRV as providing a possible first-strike weapon and thus pressures would be created to find adequate means to counteract the perceived threat. In this sense MIRV would be likely to be *destabilizing* for the strategic arms race because it would probably stimulate expenditures on weapons not really needed by either side.

A second implication of MIRV as a possible future counterforce weapon relates to its potential to erode confidence in land-based intercontinental ballistic missile (ICBM) systems, resulting eventually in a greater emphasis being placed on sea-based deterrent systems. However, the comment was later made that land-based systems might remain reliable if the other side could be made to fear that they might be "launched on warning." Nevertheless, over time the erosion of confidence in land-based systems would probably continue.

In the discussion of future technological prospects for MIRV, the accuracy variable was again emphasized. It was estimated that the likely warhead yield on MIRVs currently being deployed was about 100 KT. When coupled with current accuracy capabilities, this type of system would probably not be sufficient to make the current generation of U.S. MIRVs a credible counterforce weapon if Soviet site hardening is similar to that of the United States. In the future, the improvement of accuracy would increase the counterforce capabilities of the weapon. Since the development of the V-2, there has been an improvement in "miss" distance of missiles by about a factor of two every three or four years. Thus, MIRV could become a fairly accurate counterforce weapon for the United States against existing Soviet land-based ICBMs. Moreover, such an improvement by a factor of two in missile accuracy would probably diminish by a factor of approximately four the number of missiles that would have to be delivered on the selected targets.

Several comments were made regarding the reliability of the MIRV system. Reliability was not seen as a great problem if several warheads are targeted on each potential launch vehicle. However, if a one-to-one ratio of attacking warhead to targeted missile is desired, then a high degree of reliability would be needed. The achievement of such reliability would require extensive testing, which might be deemed provocative in the strategic arms race.

A caveat was interjected concerning the statements on accuracy and reliability improvement. MIRV technology was perceived as becoming extremely complicated. The attainment of a high degree of accuracy and reliability in order to achieve a one-to-one ratio or better was seen as becoming increasingly difficult. Sophisticated problems such as thrust termination, guidance, and atmospheric variations will become more evident as greater accuracy and reliability are sought.

Several offsetting developments were posited in regard to advancements in MIRV technology. Land-based missile sites could be hardened by, say, a factor of three. As a result, an increase in the force by a factor of two-plus would be required to knock out such "super-hardened" sites. Moreover, silos could be defended by such systems as the Safeguard missile, although George Rathjens did not feel that this particular system was valuable or advisable for deployment at this time.

It was stated that thus far in the SALT neither side seriously considered limiting MIRVs. From the U.S. point of view, certain pressures inhibit the discussion of MIRVs in the negotiations: (1) the United States is currently in the deployment stage; (2) technological momentum, because of the elegance of the MIRV concept, tends to exert pressures insuring that the concept is exploited as far as possible; (3) the military has seen MIRV as an instrument to cover more targets in the Soviet Union and thus has been against any curtailment; and (4) MIRV has been seen as assuring the United States of an ability to penetrate any possible Soviet BMD system.

Two possible reasons for a lack of Soviet interest in including MIRV at the SALT were discussed. First, the Russians are in a position of technological inferiority in MIRV development and are not likely to agree to any freeze that would leave them in a permanent state of inferiority. Second, Rathjens suggested that the Soviets may feel that an agreement on MIRV would be too complicated to achieve and, therefore, may see no reason to pursue the subject during the SALT.

In summation, there were seen to be possibilities for agreement in several areas. Accuracy development could be limited, but this would be very difficult; reliability could be limited more easily. If the number of tests could be limited, then the confidence in system reliability necessary to make MIRV an effective counterforce, first-strike weapon would be difficult to achieve. However, such an agreement would be unlikely because of the asymmetries between the two superpowers.

In his concluding observation, Rathjens suggested that it was possible, but highly unlikely, that an agreement limiting MIRV by restricting tests would be reached at the SALT. If no agreement could be reached, a substantial erosion of confidence in land-based systems might result.

Among some participants, these last remarks elicited the negative response that a diminution of any part of the U.S. strategic triad, such as the downgrading of land-based ICBMs, would make it much more difficult for the United States to tolerate the uncertainties inherent in a possible strategic arms limitation agreement. The downgrading of the land-based force, while not necessarily desirable, seemed to be a logical implication of the development of MIRV.

The panel then turned to a more general discussion of the possible offensive implications of land-based ICBMs. It was suggested that even if a quantitative limitation were to be agreed upon, the existence of extensive possibilities for qualitative improvements by either side would still make it feasible to achieve some form of land-based, first-strike counterforce capability. This would be the case more for the Soviet Union than for the United States. The existence of this possibility was seen as one way of explaining the Soviet development of the SS-9 strategic missile. In the viewpoint of one of the panelists, there is no substitute for payload that the SS-9 provides for the Soviets. With such a large payload, the Soviet options are increased.

Several comments were made as to the difficulty of establishing a hard-point defense for land-based ICBMs without making such a deployment appear as a step toward the development of a possibly credible counterforce weapon. This problem might be overcome by relying on mobile dispersion to maintain the viability of a land-based system without giving it an overly offensive appearance. One participant suggested that the key to stability for land-based deterrence in the next three to eight years would be in the area of "hiding technology" for land-based systems.

Defensive Weapons Systems and the SALT

Donald Brennan began the discussion on defensive weapons systems. In his view rational consideration of ballistic missile defense has been hampered by the continued existence of outmoded attitudes developed in the late 1950s, when the ballistic missile defense problem was characterized as one of "trying to hit a bullet with a bullet." The dramatic technological changes that have occurred since 1963–64 have made such attitudes anachronistic.

It was argued that if, under present technological conditions, strategic offensive forces were limited to existing levels, a local active defense system augmented by some form of area defense capability would be feasible and could significantly alter the outcome of a nuclear war by strengthening a society's ability to survive. The key variable would be the amount of payload that the offensive force possessed. If an offensive force targeted against the United States were limited to 1,000 tons of throw weight, then, it was argued, the United States could develop an active and effective defense system for less money than has been spent on air defense.

An area defense could be justified by the lives it would save. Thus, it would be in the interest of the United States to shift from a strategy of mutual assured destruction to one of strategic defense. Such a change in strategy will become all the more advisable as future developments in laser and other technology could improve active defense capabilities.

The United States, it was suggested, should not seek a limitation on active defense systems but rather on strategic offensive systems. A 500-ton limitation of throw weight in offensive systems would readily make active defense systems both effective and feasible. However, if a limitation on offensive throw weight at the 500- to 1,000-ton level were not possible, then a strategic defense system that emphasized both active and passive defenses could still save many lives.

Several comments from other panelists challenged the view that area defense and the protection of human life by such defense are tenable propositions. It was readily admitted that hard-site defense is technologically feasible and practical and probably stabilizing. This is much more the case for missiles than for aircraft. However, area defense was viewed as technologically difficult, if not impossible. It was remarked that because the original U.S. defensive strategy was erroneously based on area defense, the concepts and the hardware available have been somewhat out of phase with each other. Moreover, it was pointed out that the defense of human targets is difficult, since such targets cannot readily be hardened. This view elicited the reply that economical active and passive defense combinations could be constructed to defend human targets, but that the best way to do so was to limit offensive capabilities.

Several participants argued against the deployment of hard-site defense as now contemplated under the Safeguard system. The major contention was that such deployment would make it unlikely that a truly dedicated effort to develop an effective hard-site defense system would occur. It was also pointed out that the use of the Safeguard system as a bargaining chip at the SALT could inhibit the development of an effective defense. Any strategic arms limitation agreement would preclude the development of such a defense system.

Strategic Oceanic Systems and Alternative Strategic Force Configurations

The discussion on strategic oceanic systems began with remarks by John Craven. He stated that in the past the law and strategy of the sea have been determined to a large extent by surface considerations. However, in the future, commercial and military usage of the sea will take place more and more under the sea. Thus, new constraints and strategies will have to be developed.

In the technological field the development of some form of barrier lines capable of detecting clandestine activity in areas contiguous to the continents is likely. But area surveillance systems capable of detecting clandestine activity in the broad oceans will not soon be feasible. So, while it would be possible, therefore, to exclude military systems from clearly fenced-in areas of the ocean that would be subject to exploitation for human needs, it would not be possible to exclude military systems from the broad oceans unless immediate force were exerted at the barrier line to prevent such military systems from gaining access to the broad ocean areas or unless exclusion were obtained by mutual consent or restraint.

Given the above assumptions, Craven postulated that the most stable situation would be the deployment of arms-controllable underwater military systems in the broad oceans under tacit or formalized agreement, while placing extensive areas of the ocean under national or international control. Thus the placement of military systems in such areas would be at the discretion of the jurisdictional authority. Several recent developments were suggested as indicative of movement in this direction: (1) The Soviets appear to be developing and deploying a mirror image of the U.S. underwater submarine strategic system. (2) The Soviets seem to have adopted a "Mahan-Mackinder" approach to sea power—one that has emphasized controlling the seas around Eurasia, the world island. (3) The Soviets seem to be seeking a *modus operandi,* or rules to guide the extension of their naval power. (4) The United States has placed greater emphasis on its sea-based deterrent capabilities and less emphasis on strategic antisubmarine warfare (ASW) capabilities. (5) The law of the sea has increased in uncertainty and will probably do so for some time. In the past several years there has been an increasing number of national claims to territorial jurisdiction of 200 miles, which have threatened to upset projections concerning the law of the sea. In this area it was perceived as likely that the United States, the Soviet Union, and a group of other nations in the United Nations (which could be termed the "heritage of man" bloc) would seek, probably unsuccessfully, to limit the extent of claimed sovereignty to the oceans. If no agreement were to be reached, then the largest assertable claim would probably become the rule of law. (6) Finally, Japan, France, and the Scandinavian countries are outstripping the

United States and the Soviet Union in the development of sea technology for commercial uses. As a consequence, these nations will probably dominate the economic uses of the seabed, provoking even greater pressure for the extension of national control over contiguous sea areas.

In the discussion of strategic oceanic systems, symposium participants focused more on the advantages of sea-based systems compared with land-based systems. The potential erosion of confidence in land-based systems stemming from technological developments, especially those concerned with MIRV, and the resulting increased emphasis on sea-based systems were discussed. One participant suggested that it is surprising that the United States Air Force has not made greater efforts to limit the development of MIRV, since Soviet deployment of MIRVs would probably force the United States to place increasing emphasis on naval deterrent systems at the expense of land-based systems.

The case for increased emphasis on sea-based systems was underscored by several remarks from European participants. If the decision were made to develop an independent European deterrent, land-based nuclear systems in Europe would be downgraded. Instead, there would be increased submarine-launched ballistic missile (SLBM) systems as the major component of a European deterrent capacity. This view was challenged by the assertion that European-based nuclear weapons continue to have important symbolic meaning, politically and psychologically, for many Europeans. This symbolic support was stated to have greater credibility for Europeans because of the land-based location of the weapons, rather than because of any cost-benefit analysis of the effectiveness of such weapons compared with sea-based systems. The main thrust of this argument was that technological feasibility or desirability would not necessarily be compatible with psychological or political realities and constraints.

The growing U.S. reliance on sea-based systems met with a moderate degree of opposition. It was felt by some to be a mistake to assume that any one component of the strategic triad would put the United States in a position to accept the uncertainties that would probably result from an agreement at the SALT. In fact, an appropriate question might be: What can technology do to protect or enhance the viability of the strategic triad so that the United States can tolerate the uncertainties inherent in a strategic arms limitation agreement?

Additional support was voiced for the preservation of the strategic triad. Land-based systems were seen to have certain advantages over sea-based systems, including better command and control, greater physical capacity, and lower procurement cost. Moreover, the triad has the advantage of forcing an opponent to consider many more variables than he would have to consider if only one type of strategic system existed.

One of the positive aspects of sea-based capabilities is that such systems have a certain built-in "arms controllability." One of the main objectives of negotiations on strategic systems should be to get both sides to agree to develop systems with this built-in feature of controllability. For instance, sea-based systems can be designed to give the other side warning time without exposing the system itself to attack. Thus, an SLBM system, unlike a land-based system with its irrevocable commitment, could be used to motivate the other side to take political initiatives to calm the situation before the actual force capability of the system was employed.

The discussion turned to an examination of the implications of the SALT for sea-based systems. It was postulated that, in the absence of a limitation on sea-based systems, it would be possible to develop extensive sea-based counterforce weapons designed to destroy remaining land-based ICBMs. Such a development would diminish the long-term importance of a strategic arms limitation agreement.

In summary, it appeared to be a widely shared belief that sea-based systems will become more important in the future, regardless of what agreement is reached at the SALT.

Technological Innovation and the SALT

A central issue of concern regarding technology and the strategic arms race is the impact of future technological innovation on the possibilities of arms limitation under a SALT agreement. Richard Foster pointed out that several contrasting interpretations of the interaction between the arms race and the nature of superpower relations have been offered. One view, espoused by the Federation of American Scientists, argues that the Soviet Union lags behind the United States in technology. As long as the United States continues to maintain its lead, a self-defeating action-reaction pattern will exist between the two nations. Therefore, according to the Federation of American Scientists, the United States should unilaterally cease its arms buildup so that the Soviet Union will have no pattern to copy. This, in turn, would, in its view, lead to the demise of the action-reaction syndrome. According to Foster, this argument becomes circular when the idea is added that the spiraling arms race is caused by the U.S. desire to maintain its "lead" and that if the United States ceased to maintain its lead, the arms race would eventually come to an end.

Another thesis has been set forth by John Foster, Director of Research and Engineering in the Department of Defense. In his view the only way the United States can guard against Soviet secrecy and unilateral Soviet exploitation of a technological breakthrough is by maintaining an extensive research and development program designed to hedge against such possibilities. From this point of view, control of the dynamics of the technological process may be beyond the capacity of either superpower under present conditions.

Given these opposing interpretations of the arms race, the question was asked: What implications might technological advances have for an agreement at the SALT? The following answers were given: (1) technological innovation could destabilize the existing situation, and (2) agreements in phase 1 or 2 of the SALT might be delayed by certain developments, such as (a) unilateral exploitation of a technological advance or (b) the use of a marginal superiority for some political advantage.

Failure of the SALT agreement to limit R&D could lead to a search for alternative means to control the process of technological innovation. For instance, an attempt might be made to encourage both sides to initiate research that would lead to a greater understanding of the scientific process. It was suggested that neither side now understands the process very well and that a joint venture could lead to the development of more adequate concepts. Thus the dangers that uncontrolled technological innovation might pose for the world could be lessened. The Soviets have evidenced interest in a discussion of this problem, but thus far the United States has not.

Another alternative to present arrangements would be to develop self-limiting systems of such complexity that both sides would spend all their time trying to analyze the nature of the system. Deterrence in this system would be a function of the sheer uncertainty that would exist. While facetious, this suggestion could contain certain elements of plausibility, it was noted.

A third possible alternative would be an agreement to limit rationally the arms race and the process of technological innovation. The basis of such an agreement would be acceptance of the view that neither side should have the capacity to gain an exploitable strategic superiority. Both sides would have to recognize that the game being played could have no winner. Thus a motivation would exist to "automatically" limit expenditures on arms development.

Certain other alternatives can be imagined. If the offense could be made with MIRVs, why not the defense? Why could a terminally guided defense not be developed? or a "MIRVed" offensive-defensive system in which the attacked party would have the option of either continuing defensive measures or switching to offensive measures?

It might also be feasible to design a strategy that would have a built-in arms control feature that could be used to direct a nation's research and development program. Such a feature might provide a basis for future agreements on the control of technological innovation in weaponry.

The Soviet Union and the United States could also jointly study methods to reduce the uncertainty of the effects of technological innovation. The long-term ecological, medical, and genetic effects of weaponry could be the object of joint consideration.

Greater weapon sophistication could so reduce the numbers of weapons that if one system failed, a nation might be left with little bargaining power. Thus, paradoxically, it could be more efficacious to continue the proliferation of cheaper systems, thereby insuring negotiating ability.

Harold Agnew pointed out several other implications of technological dynamism for the SALT. He stated that one of the problems inherent in the pace of technological innovation is that an individual who six months previously had been deeply involved in technological work but had subsequently left the field might give outdated technical advice to a political leader. Accelerated technological innovation would in this case be an inherently destabilizing factor in the decision-making process.

An additional consideration is the possibility that after a certain stage of mutual assured destruction capability is reached, technological considerations might become irrelevant and a continued focus on them might prove dysfunctional to negotiation on key political and psychological problems.

Lead-Time Problems, Research and Development, and Budgetary Considerations

Panel remarks concerning lead-time problems were initiated by Robert Richardson. He stated that relatively little attention has been given to the implications of lead-time changes for arms control and disarmament. Lead time has been extended to a point where it takes from five to ten years to get a weapon from basic research and development (R&D) into inventory. This has necessitated extensive changes in the procurement process. Technological development has been decoupled from immediate operational needs and a separate technical war arena has thus been created. Weapon requirements are now defined not in terms of what is needed but rather in terms of what is possible. The basic question is: What can you possibly give me in ten years? rather than: What can you give me now to do a certain job? The existence of this type of decision milieu has raised the question of whether one can rationally discuss technological controls in the same context as control of arms "in-being."

A resulting question that has been raised is: Can the technical threat (not the military one arising from technology) be evaluated in order to provide a rational basis for a technical program? Richardson's answer was negative, because it has now become impossible to know what the Soviets are doing in the technological field since discussion of militarily important technological developments has disappeared from Soviet literature. The results of Soviet technological developments usually do not appear until four or five years later in the form of some operational equipment.

A rhetorical question was then asked: Would a "responsive" R&D program be a tenable proposition under the conditions outlined above? The answer was again negative—by the time a response would be initiated, it would be too late to catch up because of the lead-time problem. Therefore, it has now become necessary to have a continuous R&D program no matter what the other side does in order to make sure that the possibility of relatively immediate deployment exists if the situation demands it. This requirement of a building bloc approach to R&D might provoke a counterreaction by the other side, thus vitiating to a large extent the efficacy of arms control attempts. However, the only logical and prudent step in this case would be to risk such a counterreaction in order to protect oneself and one's capabilities "downstream."

A second problem arising from lead-time extension concerns the decision of whether or not a country should adopt a high or low risk posture in its weapons development program. A low risk approach would mean that the resultant system was likely to be three to five years obsolete by the time it was operational. Any postproduction discoveries or innovations would not go into the system except by retrofit, which would likely prove costly and unsatisfactory. The basic problem in this area was seen as a choice between systems with no waste or up-to-date systems that pose the risk of creating waste and provoking an arms race.

The change in lead time has created several other problems, including labor mobility in specialized defense industries and the difficulty of selling to Congress systems that do not exist at present and might never be operable. Finally, there is an idiosyncratic problem known in the United States: decisions on weapons systems span more than one administration and are thus subject to continuous reconsideration and even possible reversal from one administration to the next. It was noted that the Soviet Union does not have a similar problem. In the Soviet Union it appears that once R&D decisions are made, they are allowed to be carried to their projected conclusions without continuous political interference.

An immediate reaction to the above remarks was that they seemed to negate chances to control the action-reaction pattern of the arms race. It was pointed out that there is something to be said for deferring decisions on weapons system procurement, even though at a later date a crash program might be necessary. Conditions could improve, making certain weapons unnecessary. Thus, in one view, the thrust of Richardson's argument is disquieting because it assumes that, over time, little can be done to curb the arms race.

Several opinions were expressed as to the implications of lead time for research and development. Some participants drew an analogy between the effects of the treaty produced by the Washington Conference of 1922 on U.S. research and development in the naval field and the present strategic-military milieu. The 1922 U.S. decision to limit its naval development while other nations were allowed to enter an extensive R&D program led to a situation where, upon the mutual abrogation of the treaty, the United States was left in a disadvantageous position because of the R&D lead-time factor. A similar problem would exist today if limitations were placed on certain systems of one country without accompanying symmetrical limitations on the R&D outlays of the others. Current figures, if they are correct, indicate that the Soviet Union is spending approximately 40 percent more than the United States in the R&D field. It was then posited that such an asymmetrical situation might prove destabilizing for strategic deterrence.

There was a reaction among several participants to the statements concerning the disparity between U.S. and Soviet R&D expenditures. One participant held that this disparity was largely irrelevant to the strategic milieu because of the ultra stability of the strategic balance. However, at the tactical level there might be added reason for concern if the Soviet Union is not only spending more on R&D in this area, but also advancing more than the United States. Such developments could have implications for areas such as the Mediterranean and the Middle East.

The United States, given its current situation, might have to accept the development of certain Soviet advantages in the tactical area. Although in the United States a great deal of lip service has been given to providing outlays for R&D in lieu of deciding on weapons procurement, money has not been forthcoming. It was estimated that there has been a 15 to 20 percent cut in research staff over the past several years.

In a discussion of the problem of adequate planning of R&D programs, it was noted that the United States, unlike the Soviet Union, does not have a strategy that establishes priorities and linkages between force configurations and objectives. Until such a strategy is developed, no adequately formulated economic or political guidelines for research and development expenditures will exist.

Budgetary allocations for alternative force configurations were then discussed. The question was asked: What R&D programs should receive the maximum support after a "hardware" agreement has been reached at the SALT? This elicited another question: What is the relative utility to the superpowers of strategic forces vis-à-vis other forces in the attainment of the interests of the superpowers? It was suggested that answers to these questions should focus on budgetary considerations. Several different viewpoints exist on this subject. One view holds that the United States should spend as much as the Soviet Union on strategic forces. The U.S. outlay is presently about 50 percent of that of the Soviet Union. Any increased outlay on strategic forces should not come out of the general-purpose force budget; the United States is wealthy enough to afford increased outlays in the strategic area without cutting back on other areas.

The views expressed above were countered by the observation that, because of rising costs, a nation will inevitably be forced to place greater emphasis on areas more subject to technological exploitation in order to produce as much hardware as possible from the available funds. Technological exploitation was seen as more feasible in the strategic area than in the tactical area.

Another perspective was offered. Although certain societies may be able to put off the necessary adjustment to the inevitable cost squeeze, eventually they will have to make decisions whether technology should be exploited for quality rather than quantity or whether commitments should be reduced in order to compensate for the squeeze. This is the situation in which the United States finds itself at the present time. American policy-makers are faced essentially with four options: (1) a substantial increase in defense allocations, which would be very difficult under present conditions; (2) a substantial reduction of commitments, which may be under way; (3) a decrease in the cost of procurement by relying on such capabilities as tactical nuclear weapons and space systems; and (4) a change in the nature of the tasks to be performed by defense allocations through agreements at negotiations such as the SALT.

It was suggested that three considerations should determine the form of the strategic force budget: (1) the United States should spend as much as the Soviet Union on strategic forces; (2) the United States should maintain an effective offensive capability; and (3) the United States should spend as much as possible on defense after fulfilling the requirements of (1) and (2).

The general consensus among the participants was that lead-time considerations, budgetary problems, and the resultant effects on the design and structure of R&D programs were key aspects of the technological problem confronting the superpowers.

The Nature and Effect of a Strategic Arms Limitation Agreement and Technological Considerations

At the beginning of the discussion period of the session, a scenario of a possible first-stage strategic arms limitation agreement was set forth. It was suggested that such an agreement might include: (1) a freeze on new starts of land-based ICBMs; (2) no freeze on SLBM development or deployment; and (3) a roughly symmetrical ABM limitation at low levels. The question was then posed: Given the current realizable technology, to what extent would such an agreement serve to stabilize or destabilize the balance of power over the next three to eight years?

One participant suggested that the type of agreement set forth above would have little, if any, effect on strategic stability during crises. However, it was admitted that such an agreement might possibly affect the nature of the arms race over time. Another maintained that instabilities would be possible under such an agreement. For instance, one side, in a fit of euphoria, might decide that the arms race had been controlled, while the other side might use the agreement and this type of reaction to develop a way to counter its opponent's existing deterrent force. Such a development would be more likely under the terms of such an agreement because the "aggressive" side could work on circumventing a system they knew would still exist in x number of years. A second destabilizing factor might be that one side would be tempted to seek to exploit technology in such a manner as to develop systems designed to be used against the other side, rather than as a deterrent.

A further destabilizing possibility was suggested. Assuming that mutual assured destruction will continue to characterize superpower relationships, a likely effect of the scenario agreement would be a codification of the decoupling of the U.S. strategic guarantee from Western Europe through a recognition of superpower parity or even Soviet "superiority" in the European theater at levels below MAD. Thus, the Soviet Union would obtain an operable "marginal superiority" in the European milieu. Therefore, an agreement such as the one posited could be destabilizing for European security.

Objections were raised to the above point. It was contended that the Europeans have already accepted the existence of parity and are in the process of adjusting to it. As a result, there did not appear to be any features of the projected scenario that would serve to destabilize the situation.

It was pointed out that if MRBMs and IRBMs were not included in the agreement and if the Soviets insisted that all forward-based systems should be counted in the equation, the U.S. strategic deterrent would be decoupled from Europe, leaving Europe more susceptible to strategic threats from the Soviet Union. Thus, under this type of assumption concerning the scenario, a further destabilization of the European power balance would occur. However, it was stated that it would be hard to imagine that the United States would trade off such systems in Europe in a strategic arms limitation agreement without receiving an acceptable *quid pro quo*.

Several comments were made in reaction to this view of European perspectives on the SALT. If there is apprehension in Europe about the SALT, it is not about the negotiations per se, but about the extent of U.S. commitment to defend Europe. Bilateral Soviet-U.S. negotiations invariably arouse European fears that their interests will be sacrificed. But even if the SALT did not exist or if no agreement is reached, Western European concerns would still persist.

It was further noted that many in Europe see growing reason for concern about the credibility of the U.S. nuclear guarantee. This alarm does not emerge from, nor is it limited to, the SALT. For example, U.S. attitudes about forward-based systems in Europe as expressed in the SALT would be regarded in Europe as but one of many indications of U.S. intentions concerning Western European defense in general.

A caveat was interjected concerning European expectations at the SALT. It was seen as misleading to underestimate the expectations that

U.S. involvement in the SALT has aroused in Western Europe. One of the things that would alarm Western Europeans most would be a failure of the SALT. The expectation has grown in Europe that the two superpowers, for their own reasons, are relatively sincere in their efforts to place some limitations on a strategic arms race that, many in Europe feel, has gone beyond the bounds of rationality. If this expectation should prove chimerical, then failure at the SALT could have a significant impact on European perceptions of their security needs, especially in the area of a possible European nuclear deterrent force.

The expansion of limited-area defense ABMs projected under the posited strategic arms limitation agreement would tend to necessitate the deployment of a relatively large defensive missile. But such a missile, by a relatively easy process of warhead change, could become an offensive weapon. It would be difficult to build protection against this possibility into any foreseeable agreement.

In a more general vein, the question was asked: Are there any historical examples of an agreement designed to stop or delay the development of weapons systems for any period of time? The 1963 Nuclear Test Ban Treaty and the *de facto* agreement in the Middle Ages to delay the introduction of gunpowder into Europe were cited as two examples.

Finally, discussion centered on further negotiations that might follow an agreement at the SALT, phase 1. Several comments supported the view that the real purpose of the present negotiations is to prepare the way for future negotiations. However, this view was challenged by one participant, who remarked that if any agreement under phase 1 of the SALT seemed likely to be partially destabilizing to one side or the other, it would be difficult to justify such an agreement by viewing it as a preliminary step to future negotiations.

The only mention of possible topics of future strategic arms limitation negotiations was made in reference to what some Europeans hope to see as the object of such talks. Phase 2 of the SALT might be concerned with the imbalance of Soviet MRBMs targeted against Western Europe as contrasted with European national nuclear capabilities. Phase 3 of the SALT would then possibly concern itself with the reduction of land forces.

In conclusion, the discussion of the effects of a possible agreement pointed out the uncertainty of what really is desired from the SALT, especially from the Western viewpoint.

PART III

ROBERT R. BOWIE

The Bargaining Aspects of Arms Control: The SALT Experience

ANY EFFORT to analyze the bargaining aspects of the SALT suffers from one severe handicap: The parties have wisely agreed to conduct the negotiations with secrecy, and on the whole have actually done so. Thus details about the tactics and positions of the U.S. and USSR for the five sessions already held are not available.

Even so, it is feasible to analyze the negotiations on a more general plane. On this level much can be gleaned from the two Foreign Policy Reports of President Nixon, from testimony before congressional committees, from official press conferences, and from a few leaks. Beyond that, the bargaining is shaped by many basic factors, such as the relations of the parties, the strategic equation, characteristics of weapons systems, and the impact of new technology.

This chapter examines how the bargaining is affected by such aspects of its context as well as by the positions and tactics of the United States and the Soviet Union.

Limits of Negotiation

DECOUPLING STRATEGIC ARMS

How can the United States and the Soviet Union negotiate any agreement limiting or regulating strategic arms in view of their basic hostile rivalry? It would be idle to expect this hostility to be resolved or fade away any time soon. For Soviet leaders, it is a fact of life, as they stressed at their Party Congress in March 1971. The policies of "co-existence" and *détente* are based on the continuing struggle against "imperialism" and the need to expand Soviet influence.

Any hope for arms control depends on decoupling the strategic equation from this basic rivalry. Khrushchev and his successors have clearly recognized, as has the United States, that nuclear war would certainly be suicidal as long as both sides retain even modest second-strike capabilities. The vast Soviet buildup since 1965, even if it

127

continues, will hardly convince the Soviet leaders that nuclear war would serve any rational political purpose. Thus they might well share an interest with the United States in seeking to reduce the expense of mutual deterrence and in enhancing its stability, despite continuing hostility.

In practice, however, it is not so easy to divorce the military equation from rivalry in other respects. Traditionally, Soviet leaders have looked on military capacity as a political instrument. They may realize that strategic "superiority" is meaningless in strictly military terms—for winning a war—and still consider it significant for political purposes or as a plaftorm for limited uses of conventional force or threats. That may be the lesson they drew from the Cuban backdown.[1] The nature and scope of the subsequent buildup, and the fact that it continues, tend to support this interpretation. The truth is that we do not yet know whether the Soviet Union is willing to accept a strategic equilibrium that would largely neutralize strategic weapons.

The SALT might serve Soviet purposes. Even in the absence of an agreement, the talks confirm at least Soviet parity with the United States; they feed *détente;* and they could create doubts and tensions among U.S. allies whose security may be materially affected by the outcome of the negotiations.

Initially, it should be noted, Mr. Nixon did not fully accept the insulation of the SALT from other U.S.-Soviet relations. Shortly after taking office, he sought to establish some sort of linkage between the SALT and progress toward settling the Middle East crisis or other issues.[2] Later, however, this notion seems to have been put aside.[3] The SALT have gone on despite ups and downs in other areas. Thus far the *negotiations* have been largely separated from these other issues. How far any ultimate agreement could be similarly insulated from severe conflicts or tensions would probably depend greatly on their intensity and duration and on how each side interpreted their implications.

RELIANCE ON SELF-HELP

Although hostility and distrust do not preclude arms control agreements between the United States and the Soviet Union, they severely restrict the scope and nature of restrictions that might be negotiated. Clearly neither nation will accept or maintain any agreed limits that it thinks will jeopardize its security. But in judging any limitation, each side must consider consequences not only if carried out, but also if violated by the other side. In case of violation, the risks will depend on (1) whether it can be detected and how quickly, and (2) how long it will take to negate it or compensate for it.

Inevitably, therefore, the reliability of inspection to verify compliance or detect violation directly affects the extent and kinds of limitations that will be acceptable. Thus the Soviet rejection of any on-site inspection as an improper intrusion sets drastic constraints on possible limitations. Artificial satellites and other national means now make it feasible to verify some kinds of limitations without on-site inspection. They can reveal what is being done physically on the observed territory and can therefore verify limitations based on counting or monitoring installations, or objects, or activities such as flight testing. But such unilateral methods are not adequate to police restraints on qualitative changes or on research and development. Only actual on-site inspection could determine for certain whether the warhead of a missile contains MIRVs.

If there is a violation, then the other party must rely on self-help to compensate. Since resort to force would hardly be attractive, the aggrieved party must be able to offset the effects of the violation by its countermeasures in its own strategic system. Here time may be of the essence. And the situations of the United States and the Soviet Union would be quite different in these instances. In the United States any plans to develop, deploy, or modify weapons systems are likely to become public knowledge very quickly. But the Soviet Union could go quite a long way in secrecy. As Dr. John Foster has pointed out:

Because of Soviet secrecy, by the time we have firm evidence of precisely what the Soviets are doing, their development has been underway for several years. Even then we often have difficulty in understanding their new system capability. If we react only when we know precisely what they are doing and why, we generally require about four years for development and another three or four years to fully deploy a counter measure.[4]

The point is illustrated by the hundred or so holes that the Soviet Union has been digging at its missile sites. Although the United States detected these some time ago, it still does not know exactly what they are for or what weapons they will take. Thus if an agreement were in effect, it is hard to be sure how soon a particular action would be observed and then properly appraised in terms of its purpose and significance. This may be especially true when only some portion or aspect of strategic armament is restricted (as is probable for some while). Then changes in other aspects (such as upgrading) may not violate the agreement but still profoundly disturb the system and the balance justifying the agreed limitations.

There is, however, one important countervailing factor, especially in the early phases. The strategic forces of both sides are so redundant in terms of an assured deterrent that even substantial changes by the adversary (short of a major breakthrough) would not upset the *military* stalemate, whatever the other effects.

A corollary follows from the necessity to rely on unilateral inspection and self-help. Neither side will be prepared to adhere to an agreed restriction if it concludes that the effect is to impair its security. This might occur for various reasons: It may suspect that the other party is violating the agreement, or it may think that other conditions (such as new weapons) have changed the impact of the restrictions; or the agreement may simply have operated differently than foreseen.

Whatever the reasons, either nation will feel compelled to disregard a restriction that seems contrary to a serious security interest. Under these conditions, it seems far better that the party be able to escape according to the agreement rather than be faced with violating or repudiating it. In other words, any agreement (whether a treaty or a more informal agreement) should provide explicitly for the parties to renounce the restrictions or request their revision, preferably after reasonable notice to minimize surprise. Such an approach conforms to the inevitable realities. It has the further merit that the parties are constantly on notice that the validity and continuance of the agreement depend on its genuinely serving each party's interests as conditions change.

Dynamism of Military Technology

The dynamism of military technology creates several hazards or obstacles to negotiation: First, it complicates the timing of any negotiation. Weapons programs of the two sides are likely to be out of phase. Thus when President Johnson, apparently concerned about the Moscow ABM system, proposed the SALT to Premier Kosygin in January 1967, the United States was well ahead. By then, most of its present strategic forces were in operation: the planned forty-one Polaris subs, the one thousand Minutemen, and the bombers. There were already programs for improving the Polaris and Minuteman missiles and for an ABM system, though differing from that now being deployed. The Soviet Union was in quite a different stage, with its massive buildup beginning only in 1965–66. Since then its number of ICBMs has expanded five or six times to about fifteen hundred, with three hundred of the huge SS-9s; its Polaris-type subs are being produced at a rate of six to eight per year, with over twenty now operational; and it is developing MRVs and an improved ABM. Under these conditions, it was not until June

1968 that Soviet Foreign Minister Gromyko indicated that the USSR was willing to start such talks. Then the Soviet invasion of Czechoslovakia and the U.S. election produced still further delays, compounded by a slow Soviet response to beginning the talks. Thus the talks began on November 17, 1969, nearly three years after the first proposal.

Second, the same factors make it very difficult to equate the effect of any limitations on the two systems. The premise of the SALT is parity—but the concept is hard to define. Clearly each side is satisfied that it has "sufficiency" in the sense of a secure second-strike capacity adequate to deter an attack. But actually that was probably true even before the recent Soviet buildup, and would still be true with substantial changes on either side, in view of the heavy redundancy of both deterrent systems. Although both systems contain many similar elements, their mix is not the same, and the two sides may evaluate the several components quite differently.

President Nixon called specific attention to this fact in his second foreign policy report.[5] Thus, while the Minuteman and the SS-11 and SS-13 are similar, the United States has no weapon comparable to the SS-9, with its 25-megaton warhead. For the Soviet Union, our forward-based systems in the NATO area are treated as part of our strategic forces, since they can strike the Soviet Union to some degree. For us, the Soviet MRBMs, targeted on Western Europe, are the counterpart of these FBS weapons. The Soviet ABM system is centered on Moscow; ours is now designed to protect Minuteman sites and bomber forces. We have over twice as many strategic bombers as the Soviets; they have 50 percent more ICBMs. We are installing MIRVs; whether they have gotten beyond MRVs is not clear.

To attempt to agree on restraints for all the components of each system would probably be a hopeless task, at least at the start. Yet if one component is selected, such as ABMs, will both sides see it as having the same relation to their total system? If the effort is to select a single offensive system, that will raise for the United States at least (and perhaps for the Soviets) the relation among the components of the deterrent forces (subs, land-based missiles, and air forces), since the United States's concept is that all three are essential for a secure and reliable total deterrent system.[6]

Third, since any limitations will extend into the future, they are subject to the uncertain impact of advancing technology and other changes. Research and development will inexorably spawn weapons and systems outside agreed limitations, thus posing new problems in themselves and disrupting the balance achieved by agreed limitations. Other nuclear states, such as China, will grow in importance and impinge on bilateral arrangements. Changing perceptions or shifting strategic doctrines may modify the relative value or significance of specific systems or limitations.

In short, as the future unfolds, it will require agreed limitations to be modified, supplemented, or removed in ways not foreseen when they were worked out. The processes for adopting and defining such limitations must allow for adapting them to changing conditions.

The Conduct of Negotiations

The way a negotiation is organized and carried on may often determine whether it succeeds or fails. In the case of the SALT, some relevant factors are: (1) clarification of the issues, (2) criteria for selecting initial subjects for control, (3) the relating of arms decisions to the negotiations, and (4) the form of any agreement.

CLARIFICATION OF THE ISSUES

As has been said, the SALT can succeed only if both sides accept the basic premise that strategic arms are useful only for mutual deterrence. If they do not, it is hard to see any ground for bona fide limitations. Hence a prime purpose of the SALT should be to explore and determine as far as feasible whether that premise is shared.

If it is, then it would seem to be in the interest of both sides (1) to "stabilize" deterrence, especially in crises, and (2) to minimize the costs of strategic competition. Given the obstacles already discussed, it will not be easy to agree on how those objectives should be achieved. Each side starts with its own strategic doctrine about what is required for its security and with specific weapons systems designed to achieve it. In each case, the decisions about what to procure and why have been reached through processes and institutions peculiar to each country. Doubtless, in each the strategic doctrine is not entirely coherent and is interpreted in diverse ways, and the selection of weapons has not been governed only by the doctrine. Given the differences in history, geography and commitments, it is hardly likely that the United States and the Soviet Union would be able to agree on strategic doctrine or even on the relative importance of different weapons for stable deterrence. But it is not necessary that they should do so in order to agree to limit or regulate specific weapons systems or activities.

Even so, before tackling the specifics, there should be value in general exchanges to enable each side to gain a clearer understanding of the strategic thinking of the other. Such exchanges should clarify somewhat how each side (1) conceives of deterrence, (2) determines the amounts and kinds of weapons needed for its security, and (3) reacts to the weapons choices of the other.

Such a discussion is likely to have distinct limits. Neither side will be prepared to be entirely forthcoming. The discussions do not start with a clear slate, of course. The Soviet negotiators start with a vast amount of information about our strategy, concepts, weapons systems, and plans, as well as our divergences, which are regularly revealed through reports, hearings, the press, and academic writing. Given the secrecy of their system, they will hardly disclose anything like this degree of material or detail on these topics. And both sides will withhold classified data on such critical matters as the accuracies of missiles and the effectiveness of ABMs or satellite observation. But even within these limits, general discussion should assist in developing a framework for negotiation and in deciding where to start and what to attempt in the first stages of the SALT.

Apparently, this course was actually followed at the initial Helsinki sessions. According to the second foreign policy report, "we believed that progress could best be made if the initial exchanges encouraged agreement on the definition of the subject matter and the nature of the issues. . . . Instead [of starting with detailed proposals] we explored some general concepts of strategic stability and related them to the issues posed by limiting individual weapons systems." Apparently the Soviet Union fell in with this approach. In this general exchange of views, the United States and the Soviet Union "reviewed our analysis, explaining how we thought agreements might evolve and their verification requirements." According to this report, "there was broad consensus on certain general strategic concepts." [7]

These explorations also brought to light, however, a critical divergence about what should be treated as strategic weapons. By defining them as weapons able to reach the other's territory, the Soviet Union insisted on (1) including U.S. theater nuclear delivery systems, including those on carriers, and (2) excluding Soviet theater nuclear forces, including MRBMs. Clearly this line, which would be highly divisive within NATO, takes advantage of the differing geopolitical and alliance commitments of the two sides. This divergence apparently plagued the later sessions for some time.[8]

CRITERIA FOR LIMITATIONS

Whatever its merits, such general discussion is unlikely to lead to actual restraints on deploying weapons without more explicit agreements. Neither nation will be prepared to take unilateral action merely in the hope that the other will adjust its program accordingly. Suspension of nuclear testing was a special case, and even that broke down without an agreement. In the case of specific weapons, a key problem is to identify what would be offsetting or equivalent restraints within two differently constituted strategic systems. Nor would it be feasible on either side to persuade decision-makers or bureaucracies to withhold action merely on the hope that a projected threat will then not materialize in response.

The question then is: How comprehensive should any agreed limitations be? The SALT themselves already represent a narrowing of the field by focusing on strategic weapons and leaving aside conventional and tactical systems. But a "comprehensive" strategic agreement would raise extremely difficult issues. The problem of defining what is a strategic weapon in view of the differing situations has previously been discussed. Moreover, such an effort at an all-inclusive agreement would outrun the limits of unilateral inspection. Without on-site inspection, there cannot be effective control of improved accuracy or of MIRVs, once the testing stage is past. Yet either of these could be much more critical for the stability of the deterrent system than many changes in numbers.

If a limitation is partial, however, it inherently leaves loopholes in other fields. Hence the danger is that it may merely intensify the arms competition in other areas. Thus a major criterion in selecting a partial restraint should be whether the result will be to divert or to channel such competition in directions that tend to stabilize the deterrent and to reduce the scale of strategic spending. Thus the problem is to find one or more partial restraints of this kind that the parties will treat as equivalent in their effects.

In the interest of negotiating flexibility, the United States adopted what was called a "building block" approach. The purpose was to avoid freezing on a specific proposal too soon and locking in on that. In preparing for the talks, the United States analyzed each strategic weapons system in isolation, explored what would be involved in its limitation, surveyed our unilateral capacity to monitor compliance, and considered the impact of any such limitation on the United States and the Soviet Union. These studies produced a comprehensive inventory of various kinds of limitations that might be combined into a final agreement. According to the President, the United States "found in our preliminary discussions that the Soviet Union [also] . . . came in with very precise weapons systems analysis." [9]

The report outlines, in general terms, the course of the negotiations:

Initially, the U.S. suggested possible approaches involving both numerical and qualitative limitations on strategic offensive and defensive systems, including MIRVs. We also put forward an alternative comprehensive approach which would not constrain MIRVs, but would involve reductions in offensive forces in order to maintain stability even in the face of qualitative improvements.

The Soviet Union, for its part, submitted a general proposal which diverged from ours in many respects, including a major difference on the definition of strategic systems.[10]

These proposals apparently produced no progress. To take account of Soviet objections, modified proposals were submitted by both the United States and the Soviet Union. Ours provided for either limitation or total ban on ABM. Theirs partly differed and partly coincided, but was not specific or detailed enough on the offensive or defensive limitations to allow firm judgment on their overall impact.

In May 1971, in announcing the agreed framework for negotiation, the President was more blunt. He stated flatly: "The Soviet-American talks on limiting nuclear arms have been deadlocked for over a year." The joint statement issued in Moscow and Washington said that the United States and the Soviet Union "have agreed to concentrate this year on working out an agreement for the limitation of the deployment of antiballistic missile systems (ABMs). They have also agreed that, together with concluding an agreement to limit ABMs, they will agree on certain measures with respect to the limitation of offensive strategic weapons." [11]

Apparently this was a compromise between Soviet pressure for a "separate agreement limiting ABMs alone" and U.S. insistence that an agreement must limit both offensive and defensive systems in order to be stable and acceptable.[12] This difference reflects the differing functions of the U.S. and Soviet ABM systems. The Soviet system appears to defend the Moscow region, whereas Safeguard seeks to protect part of the Minuteman and bomber forces. Since U.S. officials have stressed the threat to the American forces from the SS-9, especially if equipped with MIRVs, it is probable that the "offensive" limitation will apply to the SS-9s in some way. But since restriction of installation of MIRVs would require on-site inspection, restricting numbers beyond the existing three hundred would have only limited significance for protecting the Minuteman missiles.

More basically, it appears that the U.S. negotiating position is much influenced by insistence on the need for three strategic armaments systems (land-based, bombers, and sea-based). As accuracies increase, the Minuteman seems certain to become more and more vulnerable to

Soviet ICBMs, although further hardening may slow down the process. The sensible course might well be to try to phase out the land-based systems in favor of sea-based strategic capabilities and bombers, if they can be protected.

But the Soviet Union may well have less motive to move that way than we do. The United States asserts that its missiles equipped with MIRVs will not have the capacity to threaten the Soviet ICBMs.[13] If so, it is hard to see what the Soviets would accept as a trade-off for phasing them out.

RELATING WEAPONS DECISIONS TO THE SALT

Arms control negotiations take substantial time. The processes of preparation and decision on each side in addition to the negotiations themselves are inevitably cumbersome. If a treaty or other formal agreement results, further time will be needed to ratify it and bring it into force. The SALT have already been under way for two years and may take much longer before any limitations become effective.

During this period, how should the parties handle changes in their weapons systems? For example, should the United States have unilaterally suspended installing any new or improved systems while the talks are going on? From time to time, the Soviet leaders and press, while defending Soviet measures, have criticized the U.S. decisions on MIRV and ABM as endangering the SALT.[14]

In practice, neither side has suspended its weapons programs. Throughout the period of the SALT the Soviet Union has continued to install SS-9s and other missiles at a rapid rate, to build Polaris-type submarines at the rate of eight per year, to test multiple warheads and improved ABMs, and to dig nearly one hundred new silos.[15] The United States has likewise gone forward with missiles equipped with MIRVs for the modified Polaris submarines and for Minuteman ICBMs, and with the revised ABM Safeguard systems. But the number of U.S. missiles has not been increased since 1967, despite the pace and scope of the Soviet buildup, which has exceeded predictions and created legitimate concern about their purposes. (U.S. leaders assert, however, that countermeasures cannot be postponed much longer, and in January 1972 President Nixon announced that the United States would develop and deploy submarines armed with missiles with a range of five thousand miles.)

There is no evidence that the weapons actions by either side have impeded the SALT. Indeed, it can be argued that unilateral suspension of planned improvements would remove one of the motives for Soviet agreement to restrictions in the SALT.[16]

Yet the failure to limit new MIRVs is unfortunate. Their effects on the two systems will be different and may hinder future efforts at limitation. If, as U.S. leaders assert, the U.S. MIRV missiles are not able to destroy Soviet missiles, they will merely increase still more the "assured destruction" overkill. The Soviet SS-9s with MIRVs will, how-ever, be a potent counterforce weapon against land-based Minutemen. Since MIRVs could not be controlled after development without using on-site inspection, rejected by the Soviets, the only chance to ban them would have been before testing was completed. Apparently the Soviet Union showed no interest in such proposals, probably in the belief that the United States had already perfected its systems.

For the future, what this suggests is that the methods or forms of agreement must be such as to avoid undue delay when dealing with emerging technical developments.

FORMAL VERSUS INFORMAL AGREEMENTS

What form should any SALT outcome take? A formal treaty? An executive agreement? Or less formal undertakings? There are prece-dents for a wide variety of answers.[17]

The choice of form should take account of the characteristics of any such agreement, which are inherent in the relations of the parties and the nature of the subject matter.[18] Some of these have already been referred to in the earlier discussion:

1. The agreement should define clearly the respective undertakings to avoid as far as feasible charges of violation due to ambiguity or mis-understanding.

2. It should allow withdrawal whenever a party concludes that it no longer serves its interests. This explicit privilege would emphasize the fact that the validity and continuance of the agreement depend on its continuing appeal to the self-interest of the parties and not merely on their promises. Neither the United States nor the Soviet Union will al-low its actions to be constrained by limitations that it considers unfair or dangerous to its security. It is prudent to recognize this reality in the agreement itself. To do so also underscores the necessity for either party to remain in a position to protect its security if the agreement breaks down.

3. The agreement must recognize the inevitable necessity for revi-sion. It may not operate as anticipated and may bear unfairly on one of the parties. Similarly, the progress of technology will certainly change the impact of any specific limitations, especially if restricted to one or two weapons systems. Other states, such as China, will gradually ac-

quire nuclear capacities that will affect any bilateral U.S.-USSR arrangement. The agreement should, therefore, provide for some procedure or organ for regular review of the agreed limitations.

4. Any major change in the strategic arms competition will not be the result of a single agreement but the cumulative product of a series of steps. Hence the initial agreement should be designed to make it easy to complement, expand, and adapt its coverage and application as experience is gained and new limitations become feasible.

These requirements will be difficult to meet, especially in the early stages. Many will expect any agreement to take the form of a treaty, and that does have some advantages, particularly for domestic purposes. The Soviets also often seem to prefer more formal documents. A treaty could, of course, be drafted to provide for the relationship a flexible framework, embodying provisions for extension, revision, and adaptation without repeating the ratification process. Ultimately, when the relations and structure have developed and evolved, the system of limitations should probably be formalized by a treaty.

But for the initial phases, it seems better to adopt some method that is less formal or seemingly definitive and that would lend itself more readily to adaptation in the light of experience and changing conditions. One possible method would be to exchange explicit statements, which could be reciprocally related, about programs and intentions.[19] In essence, they would amount to reciprocal exchange of a series of "if . . . then" propositions. One side would state its plans in regard to some part or all of its strategic systems over some specified time span. The other would reciprocate by stating that so long as it was satisfied that the first followed the announced course it intended to adhere to a specific program with regard to a related or similar weapons system.

This procedure could meet much of the need to combine flexibility with definiteness as well as the other requirements. It could lay the basis over the longer term for a more formal treaty if that seemed desirable. But even a treaty would need to be supplemented by more informal understandings regarding related matters.

To sum up, the United States and the Soviet Union are inescapably enmeshed in a process of action and reaction in the dynamic field of strategic armament. What each does is both a response and a stimulus to the conduct of the other. If the SALT are serious, they are efforts to manage and regulate this interaction. Given the basic hostility and distrust, and the inherent difficulty of conscious control of the subject matter, this effort is bound to involve slow groping toward piecemeal measures. Both the negotiations and any agreements should be designed to recognize the nature of this process and the complexities of controlling it by cooperation among adversaries.

NOTES

1. Thomas W. Wolfe, *Soviet Power and Europe* (Baltimore: Johns Hopkins Press, 1970), chap. XVIII, for an excellent discussion of alternative interpretations of Soviet purposes.

2. U.S. Arms Control and Disarmament Agency, Disarmament Document Series (mimeographed), August 11, 1969 (cited hereafter as DDS), no. 532, pp. 2–3, 5.

3. DDS, no. 559, October 27, 1970, p. 27.

4. Testimony to Arms Control Subcommittee of Senate Foreign Relations Committee, June 16, 1971, DDS, no. 573, June 29, 1971, p. 73.

5. DDS, no. 568, March 15, 1971, p. 34.

6. DDS, no. 573, p. 20.

7. DDS, no. 568, pp. 35–37.

8. For an excellent discussion of the values and limitations of such a general discussion, see Jerome H. Kahan, *Strategies for SALT,* Brookings Reprint 194 (Washington, D.C., 1971), (reprinted from *World Politics,* January 1971).

9. DDS, no. 559, p. 7.

10. DDS, no. 568, pp. 35–36.

11. DDS, no. 573, pp. 51–52.

12. DDS, no. 568, pp. 37–38.

13. DDS, no. 568, p. 34.

14. See, for example, Brezhnev, DDS, no. 573, pp. 59–61.

15. DDS, nos. 532, p. 23; 546, pp. 92–93; 559, pp. 19–23.

16. See, for example, Secretary Rogers and Secretary Laird before Disarmament Subcommittee of Senate Foreign Relations Committee, May 1970, DDS, no. 559, pp. 9, 35–40.

17. See George Bunn, "Missile Limitation: By Treaty or Otherwise?" *Columbia Law Review,* vol. LXX (January 1970).

18. Some of these problems were analyzed in Robert R. Bowie, "Basic Requirements for Arms Control," *Daedalus,* vol. 89 (Fall 1960), pp. 708–22, esp. pp. 720–22.

19. See Kahan, *Strategies for SALT,* esp. pp. 183–87.

ROBERT A. SCALAPINO

The American-Soviet-Chinese Triangle: Implications for Arms Control

Introduction

IN THE MIDST of rapidly changing international alignments, even short-hand descriptions of this period are in dispute. Should we assume that we are entering an era to be characterized by five major elements: the United States, the Soviet Union, the People's Republic of China (PRC), Japan, and a European Community? Or is it more realistic to eliminate the yet-embryonic European Community and concentrate upon quadrilateral relations? Is Japan truly going to be a major power in politico-military terms, or should we speak of triangular relations as holding the key to the new era, especially in a field like weapons control? But is the PRC a power in any sense other than in terms of its sheer mass, or will it become so in the near future? Despite the dramatic changes of recent years, are we still living in a world essentially dominated by U.S. and Soviet power, albeit with both of these superpowers faced with increasing difficulties in playing past roles effectively?

No doubt each of the above combinations is significant under certain circumstances, given certain issues. To raise this broad question, however, is to highlight the extraordinary complexity of this period. If we are currently in the much-heralded transition from the age of "superpower dominance" toward a world characterized by a much higher degree of multilateralism and dispersed power, the transition is progressing unevenly at this point. In traditional military terms, power relations have changed little as yet (except, possibly, *between* the superpowers). Changes in the capacity or will to use power may be a different matter. Here we are drawn into the realm of those complex psychological and political factors that underwrite authority and legitimacy *internally,* and also serve to fix a role for power—at home and abroad. As is well known, the internal cohesion of a given state, its perception of its international role, and the image that it manages to convey externally must all enter into any realistic appraisal of the effective power it possesses at a given time. Indeed, among the major powers

141

or major contenders for world roles (two potentially different conditions), the widening differences in internal restraints upon foreign policy may well become the primary source of international disequilibrium in the years immediately ahead.

Soviet-Chinese Relations

In this context, American-Soviet-Chinese relations are the most critical set of relations with respect to the general question of weapons control, and particularly to such ultimate control as is attained over nuclear weapons dispersal and use. Let us examine first the background and current state of Soviet-Chinese relations. It now appears that relations between the Stalinist Soviet Union and the Chinese Communists in the post-1945 era were more complex and less intimate than was once assumed. Although the Soviets ultimately made some important contributions to the Communist military victory over the Nationalists, and some even more significant contributions to Chinese industrial development in the years immediately after 1949, divisive issues were imbedded in Sino-Soviet relations from the beginning of the Chinese Communist era. Before the political demise of Khrushchev, they had become issues out of control, impossible to contain within any framework of compromise or solution.

The initial questions of critical importance were fourfold: how to operate international organization and decision-making processes in an age of Communist pluralism; how to establish an effective policy of containing and rolling back American power; what constituted the obligations of comradeship in matters of international aid and support—economic, political, and military; and finally, the impact of divergence in internal policies, especially economic ones, upon bilateral relations.

In retrospect, it can probably be said that none of these major problems could easily have been avoided. Communism in the post-1945 period acquired new, relatively independent bases of power outside the Soviet Union; yet the Russians found it extremely difficult to abandon old patterns of thought and methods of operation within the international Communist movement, especially since they continued to carry the heaviest burdens within that movement for defense and technical-economic assistance. The attempts to establish the principles of unanimity as the basis for decision-making among Communist parties and states, based upon their complete "equality" and absolute "sovereignty," were less than successful, moreover, because such agreements among a multitude of diverse parties were destined to be either too vague (and hence susceptible to radically different interpretations) or impossible to attain.

Similarly, the problem of the United States produced increasing friction during the decade after Stalin's death. Whereas the Soviet Union could begin to think realistically about the feasibility of nation-to-nation competition (and orient its priorities accordingly), the Chinese Communists, given their internal conditions and international status, naturally gravitated toward the more classical Leninist formula of unfolding the global revolution in order to seek the dissipation of American power.

The variant positions taken on the "American problem" merely accentuated the issue of priorities. From the outset of the postwar era, the Russians were forced to spread their resources over a number of commitments, most of them of seemingly equal urgency: the achievement of military parity with the United States, the rebuilding of their own shattered nation, competition in the wooing of "nonaligned" and "national-bourgeois" governments, and maximal aid to the desperately poor new Communist states that had emerged as a result of World War II. Soviet priorities, of course, could not be expected to accord with those desired by the PRC, especially as they pertained to the amount and terms of aid.

The issue was both exacerbated and altered, however, with the Chinese decision beginning in 1956 to diverge from the Soviet model of development and to take an independent stance on other matters as well. These decisions served as catalytic agents releasing a huge wave of pent-up nationalism and, more importantly, directing much of it against the Soviet Union. "The Soviet way or the Chinese way" became a burning issue in Chinese politics, sometimes a real issue, sometimes an artificial one, but in any case, an issue having a dramatic, seemingly irreversible impact upon Sino-Soviet relations because of the manner in which it involved each in the internal affairs of the other.

Thus, over the past ten years, the tension between the Soviet Union and the People's Republic of China has grown to classic proportions. It has taken on most of the characteristics, moreover, of a traditional struggle between two neighboring, massive, and strongly xenophobic nations having very different definitions of "national interest," each possessed of a fierce nationalism, with minimal tolerance toward external forces, a very strong orientation toward development, and the will to use a wide range of techniques in countering opponents. Subsequently, other issues were added to the initial ones. The most spectacular one was the issue of boundaries, combined with the thorny problem of governing the minority peoples living on both sides of the forty-five-hundred-mile Sino-Soviet border. On more than one occasion, as is well known, violence of considerable proportions ensued. Meanwhile, since both nations claimed to be loyal and orthodox adherents of Marxism-Leninism, and staked their legitimacy in some measure upon that claim, differences rooted in "national interest" had to be translated into ideological terms. Thereby both the style and intensity of disputation were affected, with "orthodoxy" pitted against "heresy" in the manner of medieval ecclesiastics.

The primary issues, however, continue to lie elsewhere. As just indicated, ideology affects the style far more than the substance of the Sino-Soviet debate. The boundary conflicts, moreover, have been the result, not the cause of the major split between these two allies, despite the dangerous proportions that those conflicts have subsequently assumed. At the same time, the "first causes" of the Sino-Soviet cleavage to which we addressed ourselves briefly above have in each case undergone significant alterations with time, now combining in such a fashion as to make the central issues today grouped around a single basic problem, that of national security. To understand the current status of Soviet-Chinese relations and the potentialities for the future, the evolution and transformation of those initial causes into an overweening concern by both parties for their security must be analyzed.

The struggle for control over Communist international organization and decision-making, once so prominent, is largely in abeyance simply because Communist internationalism in its broadest dimensions has collapsed. At present, there is no counterpart to the old Comintern/ Cominform, and the effort to regularize meetings of all Communist parties and states has ceased. In essence, there has been a major retreat from internationalism and toward regionalism within the Communist world. Finding it impossible to continue with a single international body, or to reach and enforce decisions by unanimous consent, the Soviet Union has concentrated upon efforts to shore up the Warsaw Pact nations and other select Communist allies such as the Mongolian People's Republic against the threats posed by the PRC.

But while the Soviets have been primarily concerned with those Communist parties and states proximate to them and affecting their security, have continued to vie with the Chinese for influence elsewhere, such as with respect to North Vietnam, and there is scarcely a Communist movement in the world that has not been divided as a result of the Sino-Soviet quarrel. Along with the divisions, of course, has come a greater possibility for independence. In point of fact, international relations within the Communist orbit today run the same gamut as relations outside that orbit, with dependence, alliance, non-alignment, and hostility all present, together with a tendency—not perfectly realized—for both of the Communist giants to have their spheres of influence.

If relations within the Communist sphere reflect the intense competition between the Soviet Union and China, so do policies toward the United States. For the moment each state is accusing the other of a policy of calculated collusion with America to the detriment of all other comrades. At last, Moscow has been able to turn the tables on its archrival in some degree, arguing that Peking's overtures to the United States constitute a cynical abandonment of those revolutionary principles espoused with such seeming ardor a few short years ago; jeopardize the Communist cause in many areas, especially in Asia; and have as their primary purpose the weakening of the Soviet Union. To underscore these points, Soviet leaders have been engaged in well-publicized visits to such "revolutionary" centers as North Vietnam and Algeria, to Yugoslavia and other East European points of contention, and to Western bastions like Canada. In this fashion, Moscow signals its availability to comrades—or near comrades—in distress; the possibilities of a "live and let live" policy toward at least some of the non-aligned states; and the global importance of the Soviet Union.

Meanwhile, despite a new stance, Peking has as yet abandoned few of its old themes. It continues to rate "American imperialism" as a major threat, and one augmented by the rise of "Japanese militarism." More importantly, perhaps, it also charges that "superpower domination" of the world constitutes one of the principal dangers of this era. Unchallenged, the United States and the Soviet Union would seek to make all critical decisions and "impose" them upon the rest of the world, treating it as their combined preserve. Peking pledges that it will *never* become a "superpower" and also that it will never abandon allies or cease supporting their positions merely to achieve a normalization of relations with the United States. Slightly defensive in the face of Soviet charges, Peking continues to use the simple rhetoric of the past as it moves toward the complexities of the future.

Understandably, the issue of what constitutes correct comradeship is of less moment at a time when the much more modest goal of reestablishing reasonably normal state-to-state relations between the USSR and the PRC has yet to be attained. Meanwhile, "the Chinese way," which commenced as an economic deviation in the 1950s, has come to symbolize the late Maoist era in most if not all of its facets. Correspondingly, "the Russian way" has been turned into a term of oppro-brium and a means of eternally damning those who are alleged to have been subverted by it. One of the chief reasons why Sino-Soviet rela-tions are so bad and why any significant improvement in the near future will be very difficult is because those relations have become in-extricably woven into the fabric of the domestic politics of both societies. Using nationalism as their ultimate weapon, Mao and his supporters fastened such labels as "pro-Soviet" and "Khrushchevite revisionist" upon those whom they wished to destroy. Fallen comrades like Peng Te-huai, Liu Shao-ch'i, Teng Hsiao-p'ing, and many others were so classified. One of them, Chen Shao-yu (Wang Ming), managed to escape to the Soviet Union, whence he periodically issues anti-Maoist philippics.

From these facts, the dimensions of the security problem for both governments take their proportions. From the Soviet perspective cur-rent Chinese policies are Leninism turned against the motherland. Not only does Peking appeal to the Soviet people to overthrow their "corrupt, decadent, and revisionist" leadership, it also seeks to apply the very policies being advanced against the United States a few years ago: Unfold the world revolution and dissipate *Soviet* power. It calls for a global revolution against revisionism *and* "Soviet imperialism." This revolution, moreover, is intended to encompass not merely the peoples of the Afro-Asian-Latin American world whom the USSR once hoped to guide, but it is also aimed at regions considered vital to Rus-sian security such as Eastern Europe and Mongolia; indeed, it is aimed at the peoples of the Soviet Union themselves, including the Asian peoples within that union.

In official and semiofficial organs, the Soviet assessment of current trends within the People's Republic of China is set forth in stark terms: Maoism has become unvarnished militarism. The army now dominates both the party and the state in a fashion totally inimical to the cause of true communism. Moreover, catering to the forces of xeno-phobia and ultranationalism, the Maoists are teaching their people to hate the foreigner, particularly the Russian, and to glorify war. Down to the smallest child, militancy is cultivated. This constitutes a menace to the world and especially to those nations that must exist on the peripheries of China.

As might be expected, the Chinese perspective is vastly different. Chinese leaders see the Soviet Union as having once threatened them with nuclear weapons and as now seeking to create against them a policy of containment very similar to that pursued earlier by the United States. Was the Soviet threat of a nuclear strike real, and if real, how seriously should it have been taken? Irrespective of the facts, the Chinese took the 1969 threat very seriously, as the construction of air defenses throughout China indicates. Moreover, Chou En-lai, in a recent interview with a Yugoslav journalist, repeatedly emphasized the continuing Soviet military challenge, and listed it first among the possible threats that China faced.[1] It is conceivable that fears of a Soviet attack have been deliberately exaggerated for internal reasons and for the purpose of soliciting world support in the event of another crisis. However, the presence of large Soviet forces on the frontier, the installation of missiles at strategic points, and the availability of the vast Soviet arsenal of nuclear and nonnuclear weapons are realities, not fiction—and realities well known to Chinese leaders.

Meanwhile, other Soviet actions add to the threat as seen by Peking. The USSR is the only major power rapidly expanding its military arsenal and its global commitments. Many of those commitments are being directed toward Asia. Since Leonid Brezhnev's call for an Asian collective security system, the Soviets have reached a significant agreement with India, which counters the Sino-Pakistan alliance. They have also made overtures to a wide range of Southeast Asian states, including Thailand, Singapore, the Philippines, and Indonesia—states that are both anti-Communist and deeply concerned about Peking's future role in the area. Even toward Cambodia, the Russians have followed an ambivalent policy, failing to accord full support or recognition as yet to Norodom Sihanouk's exile regime. To each of the small Communist states on China's border, moreover, Russia offers herself as counterweight and protector. Even with Japan, the Soviets are exploring new ties of potential significance. Do not these policies collectively constitute a more formidable policy of encirclement and containment of China than any ever advanced by the United States?

Although major changes can never be foreclosed in international politics, it is difficult to conceive of the circumstances that might lead to a dramatic improvement in Soviet-Chinese relations. Certainly the death of Mao or a change in Soviet leadership does not appear likely to produce major alterations in relations at this point. In certain terms China is already in a post-Maoist era, and obviously the shift from Khrushchev to Brezhnev-Kosygin resolved none of the basic issues. It is true that both sides talk hopefully about the emergence of a leadership "responsive to the needs and wishes of its people," and in any succession crisis the other side might try to exert some influence on the outcome. Intervention in any form, however, is likely to be counterproductive. The tides of nationalism are running too strongly both in

Russia and in China to allow for the reestablishment of the older relationship. Yet the time does not seem ripe for the creation of a new relationship. Such accommodations as are made are likely to be limited, specific, and pragmatic—and they will probably stem from bargaining situations made arduous by the style, the resources, and the will of the two parties.

If "peace" is probably remote, it does not follow that war is imminent. The costs of any full-scale war and the improbability of "victory" for either side in such a war are understood both in Moscow and in Peking. Both sides consequently proclaim their determination to be tough *and* patient. Unlike the United States, moreover, these governments do not have to contend with a media cultivating public impatience and forcing premature action. In pursuing a fixed policy indefinitely, the elites of these societies are subject to few public pressures, although external factors may intervene, or occasion splits within the elite.

Thus relations between the USSR and the PRC are likely to be characterized by hostility, intense competition, and limited movement in the period immediately ahead, posing both opportunities and dangers to the rest of the world. Before assessing the impact of these relations upon the prospects for arms limitations, let us examine the other two sets of relations in our triangle, turning first to relations between the United States and the PRC.

Sino-American Relations

Has a significant turning point been reached in relations between these two countries? No conclusive answer can be given at this point, although *certain* facts point in that direction. Nevertheless, both the motivations and the expectations of the two parties, and particularly of the PRC, are susceptible to different interpretations. It can be argued that Peking, faced with a grave Soviet challenge and fearful of a resurgent Japan, now wishes to end its isolation and achieve a greater flexibility in its foreign policies, putting the inane policies of the Cultural Revolution era firmly behind it. To attain these new objectives, some degree of rapprochement with the West, and especially with the United States, is required, and since the United States is a distant superpower, not a superpower close to China's borders, such rapprochement may be possible.

Another interpretation of Chinese motives, however, would be that the PRC leaders see this as an ideal time to weaken and divide *all* major opponents, including the United States. With weariness deeply etched into the American scene, a preoccupation of the American people with internal problems and strong resistance to additional commitments or risk-taking abroad, deep fissures opening in American-Japanese relations, and some weakening of American credibility abroad, is this not an appropriate time to "force" the United States into making major concessions and to build an Asia in line with Peking's views?

In truth, these seemingly rival interpretations are not as incompatible as they may appear at first glance. At the moment, the PRC clearly regards the Soviet and Japanese threats as the more immediate and the more dangerous, although it closely connects "Japanese militarism" with "American imperialism." Thus it was enormously revealing when extensive references were made to Mao's "On Policy," a famous tract from the Sino-Japanese War era calling for a united front with the Kuomintang and all other willing forces against *the primary enemy* of the moment until victory could be attained and the struggle moved to a new level.[2] No great acumen is required to see the analogy intended.

To support its new tactics at home and to defend itself before worried allies, however, Peking has carefully spelled out another rationale for its receptivity to American overtures. Both publicly and privately, it has given interested parties the following information: "American imperialism" is currently in unprecedented trouble at home and abroad. Now is precisely the time, therefore, to compel the United States "to accept the demands of the people of Asia" and act in accordance with them. In order to expose the enemy fully and lay bare his weaknesses, one must have contact with him—*when* the time is ripe. An appeal can now be made to the American people, moreover, over the head of the leaders in Washington. Peking makes it clear that it intends to practice people-to-people and comrade-to-comrade diplomacy intensively, even as it engages in government-to-government negotiations.

In explaining the new PRC stance, men like Chou En-lai have also implied that the current status of ongoing events in Asia plays a major role in determining the timing. To revive "Japanese militarism" requires extensive preparations. Similarly, it will take time to train Thai, South Vietnamese, Cambodian, and Laotian forces for military operations in Southeast Asia. Such efforts should be countered now. Is it not also wise to seek an international commitment against any independent Taiwan backed by Japanese and American support while the veteran Chiang Kai-shek remains alive, since he is a primary symbol of "one China" and deeply opposed to any independence for the island or its people?

Meanwhile, on these and other specific issues, at least publicly, Peking has clearly signaled that on the one hand it has a special interest in, and responsibility for, Asia and on the other hand that it is not currently disposed to make any concessions or attempt any mediation on such problems as Indochina (the United States must accept the Communist seven-point proposal and disavow the "puppet governments" of South Vietnam and Cambodia); Taiwan (the PRC will never recognize the separation of Taiwan from China, and its "liberation" is China's internal affair); Korea (the Korean issue must be settled in accordance with the "just proposals" of the People's Democratic Republic of Korea). Even with respect to broader issues, the PRC's current public stance could scarcely be more rigid: U.S. military forces must be withdrawn from *all* of Asia; the Indian subcontinent and the Indian Ocean must be "freed" from the control of the "two superpowers"; the collusion between "American imperialism" and "Japanese militarism" must be completely broken; there is no need for another Geneva conference on Indochina, since this is a matter to be decided between the Indochinese people and the United States.

Naturally, these statements need not be taken as Peking's final and eternal positions. In the past, the PRC has shown itself capable of radical policy shifts with respect to both men and issues on more than one occasion—witness the Peking reception recently accorded General Ne Win, the Burmese leader who had only a short time earlier been given the PRC's "Heinous Fascist" award; or the extraordinary changes in relations with North Korea, which moved from the sharp attacks launched against P'yŏngyang by Peking in 1967–1968 to the eternal friendship pledged in 1970. These shifts, to be sure, can be ascribed to the need to correct "ultraleftist" errors committed in the course of the Cultural Revolution—although that would not do full justice to the truth. However, taking Peking's words too seriously has been hazardous even for Americans. Only two years ago, various American scholars were arguing that absolutely no change could be expected in the deepfreeze into which American-Chinese relations had fallen unless Washington was prepared to abandon Taiwan in advance.

There are other indications that the new course upon which the PRC appears to be set presents risks to its credibility. Despite efforts of heroic proportions to convince P'yŏngyang and Hanoi that they will never be "betrayed," signs of anxiety have developed, particularly among the North Vietnamese. As might be expected, Moscow intends to exploit these as earnestly as Peking's exploitation of Soviet weaknesses in the Balkans and the Middle East, with uncertain results, as events in this area change rapidly. Perhaps a general problem is more difficult in the long run. When the process of deepening international involvement gets under way, "purity," whether of doctrine or of policy, becomes increasingly difficult to maintain. Whatever its promises of the moment, Peking will not be able to satisfy its own dynamic needs in a rapidly changing, dangerous world and at the same time satisfy fully its primary allies and clients. Already Peking has shown a growing awareness of this fact, placing ever greater emphasis upon the need for revolutionaries and new nations alike to be self-sufficient, and indicating that in any case, China's efforts would have to be confined primarily to Asia (note Chou En-lai's recent statement that water at a distance cannot extinguish fire, in explaining the limitations upon China's role in distant regions).[3]

In sum, it seems safe to assume that Peking's motivations in responding to American overtures at this point are mixed: In part they are defensive responses to the steadily increased perception of threat from the USSR and Japan; in part they are offensive preliminaries to an effort at improving the PRC's status in Asia and in the world and conducting a more active, diversified campaign in the political arena on behalf of its programs and positions. Peking's initial expectations with respect to bilateral, official ties between the U.S. and the PRC are probably very modest. It is not prepared to pay any substantial price for such ties at this point, especially since it believes that with respect to most issues in dispute, time is on its side. The gains that it expects to make lie primarily outside the official bilateral sphere; they relate to attaining a greatly enhanced world status and much wider access to U.S. allies and to the American people themselves.

The motives and expectations of the United States require a less-detailed analysis. In the broadest sense, a shift in U.S. China policy was first attempted at the outset of the Kennedy Administration. For more than a decade, the United States has desired to test out a "step-by-step" program of normalization, beginning at low levels and involving no major substantive concessions on either side initially. After 1960, however, Peking insisted that there could be "no improvement" in Sino-American relations until the issue of Taiwan was "settled," as we noted earlier. No American President was prepared to pay such a price. Nevertheless, the Nixon Administration took advantage of the deescalation of the American role in the Vietnam War and other developments in the international scene to initiate certain new unilateral actions, primarily in the economic field, and to communicate through various channels its desire to initiate a dialogue beyond that of Warsaw, at the highest levels. These efforts culminated in the President's visit to Peking and what appeared to be the emergence of a new era in American-Chinese relations.

American motives were influenced by certain negative considerations as well as positive ones. Of course, it had long been accepted as a truism that no critical issues relating to Asia could be settled without the ultimate involvement of the People's Republic of China. Moreover, the new Nixon Doctrine, predicated upon an adjusted and reduced American presence, especially of a military nature, in Asia, placed a much greater premium upon political accommodation with China. In addition, when the Cultural Revolution had concluded with the PRC still intact, and when Chinese foreign policy returned to a state of "normalcy" after the excesses of 1966–67, it became apparent that the traditional U.S. policies on China could not be sustained. Indeed, attrition set in immediately, with allies as well as "neutrals" deserting. Naturally, the U.S. stance on the UN question was the most vulnerable, and, once the PRC signaled an interest in UN admission, its entry was preordained, with only the timing dependent upon American policies.

United States expectations, like those of the PRC, are modest with respect to bilateral relations, at least in the initial phases. In this respect, the President may have some problems on the domestic front. Having opted for a spectacular method of inaugurating the new era, that of a personal visit to China, he may find it difficult to satisfy public expectations, and in this respect, the media, for whom sensationalism is the meat of life, can be expected to be of little aid. On a broader level, indeed, American impatience is a cultural-political trait upon which the Chinese are known to be counting heavily in the arduous negotiations—bilateral and multilateral—that lie ahead. Meanwhile, U.S. hopes rest less upon immediate, dramatic "solutions" to such issues as Taiwan (which, if they occurred, would almost certainly be adverse to American interests), and more in the unfolding of the *process* of Chinese international involvement. Current American policies toward the PRC are underwritten by the belief that PRC involvement at many levels in international affairs will inevitably introduce greater complexity into Chinese attitudes and policies, and that the Chinese leaders will find it to be in the PRC's interest to reach compromises and accommodations with the United States on certain issues.

What are the prospects for American-Chinese relations in the period immediately ahead, and over an intermediate period beyond? Here the critical variables seem greater in number and complexity than those present with respect to USSR-PRC relations. An impressive list of factors can be drawn up on any balance sheet supporting the thesis that American-Chinese relations will improve on balance and operate within a range that can be considered normal for states not in alliance or sharing a broad range of values. But in the case of each of these factors, ambiguous or negative elements are also present.

Let us turn first to the all-important security issue. If the United States implements the Nixon Doctrine, removing its "close-in" military forces in the vicinity of China and turning over the primary defense of Asian states to indigenous military forces, it should increasingly acquire the image of a distant superpower, one not representing an imminent threat in Peking's eyes. If the U.S. military role in East Asia is to be limited to providing its allies with the equipment and training essential to their defense, but resting that defense in their hands except for the maintenance of the nuclear umbrella so as to prevent massive external aggression, American policy will provide an element of predictability absent in earlier years. On the other hand, the Nixon Doctrine is not fully explicit on this latter matter. The United States has stated firmly that all of its treaty commitments will be kept, and it has certainly not ruled out the use of American air and naval power at least to aid an ally considered under external attack.

How does the security issue look when viewed from the Chinese side of the equation? The PRC continues to phrase its security concerns in "interior," defensive terms. Only recently, Chou En-lai, in the interview with the Yugoslav journalist noted earlier, repeated in remarkably similar language a statement made by Ch'en Yi a few years ago (and thought at the time to have been an offhand boast) to the effect that even if China were attacked from the north by Russia, from the south by the United States, from the east by Japan, and from the Tibetan frontier by India, it was ready "for all eventualities." [4] If this truly represents the current thinking of Chinese leaders, it reveals a deep consciousness of China's military weakness, a continued preoccupation with the problem of encirclement and the uniform hostility of all external forces, and an extraordinarily high level of "defensiveness" in approaching security issues. This is as befits a nation still facing multiple internal problems and destined to continue for the foreseeable future to be militarily weak in comparison with the United States or the Soviet Union. At present, moreover, the PRC needs the great bulk of its army for purposes of internal governance; its air and naval power are modest to negligible. It is not surprising, therefore, that the principal Chinese advice to aspiring revolutionists has a Khrushchevian flavor: revolution cannot be exported; we can provide moral and limited material assistance, but you must achieve as high a degree of self-sufficiency as possible if you are to succeed, depending upon external assistance in minimal degree. Can this be considered the counterpart to the Nixon Doctrine?

If these elements of Chinese policy predominate, accommodation with the United States would not seem extraordinarily difficult with respect to security issues. Once again, however, various complexities enter the scene. Current defensiveness has not inhibited Chinese leaders from signaling clearly that China intends to have its sphere of influence in Asia, *beyond* Chinese borders. Once again, Chou En-lai has openly delineated the official position: We have a greater right to speak on Asian problems, he has asserted, than others—implying specifically a greater right than the two "superpowers"—and we bear "heavier responsibilities." But unlike Europe, there are no commonly agreed "spheres" and "neutral" or "intermediate" zones. Moreover, in addition to the United States and the Soviet Union, such states as Japan, India, Pakistan, and Indonesia are likely to have a considerable interest in Chinese assertions of prior rights and interests, not to mention the small states on China's borders. Some Europeans having had recent contact with Prince Sihanouk report that he is prepared to accept a "Hungary" status for Cambodia vis-à-vis Peking, but even in the event that he regains power, such a status may not be acceptable—without struggle—to other small states on the Asian mainland.

Meanwhile, the PRC continues to threaten those governments considered hostile to it by calling for their overthrow from within and giving some support to those who are prepared to attempt it. The primary targets at present in addition to the non-Communist regimes of Indochina are the governments of Thailand and the Philippines, but the list varies, depending upon the circumstances. By altering the quotient of government-to-government, people-to-people, and comrade-to-comrade recognition, contacts, and support, Peking hopes to exercise maximum influence without overcommitment and other risks. Yet if this policy continues to be Peking's central reliance, periodic tension and crises throughout East Asia are likely to be the result. Moreover, it is clear that the PRC intends to apply similar policies to additional states, including the United States and Japan. Even the USSR and other Communist states have been the recipients of such treatment when they deviated significantly from the PRC line. Much of this is reminiscent of the early Soviet Union. Whatever progress is made in tackling specific issues and in accepting the PRC's new international status, for an indefinite period of time Peking is likely to display some ambivalence as to whether it wishes to operate wholly within the community of nations or play in addition, the role of roving revolutionary, its formal commitments to "peaceful coexistence" notwithstanding.

Meanwhile, progress is likely to be slow in "solving" such specific issues as Taiwan, Indochina, Korea, and the Japan-U.S. alliance. Currently there is every indication that Peking expects Washington to make the basic concessions with respect to each of these issues, not because Washington wishes to do so, but because a combination of domestic and foreign pressures will force it to do so. Thus bargaining on these issues may be exceedingly limited in scope and results, at least initially. Each side will present its position, seek to make that position credible, and signal the areas where some flexibility exists. Meanwhile, developments external to the bilateral discussion-negotiation process will probably have a much greater influence upon the course of events with respect to each of the above issues than official American-Chinese contacts.

Economic relations between the United States and the People's Republic of China are not likely to be of great significance for the foreseeable future. As is well known, in sheer economic terms, a number of other countries, and notably Japan, are in a better competitive position to trade with China. The U.S. advantage tends to lie in precisely those areas where issues of security are apt to inhibit trade. In any case, volume would not be great. Moreover, it is by no means clear that the PRC intends to abandon a pattern of economic development that has placed the highest premium upon self-sufficiency, relegating trade and other forms of international economic intercourse to the lowest level consistent with critical economic requirements. Favorable credit conditions and other inducements would certainly make some difference, but it is difficult to envisage major changes in this aspect of U.S.-PRC relations under prevailing or foreseeable political and economic conditions.

Thus the prospects for U.S.-PRC relations must be viewed with considerable caution. A network of contacts, official and unofficial, is now in the process of being constructed, with Paris designated as the point of regular diplomatic exchange. Unofficial contacts may be the most significant initially, but from the Chinese side, these are likely to be carefully regulated. Nevertheless, it is in this area that the first sustained interaction may take place. In all probability progress on most of the specific issues outlined above will range from limited to none, with the containment of the issue to its present proportions, or somewhat reduced ones, being the most hopeful prospect. The first agreements are likely to be essentially technical or procedural ones, building from the areas where minimal obstacles and maximal common interests already exist. The most difficult political and security issues, in any case, are only susceptible to containment via bilateral U.S.-PRC negotiations. "Solutions" are certain to require broader participation.

In sum, relations between the United States and the People's Republic of China are likely to be guarded, partial, and decidedly uneven in the years immediately ahead. If these relations will generally avoid the element of steady, escalating hostility and threat of conflict that have recently characterized Soviet-Chinese relations, they will in no sense replace American-Japanese relations as the cornerstone of U.S. Far Eastern policy. Once again, as in the case of the projection of USSR-PRC relations, "surprise" developments causing major deviation from this prognosis cannot be ruled out. Internal developments in either country could affect relations with the other in dramatic fashion. No one should be allowed to forget the extraordinary, if temporary, impact of the Cultural Revolution upon China's foreign policy. A prolonged succession crisis, economic failures, or any other event that threatened the basic stability and integrity of China would present a set of radically altered possibilities. And if isolationism captured the heights of American attitudes and policies, prospects for the future would also be decidedly affected. Drastically changed relations between the USSR and the PRC, either for better or for worse, would also have a major impact. Finally, a radical change of the balance within Asia that occurred independently of U.S.-PRC interaction, affecting Taiwan, Southeast Asia, or Japan, could also introduce decisive new factors into the bilateral equation. We can suggest here only the "most probable" outcome of ongoing events.

Soviet-American Relations

The final part of our triangle consists of U.S.-USSR relations. Without doubt, these relations remain the most crucial among the three sets of bilateral relations with which we have been concerned, both with respect to security issues and to most matters in the global political realm. Here we have certain patterns now reasonably established against which to project the future. Yet once again, a number of uncertainties, including some new elements, cloud the picture.

If we turn initially to considerations of security, U.S.-USSR relations present a striking contrast with those involving the PRC. Relations between the PRC and either the United States or the Soviet Union are clearly between unequals in military terms. United States-USSR relations, on the other hand, have moved toward military parity, at least in strategic weapons systems. Indeed, the element of stability entering into global politics in recent years has revolved in considerable measure around three closely related factors: the growing acceptance by the United States and the Soviet Union of the principle of military parity in strategic weapons, together with an increasing recognition of the need to find means of halting arms escalation and preventing nuclear proliferation; the "solution" or containment of most, if not all, situations that harbored the potentiality for direct military confrontation between the two superpowers; and the minimal threat posed to either nation from a third party.

In each of these respects, the road after 1945 has been long and tortuous. One can scarcely forget the series of crises and conflicts involving—directly or indirectly—U.S.-USSR confrontations in Europe and Asia in the 1945–49 period when the United States was the only state possessing nuclear weapons. During this period and until the death of Stalin, the Soviet Union, acting out of weakness, sought to advance its interests and protect its security by unfolding the global revolution in a fashion that cheered the hearts of the most ardent Maoists.

To recall the hazards of nuclear inequality is not to dismiss the problems of the subsequent period. In reaching rough parity, both the United States and the Soviet Union have developed defensive and offensive weapons of ever greater sophistication and in ever greater numbers. Nor is the technological race over. Despite the current achievements attained by the SALT, agreements on limiting ABM defenses and ICBMs really represent only a belated start. Meanwhile, military research and development will continue on both sides. The negotiation process, moreover, is hampered by the fact that the rules governing internal debate and discussion differ radically in the two nations, and hence comparable scientific and public pressures cannot be mounted. Under these conditions, risk-taking initiatives from either side become more difficult.

Thus, even after the principle of military parity in strategic weapons systems has been accepted, the issue of what constitutes parity in the midst of a rapidly changing technology constitutes a central difficulty, and one with extremely dangerous possibilities. The limited agreements that have been attained thus far, such as the Non-Proliferation Treaty, illustrate those specific areas where mutual interests have been easiest to discover. In the security field, these areas have been exceedingly limited to date. Meanwhile, however, a number of situations threatening confrontation have been defused. The most dramatic example has been the Cuban affair—but that case scarcely constitutes a model, representing as it does the most dangerous confrontation of the post-1945 era. More encouraging have been recent developments relating to Europe and especially with respect to Germany. Even with regard to the Middle East, where the situation remains dangerous and no solutions are in sight, the United States and the Soviet Union have found means of rapid communication and methods of containing a situation seemingly not susceptible to immediate settlement.

One major development, however, must be placed in contradistinction to the generally favorable trends just noted. In the recent past, the Soviet Union has been rapidly expanding its international commitments. Indeed, at a time when the United States is generally reducing its foreign commitments, the USSR was entering into a vigorous expansionism, in many parts of the world including the South and East of Asia, as we have previously noted. Although this expansion is not necessarily directed against the United States in every case (in Asia, as we have noted, a clear goal is the containment of China), it is certain to raise a host of complications, of both a security and political nature. Indeed, there is a growing fear on the part of some Western observers that whatever the equilibrium established between American and Soviet strategic weapons systems, an imbalance is developing in conventional weapons and related military forces. Soviet objectives and gains in this area are substantial. And even if the Soviets were merely to maintain present levels of conventional strength, it is argued, they may well be able to count on a heavy attrition with respect to American conventional power, given internal developments in the United States. Will the Soviet Union then become the only major power with both the will and the capacity to play a significant global role? In any case, current developments emphasize the close relation between new Soviet commitments and sense of role on the one hand, and Soviet concepts of both strategic and conventional weapons needs on the other.

American-Soviet relations cannot accurately be portrayed in a linear fashion, either up or down; rather, they must be represented by a series of circles on either side of a line that we may use to depict an ideal state of complete accord. A growing number of issues can be placed in varying proximity to that line on the "positive" side, denoting the substantial progress toward accommodation that has been made in certain fields. Yet there remain many crucial issues on the "negative" side, some of which continue to be subjects of near-total disagreement. In still other cases, the issue is not yet on the ledger, because it has not been raised or discussed in any systematic fashion.

The fact cannot be overlooked, however, that U.S.-USSR relations have evolved to date under circumstances where no serious threat has been perceived from any third party or force. Will this situation continue? Is it true now? It seems easy to demonstrate that the People's Republic of China cannot constitute a military threat of any substantial proportions to the USSR in the foreseeable future. As has been indicated, the Chinese themselves currently project a military strategy that is of low risk vis-à-vis the superpowers and is heavily defensive. Moreover, while the PRC can be considered to have the world's third largest military establishment, any comparison with the United States and the Soviet Union reveals an enormous disparity in both the numbers and the quality of its military hardware. At present, China has approximately three million men in the regular armed forces, but a number of these have been siphoned into the domestic economic and political structure, as is well known. According to the Institute of Strategic Studies, the PRC has some twenty-eight-hundred combat aircraft, mostly Soviet models of relatively recent vintage. MIG-19s have been produced in China in sufficient numbers to enable sales to Pakistan, but the PRC has just begun to produce the first jet fighter of its own. Similarly, while the Chinese have some forty attack submarines, diesel-powered, they have only begun to produce their first nuclear-powered submarine, according to recent reports.

Viewed from a Soviet perspective, however, these facts and others related to them may not be as comforting as might be assumed. The Russians must share a lengthy border with a nation having limitless supplies of manpower, possessed by an intense nationalism that may well be directed against them in the foreseeable future, and seemingly determined to acquire a substantial nuclear capacity in addition to a modernized conventional force. The steadily increasing psychological-political impact of these facts upon Soviet leadership *and* the Soviet people seems very probable.

Certainly there has been intense debate within top Chinese circles with respect to military-political strategies. Nor is there any reason to assume that all issues have been resolved permanently. Despite the shadowy and disputed character of the evidence, we can hypothesize that during the 1960s various discussion-debates probably involved this wide range of interrelated political and military issues: the nature of the relationships possible with the Soviet Union and the United States, and what relationships should be sought; the PRC's most probable enemy or enemies in the decade ahead; the value of a defense hinged to highly politicized, mass-mobilized military-militia forces using guerrilla techniques; the relative emphasis to be given to up-grading conventional weaponry or basic economic and scientific-tech-nological development for longer range military efforts with a strong nuclear component; and the type of modern weapons system to seek.

Personality and power rivalries undoubtedly complicated the scene, but real differences with respect to military strategy existed and may still exist. Nevertheless, certain decisions appear to have been reached, for this period at least. Chinese military strategy currently consists of the following central components: a military posture as self-sufficient as possible; a strong priority to scientific and technological development so that a few advanced weapons systems can be developed with maxi-mum speed and at the highest possible level of quality; a commitment to the updating of select conventional weapons and continued emphasis upon intense politicalization at the mass levels within the People's Liberation Army (PLA) and militia, but the allocation of primary ef-forts and resources to nuclear weapons, probably including tactical nu-clear weapons; the development of a few long-range weapons (ICBMs) for prestige and political reasons, but a primary concentration upon a regional military capacity, with first attention going to short- and me-dium-range arms.

Such a military strategy clearly poses more problems for the Soviet Union than for the United States. The critical issues are how seriously are the problems perceived by Soviet leaders, and more specifically, to what extent do "worst possible" projections now command intensive Soviet attention and what range of countermeasures is contemplated. Let us assume that the future Chinese national growth rate somewhat ex-ceeds the 5 to 7 percent per annum average that has been estimated in the past, and that a sizable proportion of the budget (up to 20 to 30 percent) goes directly or indirectly into the military sector. Although this would constitute support sufficient for a rapidly improving modern military capability, it would scarcely elevate the PRC to the ranks of the U.S. and the USSR. As of 1971, for example, the Chinese probably had 20 medium-range ballistic missiles that were operational, according to the Institute for Strategic Studies. This contrasted with the 1,510 ICBMs possessed by the Soviet Union and the 1,054 U.S. ICBMs (with the United States having, in addition, a MIRV system greatly augmenting its destructive capabilities). It was estimated that it would take the PRC eight to ten years to develop and construct a nuclear-powered submarine and missile-launching combination comparable to the U.S. Polaris. The new Chinese jet fighter is regarded as a highly competent weapon, but likely to be outperformed by the MIG-21 or the American F-4 Phantom.

Two radically different interpretations of these facts are possible. On the one hand, it can be argued that the Chinese will ultimately discover the high costs and limited value of being a second- or third-class nuclear power, and be increasingly prepared to enter seriously into discussions looking toward control over nuclear weapons as well as broader disarmament. A less sanguine view would be that the PRC will be prepared to undergo any sacrifice to achieve a deterrent capacity presenting the USSR with unacceptable costs should it consider full-fledged military operations, thereby gaining significant bargaining leverage, and at the same time enabling the PRC to assert supremacy regionally over other Asian states, particularly if U.S. presence and credibility are substantially reduced and if Japan refrains from becoming a nuclear power.

Before exploring possibilities and countermeasures further, let us briefly place these questions in the context of current trends relating to Soviet and U.S. military capacity and strategy. President Nixon himself put the major development very succinctly when he stated that from 1950 to 1966, the United States possessed an overwhelming superiority in strategic weapons; from 1967 to 1969, the United States retained a significant superiority; by 1970, the Soviet Union possessed a powerful and sophisticated strategic force approaching that of America. The Soviet decision to close the missile gap has been pursued in recent years with remarkable success, as is well known. Equally significant strides have been made by the Soviets in expanding their naval forces and their air-transport system. Both superpowers now have approximately the same number of nuclear-powered submarines (ninety-two operational); and with respect to military aviation also, differences in overall capacity have been greatly narrowed.

Thus it is frequently asserted not only that the United States and the Soviet Union have attained strategic nuclear forces sufficient to destroy each other, but that each possesses the capacity to maintain that capability. Hence the strategic balance cannot be upset, assuming that appropriate countermeasures are taken and that efforts on either side to achieve a major military advantage will merely result in raising the levels of armament and the costs—not in altering the balance. Although these propositions may be true, they do not necessarily resolve a number of the obstacles now blocking major progress in arms control. United States-USSR arms control negotiations have reached their current status by a mutual acceptance of the concept of "bargaining from strength"—specifically, from an implicit acceptance of rough military parity. Thus the technical issues of what constitutes parity, as well as the need for guarantees against cheating, make up much of the lengthy background against which present discussions take place.

Beyond these issues, however, there are certain more complex elements in any such scenario. Since the political systems of the two superpowers are fundamentally different, the role of internal interest groups, the media, the political opposition, and the public cannot be the same, as was noted earlier. This affects such vital elements as the dynamics of concession and the relative capacities for risk-taking. For example, the respective pressures to reduce or refrain from military-oriented research and development could be radically unequal in the two nations, and this is surely one central key to the issues of strategic balance and arms control.

It is also apparent that "national interest" concepts, with their military-political corollaries, have recently undergone changes, and generally changes in opposite directions. Reference has already been made to this fact. The Soviet Union now gives every indication of seeing its security interests in much broader dimensions than in the past. Although this fact in itself has been widely acknowledged, its implications have scarcely been probed. The enlarged scope of its new commitments would naturally be expected to have some impact upon the Soviet sense of total military need. Such an impact, however, might not necessarily in and of itself be adverse to strategic arms limitations. Beyond the immediate horizon, moreover, lies an intriguing question: Is the Soviet Union moving toward its own crisis of priorities, with internal pressures mounting for much greater commitments to domestic concerns?

If American and Soviet definitions of their respective security interests appear to be moving in opposite directions, this is not the case with respect to basic doctrines of military strategy. Here both states have undergone similar oscillations, with Soviet fashions possibly influenced in considerable measure by prevailing U.S. styles. The Eisenhower doctrine of "massive retaliation" had its counterpart in the heavy Russian reliance upon nuclear deterrence of the Khrushchev era. Now both states appear to accept the need for preparations for a variety of contingencies, including full-fledged nuclear war, wholly conventional war, or some mix between nuclear and conventional operations.

The SALT up to date have made it clear that the bilateral U.S.-USSR agreements most easily reached are those pertaining to the avoidance of conflict through error or miscalculation; in addition, agreements relating to limitations upon defensive weapons represent a step of intermediate difficulty; and most complex are limits upon offensive weapons. Both states show a genuine interest in reducing the 9 to 11 percent of the GNP being expended annually by each nation in the military field (some authorities believe that Soviet expenditures are considerably greater) and in recognizing the risks of arms escalations. Mutual trust, however, is far from being achieved. Meanwhile, the broader mosaic of U.S.-Soviet relations remains one of varying circles of agreement and disagreement, rapprochement and discord, with progress in the most critical areas painfully slow and much labored but generally discernible.

Prospects for Arms Control

In such a setting, what influence is the PRC likely to have, given the data and hypotheses concerning its position advanced earlier? Once again, we must emphasize the "most probable," acknowledging that dramatic factors, domestic or international, could intervene to negate the following likelihoods. First, it should be noted that the PRC is currently progressing along the path taken earlier by the USSR with respect to strategic weapons controls. It is seeking to extract from the two superpowers a pledge that they will never be the first to use nuclear weapons as a substitute for concrete limitations. This was the Soviet stance at a much earlier point, and it is clearly intended to offset current Chinese weakness. At the same time the PRC is rejecting the Soviet call for a five-power conference on nuclear weapon controls and asking instead for an all-nations parley on general disarmament.

The available evidence thus suggests that the PRC has no interest in participating in a nuclear weapons control agreement at this time or in the near future. It cannot seriously believe that either the United States or the Soviet Union would agree to the pledge proposed in the absence of other, far-reaching agreements relating both to nuclear and conventional weapons. The Soviet Union has also proposed an all-nations disarmament conference in addition to a conference of the nuclear states, but it is extremely difficult to envisage concrete results from such a conference, and its advocacy must be assigned primarily to the realm of political propaganda.

Thus, while internal changes might alter the situation, it is now reasonable to assume that the PRC will eschew strategic arms controls, continue to develop its military capacities as rapidly as possible, and—without neglecting selective conventional weapons—place its primary emphasis upon a few modern nuclear weapons systems oriented toward a regional capability. Meanwhile, if current conditions hold, Soviet-Chinese relations will continue to be largely competitive and hostile. China's relations with the United States will show somewhat greater flexibility, and certain areas of accommodation or even agreement may emerge. "Normalization," however, is likely to be a long and thorny path, with factors of difference and fundamental disagreement the more prominent for the foreseeable future.

Under these circumstances, the Soviet Union will incline toward the following political and military policies: to avoid the risk of a two-front war, it will find ever-greater advantage in a *détente* in Europe with the West, and an accommodation—insofar as possible—to variations in relations with East European states so as to deny the Chinese extensive access to this vital region. These trends, of course, are already under way. To the Soviets, however, *détente* will continue to mean a legitimization of post-1945 boundaries, and in a broader sense, a de jure acceptance of the prevailing balance of power. It certainly will not mean a movement toward "self-determination" for the East European Communist states in its orbit or any radical departure from the status quo. Since the West has moved ever closer to accepting the Soviet premises with respect to European *détente,* however, it is entirely possible that present trends can continue or even be accelerated. On the military front, this would involve a mutual reduction of conventional forces, and at some point, a reconsideration of the continued existence of NATO and the Warsaw Pact. The difficult problem of nuclear weapons demands a more comprehensive solution, centering upon U.S.-USSR agreement.

Meanwhile, there would seem to be no reason why limited progress could not be continued at the SALT. Those limitations posed by "the Chinese problem" would appear to be primarily of a middle- and longer-range character, and to relate more to the issue of offensive weapons limitations. This may add to the value of specified "reexamination" periods being incorporated into any agreements, or the "overriding national interest" escape clause currently being employed. If containment of China, however, is a central concern of the Soviet Union, as currently appears to be the case, and such a policy envisages a wider range of economic and political as well as military activities in the Asian region, then contemporary agreements with the United States on strategic weapons control might have an enhanced value for the Soviets, enabling them to divert resources into these more immediate tasks without substantial risks to either their short- or long-range security. Such a prospect would be all the more logical and feasible if the Middle Eastern crisis could be defused and gradually settled. It is now here that the highest possibility of Soviet-American confrontation exists, although recent dramatic events in Egypt appear to have reduced that risk.

If we assume a less likely possibility, namely, a meaningful rapprochement between the Soviet Union and China in the near future, what would the impact be upon arms control negotiations? Although undoubtedly such a development would make all negotiatory relations between the United States and the Soviet Union more difficult and stiffen the Soviet position with respect to many issues, especially those concerning Europe and the Middle East, it is difficult to see why the Soviet Union would not continue to be deeply interested in placing a ceiling upon the development and dissemination of strategic weapons. China's interests might be given greater support by Moscow under such circumstances, at least in a *pro forma* fashion, but even in the event of rapprochement, memories of the past—and concern about the future—would project themselves into the attitudes and policies of the Soviets. This, together with the fact that the United States would continue to represent the primary competitive power, and one possessed of greater immediate resources, would provide the perimeters of Soviet policy.

We return to the point whence we began. With respect to the critical issues of arms control, the American-Soviet relationship is the vital one. Nothing must be allowed to interfere with the intensive American-Soviet negotiations on strategic weapons control. Approaches to the broader issues of *détente* and disarmament, moreover, must be pursued most vigorously at regional levels for the time being—Europe has to be the central region of endeavor, together with a concentration upon the Middle East as the principal target for crisis management and resolution.

The Pacific-Asian region is not yet ripe for regional efforts of the same scope and direction. No military-political equilibrium has yet had the common acceptance of the states in the region. In many cases —including that of the People's Republic of China itself—economic and political uncertainties becloud the future. The immediate tasks presenting themselves are therefore different in character. Agreements upon the requirements for peaceful coexistence and acceptance of the principle that all de facto states warrant de jure recognition must precede any meaningful and comprehensive regional agreements upon arms control. In sum, only when the Pacific-Asian region has acquired a greater degree of stability and mutual acceptance can arms control become a commonly accepted objective. For the immediate future, it must be assumed that the People's Republic of China will not contribute positively to controls over weapons, nuclear or conventional. A combination of bilateral U.S.-USSR negotiations and regional, multilateral efforts attuned to different stages of development and hence different problems in the two key regions, Europe and Asia, represent the most realistic approaches to the central problem of the late twentieth century.

NOTES

1. Chou En-lai interview with Dara Jankevich, reported in *Vjesnit* (Belgrade), August 28, 1971.

2. See "A Strong Weapon to Unite the People and Defeat the Enemy: Study 'On Policy'," an article written by "the writing group of the Hupeh Provincial Party Committee," and first published in the party's theoretical journal, *Hung Ch'i* (*Red Flag*), no. 9, August 2, 1971; reprinted in *Jen-min Jih-pao* (*People's Daily*), Peking, August 17, 1971, p. 1; and reproduced in part in English, *Peking Review*, 35, August 27, 1971, pp. 10–13.

3. Interview with Dara Jankevich, in *Vjesnit*.

4. Ibid.

WILLIAM R. KINTNER

Arms Control for
a Five-Power World

IN HIS STATE OF THE WORLD MESSAGE in 1971, President Nixon summarized the nature of the changes that have taken place in the global system since the end of the Second World War.

No single sudden upheaval marked the end of the postwar era in the way that the World Wars of this century shattered the prewar orders of international relations. But the cumulative change since 1945 is profound nonetheless:

Western Europe and Japan, nations physically or psychologically debilitated by the war, have regained their economic vitality, social cohesion, and political self-assurance. Their new vigor transforms our relationship into a more balanced and dynamic coalition of independent states. . . .

In the last twenty years, the nature of the Communist challenge has been transformed. The Stalinist bloc has fragmented into competing centers of doctrine and power. One of the deepest conflicts in the world today is between Communist China and the Soviet Union. . . .

At the same time, the Soviet Union has expanded its military power on a global scale and has moved from an inferior status in strategic weapons to one comparable to the United States. This shift in the military equation has changed both defense doctrines and the context of diplomacy.

Around the globe, East and West, the rigid bipolar world of the 1940's and 1950's has given way to the fluidity of a new era of multilateral diplomacy.[1]

The common recognition among the major world capitals that a new global system is coming into being is reflected in the unusual spate of diplomatic activity that has marked international intercourse for the past several years. The aim of this diplomatic activity has been to seek to reach international agreements, through negotiations, or to establish new relationships that apparently aim to achieve greater national flexibility, even at the expense of weakening prior ties and commitments.

The 1972 Nixon visit to Peking is perhaps the most striking example of a diplomatic response to the changing array of global power. But the President's announcement of a new American economic "game

167

plan" on August 15, 1971, also can be interpreted as a declaration of American independence from the paternal role it has played toward its European allies and Japan for two decades.

The Soviet Union has also been pursuing an active diplomatic engagement in many parts of the world, with particular emphasis on relations with Western Europe, the Middle East, and the Indian subcontinent. The Soviets appear to be seeking to tidy up their western front and strengthening their position in South Asia and the Indian Ocean in order to obtain greater freedom of action vis-à-vis the People's Republic of China.

In the past few years the German Federal Republic has apparently replaced France as the European power most anxious to obtain a new relationship with Eastern Europe and the Soviet Union. In Europe itself French acceptance of British entry into the Common Market is reviving the once moribund vision of a European community.

China has likewise demonstrated a capacity to open a new era in United States-Chinese relations, even though Peking continues nonetheless to denounce the United States as an imperialist power. In Chinese official statements, American activities are often equated with those practiced by "revisionist" Moscow.

Part of the explanation for the emerging world system has been the declining capacity and interest of the United States to engage in the world as it has in the past. Since 1968 American aversion to the war in Vietnam and internal social crises have forced the American people to focus on domestic issues to the neglect of some of their long-standing commitments abroad. These changes in the global system have added new dimensions to the problem of strategic nuclear arms control.

Soviet Design for a Post-SALT Arms Conference

Even during the SALT, the Soviets advocated the expansion of bilateral U.S.-Soviet talks into a conference of the five nuclear powers, to be followed by a conference comprising the United Nations. On June 24, 1971, the *New York Times* reported:

The Soviet Union gave extensive publicity to its call for a conference of the five atomic powers to discuss nuclear disarmament questions. But Western diplomats were less than enthusiastic about the proposal.

Every Moscow newspaper published the text of a note delivered to the United States, Britain, France and China in recent days, calling for talks on "the whole range of nuclear disarmament measures." [2]

The proposal, which was presented to the White House by Ambassador Anatoly F. Dobrynin, suggested that the five powers exchange views on holding such a conference. "As for the Soviet Government, it believes that the sooner a conference of the five nuclear powers is convened, the better," the note said.

"With regard to the site of the conference, its position remains open. Any place convenient to all the participants is acceptable. If the other parties agree, the Soviet Government would not object to setting up a preparatory committee for the conference."

The United States said it would study the proposal, but diplomats here indicated that Washington saw no reason to divert attention from the talks on limitation of strategic arms. . . .

France expressed her readiness to take part in a five-nation conference if the other parties agree. But French diplomats believe the Soviet proposal is more a political gesture than a realistic move towards arms control. . . . At a Moscow diplomatic reception at the Hungarian embassy a Chinese embassy official expressed reservations about the proposal. He said the "nuclear superpowers," meaning the United States and the Soviet Union, "are trying to dominate the world and want to disarm China." [3]

In his speech to the United Nations on September 28, 1971, Soviet Foreign Minister Andrei Gromyko conceded that the June proposal had not been well received, and he presented another plan. His statement follows:

The Soviet Union recently made a proposal to convene a conference of the five powers possessing nuclear weapons—the Soviet Union, the United States, the Chinese People's Republic, France and the United Kingdom—to consider questions of nuclear disarmament.

One of the nuclear powers we approached, France, supported this initiative of the Soviet Union. But another one declared its negative position: and then the two remaining powers hastened to state that under these circumstances the convening of the five nuclear power conference had already become an "academic" question.

The Soviet Union does not believe that the other nuclear powers have already said their last word. All those who view things realistically realize that nuclear disarmament can only be achieved with the participation and consent of all the five nuclear powers.

The Soviet Government believes that the convening of a world disarmament conference with the participation of all states of the world would meet the task of still further enhancing efforts in the struggle for disarmament and that it is expedient to discuss this question at the present session of the General Assembly. Accordingly we have asked for the inclusion of the relevant item in the agenda of the session of the General Assembly. [4]

It appears that the Soviet government is anxious to have any agreement that might be reached in the SALT ratified by the other existing nuclear powers as a means of preventing other states from acquiring nuclear arms.

An Alternative Five-Power Strategic Arms Control Conference

Now that Mainland China has joined the United Nations and occupies Taipei's seat, the five nuclear powers are also the five permanent members of the Security Council. In short, the victors of World War II occupy the driver's seat in both UN security and nuclear affairs. It is in the Soviet interest to sustain this arrangement indefinitely because it effectively isolates two powerful states, Japan and West Germany, from political influence commensurate with their economic strength. The international system will be disturbed as long as this disparity between power and political influence exists. Consequently, it is in the interest of world stability to design a global system that accommodates these states and their nuclear possibilities—*unless truly effective means of nuclear arms control or reduction can be devised among the present members of the "nuclear club."*

To move this question into the open, a new five-power group should be convened to discuss strategic arms control. This grouping would be comprised of delegations from the Western European Union,[5] the Soviet Union, the People's Republic of China, Japan, and the United States.

Contemporary and Projected International Power Distribution

A five-power arms control conference between the United States, Soviet, Chinese, Japanese, and WEU delegations would assemble representatives from those states which already possess strategic nuclear weapons and those states able to develop strategic weapons systems quickly.

Intuitive and objective judgments can be made concerning the capacity and potential of various nations to deploy or develop nuclear weapons and their delivery systems. An index of nuclear capability can be constructed by combining judgmental indexes for (1) GNP; (2) scientific talent (sufficient and of high quality); (3) technological base (as judged by quality and capability rather than extent of technical output); (4) nuclear base (as judged by a domestic source of plutonium or enriched uranium); (5) nuclear weapons (existing); and (6) strategic delivery systems. By these criteria and in descending order the United States, the Soviet Union, the Western European

Union, China, Japan, and India possess the most significant existing or future nuclear potential.

But some intangibles are more important than objective factors. These include how national leaders perceive their country's security environment and the strategy they adopt to safeguard its interests in the nuclear age. And since deterrence—a key component of every nuclear strategy—rests on psychological factors, national *will* as expressed through national leadership is the ultimate determinant of strategic nuclear capacity. A thousand nuclear warheads and launchers and zero *will* would be the equivalent of something times nothing. These intangible factors cannot be quantified, but their significance must be grasped in assessing future centers of world power.

In comparing the nuclear potential of the United States, Western Europe, the Soviet Union, China, Japan, and India, attention must be given to the economic base of each major nation as reflected in its gross national product. It is also useful to compare the economic position of these nations with respect to dynamic features in the shift of economic roles. Lawrence B. Krause has summarized this perspective in a publication entitled *Sequel to Bretton Woods:*

Because of their differing attributes, three centers of economic power now exist in the noncommunist world: the United States, the European Economic Community (EEC), and Japan. The United States, because it accounts for a large percentage of the total GNP of the world and has a high level of per capita income, remains a major force through its activities as an international investor and provider of financial services. The EEC dominates international trade in goods and it is therefore the primary force in commodity markets. Japan has gained prominence because its economy is the fastest growing—which gives it leverage through expansion of trade and investment—and because it is a model that other countries may try to emulate.

The increase in the EEC's importance in world trade is most striking. The trade gains made by the individual member countries in the 1950s continued through the 1960s as a result of the Common Market. While world trade increased to two and one-half times its former value over the past ten years, EEC trade more than tripled. By 1970 the EEC's share of world trade (even when intra-Community shipments are excluded) was greater than that of the United States, although in 1960 the U.S. share was the larger. Furthermore, as the United Kingdom and other countries join the EEC, the Community's share will certainly rise even higher. . . .

There are countries with greater influence on international finance than Japan, but none has increased its influence as much as Japan has since 1968. Likewise there are countries with a larger share of world trade, but none has increased its share as much over the last decade. From less than 4 percent in 1960, Japanese exports now make up nearly 7 percent of world trade.[6]

The analysis clearly indicates the leading economic centers of the non-Communist world.

The Rationale for WEU Participation in Nuclear Arms Control Discussions

While none of the larger individual European nations (the United Kingdom, France, and the Federal Republic of Germany) can be considered a major power center, collectively they and their WEU associates may well qualify. The United States has held that the Non-Proliferation Treaty does not preclude the creation of a nuclear consortium in Western Europe that might reduce the number of nuclear powers there from two to one. This requires the creation of a political community that may eventually come into being with British entry into the Common Market.

The United States and the Soviet Union hold different public views concerning one aspect of the Non-Proliferation Treaty. The United States maintains that the transfer of French and British nuclear assets to a European political authority would not constitute proliferation but in fact would represent a reduction in the number of nuclear powers. The Soviets, apprehensive about the Federal Republic of Germany's obtaining even the semblance of control over nuclear weapons, interpret the Non-Proliferation Treaty differently. In short, the creation of a European nuclear consortium is a moot question unless a true political community emerges in Western Europe.

An existing institution that has the potential for becoming a political community is the Western European Union, comprising the six members of the European Economic Community and Great Britain. Britain's entry into the Common Market and the more positive attitude displayed by France toward the Western European Union recently suggests revived prospects for the development of a political community in Western Europe. In this context, if WEU, the security instrument of Western Europe, participates as an element in the five-power nuclear disarmament talks, it will enhance the movement toward the political unification of Europe by giving WEU a major substantive role.

A New Role for Japan [7]

In the long run, it seems unlikely that Japan can entrust its security entirely to the United States. Is it possible for Japan to become an ever stronger economic giant without possessing commensurate sup-porting military force? The alternative of disarmed neutrality is un-likely; the greater possibility is that Japan will eventually attempt to develop an independent military position.

It may be argued that if Japan ever wishes to play a major role in Asia she will have to acquire her own independent nuclear force. The Japanese have made no effort to ratify the Non-Proliferation Treaty (NPT), and they are most unlikely to do so. Consequently, American efforts to force Japan to ratify the treaty might create a major break in U.S.-Japanese relations.

In his discussion with Chou En-lai, James Reston suggested that if the U.S.-Japanese security pact were broken, Japan, confronted by a nuclear China and a nuclear Soviet Union, "would almost certainly have to go nuclear." Chou En-lai responded by stating that Japan would acquire nuclear weapons, treaty or no treaty.

Despite this treaty, Japan with her present industrial capabilities is fully able to produce all the means of delivery. She is able to manufacture ground-to-air, ground-to-ground missiles and sea-to-ground missiles. As for bombers, she is all the more capable of manufacturing them. The only thing lacking is the nuclear warhead.

Japan's output of nuclear power is increasing daily. The United States supply of enriched uranium to Japan is not enough for her requirement, and she is now importing enriched uranium from other countries. And so her nuclear weapons can be produced readily. She cannot be prevented from doing so merely by the treaty. You have helped her develop her econ-omy to such a level. And she is bound to demand outward expansion.[8]

Future Japanese defense policies in both the conventional and nuclear field will be conditioned by the extent of the commitment of the Japanese to Article 9 of their Constitution prohibiting rearma-ment, as well as Japanese attitudes toward the military (see n. 13, p. 294). Any significant immediate increase in the role of the Japanese military is unlikely; every increase in the self-defense force has been very difficult to obtain. The present Japanese coalition rulers were all under the thumb of the Japanese militarists in the period of the thirties, and they have never forgotten that. It is most unlikely that Japan's leaders now or in the future will let the admirals and generals of Japan get out of hand. Hence, if there are changes in Japanese defense policy, they will be made by political leaders and not dictated by the Japanese military.

Japan has three choices regarding security policy. The first is to accept the peace constitution in its purest form and renounce the use of arms. The second is to carry on the present policy of a limited conventional buildup, combined with the renunciation of nuclear weapons sealed by signing the NPT. The third choice would be to work with the United States to build up a regional balance of power in the Western Pacific. Implicit in this course would be the eventual acquisition by Japan of nuclear weapons. Discussion of this subject in Japan is no longer taboo, although most members of the Japanese Diet (National Assembly) will not openly state their true position regarding nonproliferation.

change –   In the 1970s there may be a change in Japanese public opinion about the U.S. nuclear umbrella. For Japan, the American nuclear umbrella is an abstract concept unless it is associated directly with the U.S. Seventh Fleet. If the Seventh Fleet is ever removed from East Asian waters the Japanese people would think more seriously about their own defense. At the same time, the Japanese psychological mood about the Soviet Union and China may change. As Japan faces new situations there will be a shift in Japanese attitudes. Toward the latter part of the seventies the Japanese attitudes about the position of nuclear weapons may develop in a way that will be worth watching.

No one doubts that Japan has the potential for becoming a nuclear power in short order. As of now, the great majority of the Japanese people support the defense policy of the present government. The remainder tend to be pacifist, neutralist, or even antimilitarist. Whether or not a democratic Japan will go nuclear remains to be seen, but thus far Japan has kept this option open.

Japan's decision to adopt a disarmed neutrality or to acquire the great power status associated with the possession of nuclear arms will most likely be triggered by the failure of the existing nuclear powers to reach arms-control agreements that will safeguard Japan's legitimate security interests. The participation of Japan in crucial nuclear arms conferences may be the best way for her to find security while eschewing nuclear weapons.

Implications for India

Among the possible adverse effects of the proposed five-power nuclear arrangement is the motivation of the Indian government to develop its own nuclear weapons. There are two arguments against this prospect. The first is that the quasi-alliance formed between India and the Soviet Union should provide a nuclear guarantee against any Chinese attack—the only conceivable major threat confronting India.

The other is the state of the Indian economy. India's resources are fewer than those of China and far below the other members of the proposed nuclear club. Nevertheless, India does have the scientific and technical capacity to make nuclear weapons and may choose to do so in the next several years. For these reasons India should be invited to the proposed five-power conference as the spokesman of the nonnuclear nations. Her principal contribution would be to exert pressure upon the Big Five to stabilize the nuclear equation and hopefully reduce the power gap between the nuclear powers and the other countries. If this endeavor is unsuccessful and India does acquire political stability and sufficient economic potential, India might eventually be recognized as a major power center and treated accordingly. India's aspirations to become such a center were revealed in the 1971 war with Pakistan.

Changes in the UN Security Council

The best way to help design the new world of tomorrow is to endeavor to adjust the changing realities of the present to correspond more precisely with those which appear to be most significant in the future. The proposed five-power arms control conference points this way. Another major step in this same direction might be a realignment of the permanent membership of the United Nations Security Council to correspond with the major world powers of the seventies rather than to represent those regarded as most important at the time of the formation of the United Nations in 1945. This, in fact, is what is being done in the process of bringing the People's Republic of China into the United Nations and the granting of China's seat on the Security Council to Peking in place of Taipei.

If such realignment is carried to its obvious conclusion, Japan should also qualify as a permanent member of the Security Council. (Japan is already a senior member of two other major international organizations, namely, the World Bank and the International Monetary Fund.) There are obviously objections to such a move or there might be other claimants to a permanent seat on the Security Council, including the Federal Republic of Germany and perhaps India (Germany because of its tremendous economic vitality and India because of its large population).

There should also be created one European seat in the Security Council. This seat might help to foster the political cohesion of Western

Europe and at the same time assure that the most prestigious organizational structure of the United Nations would correspond to the overall power realities of the major political, economic, and military centers.

Multiple Power Centers and Global Stability

There is no present way of determining whether any specific array of power centers existing in the global system during the nuclear age will prove to be more stable than another. The only experience we have had thus far has been the bipolar system centering around the United States and the Soviet Union. There is the early possibility of the emergence of a tripolar system, comprising the United States, the Soviet Union, and China. This chapter suggests the subsequent emergence of a pentagonal power system, consisting of the United States, the Soviet Union, China, Japan, and Western Europe.

It is an underlying assumption of this chapter that the bipolar system, characterized by the unique superpower status of the United States and the Soviet Union, was inherently stable as long as the United States enjoyed a significant strategic advantage over the Soviet Union. This statement can be substantiated by the fact that there was no war between the two superpowers and that despite the frequency of local and limited conflicts in which both of the superpower protagonists were involved, either directly or indirectly, none of these various conflicts was escalated into an all-out global war. In addition, the one direct confrontation between the superpowers in the Cuban missile crisis came to a satisfactory conclusion for the United States primarily because of the immense strategic advantage enjoyed by the United States as well as the local conventional advantage the United States possessed in the waters and airspace surrounding Cuba. As to this point, McGeorge Bundy, Special Assistant to President Kennedy, in reflecting upon the value of strategic superiority during the missile crisis, stated that "this power should exist and . . . there should be confidence in its future as well as present effectiveness." [9]

Throughout the unique bipolar era of United States-Soviet superpower status, the Soviet Union engaged in the cautious pursuit of expansionist policies, whereas the United States adopted the broad political stance of the defense of the status quo. In the approximately twenty-five years of the confrontation between the two superpowers, Soviet power and influence have expanded relative to that of the United States. But it is a common observation among students of history that if a status quo power wishes to restrain an expansionist and/or revolutionary power, it must enjoy a preponderance of force, particularly in the more decisive areas of armaments. The United States enjoyed such an advantage until approximately 1970.

Since approximately 1970 the Soviet Union has surpassed the United States in some elements of strategic power, specifically in land-based intercontinental ballistic missile systems, in intermediate-range ballistic missiles poised against NATO Europe, in the payload of many of its intercontinental ballistic missiles, and in the associated higher explosive power of its nuclear warheads.

The United States enjoys a declining advantage in its strategic air forces. The unique advantage that the United States once had in sea-launched ballistic missiles is rapidly disappearing. In fact, the Soviet deployment of Polaris-type submarines is proceeding at such a rate that the United States lead in this area will be overcome by late 1972 or early 1973.[10] For these reasons it will no longer be credible for the United States to threaten to use its nuclear strike forces to sustain an extended deterrent to provide a nuclear umbrella for its allies in Western Europe and Eastern Asia. Consequently, unless some counter can be found for the growing Soviet strategic advantage, the world is likely to become increasingly unstable during the seventies.[11]

One need not impugn Soviet motives in entering into arms control discussions, including the present SALT, by observing that the Soviet military buildup has been most successful relative to the United States since the attainment of the Nuclear Test Ban Treaty of 1963 and the Non-Proliferation Treaty of 1968, and during the course of the SALT, which began in November 1969. In fact, Soviet intercontinental ballistic missile capabilities have increased at least 50 percent during the course of the SALT.

If we are moving into a situation in which the bipolar world seems to be disappearing, and if the relationship between the super-powers is tending to become an unstable one, what are the prospects for stability in a tripolar world—of the United States, the Soviet Union, and China?

A stable tripolar world requires that each point in the triangle must operate independently of the other two and resist the temptation to form bipolar alignments. Only in this fashion can a rough tripolar equilibrium be achieved. Theoretically, each state should keep its bilateral relationships to the others as limited as possible and only to those necessary for the maintenance of the equilibrium. Yet two of the pillars of this tripartite world operate under the philosophy of the dialectic that postulates a world of constant change and flux, in which equilibrium for the global system is sought while one's own advantage is promoted. But the stability or equilibrium is temporary and relative. It would appear that unremitting effort must be applied to seek, let alone achieve, or even further, to maintain, even a relative equilibrium. From the Chinese point of view, neither the Soviet Union nor the United States can be allowed to maintain a significant advantage over China. Consequently, as long as China lags far behind in the "objective" forces of power, Chinese relations with the other two members of the triangle are likely to be characterized by devious manipulations that cannot help but threaten the stability of the triangular world, since there would be no outside forces to regulate the stability of the tripolar system.

Until the Chinese acquire an assured second-strike capability, the stability of the deterrent of the tripolar system will probably be lower than at the present stage of the bipolar relationship between the United States and the Soviet Union.

Despite the disadvantages of a tripolar world, it would seem that the new diplomatic opening between the United States and China is a recognition on the part of both parties that there is some advantage in the tripolar world that cannot be found in the present superpower confrontation between the United States and the Soviet Union, and in a military clash between China and the Soviet Union. Whatever equilibrium that may be obtained in the tripolar world will be extremely sensitive to small fluctuations in relationships between the parties of the triangle. It may ultimately require that the three members of this system refrain as much from extensive cooperation with one another as from promoting irritations and conflicts with one another. The most sanguine hopes for the stability of the tripolar world require that ideological considerations be ignored. But the only conceivable tripolar system would comprise one nation having the traditional goals and objectives of a great power with two Communist states that appear committed to the ultimate reduction of the United States' influence and power. Ultimately, stability in the tripolar world would rest on the hope that neither of the Communist states would threaten the peace for fear that the other two world powers would combine against it.

This chapter argues that the tripolar world will be transitory and unstable and therefore that the United States should anticipate a transformation of the system by promoting the inclusion of two other power centers, namely, Western Europe and Japan. There is a good possibility that the transformation of the transient tripolar world into a pentagonal system will initially bring with it associated instability.

But if the five-power world seems inevitable, these instabilities must be anticipated, and the phasing of progress from the present into the future should require the diligent attention of the leaders of the power centers concerned.

Once the five-power world arrives, a logical case can be made for its inherent stability. In the first place, the expansionist powers [12] are likely to be the Soviet Union and China. Their ambitions will be restrained, unless there is complete elimination of their hostility, by their deep and pervasive conflict with each other. They will also be restrained by the fact that other power centers will be located nearby, namely, Western Europe, near to the Soviet Union, and Japan, near to both China and the Soviet Union. In the event of bilateral disputes between Western Europe and the Soviet Union, China and Japan, or the Soviet Union and Japan, there will be considerable incentive on the part of both Western Europe and Japan to seek the tacit support of the United States. This tacit support may help to ensure that conflicts and disputes between the Communist powers and the nearby non-Communist power centers will never reach the stage of major crisis or conflict.

Critique of Arms Control Conference Proposals

It seems obvious that the Soviet proposal for convening a conference of the five existing nuclear powers is advantageous from the Soviet point of view. My alternative—namely, the convening of a conference of the five most significant world power centers—is not necessarily advantageous to either the United States or the Soviet Union. Even if such a conference accelerated the development of a five-power global system, it cannot be demonstrated conclusively that such a world would be more inherently stable than the present one. Yet this possibility appears sufficiently high to justify presenting this concept in its present sketchy form.

The five-power conference for the purpose of creating a stricter climate of nonproliferation is especially desirable from the Soviet point of view. The minor nuclear powers (France, Britain, and China) are either allies of the United States or antagonists of the Soviet Union. Japan is an American ally. Hence a Soviet strategy to retain *U.S.* control over its allies' armaments, especially in Europe, is understandable. A nuclear Japan would probably distress China as well as the Soviet Union; West Germany with any form of access to nuclear weapons would be opposed by the Soviet Union. (It should be noted, however, that in the event of a war in Europe West German forces could be provided nuclear weapons under U.S. custodial arrangements.)

A Soviet-style five-power arms control treaty would be designed to achieve a long-standing Soviet goal: the reduction of the U.S. military presence in Europe. If we presume that the forces committed by the United States to Europe could reinforce the American deterrent, what the Soviets seek is the rapid decline of the U.S. strategic guarantees through a weakening of the American conventional link. In other words, before the Europeans create a joint nuclear force to substitute for, or assist, the U.S. deterrent, the viability of NATO's flexible response strategy could be greatly weakened.

A cursory examination of European security and our own defense planning reveals that the Soviets have about five years to whittle down NATO's defense capabilities. However, it will be at least that long also before the Chinese can really create a nuclear force that would be more than worrisome to the Soviets.

The Soviet Union hopes to forestall or at least slow the development of a significant European nuclear force by (1) convincing the United States that continued *détente* depends upon nonproliferation, and (2) exploiting a U.S. conventional winddown with (a) a powerful conventional "force in being" and (b) a superior nuclear counterforce capability, which is already coming into existence. The Soviet five-power conference, a conference on European security, and mutual and balanced force reductions (MBFR) are the political instruments chosen to achieve the reduction of U.S. presence in Western Europe.

My alternate proposal (a five-power-center conference) questions the assumption that limited proliferation is dangerous for the world and hence dangerous for the United States. The chief problem, however, is how to gain time to allow Western Europe to take significant strides toward political unification in the face of Soviet tactics aimed at sapping U.S. alliances before the new centers of power can emerge in Europe and Asia.

Under conditions of increasing integration in both economics and defense, Western Europe can be expected increasingly to go its own way. With recent U.S. economic contentions with Japan, that country, too, may be expected to loosen its policy dependence on the United States. Thus an offer by the United States to exercise nuclear restraint on WEU and Japan may be affected by its reduced influence vis-à-vis those countries. With U.S. rapprochement with China a possibility, and with continuing Sino-Soviet hostility, the Soviet Union cannot be expected to reduce its forces directed at the People's Republic of China.

A nuclear consortium for a politically integrated WEU (including Germany) and a nuclear Japan would create two strong, independent power centers geographically close to the western and eastern flanks of the Soviet Union. Soviet relations with these centers need not be hostile.

With a European nuclear consortium accompanied by increasing European integration, and with a nuclear Japan, the nuclear calculus would become vastly more complicated. Europe and Japan would surely act much more freely of the U.S. position on any matter. The resulting five-power world, even if more stable, would surely be a world of diminished U.S. influence. It is true that a five-power world may not be more unstable than a two-power one; still, such a world could demand greater sophistication in U.S. foreign policy moves.

A U.S. willingness to tolerate the acquisition of nuclear weapons by Japan and the development of WEU as a political community based initially on a British-French nuclear consortium might temper Soviet desires to continue the expansion of its strategic nuclear forces. There are conflicting views as to whether the United States or the Soviet Union would be most benefited if the international system evolves from the residual bipolarity through a triangular world to a five-power system. There is much to suggest that the Soviet Union is even more opposed to sharing nuclear power than is the United States. On the other hand, the Soviet effort to increase its intrinsic power position through the development of its strategic forces, through the development and ever-wider deployment of its naval forces, through its continued efforts to achieve a superior position in space, and through its quasi-military alliance and implied commitments to Egypt and India would indicate that the Soviet Union finds the prospect of the future world somewhat attractive, despite President Sadat's decision in 1972 to remove Soviet personnel from Egypt. Whether or not nature abhors a vacuum, the Soviet Union appears to anticipate with some pleasure the diminution of U.S. influence in many parts of the world and likewise the unwillingness or incapacity of the United States to maintain an equivalent position with it in the R&D race and in other aspects of national power.

The United States might find the conditions of a five-power world in general more attractive than continued competition with the USSR by sustaining or re-creating the conditions of a bipolar world. On the other hand, a very impressive case has been made by John R. Swanson that the transition from a bipolar to a multipolar world would involve a transition from Pax Americana to Pax Sovietica. Swanson's article to this effect concludes as follows:

> The mere equalization of American and Soviet power and influence would mean enormous changes in the character of international politics and spell the end of the *Pax Americana* which underlay nuclear bipolarity. It would mean a great increase in Soviet influence, largely at American expense. The fact that two of the likely future superpowers are present American allies, Western Europe and Japan, and the probability that the Soviet Union can keep its influence in Eastern Europe substantially intact while being able to withstand Chinese competition suggests at least an equalization of the American and Soviet power positions vis-à-vis the future superpowers.[13]

The outcome as stated above is not inevitable. Much will depend upon American willingness to maintain adequate forces and to sustain sufficient economic engagement with the rest of the world to play the role of "balancer." If this can be done, Pax Americana can disappear without being replaced with Pax Sovietica.

On September 30, 1971 the texts of a United States-Soviet agreement on measures to reduce the risk of nuclear warfare between the two countries and of an agreement to improve the direct communications link between them was signed by United States Secretary of State William P. Rogers and Soviet Foreign Minister Andrei A. Gromyko. Following the ceremonial signing, Mr. Gromyko stated: "The agreements signed today do not yet solve in any way the substance of the problem of limiting strategic armaments. This task is still outstanding and the participants in the talks should seek ways to solve it." [14]

Meanwhile, as the SALT continue, the United States government cannot safely overlook the immense increase in Soviet strategic forces that has taken place since the talks were begun in November 1969. If an agreement at the SALT is soon reached, the United States could urge nuclear restraint on both WEU and Japan if the Soviet Union reduced its nuclear missile capabilities in relation to WEU, China, and Japan (these are now far greater than those of the United States).

If, however, the Soviet strategic buildup continues with the conclusion of the SALT, the United States should change its policy. In this case it would seem evident that the Soviet Union is developing its nuclear capabilities for a *tous azimut* strategy. In response, the United States should advocate a nuclear consortium for WEU and the movement of Japan toward the acquisition of nuclear weapons.

As of now, Western Europe is not a power center in the sense of the United States, the Soviet Union, China, and Japan. Unless and until it becomes a political community, possessing an executive authority that will be responsible for West European security and foreign policy, Western Europe cannot be reckoned in the same scale with the other existing and emerging power centers. Further, Western Europe is caught between the United States and the Soviet Union. The Soviets have no interest in promoting the economic and political unity of Western Europe and are opposed to European moves toward integration, particularly if they are supported by the United States. Yet there is the possibility that the integration movement will receive a new impetus and may achieve sustained momentum after the British entry into the Common Market. If this happens and spurs the creation of a political community, a new and positive role for Western Europe on the world scene will become inevitable.

To some, the proposal presented might appear to be retrogressive, for by it the Germans could, through the WEU, have a different kind of access to nuclear weapons and the Japanese would also acquire nuclear weapons for the first time. On the other hand, this policy in a direct sense would encourage the creation of a genuine five-power world, which may prove to be inherently far more stable than the bipolar world that until very recently has characterized the global system since the end of the Second World War. It will be far more stable than the transitory tripolar world that may be emerging.

It would be far preferable if the five-power constellation could be created without nuclear strategic weapons. Whether this is possible rests largely on the conduct of the leaders of the USSR, who have apparently perceived the utility of a strategic military buildup as the necessary tool for making the Soviet Union the dominant world power.

Conclusion

The possibility of the world being organized around a five-nuclear-power core is not one advanced with great enthusiasm. It provides one method of preventing the Soviet Union from becoming the dominant world center, and this is the primary attraction of a new global power structure.

But efforts to move in this direction, which are implicit in the Nixon Doctrine, are made at the expense of the principles that dominated American foreign policy for a quarter of a century following the end of World War II. These were to contain communism within its geographical frontiers and simultaneously to construct a community of nations governed by the process of representative democracy. The United States and its allies achieved less success with containment than they did with building an association of free nations.

The idea that communism, contained within fixed geographical frontiers, bore the seeds of its own dissolution was never really tested, for the operational requirement—containment—was never fully achieved.

On the other hand, the creation of NATO, the World Bank, the European Economic Community, and the OECD, in which Japan was included, indicated a remarkable capacity for organizational innovation. Except for the European Common Market, the United States took the leadership role in the development of these political-economic infrastructures. The high tide in the effort to create an organized community of free nations based upon an Atlantic partnership was reached when President Kennedy delivered an inspiring speech—the Declaration of Interdependence at Philadelphia on July 4, 1962.

Unfortunately, the political will required to translate this dream into reality never materialized. In January 1963, President de Gaulle set back the Western march toward unity by several years when he vetoed Britain's first application for common market membership. The deep American involvement in Vietnam has helped divide the United States from Europe and even from Japan. When President Nixon took office in 1969, his options were severely limited because of popular antipathy toward the war in Vietnam and opposition to American foreign and national security policies premised on the principles we had pursued for the past quarter of a century.

Politics is the art of the possible. Support for the creation of a five-power world may be the best that can be done from the vantage point of Washington in 1972. A world with five nuclear power centers has obvious drawbacks. An adverse by-product of its development, as suggested in this chapter, would be the increased difficulty of policy coordination between Washington, Tokyo, and whatever might be the capital of the emerging new Europe. One of the difficulties of coordinating United States policies with those of its NATO allies during the past decade has been that no American President has wanted to permit London, Paris, or Bonn to have the opportunity to expose the United States to a nuclear risk that would automatically trigger a nuclear war with the Soviet Union. The problem has thus far been manageable because of the vast U.S. nuclear dominance within NATO. The Suez crisis of 1956 gave some insight as to what can happen if some members of an alliance act independently in ways that raise the nuclear specter. The failure, however, of the United States to support its British and French allies in their Suez adventure accelerated the development of independent nuclear forces by Britain and France.

This chapter does not suggest that the achievement of either an integrated Western European nuclear force or an independent Japanese nuclear capacity is inevitable; it does suggest that these developments are quite possible. If a de facto five-power world emerges, the United States will find that its interests are likely to be compatible with those of Western Europe and Japan. Consequently, the problem of nuclear collaboration is perhaps solvable if the will exists between the United States and its European and Japanese allies to coordinate their foreign and military policies and create practical arrangements for planning and coordinating the systems under which nuclear weapons might be employed. To create these arrangements will be a complicated and vexing problem. But if the emerging new world takes the form suggested in this chapter, arrangements for nuclear cooperation will inevitably become a key item in the analytical agenda of Japan, Western Europe, and the United States.

The foregoing problem can be avoided or reduced in scope if the leaders in Western Europe and Japan see greater utility in the earlier "grand design" for U.S. collaboration with them and if there are sufficient resources and time to bring it into being. Then the nations committed to representative government could sustain the efforts required to confront, negotiate, and deal with their totalitarian opponents.

But time is of the essence. The Soviet strategic arsenal has increased very considerably while the SALT have been in progress. Satellite photos, analyzed by the U.S. government, indicate that there has been a substantial buildup of more and better strategic weapons in the USSR and a doubling of the "production facilities for Soviet missile submarines." [15] Unless an arms control treaty on offensive strategic systems is quickly reached, the United States may feel impelled to expand its own nuclear arsenal to maintain strategic parity. In addition, we can also threaten the Soviet Union with a speedy proliferation unless a mutual winddown of strategic forces is agreed upon. We can delay proliferation by withholding information and assistance; we can accelerate it by providing our allies with both. In this context, the strategic arms limitation talks are far too important a matter to be left only to the United States and the Soviet Union. The other power centers discussed in this chapter have a direct interest in their outcome, and those world centers that have the greatest capacity to influence the world of tomorrow should begin dealing with those issues today.

NOTES

1. "U.S. Foreign Policy for the 1970's: Building for Peace," A Report to the Congress by Richard Nixon, President of the United States, February 25, 1971, pp. 4–5.

2. For the complete statement of the Soviet position, see *The Current Digest of the Soviet Press,* XXIII (July 20, 1971), p. 17.

3. *New York Times* (June 24, 1971), p. 10.

4. *New York Times* (September 29, 1971), p. 2.

5. The Western European Union (WEU) includes as members Belgium, France, the Federal Republic of Germany, Italy, Luxembourg, the Netherlands, and the United Kingdom.

6. Lawrence B. Krause, *Sequel to Bretton Woods: A Proposal to Reform the World Monetary System* (Washington, D.C.: The Brookings Institution, 1971), pp. 47–48.

7. Based upon William R. Kintner, "Japan and the U.S.—New Directions," *Freedom at Issue,* 9 (September-October 1971).

8. *New York Times* (August 10, 1971), pp. 14–15.

9. McGeorge Bundy, "The Presidency and the Peace," *Foreign Affairs,* 42, no. 3 (April 1964), p. 354.

10. "The Russians now have about 41 Y-class missile submarines ready or under construction, thus drawing abreast of the American Polaris submarine force" (*New York Times* [October 11, 1971], p. 9).

11. For an analysis of this situation, see William R. Kintner and Robert L. Pfaltzgraff, Jr., *Soviet Military Trends: Implications for U.S. Security,* American Enterprise Institute and Foreign Policy Research Institute Special Analysis, no. 6 (Washington, D.C., June 1971.).

12. Not necessarily with respect to territory.

13. John R. Swanson, "The Superpowers and Multipolarity: From Pax Americana to Pax Sovietica?" *Orbis* (Winter 1972), p. 22.

14. *New York Times* (October 1, 1971), p. 14.

15. *New York Times* (October 11, 1971), p. 1.

Dynamics of the Bargaining Process in a Bureaucratic Age

THE PAPERS PRESENTED in this session studied a range of problems in negotiating arms control agreements. They examined these problems in several contexts, including the effect of a changing international system upon negotiations between the United States and the Soviet Union, the nature of the arms control bargaining process, and the major asymmetries between the superpowers that affect bargaining outcomes.

The discussion focused on the following general topics:

1. the international system: milieu for the SALT,
2. the nature of the bargaining process,
3. the components of an agreement, and
4. the possible effects of a strategic arms control agreement.

The International System: Milieu for the SALT

TRANSFORMATION OF THE SYSTEM

A widespread consensus that a fundamental change is occurring in the nature of the international system exists among knowledgeable international relations analysts. The views expressed during this session of the symposium reflect this consensus. The general transformation was seen as being one from superpower dominance to multilateralism and greater distribution of power. To this was added the viewpoint that the international system will probably go through a tripolar phase before attaining a multipolar configuration. During the tripolar phase, the relationships among the People's Republic of China (PRC), the Soviet Union, and the United States will be of major importance. This triangular phase will be a critical factor in the evolution of strategic arms control agreements in the 1970s.

It was posited that as tripolarity changes to multipolarity, two other

---

In addition to those presenting papers discussants included Amrom Katz, Evgeny Kutovoj, Charles Burton Marshall, Uri Ra'anan, and Seymour Weiss. Edmond A. Gullion served as chairman for this session.

states will become important factors in the system. Japan will exert an increasing influence based principally on its economic strength. The other "state" will be a conglomeration of European nations, possibly represented under the designation of the Western European Union (WEU). Included in such a European grouping would be the United Kingdom, France, Italy, the Benelux, and the German Federal Republic. The assumption that Japan and Western Europe will emerge as global actors is based on the premise that both will possess a credible nuclear deterrent capability. If such a capacity is attained by each in a manner that limits proliferation, the resulting nuclear configuration might serve to (1) constrain Soviet expansionist tendencies; (2) stabilize the international system; and (3) promote, to some extent, conditions more conducive to attaining a form of world "peace." In such a system neither of the two superpowers would have hegemony.

If no agreement is reached at the SALT and the Soviet buildup continues, the United States might be forced to acquiesce in the development of a nuclear consortium for the Western European Union and the acquisition of nuclear weapons by Japan. These remarks spurred comment that encouraging a limited proliferation of nuclear weapons would possibly result in an unwillingness on the part of the superpowers to make any limiting agreement on strategic weapons now or in the future if they felt that others might be seeking ways to overcome their leads in the nuclear field.

Several possible implications arising from the pentagonal model were mentioned. First, if the nations of Europe, under the WEU arrangement, were included in disarmament talks, there would be a greater incentive for European unification than would otherwise be the case. Such an arrangement would limit the growth of pressures in the German Federal Republic to seek on its own some means of reconciling its lack of political influence with its great economic strength. Although a West German "finger-on-the-trigger" possibility would be excluded, access to some form of command and control participation could serve to enhance Bonn's prestige in its own eyes and in those of the world.

In addition to emphasizing the possibility of a nuclear Japan and a European nuclear capability, it was proposed that India might be included in disarmament arrangements as the spokesman of the nonnuclear nations if it chose to eschew the development of atomic weapons. Moreover, the need would develop for some structural rearrangement of the United Nations to compensate for the changed nature of the international system.

CURRENT RELATIONSHIPS IN THE INTERNATIONAL SYSTEM

On a less theoretical level the current relationships among China, the Soviet Union, and the United States were analyzed by several individuals. In presenting his paper, Robert Scalapino outlined the general nature of the Sino-Soviet relationship, the Sino-American relationship, and the Soviet-American relationship. In the Sino-Soviet split the complexity of the causation matrix was stressed. Simplistic views emphasizing contemporary factors but ignoring historical cleavages between the two powers were regarded as of little use in understanding the problem. Nevertheless, if emphasis is placed on current developments, two considerations should be taken into account. First, ideology must be understood as affecting more the style than the substance of the Sino-Soviet rift. Second, the difficulty of reconciliation was noted, especially in regard to the fact that the basic hostility between the two powers has domestic roots in both societies. These and other factors make it likely that future relations between the Soviet Union and China will be characterized by hostility, intense competition, and ideological polemics, which, however, will not result in open warfare.

The remarks during the discussion on the new developments in Sino-American relations reflected uncertainty over the future direction of the rapprochement. It was suggested that the main reason that the United States has decided to seek a new relationship with China at this time is that no critical issues in Asia can be settled without the involvement of Peking. In addition, several possible mutual interests between Peking and Washington were suggested. First, it is probably in the interest of both powers to deter any possible Soviet military move against China. An open conflict between the two Communist giants would have too many dangerous ramifications to be encouraged by Washington. Second, China and the United States appear to have a common interest in supporting greater autonomy for countries on the periphery of the Soviet Union, especially those in Eastern Europe.

Several factors were seen as possibly leading Peking to improve its relationship with Washington. First, fear of a possible resurgence of Japanese militarism may have motivated China to seek some understanding with the United States in order to impede the possible development of a Japanese nuclear capacity. Second, with growing pressure from the Soviet Union, China might be trying to lessen the possibility of a two-front confrontation with the superpowers. This argument was similar to the one that sees the Soviet *détente* diplomacy in Europe as a prelude to keeping the Western front quiet while focusing on China. It seemed possible that the Chinese may be thinking in similar terms. Third, China may perceive the Nixon Doctrine as a signal that the United States, in the withdrawal stage, can be pressured into accepting Peking's hegemony in Asia. Moreover, believing that the American arming of countries such as Thailand and the Philippines will take time, the Chinese may believe that some agreement that would halt these developments might be reached with the United States. To be sure, Chinese motivations were seen as more extensive and complex than these three possibilities indicate.

The Soviet-American relationship received extensive attention in the first session of the symposium. Therefore, only a few general remarks were addressed to this subject during this meeting. It was again emphasized that the relationship remains a conflictual one. Basic asymmetries (discussed more fully in the next section) were seen to exist between the two nations, making difficult any substantial mutuality of interests on a wide range of issues.

In summary, the triangular relationship that now exists in the system was seen as one marked mainly by extensive conflicts that are likely to continue but at a level below open warfare. Under such conditions the question of the stability or instability of any specific agreement or relationship would have to be couched in terms of who finds it stable and in what context.

The Nature of the Bargaining Process

Negotiations on strategic arms limitation are likely to remain bilateral. China, it was noted, has not evidenced any appreciable interest in participating in the discussions. Peking was seen as being more interested at present in expanding its strategic capacity in order to deter the Soviet Union in a more credible manner and exert greater influence in Asia. It is unlikely that Peking would be interested in the proposed Five-Power Nuclear Disarmament Conference. The only Chinese initiative in the arms control area has been the call for a no-first-use pledge from the existing nuclear powers. Although it was suggested that now is the best time to include China in the SALT structure (because as Peking expands its nuclear capacity, the possibility will grow that the United States and the Soviet Union will be motivated to scrap any agreement on limitation in order to remain ahead of the Chinese), there was little conviction that China is inclined to join in the talks at the present time. This prompted the observation that since the European and

Asian milieus are dissimilar, separate regional approaches to arms control are required. To include the Chinese in the process may entail the formation of a distinctive approach to Asian concerns.

The continued bilateral nature of the negotiations led to a consideration of the approaches of the two sides to the negotiations. Basic asymmetries exist between the two parties, but it was noted that a prerequisite for strategic arms control is a mutual interest in decoupling the strategic equation from their basic hostility and intense rivalry. The United States appears willing to do this. It was seen as questionable that the Soviet Union is similarly inclined. Soviet emphasis on the political uses of military power at least makes it unlikely that such a decoupling has taken place. Thus, although the SALT might serve Soviet purposes by codifying strategic parity, "feeding" *détente,* and promoting the decoupling of the American guarantee from Western Europe and Japan, it might prove impossible to reach a comprehensive agreement because of Soviet refusal to decouple the issues. However, as was noted by several participants, an agreement might result if the United States desired one so much that it would risk giving the Soviet Union a psychological, if not moral, edge in nuclear weaponry.

A second asymmetry was posited to exist in that the Soviet Union has continued to advocate expansion of the SALT into a general conference on disarmament, whereas the United States has sought to maintain a conservative building-block approach to the problem of arms control.

A third area of asymmetry exists in relation to the differing strategic calculi used by the parties. An example of this difference would be the difficulty that the United States has had in understanding the rationale behind the Soviet development of the SS-9. From this experience, one participant remarked the United States should have learned that it did not understand the Soviet strategic calculus and vice versa.

Another possible area of asymmetry was brought out by the question: What part does the Soviet strategic buildup play in the bargaining process? This evoked several answers. There was general agreement that the Soviet arms buildup should be viewed as part of the bargaining process but in a wider perspective than just the SALT. The Soviet reaction to the Cuban missile crisis was emphasized as a key determinant in understanding why the Soviet Union continues to accelerate its strategic weapons program. The Soviets do not wish to be in a position of inferiority again should a direct confrontation with the United States occur. Currently, the Soviet buildup could also be viewed as a concentrated effort to gain increased influence in Europe and Asia. This aspect of the Soviet approach is linked closely with the problem of the political influence issuing from nuclear weaponry.

One participant offered an alternative explanation, stating that conceivably a momentum builds up in arms procurement beyond the military needs of a nation. Although this comment was made in reference to China, it could apply also to the Soviet buildup.

Several other asymmetries were suggested in the form of questions. Is there an asymmetry in the positions of Washington and Moscow regarding (a) both short- and long-term political objectives, (b) domestic constraints on policy-making and implementation, and (c) the credibility of national will to do whatever is necessary to attain political objectives deemed important? If the SALT are viewed as politics carried on by other means, then strategy and tactics at the SALT and the potential political and psychological fallout from such negotiations would have to be examined in the light of such asymmetries.

Aside from the effect of asymmetries in determining the general milieu in which the SALT take place, other important considerations were raised. First, it was pointed out that the U.S. approach to the SALT has changed. Originally, the Nixon Administration approached the SALT from the viewpoint that the United States would cooperate with the Soviets in the SALT if they embarked on policies of accommodation elsewhere. This linkage pattern has been inverted to the point that the United States appears to be "cooling it" in certain areas in order to keep the SALT going. Thus, the SALT, instead of being used by the United States as the stick, have now become a driving force in U.S. diplomacy.

Several participants commented on the need to give greater emphasis to Soviet internal considerations, both for an understanding of their bargaining postures and as an aid in determining the best posture for the United States. Concerning the Soviet buildup, it was noted that it is not in the nature of internal Soviet decision-making to supply large numbers of missiles only to remove them because of an arms control agreement. Therefore, it would be erroneous to conclude that the missiles now in place can be assumed to be part of the bargaining trade-offs that the Soviet Union would offer in the SALT.

Some discussion focused on developing U.S. bargaining positions in the light of certain internal Soviet realities. It was suggested that the existence of factional rivalries in the Soviet Union makes it important that the United States determine what bargaining position will best support those groups in the Soviet Union which hold views most favorable to U.S. interests.

Several comments during this session raised the issue of the economic costs of the arms race. Several participants suggested that one cannot really tell how much is being spent on the arms race. Neither can one determine from present statistics if an increase has occurred during the last ten years in terms of real dollars. It is likely that any savings arising from a strategic arms limitation agreement would be reinvested by the Soviet Union in other types of weaponry. If this is the case, then it would be very difficult to conclude that one of the Soviet rationales for participating in the SALT is the possibility of economic savings that could be rechanneled into the domestic area.

The issue of developments that might pose special problems during the negotiation process was mentioned. A central problem is the effect of ongoing weapons programs during the negotiations. Neither side can afford to restrain itself unilaterally for very long in the hope that the other side will reciprocate. Thus, if a Soviet buildup continues, the chance that it will trigger a reaction leading to a mobilization of the superior U.S. resources and productive capacity designed to strengthen U.S. weaponry programs will increase. If the current domestic milieu in the United States, which militates against such a reaction, turns out to be transitory, then such a development could become a real Soviet concern.

Robert Bowie's remarks emphasized the need to examine how the process of negotiation itself is organized. One factor that will surely affect the outcome of the SALT is the general exchange of information that might lead to a clearer understanding of the strategic thinking of the other party. A second characteristic of the negotiations might be that the participants will begin to identify and argue about off-setting advantages in the two asymmetrical force postures. Such arguments would make agreement more difficult to achieve but more stable once it was achieved.

Some concluding remarks on the nature of the bargaining process focused on the question: Why the SALT? Several answers were given. First, there may be actual intrinsic value in the type of agreement that was concluded in the SALT. Second, the SALT may be quite valuable as a precursor of future developments. Several participants suggested that the SALT will probably continue as a process after initial agreement is reached, even if only in the form of modification and refinement of the original agreement. Third, even if no agreement is reached, the process of negotiation might prove beneficial since it brought the superpowers together in a discussion of highly complex issues that may serve to clear up several dangerous misconceptions that may have existed. However, this view of the possible benefit of the SALT was countered by the suggestion that parties to such negotiations usually talk past each other. From the U.S. viewpoint, agreement now may be the best available option. Besides, if parity already exists in fact, why not codify it now? The opportunity to do so is likely to decrease over time.

The Components of an Agreement

Several general requirements of an agreement were outlined in the discussion. First, explicit understanding as to what had been agreed upon would be necessary. Second, there should be an unlimited right of withdrawal, given certain violations or changed conditions that would make continued adherence to an agreement dangerous from a national point of view. Third, the agreement should provide for periodic reexamination that would allow needed revisions of the agreement or the addition of new signatories. Finally, the agreement should be designed in such a manner as to make it provisional and recognizable as only a first step rather than a completed transaction.

The outlining of these general requirements stimulated a consideration of certain important technical problems. The problem of verification received the most attention. It was noted that under other agreements the failure rate in verification could be relatively high without leading to abrogation or extensive destabilization. However, under certain forms of a strategic arms limitation agreement, it would be important to have a relatively high successful rate of verification, since one failure might be fatal.

It was further pointed out that one of the main problems of verification was the differing nature of the U.S. and Soviet political systems and the resulting idiosyncratic natures of information disclosure. It has been necessary that both sides know as much about the capabilities of the other as may be necessary to ensure the preservation of deterrence. It was noted that the United States has a fairly open system of disclosure whereas the Soviet Union, by the nature of its society, is not given to open disclosure. Nevertheless, the Soviets have made qualitative disclosures through such means as parades, photographs, or intelligence networks by which the United States monitors developments in the Soviet Union. However, if the Soviet Union should ever decide that it is not in its interest to cooperate with the United States in disclosing Soviet developments, then knowledge of these developments would be difficult for the United States to obtain. Therefore, the verification problem must remain a central concern to U.S. planners in evolving the type of agreement at the SALT that would be acceptable to the United States.

Discussion then turned to the domestic political problems that would confront the U.S. government if the national interest demanded abrogation of the SALT agreements. It was noted that the Soviet leadership would not face similar problems in such an instance because of the authoritarian nature of the Soviet political system. In accord with this asymmetry, two factors would largely determine how readily the United States could withdraw from an agreement in case of Soviet violations. First, if the evidence of a Soviet violation were unequivocal in nature, it would be much easier to rally domestic support for abrogation. Second, if the type of evidence of such Soviet violation were convincing in its sophistication, then elite support would probably be relatively easy to obtain. However, it would be more likely that, since neither of these conditions would be met completely, domestic disquietude over U.S. moves to abrogate an agreement would arise. To compensate for this problem, an extensive effort might be made to educate the public as to the real implications of an agreement in the SALT and the need to be able to invoke a criterion of self-help if dangerous violations occur.

The concluding remarks regarding the components of a possible agreement emphasized the point that under the conditions peculiar to the SALT, an informal agreement might be best suited to achieving constructive purposes. However, given the expectations engendered by the negotiations themselves, informality may not be a viable alternative.

The Possible Effects of a Strategic Arms Control Agreement

Several comments were made regarding the possible results of a strategic arms limitation agreement:

a. The key consideration was the effect that an agreement would have on the political aspects of the continuing technological competition with the Soviet Union.

b. Success or failure of the agreement would be determined by subsequent, at present unforeseeable, developments.

c. No matter what the form of agreement, the possibility of a Soviet temptation to initiate nuclear war was seen as practically nil.

Thus the real question would be: What are the possible *political* implications of the situation? In the United States there would be a great danger of a euphoria developing, which might decrease American ability to respond to future Soviet threats.

d. After the patterns of agreement become somewhat fixed, it would be more difficult to bring other parties into the process.

PART IV

GEOFFREY KEMP

IAN SMART

SALT and European Nuclear Forces

Introduction

WHETHER OR NOT the United States and the Soviet Union reach a formal agreement to impose limits on their strategic armaments, the European NATO countries, and especially Britain and France, will soon have to make some decisions concerning their own actual or potential nuclear forces—even if they are only decisions to do nothing. The precise nature of the issues they will face must, however, owe something to the formal and informal outcomes of the SALT. It is the purpose of this chapter to point out some of the questions about nuclear forces that West Europeans will have to face over the next ten years, to suggest some of the major constraints that will influence European options, and to indicate how those options might be weighed against each other.

The emphasis of this chapter is upon technical, economic, and strategic considerations rather than upon political questions. We should stress at the outset that we intend to be deliberately vague in our interpretation of the terms "Europe" and "Europeans," as well as about the possible political context for future European nuclear co-operation. We do not wish to imply any judgment about the possible ways in which Western Europe might organize itself politically or about the possible identity of the West European units that might, in the future, exercise political control over nuclear forces. Obviously, such political questions are of vital importance and cannot, in the last analysis, be dissociated from the strategic, technical, and economic factors upon which we do intend to focus. However, a case can be made for initially analyzing the West European situation in a way that excludes politics. Although there have been many general statements about the political desirability—or undesirability—of West European cooperation in nuclear matters, and even about the political advantages of specific joint research, development, testing, evaluation, procurement, and deployment arrangements for nuclear forces, very little factual analysis of alternative strategic requirements and costs seems to have been carried out, at least for public consumption. A chapter that avoids the temptation to make easy judgments about what is politically desirable, in order to examine what is technically and economically feasible, may conceivably offer a useful antidote.

The political reasons for nuclear cooperation among allies obviously reflect something more than calculations about force requirements, economic costs, and technical measures of effectiveness. They mirror a wide spectrum of motives, including the desire for national or regional prestige, the belief that nuclear weapons buy a "ticket to the top table," and the urge to have insurance against future changes in the world alliance system. (It is not totally absurd to argue, for instance, that one reason why Britain and France would not wish to abandon their current nuclear forces may be uncertainty about the behavior of future United States and German governments, rather than more traditional fears regarding Soviet or Chinese behavior.) In other words, the political arguments for and against certain levels of nuclear force cannot be neatly summarized in a quantitative fashion. They are based, in part, upon subjective interpretations of national or regional interest that defy quantification or exact definition.

Although the political aspects of European nuclear cooperation can be *discussed* without reference to the technical, economic, and strategic factors (just as the latter can also be discussed without reference to the former), political *decisions* cannot avoid the realities that these factors represent. One purpose, then, of this chapter is to suggest a method for preparing an apolitical agenda of European nuclear options from which criteria could be drawn for assessing the practical relevance of politically founded propositions.

For obvious reasons, most of the available examples of medium-power nuclear options in Europe refer to British and French experience in this field.[1] The types of technical and economic calculations that have to be made by these two countries are not dissimilar, however, to those that a government in, say, Bonn or Rome would need to make if it wished to cooperate with Britain or France or to develop its own "independent" capability—nor, indeed, to the calculations that would have to be made in connection with a nuclear force to be controlled by some future West European political entity. Thus, although most of the arguments in this chapter may appear to have a direct application to British and French alternatives, we are, in reality, discussing West European alternatives in general.

Although we have made no judgment about the future political organization of Western Europe, we have made certain assumptions, which should be explicitly stated, about the strategic expectations and aspirations of the West European countries within the North Atlantic Alliance.

First, it has been assumed that "Europe" (which we shall use here as a shorthand expression for the *West* European members of NATO) will continue to wish to maintain some strategic nuclear capability within Western Europe during the late 1970s and 1980s, irrespective of SALT outcomes, of a European Security Conference agreement on conventional force levels, or of greater cooperation among the NATO allies.[2]

Second, although the only European countries that now possess some independent nuclear capability are Britain and France, standing separately, we have assumed that future cooperation between these two powers, possibly in a wider association with other European NATO members such as West Germany and Italy, is not ruled out.

A third assumption is that, *for purposes of force design and planning,* the Soviet Union will continue to be the adversary against which a European nuclear force is to be directed. This is not meant to downgrade the importance that independent nuclear forces may have, in the present or future, vis-à-vis other powers. It does, however, simplify the analysis to focus solely upon the Soviet contingency. Moreover, it seems reasonable to suppose that, in the foreseeable future, any European nuclear force will at least have to be rationalized publicly in terms of its utility against the Soviet Union.

Against this background, a fourth, and qualifying, assumption is that the options practically available to the Europeans over the next ten years do not include either the procurement of nuclear delivery systems capable of launching a successful counterforce first strike against Soviet strategic weapons or the adoption of a "launch on warning" policy for second-strike forces. Thus, in all planning, the Europeans will have to assume that their nuclear forces must be prepared to ride out a Soviet first strike against military and civilian targets.

A fifth, critical assumption is that, for the foreseeable future, the Soviet Union will continue to see the United States as its primary nuclear adversary, with China as a secondary preoccupation of growing importance. Thus, in planning for its own national security, the Soviet Union will not be able to treat the threat posed by a European nuclear force in a way that has no reference to American and Chinese nuclear and nonnuclear force levels and capabilities. It can be argued that this constraint would continue to have major implications for a West European-Soviet deterrence relationship even if, for example, no formal United States commitment to the strategic defense of the European members of NATO were to persist. Only if the Europeans had to assume a joint Soviet-American or Soviet-American-Chinese threat to Western Europe would the problem of maintaining "adequate" deterrent forces be very different from that which we have here assumed to exist.

A sixth assumption is that the primary purpose of a European nuclear force would be to deter the Soviet Union from behavior considered to threaten some security interest asserted, and recognized, as vital to the political unit in control of the force. An assumption that will not be made, however, is that an ability to inflict any *unique* level of second-strike damage on Soviet targets is required to attain this necessarily flexible goal. The critical judgment concerning the capabilities required to deter Soviet leaders in specific circumstances (which we do not purport to predict) falls outside our defined terms of reference. Instead, therefore, a plausibly wide range of alternative force levels required to inflict different levels of damage upon Soviet targets will be suggested.

A seventh assumption, deriving from those already stated, is that the purpose of a European nuclear force will be to threaten certain levels of damage to Soviet population and industrial centers, rather than to Soviet military targets. In very broad terms, the concept of "assured destruction," as it is generally understood in Western circles, will be assumed throughout this text, to the exclusion of more recondite strategies.

An eighth assumption is that the future design of European strategic nuclear forces will be based upon submarine-launched ballistic missile (SLBM) systems broadly comparable to the U.S. Polaris and Poseidon and to their British, French, and Soviet counterparts. This assumption reflects two preliminary assessments we have made concerning the scope of European options and the strategic environment over the next ten years. First, we have judged that a mix of land-based and sea-based nuclear forces, analogous to the combined U.S. force of intercontinental ballistic missiles (ICBMs), bombers, and submarines (the so-called "triad" system), would prove too expensive for any realistic coalition of European powers within the next decade. Second, we have judged that a major breakthrough in Soviet antisubmarine warfare (ASW) capabilities, *sufficient to pose a greater threat to European submarines than could be posed, at comparable cost, to European land-based systems,* is most unlikely to occur, at least during the next ten years.

The method of analysis used in composing the following paragraphs has been based upon developing and examining a representative selection of the types of technical, economic, and strategic questions that Europeans will need to face, given the above list of assumptions and given also what seem to be plausible alternative outcomes of the SALT. A brief discussion of the current status of British and French nuclear forces in relation to current Soviet capabilities is followed by a more speculative discussion of the range of nuclear options that face Europeans, given alternative Soviet strategic force levels.

The Present Status of British and French Nuclear Forces

Britain's strategic nuclear delivery systems now (1972) consist of four nuclear-powered submarines (SSBNs), each with 16 *Polaris* A3 missiles procured from the United States but fitted with British re-entry vehicles and warheads. The original decision to build a fifth SSBN was rescinded by the British Labour Government in 1965 and plans for it were placed in suspense.

Britain retains some 56 operational Vulcan bomber aircraft, with a maximum theoretical range, unrefueled, of about 4,000 miles. These previously constituted the British strategic force but have now been relegated to a tactical role. They are no longer considered by the British government to serve any strategic purpose but, given their low-level penetration capability and the ability of many of them to deliver the Blue Steel standoff missile, they could not be entirely ignored by the Soviet Union, especially since they might now be used in conjunction with other, more sophisticated delivery systems.

In addition, Britain operates 13 strike/light bomber squadrons containing about 150 nuclear-capable strike aircraft, which are now equipped with nuclear weapons of British construction; these weapons are under British control. These aircraft, which include Canberra (i.e., B-57) light bombers and Buccaneer and F-4 Phantom strike aircraft, are based in Britain, on the European mainland, and on the two remaining aircraft carriers currently in service with the Royal Navy. In theory, all have sufficient range to reach certain Soviet targets.[3] They are not, however, intended to play a strategic role and, in practice, cannot be considered to enhance Britain's strategic capability against the Soviet Union to any significant extent.

France's strategic nuclear forces consist, at present, of three squadrons of Mirage IVA light bombers (36 operational aircraft plus some 22 in reserve) and one squadron of nine intermediate-range ballistic missiles (IRBMs) (SSBS, *sol-sol balistique stratégique*). A second squadron of nine IRBMs is to become operational during 1972. Meanwhile, the first French nuclear-powered ballistic-missile submarine (SNLE, *sous-marin nucléaire lance-engins*) was scheduled to enter operational service in 1972, to be followed by at least three more SNLEs by 1976–77. (Plans for a fifth SNLE exist, but no firm decision to build it seems yet to have been taken.) Each SNLE will carry 16 missiles (MSBS, *mer-sol balistique stratégique*) of French design and manufacture.

France is also developing a short-range tactical missile, Pluton. However, its range will only be 60 to 75 miles and it is, in any case, not expected to be in operational service until 1973 or later.

France operates 16 squadrons containing about 175 strike and fighter-bomber aircraft (Étendard IV, Mirage III, Mystère IV, and F-100). A number of the carrier-based Étendard IVs and land-based Mirage IIIs are capable of delivering free-fall nuclear weapons. None of these, however, can be considered to have a plausible strategic capability against Soviet targets.

The characteristics and capabilities of British and French strategic delivery systems vary widely. On the British side, the Polaris A3 missiles have a range of 2,500 nautical miles (n.m.) and are equipped with three British-made multiple re-entry vehicles (MRVs), each of which is capable of carrying a nuclear warhead with an approximate yield of 200 kilotons (KT) and of delivering it with an estimated accuracy of 0.8 n.m. (4,864 feet) CEP.[4] On the French side, the Mirage IVA aircraft have a maximum speed of Mach 2.2, a maximum theoretical range, unrefueled, of about 2,000 miles, and are equipped with free-fall bombs of about 60 KT yield. The SSBS missiles carry a single re-entry vehicle (RV), with a warhead of some 150 KT, and have a range of about 1,600 n.m. The first French MSBS missiles, when they enter service, will have a 1,200 n.m. range and will carry a single warhead of about 500 KT. No reliable estimates of SSBS and MSBS accuracy are available.

Some of these characteristics are significant. The limited range of French IRBMs means, for example, that they can only reach targets in the western part of the European territories of the Soviet Union, their maximum range being roughly indicated by an arc from Onega, on the White Sea, through Gorkiy and Volgograd, to Leninakan, on the Turkish frontier. Even with in-flight refueling, for which they rely on 12 KC-135 tanker aircraft (procured from the United States), the maximum operational radius of the Mirage IVA squadrons is likely to be even more narrowly circumscribed, barely taking in Leningrad and Moscow. French SNLEs, when they are available, will obviously provide much greater targeting flexibility. Even then, however, the short range of their original MSBS missiles will act as a constraint. From the SNLE base at Brest, only the Baltic states and the western borders of Byelorussia and the Ukraine will be accessible, while their major patrol options would appear to be restricted to threatening the Moscow and Leningrad areas from the North or Norwegian Seas or threatening the Donets-Dnepr basin from the eastern Mediterranean.

In contrast, the British strategic force is, in this respect, much less seriously constrained. The greater range of the Polaris A3 missile enables British SSBNs to threaten all of Soviet territory by exploiting alternative firing positions in the Greenland Sea, the eastern Atlantic, the Mediterranean, the Arabian Sea, the Bay of Bengal, and the north-western Pacific. Indeed, A3 missiles fired even from the British SSBN base at Faslane, on the River Clyde, can reach Soviet targets as far eastward as Omsk.

British SSBNs have another apparent advantage over the current French forces in terms of their survivability. The Mirage IVAs, even if dispersed in small numbers to "alert" bases, are necessarily vulnerable to a Soviet first strike, as are the associated KC-135 tankers. Because of their short endurance and the heavy expense involved, no attempt has been made to maintain elements of the Mirage IVA force on airborne alert. It must be assumed, therefore, that the whole of the force will be on the ground at the moment when a Soviet attack is launched. By depending upon the NATO air defense ground environment (NADGE) system, its French commanders might expect to have some brief warning of an attack by Soviet aircraft. There is no evidence, however, that they could expect sufficient warning of a Soviet missile attack to "scramble" more than a very small proportion of the force. As to the SSBS (IRBM) force, its silos, although hardened, could hardly withstand a large-scale Soviet missile attack, while the ability of the French President to launch it "on warning"—even if such a policy were politically acceptable—would again be restricted by the lack of any adequate ballistic missile early-warning system.

The survivability of British SSBNs (and, in the future, of French SNLEs) must be rated much more highly. It can be assumed that a Soviet first strike would destroy the submarine bases at Faslane and Brest, with all their contents, including any submarines then in port. The British, however, normally maintain two of their four SSBNs on firing station at all times—a task made easier by the proximity of the Faslane base to several of the potential patrol areas (although, for relatively short periods, the effect of the long refit cycle is to reduce this number to one). Some part of the British deterrent force is thus always invulnerable to a Soviet missile or aircraft attack on British territory. By 1976–77, when the fourth French SNLE is expected to enter service, France will be in a similar position. Indeed, at least one French SNLE should always be on firing station by 1974–75. Until then, the insufficient number of SNLEs and the demands of the long refit cycle will mean that, for about one-third of the time, there will be no French SNLE on patrol.

On the assumption, already stated, that future West European strategic forces will have to be based upon submarine-launched missile systems, it is reasonable to concentrate attention here upon the British and French SSBN/SNLE forces in considering the utility of the deterrents that Britain and France now have available. The choice is further justified by the apparently high vulnerability of other available systems to a Soviet first strike. Indeed, for the sake of simplicity and because French SNLEs are not yet in service, the area for examination can be narrowed still further, to the British SSBN force alone. Much of what will be said about that force can be extrapolated to apply to the French SNLEs when they become operational. It must be borne in mind, however, that the relevant French missiles will have a shorter range than the Polaris A3 and that there may be significant differences between the two systems in terms of their ability to withstand Soviet countermeasures.

Assessing the deterrent utility of the British SSBN/Polaris A3 force demands, at least, the evaluation of four separate, composite probabilities:

1. the probability that the British SSBN or SSBNs on firing station or at sea en route to firing stations will survive the efforts of Soviet ASW forces for long enough to fire at the selected second-strike targets;

2. the probability that the SSBN or SSBNs will receive any necessary commands from the British government and will, in fact, launch missiles against Soviet targets;

3. the probability that the missiles fired will perform efficiently, will, where relevant, penetrate any Soviet defenses (e.g., the Galosh Antiballistic Missile [ABM] system around Moscow), will reach their targets, will detonate, and will inflict the planned level of damage upon population and industry;

4. the probability that the targets threatened by this capability will

be of sufficient value to the Soviet government to constitute a foundation for deterrence.

It would, of course, be impossible in a chapter of only this length to consider each of those factors in detail. In addition, a precise evaluation would require access to classified information, which we do not have. It would also require us to make judgments concerning the psychology of the Soviet leadership in time of crisis—an area in which information is, perhaps, even more difficult to come by. What we can do is make some brief points under each of the four headings mentioned.

SURVIVAL FROM ASW ATTACK

Given the present state of ASW techniques, the odds seem still to be in favor of the hunted and against the hunter. Moreover, British SSBNs can exploit certain natural advantages. Egress from their home port, which can be masked by other submarines and surface activities, takes them into a continental shelf area that presents serious problems for the effective operation of ASW sonar. Passage to many of their likely firing stations involves relatively short transit distances, during all or most of which they can continue to exploit continental shelf characteristics. Some patrol areas are likely to be used also by United States SSBNs, the presence of which may both confuse and diffuse Soviet operations; it is unlikely, in fact, that more than a small proportion of the total Soviet ASW effort would be directed at the one or two British SSBNs on patrol. Taking all factors into account, we have no reason to suppose that the probability of a British SSBN surviving Soviet ASW action for long enough to fire all its missiles would be less than 0.5.[5]

COMMAND AND CONTROL

The main British very low frequency (VLF) radio station, reported to be at Rugby, must be considered vulnerable to a Soviet first strike. However, a great deal of redundancy is alleged to be built into the system for communicating with British SSBNs. In any case, the putative existence of alternative systems, coupled with the theoretical possibility of "negative control" orders (i.e., orders to fire if communication is broken and if, after a given time, efforts to make contact by other means prove unsuccessful), makes it unlikely that any attacker would rationally judge that an SSBN that had not been located and destroyed had nevertheless been neutralized. On balance, therefore, we are inclined, for present purposes, to disregard this factor, that is, to take the probability that a surviving SSBN will be able to interpret orders to fire or not to fire after a Soviet strike as 1.0.

MISSILE PERFORMANCE AND ABM SYSTEMS

The Polaris A3 missile is well tested and highly reliable. We would expect the overall system reliability, including launch, boost, separation, guidance and re-entry, to fall between about 0.7 and about 0.9.[6] The reliability and performance of the present Soviet ABM system against a SLBM attack of comparatively small proportions is very much harder to assess. Moreover, we have no evidence on which to base a judgment concerning the effectiveness of the hardening techniques and penetration aids used in constructing the Polaris A3 vehicle and its British re-entry vehicles (RVs). In a fuller analysis, we would want to consider a wide range of probabilities concerning Soviet ABM performance. One possibility, for example, would be to apply alternative probabilities between, say, 0.6 and 0.9 for the reliability of the Soviet Galosh missile system and between, say, 0.4 and 0.9 for the overall "kill" capability of a single Galosh missile fired at a single exoatmospheric target (covering detection, identification, and tracking of an incoming RV, as well as interception and destruction by the ABM system warhead). Points that would also have to be considered include:

1. that the three RVs of a single Polaris A3 presently achieve only limited in-flight separation and can therefore be taken to constitute a single target for exoatmospheric interception;
2. that more than one Galosh missile may be fired at a single target;
3. that the present Galosh system protects only a limited area of Soviet territory and is further constrained by the existence of only sixty-four launchers and by the primary orientation of the associated radars toward the "threat tube" relevant to an attack by American land-based ICBMs.

TARGET AVAILABILITY AND VALUE

It is obviously impossible to offer any quantification of the subjective value that the Soviet government would attach to civilian and industrial targets within its own territory, or of the crucial relationship between such values and the value that it would attach to the outcome of a successful attack on Britain. The targeting options open to a British second-strike force are, however, numerous. One working assumption that might be made is that British Polaris vehicles will be programmed to attack a maximum of sixteen targets (this reflects not only the fact that there are periods during which only one SSBN is on firing station but also the possibility that, even when two boats are on station, the chance of one being destroyed by ASW action will be taken to demand a considerable overlap of their target plans). Much would then depend upon the degree of importance attached to attacking Moscow and the surrounding area, protected as this is by an ABM system.

Moscow clearly offers the most attractive countervalue target of all, since it combines being the largest single Soviet concentration of both population (7 million) and industry with being the political, administrative, and economic nexus of an intensely centralized national and international system. There are, however, many other potential Soviet targets of high value. About one-sixth of the Soviet population of 243 million is concentrated in 33 cities of 500,000 or more inhabitants. If the maximum coverage of the Soviet ABM system is taken, as a first approximation, to be a circle of 500 miles radius around Moscow, at least 23 of those cities lie outside it. Indeed, the 16 most populous cities outside that protected area, all of which could be attacked by a single British SSBN, contain approximately 15 million people, together with some of the most important segments of Soviet industry.

Other potential countervalue targets outside the present estimated ABM coverage include major dams and waterways (such as the Volga-Don Canal or the dams at Kuybyshev, Volgograd, Bratsk, and Krasnoyarsk), major oil refineries (such as those at Omsk, Ufa, Groznyy and Irkutsk), major naval shipyards (such as those at Komsomolsk, Nikolayev and Arkhangelsk), major iron and steel plants (such as those at Magnitogorsk, Nizhniy Tagil, and Novokuznetsk), and major nuclear reactor establishments (such as those at Troitsk, Beloyarsk, and Shevchenko)—any selection of which could be attacked by a single British SSBN patrolling, for example, in the Greenland Sea.

Availability of targets is not a major problem; the problem that the British force would face would be whether to expend all its resources upon penetrating the Soviet ABM system in order to attack Moscow (or neighboring areas), to concentrate upon targets outside ABM coverage the aggregate value of which, although impressively high, may not be perceived by Soviet leaders to be as high as that of Moscow itself, or to attempt some mix of targets to include defended and undefended areas.

It would clearly be inappropriate to attempt here an overall assessment of the options open to the British second-strike force or of the effectiveness of choosing any particular targeting option. One point may, however, be worth making. It should not be assumed that the existence of an ABM defense of the Moscow area effectively precludes even a very small second-strike force from launching its attack on soft targets within that area. ABM systems may provide a means of reducing the damage caused by a ballistic missile attack but, unless they are extraordinarily excellent in performance and reliability, they are not likely to prevent all damage to a critical target. Let us, for example, consider a case in which one British SSBN, faced by Soviet ASW forces, seeks to launch all its sixteen missiles at Moscow in circumstances that prompt Soviet commanders to fire two Galosh missiles at each incoming target (thus expending half the immediately available ABM force). Let us also, for purely illustrative purposes, assume the probability of the British SSBN surviving the ASW attack to be 0.6, the reliability of a Polaris SLBM (i.e., the probability of the booster/RV system performing within design limits at launch and throughout the flight) to be 0.8, the reliability of a Galosh missile to be 0.8, and the probability of one Galosh warhead destroying one incoming target to be 0.7. There will then be a probability of 0.91 that any particular British RV will fail to reach the target. With sixteen missiles, however, there will also be a probability of rather more than 0.81 that at least one cluster of three British RVs *will* reach Moscow, with a total explosive effect of up to 600 KT. As between superpowers, that prospect may have come to be thought of as marginal, but it is not entirely clear that any rational Soviet leadership could ignore its bearing upon a decision to attack Britain.

Alternative SALT Outcomes and Soviet Force Levels

SALT

Many proposals and counterproposals have been advanced by the American and Soviet negotiating teams in their numerous sessions at Helsinki and Vienna. They have covered a wide range of possibilities, including a limit on ABM system deployment, qualitative restrictions upon ballistic missile system configurations, a restriction on the total number of offensive strategic nuclear delivery vehicles (ICBMs, SLBMs, and strategic bombers) on each side, and a broader restriction on all nuclear delivery vehicles capable of attacking the territory of either superpower.

Some of the SALT proposals, at least in outline, have been allowed to become public knowledge. For instance, it has reportedly been suggested that a ceiling be imposed on the number of ABM launchers on each side but that flexibility be allowed as to their location and deployment. The number of ABM launchers that each side would be permitted had not been agreed upon by the beginning of 1972. For any potential European force, this, however, is a major issue. If there were an agreement that allowed the Soviet Union to expand its Moscow ABM system from the present number of 64 launchers to the total of 128 that was apparently intended by its designers, the effect upon the utility of a very small European force, such as the current British Polaris fleet, would be significant—assuming that its commanders wished to threaten the Moscow area. An agreement that permitted—or prompted—the Soviet Union to deploy ABM defenses around population and industrial centers outside the coverage of its present system would also be of considerable importance.

One version of the proposal for ABM limitation has allegedly been an American suggestion that each nation should choose between defending its capital with 100 launchers and employing up to 300 launchers to defend land-based ICBM silos. If this were accepted, and if the Russians opted for the second alternative (which, in late 1971, was believed to be the preferred U.S. option), the present Moscow system would have to be dismantled with the result that no significant component of Soviet population and industry would be protected against a European second strike. Whether they would, in fact, choose that course is anyone's guess. The circumstances of the Soviet political and economic system, the tradition of Soviet strategic thought, and the objective importance of the Moscow area's resources arguably make it more likely that Soviet leaders would wish to protect Moscow than that American leaders would wish to protect Washington. It is not, however, impossible that the Russians would ultimately choose an ABM system for ICBM defense. Much would presumably depend upon how reliable they thought the available system to be, how highly they estimated the first-strike threat to their ICBM silos, and how far they considered their second-strike capability to depend critically upon land-based missiles.

Several different suggestions have reportedly been made in the SALT for a freeze or upper limit on the quantity and quality of ICBMs, SLBMs, and their warheads. Although this aspect of a SALT agreement may have far-reaching implications for the overall balance of strategic power between the United States and the Soviet Union, outcomes in this area would not affect the technical viability of European nuclear forces as decisively as outcomes involving ABM and/or ASW capabilities. There is very little the Soviet Union could add to its current strategic offensive forces relevant to Western Europe (medium-range ballistic missiles [MRBMs], IRBMs, ICBMs, SLBMs, submarine-launched cruise missiles and bombers) that would significantly increase its ability to conduct an effective first strike against European military and civilian targets on land. That ability is impressive today and will almost certainly remain so, irrespective of decreased, constant, or increased ICBM, SLBM, and multiple independently targetable re-entry vehicle (MIRV) deployment.

Future quantitative and qualitative improvements in Soviet ABM and ASW capabilities pose the more serious problem for the Europeans. Although the SALT talks have focused upon the ABM issue, there appears to have been no serious attempt to reach an agreement limiting ASW capabilities. Quite how an agreement of this sort would, in fact, be designed is difficult to imagine, given the extraordinary problems of defining ASW forces and force components, let alone those components of R&D budgets devoted to ASW. However, if both the United States and the Soviet Union were to agree on limiting the size of their ICBM and SLBM forces, there would be arguments for a concomitant under-standing on holding down the construction of new hunter-killer sub-marines. A rapid, unilateral expansion of ASW submarine forces at a time when each side was pledged to an upper limit on offensive stra-tegic forces (including SLBMs) would probably be regarded as a strongly destabilizing move.

SOVIET ALTERNATIVES

If no explicit or tacit SALT agreement were reached, it can be speculated that both the United States and the Soviet Union would have certain unilateral options available in terms of future weapons procurement and deployment, any of which would be well within the reach of their technology and their defense budgets. At one extreme both sides could expand their current modernization programs to include the deployment of nationwide ABM systems for city defense, the maintenance and expansion of current air defense systems, deploy-ment of MIRVs on both SLBMs and ICBMs, development of new generations of supersonic bombers, submarines, ICBMs, SLBMs, and ABMs, and accelerated R&D efforts in the general area of strategic nuclear forces. At the other extreme each side, for its own internal bureaucratic and domestic political reasons, could well decide uni-laterally to slow down the current rates of deployment and research and development, either to save money on defense as a whole or to free scarce defense resources for the expansion of general-purpose forces.

Considerations of external policy may press the Soviet Union in the latter direction. In particular, the China contingency may argue for increasing expenditure on Soviet general-purpose forces (although it can also be argued that a growing Chinese missile threat may increase pressure to expand the Soviet ABM program to protect targets in Siberia and Central Asia). Meanwhile, in the United States the transition to more expensive all-volunteer armed forces, even of reduced size, may demand that a proportionately larger share of the defense budget should be devoted to manpower costs and to the procurement of conventional equipment needed to maximize the effectiveness of such smaller forces.

In order to illustrate the possible effects of alternative Soviet deployments upon European nuclear choices, three arbitrary Soviet strategic nuclear force structures have been selected to represent the options potentially open to the Soviet Union during the next eight to ten years. The first option, which we shall call the "high" posture, assumes that there will be no SALT agreement between the two superpowers but that there will instead be a rapid modernization of Soviet strategic nuclear forces, including the deployment by 1980 of a nationwide ABM system at least equivalent in performance to the U.S. system composed of Spartan and Sprint missiles and their associated radars. This posture would include MIRV deployment on land-based Soviet SS-9, SS-11, and SS-13 ICBMs and on sea-based SS-N-6 SLBMs, together with increased R&D budgets for the strategic nuclear forces, with a particular concentration on ABM and ASW technologies. The "high" posture would also include maintenance of the in-depth air defense system that the Soviet Union has developed over the past fifteen years.

A second alternative, which we shall call the "medium" posture (and which can be assumed to exist as an option with or without a SALT agreement), assumes increasing financial constraints on the Soviet defense budget. This posture would still, however, permit limited modernization of ICBM and SLBM forces, including slower deployment of MIRVs, and gradual completion and upgrading of the Moscow ABM system to 128 launchers with a Spartan/Sprint-type mix. It would also include limited ABM deployment outside the Moscow region, to cover not more than three other major concentrations of population and industry. Finally, it would assume continued but limited ASW deployment (without any acceleration of hunter-killer submarine construction or technical breakthroughs in ASW technique), together with continued in-depth bomber defenses.

The third alternative, which we shall call the "low" posture, assumes a SALT agreement that limits ABM deployment around the Moscow area to not more than 128 launchers, with allowance for qualitative upgrading to Spartan/Sprint standards. The primary focus of the Soviet defense budget in this posture would be on general-purpose forces for the China and limited-war contingencies. There would be a maintenance of the Warsaw Pact continental air defense system but a phase-out of the most vulnerable of the force of static IRBMs and MRBMs based in the western Soviet Union.[7]

To what extent are these three alternatives a fair representation of the range of options that the Soviet Union may possess? Obviously, the other possibilities that could have been listed include more extreme definitions of the "high" and "low" limits. It is possible to imagine a "high" Soviet strategic posture that would include very little increase in the quantity of offensive strategic forces but a massive expansion of ABM systems and of civil defense investment. Conversely, it is possible to imagine a "low" posture that would include no ABM defense at all, coupled with an overall reduction of general-purpose forces.

Although it is thus possible to define "high" and "low" postures that represent more extreme limiting cases than the ones we have, in fact, chosen, the three alternatives described are based upon our judgment of the bounds of plausibility, viewed from the perspective of early 1972. We may be wrong in our selection, in gross or in detail, but, provided our force alternatives are at least "representative," we can proceed to relate them to alternative European strategies and force requirements that are equally vague but hopefully not unrealistic.[8] We have also been moved, to a lesser degree, by considerations of analytical utility. In particular, we have felt that it would be more useful to assume *some* Soviet ABM capability in the "low" posture, since even a few Soviet ABM launchers might pose considerable problems for the Europeans, and it is the difficult problems the Europeans will face, rather than the simple ones, that primarily interest us.

The Requirements for European Nuclear Forces

TARGETING

In the introduction to this chapter, certain assumptions were made about the types of strategic nuclear forces the European powers would wish to maintain in the 1970s and 1980s. We assumed, for instance, that the main purpose of any European nuclear force would be to threaten Soviet population and industry with a second strike, and that the second-strike force would be sea-based. There are many additional factors to take into account, however, before any meaningful calculation can be made relating Soviet capabilities to European requirements.

The first important problem concerns target selection. Given the scale of the territory, population, and industrial capacity concerned, there are thousands of targets to be identified on a map of the Soviet Union. There are also many ways in which such targets can be classified. The most common classifications used in popular writing distinguish between "hard" and "soft" targets, "military" and "nonmilitary" targets, "industrial" targets and "population centers," "countervalue" targets and "counterforce" targets. These types of distinction are important but they do not provide enough information to be of much use to a planner. There are, for example, many gradations of "hard" target, ranging from superhardened missile silos, which might withstand overpressures of up to 900 pounds per square inch (psi), to reinforced concrete bunkers and revetments to protect tactical aircraft from the blast effect of low-yield nuclear weapons, which might be totally destroyed by an overpressure of 30 psi. Similarly, distinctions between degrees of "softness" are readily apparent. A widely dispersed suburban area (such as southern Maryland) presents a very different type of target from Manhattan Island. Distinctions between "military" and "nonmilitary" targets become very blurred when ground transportation facilities are included, as they are, in some lists of military targets. The coincidence between the location of industry and large population centers is often sufficiently close to make demarcation difficult if the use of medium- to high-yield weapons (200 KT and above) is considered.

The ability to draw up a series of alternative target plans is not only a question of precise definition, but also a function of the number of weapons in inventories and of their yield, accuracy, and reliability. Given that it is possible to construct some useful target plan that associates different types of targets with the weapon capabilities required to destroy them, there remains the all-important but unknowable factor of "target value." Although it is possible to calculate the expected levels of damage that would be caused to, say, Moscow, Leningrad, and Kiev by three 1-megaton (MT) warheads, it is much more difficult to judge how the Soviet leadership would compare the potential damage to Moscow with the potential damage to the other two cities, simply because, for the reasons mentioned earlier, it can be assumed that Moscow ranks above any other single civilian target in terms of Soviet perceptions. It may be that the loss of any major city would be regarded by many Soviet leaders as an "unacceptable" penalty for attacking Western Europe, despite the well-worn and somewhat precarious proposition that the loss of 20 million Russians in World War II marks some minimum level of Soviet "casualty tolerance." Nevertheless, insofar as Moscow represents a target of unique value, it becomes important in any discussion of European options to indicate whether or not Moscow is on the target list.

As we pointed out earlier in this chapter, the exclusion of Moscow from a target list would still leave an impressive array of countervalue targets for a European force. Out of a total Soviet population of 243 million in 1970, 136 million people (56 percent) were concentrated in urban areas. Ten cities (Moscow, Leningrad, Kiev, Tashkent, Greater Baku, Gorkiy, Kharkov, Novosibirsk, Kuybyshev, and Sverdlovsk) had populations of over 1 million each, with a combined total of 20.8 million. Another twenty-three cities, together containing 16.5 million people, had individual populations of between 500,000 and 1 million. A further 38.3 million lived in 188 cities of 100,000 to 500,000 population. Thus, 15 percent of the total Soviet population was concentrated in only 33 urban areas, with another 100 areas containing an additional 16 percent.

As to industry, 25 percent of all Soviet industrial capacity is concentrated in only ten cities—with a further forty cities containing an additional 15 percent. Moreover, many of these industrial centers are themselves in close proximity to each other: in the Moscow-Gorkiy area, the Leningrad area, the Donets-Dnepr basin, the area from Volgograd to Kuybyshev, the Urals area around Sverdlovsk, the Central Asian cities from Tashkent to Alma Ata, and the Siberian industrial complex focused on Novosibirsk. When the dependence of the Soviet Union on relatively constricted road and rail routes, on well-defined waterways, and on hydroelectric power from major dams is also considered, it can be seen that the country, despite its enormous size, has an arterial vulnerability coupled with a surprisingly tight concentration of population. Even for a relatively small second-strike force, countervalue targets outside the Moscow area itself would not be hard to find.

The fact remains that a crucial decision for the Europeans in designing a second-strike force would be whether to prepare it for an attack only on Moscow and its environs, whether to target only cities and industrial centers outside the coverage of the Moscow ABM system, or whether to target both the Moscow area and other areas. This decision is crucial not only because of the peculiar material, organizational, and psychological importance of Moscow but also because we have assumed that some level of ABM defense will be provided for the Moscow area in all three alternative Soviet postures. (Even in our "high" posture, it can be assumed that a major upgrading of the Soviet ABM system for the area defense of several urban complexes would lay greater emphasis upon the defense of Moscow than upon that of other areas.)

LEVELS OF DAMAGE

We specified at the outset that we were not prepared to select any one level of damage and to assume it to be sufficient for all purposes of European deterrence of the Soviet Union. Instead, we have arbitrarily selected three levels of damage (D_1, D_2, D_3) and have applied them in two different modes (A and M)—thus sampling a representative spectrum of alternatives.

D_{1A} represents an ability to inflict "major" damage in a second strike on at least one Soviet city (excluding Moscow) that has a population in excess of 1 million and that is also a major industrial or communications center. D_{1M} refers to the ability to inflict similar "major" damage on Moscow and its environs.[9] Both D_{1A} and D_{1M} can be classified as *low-level deterrent postures*. If the only measure is the percentage of population and industry destroyed, they are, indeed, exactly similar. If, however, qualitative factors are taken into account, D_{1M} clearly represents a more significant capability.

D_{2A} and D_{2M} can be regarded as *medium-level deterrent postures*. D_{2A} represents an ability to cause 9.5 million "primary" fatalities and to destroy 25 percent of Soviet industrial capacity by attacking, in a second strike, a sufficient number of cities and industrial centers outside the Moscow area. D_{2M} refers to a similar capability but demands that at least 500,000 of the "primary" fatalities (and a commensurate proportion of the industrial capacity destroyed) should be in the Moscow area.

D_{3A} and D_{3M} can be called *high-level deterrent postures*. D_{3A} refers to the ability to attack enough Soviet cities and industrial centers in a second strike to result in at least 50 million "primary" fatalities and the destruction of up to 70 percent of Soviet industrial capacity, all of this damage being caused outside the Moscow area. D_{3M} represents the same level of total damage but requires that 2.5 million of the "primary" fatalities should be in Moscow.[10]

EUROPEAN FORCE STRUCTURES AND COSTS

We now have the material for a very simple matrix that will relate the three chosen Soviet force postures—"high," "medium," and "low" —to the six chosen damage requirements for a European force— D_{1A} to D_{3M}. See table 1.

Table 1
ALTERNATIVE EUROPEAN FORCE STRUCTURES AND COSTS

| | | Soviet Force Levels | | |
		Low	Medium	High
European Damage Requirements	D_{1A}	F_1B_1	F_2B_2	F_3B_3
	D_{1M}	F_4B_4	F_5B_5	F_6B_6
	D_{2A}	F_7B_7	F_8B_8	F_9B_9
	D_{2M}	$F_{10}B_{10}$	$F_{11}B_{11}$	$F_{12}B_{12}$
	D_{3A}	$F_{13}B_{13}$	$F_{14}B_{14}$	$F_{15}B_{15}$
	D_{3M}	$F_{16}B_{16}$	$F_{17}B_{17}$	$F_{18}B_{18}$

Note: F stands for Force Requirement; B stands for Budgetary Requirement.

The next problem is to estimate the optimum structure of the alternative European forces, F_1 to F_{18}, that would be required to achieve the alternative levels of damage, D_{1A} to D_{3M}, in the three alternative environments, together with the budgetary costs, B_1 to B_{18}, of procuring and operating those forces. The difficulties of translating F_1B_1 to $F_{18}B_{18}$ into actual systems requirements and costs are very great and cannot be attempted in detail in this chapter.[11] Apart from anything else, the scope of these alternatives is considerable. At the one extreme (F_1B_1), we have the problem of designing a force that need only threaten one major Soviet city, other than Moscow, in an environment in which the Soviet Union has deployed no nationwide ABM system. At the other extreme ($F_{18}B_{18}$), we have the requirement to destroy at least 50 million Soviet citizens, including 2.5 million Muscovites, and up to 70 percent of Soviet industry in an environment where the Soviet Union has deployed a nationwide ABM system and is actively expanding and modernizing its ASW forces. It needs little reflection to see intuitively that a force as small as the current British Polaris fleet may well be sufficient to cope with the former task but will be totally inadequate for the latter.

What is also intuitively obvious is that the financial burden of procuring forces for the latter task—the destruction of 50 million Soviet citizens in a heavily defended environment—would almost certainly be well beyond the economic capabilities of any individual West European power during the period considered here. After all, the infliction of damage on this scale would require a great many delivered warheads (i.e., warheads that have survived a Soviet first strike, have successfully penetrated a Soviet ABM system, and have been detonated on target). In testimony in February 1968 on the Fiscal Year (FY) 1969 Defense Budget and FY 1969–73 Defense Program, U.S. Secretary of Defense Robert McNamara estimated the requirement for killing 52 million people in the Soviet Union to be 200 delivered megaton equivalents. In order to reach this figure one would have to procure and deploy many more than that number of nuclear weapons, especially if the warheads available had an explosive yield significantly below 1 MT each.[12]

The extent to which the M modes in the matrix above (targets including Moscow) impose force requirements greater than those relevant to the A modes (targets excluding Moscow) will naturally be a function of the alternative Soviet force capabilities mentioned earlier. In particular, the degree of difference will depend upon the scale and effectiveness of ABM defenses around the Moscow area and, conversely, upon the presence or absence of ABM defenses around other population centers. By the same token, the costs of the European force requirements relevant to the A and M modes will converge or diverge in accordance with varying Soviet capabilities. At the limit, it is not inconceivable that F_6B_6 would be greater than $F_{15}B_{15}$ (if Moscow were intensively defended), or that $F_{16}B_{16}$ would be smaller than $F_{13}B_{13}$ (because of the heavy concentration of population and industry in the Moscow area).

The two limiting cases, F_1B_1 and $F_{18}B_{18}$, are relatively easy to discuss, since the answers to the question "Could Europe afford this alternative in the foreseeable future?" would respectively be a simple "Yes" and "No." The other alternatives pose greater problems. Consider, for example, F_5B_5, where we have a Soviet medium posture and a European requirement to inflict "major" damage on Moscow alone. What type of strategic force would this require and what would it cost? Although it is impossible to give a precise answer to this question, some calculations can be made, given the data publicly available on U.S. systems performance and provided some estimates are made of Soviet systems performance. Having made them, it turns out that it is at approximately this level of force requirement

(F_5B_5/F_6B_6) that the Europeans might first have to consider acquiring a new generation of missiles, such as the U.S. Poseidon. It is extremely difficult, however, to judge the exact point at which a decision on this would have to be made, even though such a decision would have a major effect on budgetary expenditure. Calculating values for B_5 and B_6 is thus likely to be especially difficult, since a relatively marginal change in the level of F will here have a much greater proportional effect on the level of B.

We cannot examine each of the eighteen alternative force structures and budgets listed above in this chapter. We can, however, make some general comments concerning the types of requirements that in any case would have to be satisfied before a European force could cope with different Soviet strategic capabilities.

STANDARD FORCE REQUIREMENTS

Irrespective of the variation in second-strike force structures required to confront alternative Soviet capabilities, there are some standard problems that any European force must overcome in order to achieve a certain level of destruction in the event of war with the Soviet Union.

First, there are problems connected with the vulnerability of submarines, submarine bases, and command and control systems to a Soviet first strike.[13] Although we have made assumptions concerning the relatively lower vulnerability of submarines when compared with land-based systems, the Soviet Union could always be expected to destroy a proportion of European submarines in a first strike, including at least those then in port for normal maintenance or long refit. The percentage of submarines that could be intercepted at sea as part of a Soviet first strike would be a function of many factors. These would include the number of European and other submarines at sea and the effectiveness of European evasive tactics, the proportion of its total ASW effort that the Soviet Union had allocated to finding and destroying European (as distinct from American or—potentially—Chinese) submarines, the patrol areas allocated to European submarines (which, in turn, would depend upon targeting requirements and the range of European SLBMs), and prevailing atmospheric and sea conditions.

It follows that extra money could be spent in an equally varied number of ways in an effort to improve the ability of European submarine forces to survive a Soviet first strike. Of the many options, some of the most obvious include the construction of more submarines in order to increase the number of delivery platforms at sea at any given time, more widely dispersed basing and communication facilities to permit deployment in several different oceans, greater European investment in ASW in order to counter Soviet hunter-killer submarines, and qualitative improvements in European SLBM systems in order to produce greater range, greater accuracy, and/or greater warhead yield. (This last course could be pursued in several ways; one option—procuring a Poseidon-type system to supplement or replace the existing Polaris A3 and MSBS missile systems now in Europe—is considered later.)

The vulnerability of submarine command and control facilities is one of the more difficult problems the Europeans have to face. Whereas it can be argued that sea-based missile systems are relatively less vulnerable to a Soviet attack than land-based systems, it is generally agreed that land-based systems, especially aircraft, would be easier to command and control in a postattack environment. Moreover, the most readily available means of communicating with submerged submarines—VLF radio—requires very large transmitting stations, which are likely to constitute "soft" first-strike targets; high redundancy of communications is therefore essential to any submarine command and control system.

For these reasons, there are both strategic and economic costs involved in relying solely upon submarine systems if independent, effective, and positive command and control at all stages is an important requirement for a European force. Britain and France have already developed independent communication systems for the command and control of small submarine forces. It is unlikely, however, that their systems compare, in capacity or in redundant survivability, with the elaborate system of submarine communications that the United States has developed for its own SSBN fleet. If the Europeans wished to develop communication systems that offered a significantly higher probability of remaining effective after a Soviet first strike and in spite of all subsequent Soviet efforts to degrade their performance, they might have to accept some fairly impressive additional capital costs, irrespective of the total size of the submarine force to be controlled. This would be especially true if they found it necessary to develop and deploy independent satellite relay systems in order to provide an additional, and possibly less vulnerable, method of communicating with their submarines.

The second major category of general problems is also one that raises the issue of satellite development and deployment. At present, no European country has a comprehensive set of systems for the independent collection and analysis of strategic intelligence on the Soviet

Union. The amount and variety of strategic intelligence needed to target a second-strike force effectively in a purely countervalue role against undefended urban and industrial targets should not be overrated. The location of large cities and industrial centers and their general configurations can be reliably analyzed using only data that it is well within current European capabilities to obtain. The problem becomes much more difficult, however, when the relevant targets are defended—by air defenses against aircraft attack, or by ABM defenses against ballistic missile attack. In the case of a European SLBM force, penetration (or evasion) of a Soviet ABM system would depend heavily upon having a steady flow of accurate intelligence concerning the location and performance of the defensive systems. That would, almost certainly, be impossible without access to information gathered by reconnaissance satellites. Ideally, it would also require a capability to detect and analyze the testing of Soviet ABM components (missiles and radars). Finally, it would, in any case, demand a highly developed system for the retrieval and interpretation of the information acquired. These requirements could only be met, directly and independently, at considerable economic cost—in terms of R&D effort as well as in terms of procurement and operations. The impact of any major expansion of Soviet ABM defenses on the cost of a European second-strike SLBM force would not be limited to the price of additional offensive delivery vehicles and warheads; it would also reflect the potentially high price of obtaining and analyzing essential information about the defenses themselves.

The third major series of problems that affect the viability of any nuclear force structure is concerned with the penetration of opposing defenses and the successful detonation of warheads over targets. Two groups of problems can be identified in this context. The first concerns the technical reliability of missile launch platforms, of the missiles themselves, of their re-entry vehicles, and of their nuclear warheads. The second concerns the technical effectiveness of Soviet active defenses, especially ballistic missile defenses, against incoming warheads.

The operational reliability of submarine-based missile systems can be estimated within certain limits provided a sufficient number of real or simulated test firings is conducted covering all systems components. This is easier said than done; none of the European powers possesses the range of test facilities that the United States has developed. In particular, neither Britain nor France appears to have the independent means to conduct test firings of multiple-warhead missiles and penetration aids against a simulated ABM environment. Britain has no missile testing range of its own that is capable of handling full-range, full-system test firings of SLBMs. France does have an instrumented missile test range in the Atlantic, based upon launching sites and tracking/telemetry facilities in southwestern France (near Biscarosse), a fixed tracking/telemetry station in the Azores (on the island of Flores), and mobile tracking/telemetry equipment in surface vessels and aircraft. It is doubtful, however, whether the French range is capable, in its present form, of handling multiple-warhead tests and almost certain that it lacks the capability to simulate a sophisticated ABM environment. Even if facilities existed for entirely simulated testing of SLBM/ABM interactions, there would remain a question about the reliability—and therefore credibility—of any European multiple warhead or penetration technology that had not been subjected to full-range flight testing. The investment costs of building facilities for such testing, and especially of building elaborate ABM simulations and their extremely complicated radars, are, however, very great.

The effectiveness of any Soviet ABM system against European missiles is not easy to guess at and still more difficult to calculate with any precision. It is generally assumed that the present (1972) Galosh system installed around Moscow is less sophisticated than the Safeguard system that the United States is now deploying with its declared purpose of protecting certain Minuteman sites. In particular, the United States is believed to be ahead of the Soviet Union in the development and deployment of the phased-array radar equipment and the associated computer software essential for the successful operation of an ABM system against a large-scale attack. However, it is reasonable to suppose that, by 1980, the Soviet Union, if it were permitted and chose to do so, could develop a system at least as effective as, and possibly more effective than, the current version of Safeguard. Moreover, the demands made upon radar and, above all, data processing systems by relatively small-scale attacks similar to that which the current British Polaris force could launch are very much less heavy than those for which the components of the Safeguard system have been designed. It must be assumed, therefore, that the Soviet Union has the technical capability to increase considerably, by 1980, the probability of its ABM defense intercepting a high percentage of the warheads that might be fired within its coverage by current European strategic missile forces. It is impossible to put precise numbers either upon the maximum size that a Soviet ABM system might reach by 1980 or upon the probability that its missiles could then successfully intercept and destroy a single European SLBM re-entry vehicle. Even without precise numbers, it is not, however, difficult to illustrate the problems that an expanded Soviet ABM defense would present to a European attacking force.

For example, a system of 128 ABM launchers around Moscow that could offer a 0.9 probability of destroying each of up to 128 incoming targets would obviously have a major effect on small SLBM forces, such as Britain's, which at present can muster a theoretical total of 64 SLBM launcher tubes (with a realistic maximum of 32 of these at sea and on firing station). In such a situation, one alternative for the offense, if it were determined to reach a defended target, would be to increase its forces to the extent necessary to overwhelm the defense with more offensive targets (i.e., individual RVs or closely spaced clusters of MRVs) than the defense had interceptors.[14]

In essence, there would be three possible ways of seeking to overwhelm the defense in this manner. The first way would be to buy enough extra submarines to increase the probability that, at any given moment, more than 128 incoming offensive targets could be presented to the defense.

The exact number of extra boats required would be dependent upon many factors. These would include the expected vulnerability of the submarines to Soviet ASW efforts, the expected reliability of each surviving submarine performing without systems failure, and the range of confidence in total systems performance believed to be required for deterrence purposes. As suggested earlier in this chapter, there are extreme difficulties in assigning realistic probabilities to these factors. If the ground rules require a 0.99 certainty that over 128 missiles will reach Moscow but assume relatively low probabilities that submarines will survive a Soviet attack and that the surviving system will perform without failure, the total number of boats required will be very high. If the ground rules were changed to include lower confidence requirements and higher probabilities of submarine survival and missile reliability, the number of boats needed would fall dramatically.

A second course would be to use a significant part of the payload capacity of European SLBMs to carry sophisticated and highly effective penetration aids. In theory, this might enable a force of even 64 (or 32) launchers to saturate an ABM defense of 128 launchers, by forcing the defense to fire at an adequate number of spurious targets or by otherwise critically degrading its performance. In practice, the design and operation of penetration aids with such a capability is an extremely difficult technical task, as well as being very expensive. Moreover, it requires comprehensive and accurate intelligence concerning all aspects of the opposing defensive system (radar frequencies, operational modes, and coverage; ABM missile guidance systems, ranges, and velocities; ABM warhead weapon effects, etc.). As we have already pointed out, West European countries have no independent capability to collect or analyze such information on an adequate scale and would find it both technically difficult and economically costly to develop such a capability.

The third alternative would be to equip European SLBMs with an adequate number of MIRVs. One great advantage of MIRVs over MRVs is the wider separation achieved during the ballistic, midcourse phase of flight as well as during the re-entry phase. Given the current state of the art, this would mean, for example, that a Polaris A3 warhead equipped with three MIRVs instead of three MRVs could probably force an exoatmospheric, area-defense ABM system to commit at least one interceptor to each MIRV instead of sending only one interceptor against a cluster of three MRVs. Thus an ABM system of 128 launchers might, in this case and in very crude terms, be saturated by one-third as many MIRVs as MRVs. This, in turn, would reduce the number of boats required on firing station. Moreover, in theory, more than three MIRVs could be fitted to a single missile such as the Polaris A3 while, if a more advanced SLBM delivery vehicle, such as the U.S. Poseidon, were procured, at least 14 MIRVs could be fitted to each vehicle. These 14 warheads would each, of course, have a lower yield than the MRVs carried by the present A3 missile, but the total expected damage to "soft" targets from a 14-warhead missile would, in most circumstances, be considerably greater.

SPECIFIC FORCE REQUIREMENTS

In the light of these cursory statements about standard systems requirements, what can be said concerning the specific requirements and costs of the alternative European deterrent postures?

1. Soviet "low" posture. The limitation of Soviet ABM defenses to a small, 128-launcher Moscow system suggests that the primary problems involved in designing the six alternative European force structures under this heading concern the total number of submarines and warheads that could be expected to survive a Soviet first strike. The planning decisions would be more concerned with the survivability of the missiles and the gross quantity that would be available to fire against Soviet targets than with advanced penetration technologies. In theory, achieving damage levels D_{1A}, D_{2A}, and D_{3A} (where no ABM defenses are involved) would not necessitate large expenditures on refined penetration techniques (MIRVs, decoys, etc.). Expenditure would nevertheless vary widely. Firing 16 Polaris missiles, each with 3 MRVs, against a mix of undefended Soviet targets would cause a level of damage much greater than that required for D_{1A}.[15] However, to achieve D_{3A} would require many more delivered warheads (approximately 200 megaton equivalents, which represents the current capacity of about 194 Polaris A3s). Thus the total cost of buying forces for D_{3A} in this environment would be several times that required for D_{1A}, with D_{2A} standing as an intermediate case.

In the case of D_{1M}, D_{2M}, and D_{3M} (an attack that had to overcome the Moscow ABM system), the problem would be one of both quantity and quality. If the Moscow system only had 128 ABM launchers but also had an extremely high "kill" probability within the limits thus set, it could still obviously be saturated by a force that could guarantee to present over 128 offensive targets. It might also be defeated by a force that could avoid being intercepted by the use of penetration decoys or refined penetration techniques.[16] Whichever option were chosen to overcome such a Moscow ABM system would not be free of cost, and it is possible that the cost requirements for D_{1M} would be closer to the cost requirements for D_{3A} than to those for D_{1A}. In that case, a decision to include Moscow in the target list and to build forces for that purpose would also allow one the option of ignoring Moscow and inflicting major damage elsewhere.[17] (It should be repeated that this assumes the Moscow ABM system will have an extremely high effectiveness against very small nuclear forces by 1980. Given the way in which marginal probabilities of penetration accumulate, any lower level of effectiveness would make planning a lot easier for the Europeans. Indeed, the cost of D_{1M} might then be little, if any, higher than that of D_{1A}.)

To build forces for D_{3M} would obviously require the most money, but it could be argued that, given European willingness to invest resources capable of meeting the requirements of D_{3A}, or even D_{1M}, the incremental cost of opting for D_{3M} would not represent as dramatic a jump as the incremental cost of opting for D_{1M} rather than for D_{1A} if the Moscow ABM defense became extremely effective.

In sum, Europe could probably sustain a deterrent posture matching D_{1A} in the late 1970s and early 1980s without making large investments in new technologies. The same would be true for D_{1M} in any circumstances in which the limited effectiveness of the Moscow ABM system left a high probability of *some* European warheads penetrating it. In these cases, the current costs of the British Polaris fleet might be representative of the types of costs that would be needed by 1980. However, all other damage requirements (including D_{1M} against an extremely effective ABM system) would certainly require additional funding and, although there are some unresolved trade-offs between buying quantity and buying quality, there can be no doubt that costs would rise well above the present level of British expenditure on strategic forces.

A conclusion would be that, in this Soviet "low" posture environment, the primary problem would be to ensure that a sufficient number of European missiles survived a Soviet first strike. The secondary problem of penetration would be important for the three cases that demand an anti-Moscow capability. However, the requirement for very sophisticated and costly penetration techniques is not self-evident since there are other, less sophisticated ways of overwhelming a small ABM system. A Soviet "low" posture, negotiated as a result of the SALT or emerging from unilateral decision, would enable the Europeans to consider their own alternative postures in an environment in which technical uncertainties would probably not present major obstacles to planning. In this Soviet posture, the Europeans would at least be able to cost out their alternatives with reasonable confidence that, if they were prepared to make plausible financial sacrifices, they could procure the required forces.

2. Soviet "medium" and "high" postures. These environments include nationwide ABM defenses, of varying degrees of sophistication, and improvements in Soviet ASW capabilities. The problem facing the Europeans would thus be of a more uncertain nature. Although it is theoretically possible to escape ASW attack and to overwhelm such ABM capabilities by multiplying the number of submarines and by using very large quantities of single and MRV warheads, the costs of doing so quickly become exceedingly high. It is at this stage that the procurement of advanced missile systems such as the U.S. Poseidon may become a much more attractive option in terms of comparative costs and capabilities.

The Poseidon system with MIRV warheads would enable the British to convert their present SSBNs without encountering the full capital cost of new submarine construction. (It is unlikely that French SNLEs could be converted with the same ease to fire Poseidon missiles.) The Poseidon might carry up to 14 MIRV warheads, as compared with 3 MRVs for the British Polaris A3. Thus, in the case of the British boats, converting to Poseidon could raise the number of separate targets open to attack by one submarine from 16 per boat to a maximum of 224 —a dramatic increase.

Procuring Poseidon is by no means the only qualitative improvement that the Europeans might consider. A less costly and complicated option might be to equip the Polaris A3 missile with MIRVs. At the other extreme, the Europeans could attempt to build or buy a new generation of submarines and longer-range undersea missiles similar to the American Undersea Long-range Missile System (ULMS). The first alternative would probably be cheaper but less effective than the Poseidon option.[18] It should not, however, be dismissed lightly; the Polaris A3 missile has an ample payload capacity to carry a useful number of MIRVs. The latter alternative is hardly feasible at the present time, given the lack of experience in Europe with very advanced missile technologies, unless Europe were to cooperate with the United States in ULMS development.

OPTING FOR THE POSEIDON MISSILE SYSTEM

It is reasonable to consider the Poseidon option with particular care, both because it is often mentioned as an alternative for Britain and because some cost data on the U.S. experience with Poseidon are available. At the same time, it is apparent that the pursuit of this option would face the Europeans with substantial problems, whether they wished to obtain the U.S. Poseidon system itself or to produce their own equivalent to it.

The first problem would clearly be the political one. Would the United States be willing to transfer a Poseidon system to European control and, if so, what would the terms be? In this context, any agreement between the two superpowers, at the SALT or elsewhere, to restrict the transfer of systems as sophisticated as Poseidon to allies would be of crucial significance. If no such agreement were reached, it is not entirely impossible that the United States might perceive an interest in selling the Poseidon system to Britain or France, or to some combination of European powers. The exact terms of such a transfer could, however, take many forms, including a purchase "off the shelf" or a cost-sharing arrangement covering all or part of RDT&E expenditure.

If the United States were not willing to provide Poseidon, an alternative would be for European powers to develop a missile system of their own equivalent to Poseidon. In those circumstances, a great deal would still depend upon the amount of technical assistance that the United States was prepared to give.

In either case, the next problem that the Europeans would have to face would be an economic one. Some U.S. figures have been released indicating the estimated costs of the total projected Poseidon program, including the cost of converting Polaris boats to Poseidon. Unfortunately, these cost data are incomplete, and using them without caution to infer potential European costs would expose the calculation to many errors. Nevertheless, U.S. costs do give general indications that can be expected to have some relevance to European options.

On the basis of the official U.S. figures that are available, it can, in fact, be shown that, at 1970 prices, the U.S. Navy's capital outlay for the Poseidon program has been expected to amount to about $179 million per boat for a 31-boat program. Of this total, $75 million per boat represents the cost of conversion from a Polaris configuration, concurrent overhaul, and tender conversions. Thus the average cost per boat, excluding both these elements and nuclear warhead costs but including Poseidon RDT&E and procurement for an initial operational capability, has been estimated at $104 million (at 1970 prices).[19]

Before it would be possible to use figures such as these as a basis for specific estimates of European costs for submarines, missiles, RVs, and warheads, some very involved calculations and many qualifying statements would be needed. If, for example, an agreement were reached to sell Europe the Poseidon missile system, what proportion of the RDT&E costs would Europe have to pay? What rates of inflation would need to be applied to make realistic cost estimates of a European program? What proportion of procurement and conversion costs would be incurred in the United States and what proportion in Europe? Would the U.S. include MIRV re-entry systems for Poseidon in any sale?

Although the answers to all these questions would have a major bearing on European costs, the answer to the last of them could be crucial. The expense to the Europeans of designing, constructing, and testing a sophisticated MIRV system, of a type appropriate to the Poseidon missile, would be extremely heavy. It might be, of course, that the United States would be prepared to sell to Europe either complete Poseidon RV systems (minus warheads) or, at least, the complete design plans for them. Even then, the additional cost of developing appropriate warheads would be substantial. Costs would be far greater, however, if the Europeans also had to conduct their own RDT&E in connection with a re-entry system for Poseidon, as they would, in any case, have to do in connection with the warheads themselves.

As earlier paragraphs have suggested, if Europe wished to develop a Poseidon-type system without U.S. cooperation, some very much more substantial capital investments would need to be made, quite apart from the costs of missile, re-entry vehicle, and warhead procurement and of submarine conversion. In particular, the Europeans would need to develop test facilities that would include ABM radar simulation to test MIRV technologies, advanced communication and navigation facilities, and advanced warhead technologies. Given that RDT&E efforts would have to cover all aspects of missile and RV development, the capital costs of test-range construction and the associated sophisticated equipment, especially radar and computers, could easily exceed $1 billion, especially if a crash program were thought necessary.

It needs little imagination to see that an entirely independent European Poseidon equivalent would be very expensive, even if the technical problems could be solved. Although it is no doubt true that in certain technical areas the Europeans would not need to duplicate work already done in the United States, simply because the broad results of that work would be known to European experts, the consequential cost savings here could be more than offset by the need to build so many new test facilities.

The main conclusion to be drawn from this is that the costs of a Poseidon-type option to Europe are bound to be heavy, but that their full extent is very much in the hands of the U.S. government. If it were prepared to share its own program with Europe, including its work on re-entry systems as well as missiles, the proportional costs for a European force might not be very much greater than those incurred by the U.S. Navy for a force of thirty-one boats. If the United States were not prepared to cooperate, however, the costs would be very much higher and there would be no certainty that the end product would be technically viable.

Summary

Given the assumptions of this paper, the primary conclusions would seem to be as follows:

1. The outcome of the SALT has potentially major consequences for the future of any West European nuclear forces. In particular, U.S.-Soviet agreement (or disagreement) on ABM deployment for area defense must affect the various options open to the European powers in designing nuclear force structures for anti-Soviet deterrent purposes. Given the probability that the Europeans would, in the future, rely upon submarine forces for deterrence, agreement—or the absence of agreement—on the restraint of Soviet and American ASW efforts will also be of major significance.

2. Since future Soviet force levels can only be guessed at, it is not possible to analyze in any precise manner the alternatives open to the

Europeans. However, by making some estimates as to the range of future Soviet force levels and by relating these to various levels of damage the Europeans might wish to be able to inflict upon Soviet population and industrial centers in a second strike, it is possible to indicate the major technical, economic, and strategic implications of alternative Soviet and European postures. The relative levels of European investment would, in any case, be contingent upon the relations between Soviet force levels, on the one hand, and European damage requirements, on the other hand.

3. If the Soviet Union significantly improves the effectiveness of its present ABM system and/or expands its coverage, the Europeans would probably not, by 1980, be able to rely on force levels equivalent to the current programmed British or French capabilities, even if their damage requirements were fairly low. The same would be true, even without such Soviet action, if the Europeans conceived a need to threaten substantially greater damage to the Soviet Union than that which might be inflicted by existing British and French second-strike forces. In either of those cases, the main choice would be between increasing the size of existing European SLBM forces, using existing technology, and making major qualitative improvements in their operational performance. Conversely, any SALT agreement that had the effect of freezing or prohibiting ABM systems designed to protect cities and industrial centers would lower the cost to Europe of threatening certain damage levels against such targets.

4. Similarly, if the Soviet Union achieves a technical breakthrough in ASW, or if it substantially increases its investment in ASW forces based upon existing technology, the Europeans would need to spend more money to ensure that a proportion of their submarines could survive a Soviet first strike. Again, this could mean either quantitative increases or qualitative improvements in their SLBM deterrent systems.

5. The choice between quantitative and qualitative means of enhancing European deterrent forces depends largely upon the ways in which the posture of the Soviet Union and the perceived second-strike requirements of the Europeans do, in fact, develop. Greater Soviet ABM capabilities might, for example, be offset most economically by the qualitative development of SLBMs themselves, whereas a technical breakthrough in ASW might argue more strongly for a quantitative increase in the number of submarines (since the quality of the missiles installed in a submarine destroyed by ASW action is irrelevant). If some need were felt for qualitative improvement, this might raise the issue, for the Europeans, of acquiring an advanced missile (SLBM) system such

as the U.S. Poseidon. The further choice would then be between attempting to develop and produce such a system within Europe and attempting to procure Poseidon, partly or wholly, from the United States. The latter option, despite its high cost, would probably be a much less expensive course than the former. Whether it were also an available option would, however, depend upon the willingness of the United States to cooperate in the reinforcement of independent European nuclear deterrent capabilities.

6. The relationship between the SALT and future U.S.-European nuclear cooperation is thus another crucial factor. Any U.S.-Soviet agreement that inhibited the further transfer of advanced nuclear delivery systems and technologies to U.S. allies would diminish the chances of a U.S.-European arrangement, for example on Poseidon procurement. At the same time, the economic cost to Europe of developing its own Poseidon-type program "from scratch" would probably be exceedingly high, and it is doubtful whether any one European state could or would want to undertake such a program unilaterally. Thus a U.S.-Soviet agreement to restrict further assistance to allies might conceivably increase the economic and technical motives for greater European cooperation in the joint development and procurement of nuclear forces.

NOTES

1. The basic characters, strengths and weaknesses of the British and French strategic nuclear programs are discussed in Ian Smart, *Future Conditional: The Prospect for Anglo-French Nuclear Co-operation,* Adelphi Paper no. 78 (London: Institute for Strategic Studies, 1971).

2. By a "strategic" nuclear capability we mean a capability to use nuclear weapons against targets that are not within a battlefield or directly connected with the maneuver of combatant forces. By extension, when we speak of "strategic" weapons (or forces), we do not mean to imply the existence of a qualitatively discrete category but only to refer to weapons whose primary utility appears to lie in the contribution that they make to such a strategic nuclear capability.

3. The Canberra has a maximum speed of Mach (M) 0.83 and a maximum theoretical range, unrefueled, of about 3,800 miles. The Buccaneer has a maximum speed of M 0.95 and a maximum theoretical range of about 2,000 miles. The F-4 has a maximum speed of M 2.4 and a maximum theoretical range of about 1,600 miles. The combat radius, as distinct from the range, of each aircraft is a function of the ordnance carried and the speed and height flown to the target. For example, an F-4 Phantom, carrying 3,000 pounds of ordnance and

flying at optimum cruising speeds for range at high altitude (35,000 feet), has a combat radius of approximately 700 statute miles. Squadrons of all types of aircraft are land-based; only Buccaneers and F-4s are also carrier-based.

4. CEP means circular error probable, the radius of a circle centered on the aiming point within which 50 percent of the projectiles will fall.

5. We are well aware of the difficulty and risk involved in attaching specific numbers to this and to the other probabilities discussed here. Moreover, this particular number has no basis beyond that of our intuitive assessment of the current effectiveness of ASW techniques against nuclear-powered submarines. In its defense, however, we can say three things: that it has been chosen from the lower end of the range of probabilities that our intuition suggests; that it is consistent with the statement by the U.S. Secretary of Defense, Melvin Laird, before the House Armed Services Committee on March 9, 1971 that he has "no immediate concern about the survivability of our Polaris and Poseidon submarines at sea" (U.S. House of Representatives, Committee on Armed Services, 92 Cong. 1 Sess., *Hearings on Military Posture and HR 3818 and HR 8687* [Washington, D.C.: G.O.P., 1971], p. 2362); that we are not aware of any authoritative suggestion of a lower probability, even for the small number of submarines that Britain possesses. In the more substantial study that we hope to publish later in the Adelphi Papers series of the International Institute for Strategic Studies (IISS), we shall want to consider a range of probabilities, here and elsewhere, rather than a single number.

6. Again, we are aware of the fragility of the figures mentioned in this paragraph. Some figures are, however, needed for exemplary testing, and these have not seemed to us to be entirely unreasonable. In the case of Polaris reliability, for example, general evidence suggests that a 0.7–0.9 range is plausible. The launch availability of U.S. Polaris missiles has been stated on a number of occasions to be substantially better than 0.99 for each missile, while it is not, in general, implausible that a solid-fueled, two-stage missile that has been in service for as long as the A3 will have an in-flight performance reliability of at least 0.75.

7. It should be emphasized that these alternative postures refer primarily to Soviet strategic nuclear forces and not to the total Soviet defense establishment. As suggested, it is quite possible that a "high" strategic nuclear posture would be combined with a "low" general-purpose forces posture and vice versa.

8. Our arbitrary method for selecting alternatives is similar to that used by the Brookings Institution team in its 1971 assessment of U.S. strategic nuclear options; see "Major Defense Options" in *Setting National Priorities: The FY 1972 Budget* (Washington, D.C.: The Brookings Institution, 1971), pp. 47–49.

9. By "major" damage, we mean the physical destruction of most important buildings, public facilities, and factories and the infliction of at least 500,000 "primary" fatalities.

10. Although the choice of these damage levels is arbitrary, and may even seem to be capricious, there is some quantitative relationship between them. The low-level postures (D_{1A}, D_{1M}) are "single city" options; the relationship between them is direct, implying a simple choice between Moscow and any one of nine other cities. In the case of Moscow, however, 500,000 casualties represent about 7 percent of that city's current population. The medium-level postures (D_{2A}, D_{2M})

have thus been constructed by applying that percentage to the total Soviet urban population (for which reason D_{2M} demands the same level of damage to Moscow as D_{1M}). The high-level postures (D_{3A}, D_{3M}) have been developed more arbitrarily, but the same course has been followed in requiring that D_{3M} should include a percentage of the Moscow population comparable to the proportion that the D_{3A} level of casualties bears to total Soviet urban population (i.e., about 37 percent).

11. The authors hope to include more quantitative data on alternative force structures and costs in the more substantial study of the subject that has already been mentioned.

12. The value of any warhead in megaton equivalents can be calculated by taking the two-thirds power of its yield ($Y^{2/3}$) expressed in megatons.

13. There are many types of first strike that the Soviet Union could, in theory, launch. At the one extreme, there might be a massive, co-ordinated attack on all major European military and civil targets. At the other extreme, there might be a clandestine attack on one submarine. In this chapter, we consider primarily a coordinated Soviet attack on European military installations, with the main thrust being against European second-strike capabilities.

14. It should be pointed out that this represents only one effective option and that the choice between options would be strongly influenced by the attacking side's view of its requirements. As we have explained earlier, a high defensive probability of intercepting *each* incoming offensive target may only be equivalent to a low probability of intercepting *all* such targets. A 0.9 probability of destroying each of 64 incoming offensive warheads would hardly give the Soviet Union overwhelming confidence that it could deny the attacker *any* successful penetration, since there would then be a greater than 0.99 probability that one of the 64 would, in fact, penetrate.

15. Assuming, of course, that a sufficient percentage of the missiles reached their targets and detonated successfully.

16. It has been suggested that one option would be to fire Polaris missiles from a location sufficiently close to Moscow (less than 1,000 miles) to allow the use of a low-angle trajectory, thus reducing the warning time available to the defense. In practice, however, this would mean firing from the Baltic or the southern Barents Sea, neither of which positions is attractive from the ASW point of view.

17. It should, however, be pointed out that *for the same cost* it may be possible to buy very different force structures. Thus if it were decided to build forces for D_{1M} and to opt for sophisticated penetration aids, the alternative options of targeting outside Moscow would be different from those which would be available if D_{1M} were achieved by adding sheer numbers of missiles.

18. It is not axiomatic that a decision to equip A3 missiles with MIRVs rather than to buy Poseidon would result in major savings. Since the United States has not equipped its own A3 missiles with MIRVs, the costs of research, development, test and evaluation (RDT&E) for this program would presumably have to be carried by the Europeans. If U.S. technical assistance were not forthcoming, this could add up to a high figure and would involve some major investments in testing facilities. Some of these are mentioned in the section on the Poseidon option.

19. The sources of these figures are found in:

a. U.S. Senate, Committee on Armed Services, 91 Cong., 2 Sess., *Authorization for Military Procurement, Research and Development, Fiscal Year 1971* (Washington, D.C.: GPO, 1970).

b. U.S. House of Representatives, Committee on Appropriations, 91 Cong., 2 Sess., *Hearings before the Subcommittee on Department of Defense Appropriations for 1971; Part 5: Procurement Reprograming Actions* (Washington, D.C.: GPO, 1970).

WYNFRED JOSHUA

SALT and the Middle East

THE PAST DECADE has witnessed a tremendous growth in Soviet military might. In the realm of strategic nuclear weaponry, the USSR is close to attaining a status of rough parity with the United States. It has overcome the American lead in the number of ICBMs, even though it is still behind the United States in the number of deliverable nuclear warheads. Unlike the United States, the Soviet Union has continued to expand and improve its air defenses and its civil defense program. The Soviets appear to perceive psychological and diplomatic benefits from closing the strategic gap between Moscow and Washington. The USSR has also markedly upgraded and expanded its navy and is modernizing its ground and air forces. A rapidly growing naval and airlift capability permits the Soviets to project their power and influence in areas of the world in which Western hegemony had heretofore gone unchallenged. In the Mediterranean the presence of a Soviet naval squadron has largely neutralized the effect of the Sixth Fleet. Soviet warships have been introduced in waters where they were rarely seen before, such as in the Indian Ocean and Persian Gulf. Thousands of Soviet military advisers are attached to Arab armed forces, and some twelve thousand Russian air troops have helped protect Egyptian air space. In addition, Moscow has been taking daring diplomatic initiatives in Europe and elsewhere to try to reap political gains and determine the limits of Western flexibility.

The United States, on the other hand, reflecting the domestic disenchantment over the Vietnam War, has sought to curtail commitments that it had assumed in the days of the cold war. In response to disillusionment with the political utility of some of the U.S. overseas forces, and in reaction to domestic pressures to reorder national priorities and limit defense spending, President Nixon has called for a lower American profile abroad. In proclaiming the notion of sufficiency for American strategic forces, Washington apparently no longer believes it can attain strategic superiority, even if it should engage in an arms race; nor does it believe it could derive political benefits from engaging in such a race. A desire for strategic stability, compounded by concern over the risks and burdens of the nuclear arms race, has caused the

United States to invite the Soviet Union to explore the possibility of strategic arms limitations.

Although it is too early to conclude that the USSR is striving for strategic superiority, it may be suggested that Moscow and Washington entertain quite dissimilar perceptions of the political value of nuclear forces. As one observer warned, the potential for instability and serious problems in the future may lie precisely in this divergence of views.[1]

The outcome of the Strategic Arms Limitations Talks (SALT), even if producing an agreement, would not necessarily reveal whether such varying conceptions of military power had been reconciled. Nor is there a particular reason to assume that Soviet acceptance of a SALT agreement would be accompanied by a corresponding willingness to limit the competition at lower levels of conflict. Even though the Middle East is generally mentioned as an area in which the potential for Soviet-American collision appears greatest, it would be very difficult to say whether a SALT agreement would have implications for security in that region. For one thing, much depends on the motivations that led the Soviets to negotiate a strategic arms limitation accord in the first place. In analyzing a nation's motivations, moreover, political and basically subjective estimates inevitably come into play. For another thing, there is no linear relationship between the strategic nuclear equation and American-Soviet rivalry in the Middle East. In neither U.S. nor Soviet strategic calculations does the Middle East play a central role. The possible effects of a strategic arms limitation agreement on the Middle East would therefore be highly indirect and felt only over a period of time.

How an agreement in the SALT would affect the Soviet-American confrontation in the Middle East can perhaps best be approached by examining the objectives of the Russians in the SALT and their ambitions and policies in the Middle East. Against this background, the impact the SALT may have on the interactions between the USSR and other actors in the Middle East will be delineated.

Soviet Motivations in SALT

Without the foreknowledge of the terms of a strategic arms control agreement, it is not too easy to suggest what the objectives of the Soviet Union might be. Although this uncertainty remains unresolved, the observer must strike a cautious balance between optimism and pessimism, tempered by the recognition of some of the basic features of Soviet politico-military policy: the enhancement of the USSR's national security and the advancement of its power and influence in the world at the expense of the West, particularly of the United States.

Thomas W. Wolfe and several other Soviet experts have come up with a range of factors that have triggered Soviet participation in the SALT.[2] The experts generally concede the possibility that the USSR may sincerely seek to stabilize the strategic environment through an agreement at the SALT. They warn, at the same time, that persuasive arguments can also be made for a different case. There are indications that the Soviets are using the SALT to fashion an outcome that may permit them to obtain a margin of superiority over the United States.

GENUINE SOVIET CONCERNS IN ACCEPTING PARITY

Soviet experts suggest that the USSR may be willing to accept the current status of nuclear parity and is prepared either to forgo the promise of strategic superiority or to recognize that it cannot achieve superiority. Moscow is trying to win formal worldwide recognition of its strategic equality with Washington in a strategic arms control agreement. According to this argument, such an agreement would satisfy Russian aspirations for prestige.

Those who believe that the Soviets will abide by the present situation usually argue that the USSR has a genuine concern in relaxing the arms race through conclusion of an arms limitation agreement. They reason that the Soviet military budget has been a considerable burden on the Soviet economy.[3] Soviet growth rates in the industrial and agricultural sectors have declined, notably during the first half of the 1960s, although they seem to have recovered in the latter part of the decade.[4] Yet the Soviet Union needs to show that its system can compete with that of the capitalist world. The Russians are, moreover, under increasing domestic pressures to meet consumer demands. In addition, within the Soviet defense establishment there are rising pressures to expand the ground and overseas projection forces and to reallocate funds from the strategic forces. Inasmuch as the USSR has finally achieved rough quantitative equality in strategic weaponry with the United States, the argument goes, it may now be prepared to curtail further expansion of its strategic power and devote more resources to meeting consumer needs, solving the problem in the agricultural and industrial sectors, or increasing its nonstrategic forces.

A third factor, which is often cited to explain the potential Soviet acceptance of a strategic arms control agreement, derives from the Chinese challenge to the USSR. Although the future dimensions of the Chinese threat are uncertain, no Soviet planner can afford to neglect them in his calculations. Soviet willingness to accept a strategic arms control accord reflects the need to avoid facing two opponents at the same time. The USSR would not wish to have to cope with the classical dilemma of a two-front war, either in the political or in the military phase of the conflict. Closely related to this consideration is the possibility that Moscow may even foresee the need to enlist American cooperation in case it would be confronted with an increasingly militant Peking at a future date. The USSR might feel that a relaxation in tensions with the West, and especially with the United States, would be necessary in order to deal with an intensely hostile China.[5]

In arguing for Soviet willingness to accept the current equilibrium, another point can be made. The Soviet Union may feel that a SALT agreement would reinforce the *détente* climate. Moscow may believe that such a climate would facilitate the attainment of a number of their politico-military objectives, notably those in Europe. The purpose of the *détente* would be to persuade the American allies in Europe that the confrontation of the cold war days had ended and that they did not need to fear a Soviet military threat. From a Soviet point of view, such a situation would hopefully lead to a further erosion of the cohesion in NATO, an increased isolation of West Germany, and a progressive reduction in the American military presence in Europe.[6] In the 1971 agreement on Berlin, for example, the USSR undoubtedly sought to reassure the NATO allies that it had no designs on Western Europe.

Thus, desire for prestige, economic considerations, concerns about the Chinese threat, and the perception that a *détente* is conducive to the realization of Soviet goals are among the main arguments made to suggest that Moscow is sincerely interested in reaching an accord at the SALT. This line of reasoning does not necessarily imply that the basic contest between the superpowers is over. It assumes instead that mutually perceived advantages in strategic stability permit superpower rivalry to be conducted in areas other than the strategic realm.

SOVIET INTERESTS IN SUPERIORITY

Most Sovietologists also caution that a very different analysis of Soviet motivations can be made. They point to the continued evidence of a substantial Soviet buildup of more and better strategic weapons.[7] Examining the past trend in Soviet allocation of domestic resources, they argue that the USSR may be trying to overcome the American lead in strategic forces and intends to continue Soviet military expansion. According to close observers, the annual growth rate of the Soviet economy is acceptable to the Soviet leaders, who apparently believe that the current pace can be maintained.[8]

This group of analysts is deeply concerned that the SALT, or even most agreements likely to come out of the SALT, merely serve as a device to win time for the Soviets. Voluntary curtailment of U.S. strategic development for the duration of the negotiations may offer Moscow the opportunity to catch up with Washington in certain areas of military technology where it suffers a conspicuous though decreasing lag, notably in MIRV technology, ballistic missile defense, and high-accuracy guidance systems.[9] Such an attempt would indicate that the USSR still seeks to attain some margin of strategic superiority. That Moscow continues to entertain this hope should not be prematurely discounted. Soviet strategists have never renounced this goal. Indeed, Soviet writers publicly profess their nation's objective of winning quantitative and qualitative military superiority over the United States.[10]

Although such claims may be designed for both foreign and domestic consumption, one student of the USSR points out that there has been a marked consistency between military doctrine and force development in the Soviet Union. The debate over military strategy that broke out in 1954 evidently resulted in a consensus by 1960. In those areas in which doctrine and force structure do not correspond, as for example in the continued absence of the deployment of a national ballistic missile defense, technological limitations may provide the answer.[11]

In the opinion of this group of Western analysts, the Soviets may still be interested in fielding superior offensive and defensive forces. Such a policy is by no means incompatible with an agreement in the SALT, particularly if the agreement does not involve ballistic missile defenses and if the problem of verification is kept in mind. Neither Moscow nor Washington is likely to consent to on-site inspection of its strategic arsenals. Monitoring of any agreement will therefore be restricted to national means. Verification involves a wide spectrum of problems, but it appears reasonable to suggest that national means of verification are best suited for monitoring agreements that call for quantitative rather than qualitative limitations. To illustrate, satellite surveillance can detect and count silos and can indicate the size of the missile inside the silo, but it cannot discover the number of warheads nor the degree of delivery accuracy.[12]

Unfortunately, the technological factor has become increasingly important in assuring the effectiveness of an arms control arrangement.[13] Assuming that the Soviets can perfect their MIRV capability for the SS-9 and their other new missiles, they are not far from obtaining a counterforce capability, even though the American Polaris- and Poseidon-armed submarines continue to be relatively secure in the near future. The Soviets appear to be equally concerned about strengthening their defensive forces. They continue to modernize their air defenses through expensive weapons systems, such as the impressive Foxbat interceptor. Their civil defense program is considerable. They are gaining in all elements of the strategic balance with the exception of the Ballistic Missile Defense (BMD) area, in which they are behind.

The issue of BMD limitations will be the key to a meaningful strategic arms control agreement. An agreement that would permit the Soviets to establish an ABM defense around Moscow and the United States to erect similar protection around its ICBMs implies Soviet acceptance of mutual deterrence through assured destruction. An agreement that would permit protection of Moscow but not of U.S. ICBMs, or an arrangement that would permit BMD for Soviet urban-industrial centers without similar protection for American cities, might enable the USSR to attain eventually a politically usable margin of strategic superiority over the United States.[14]

There is a growing acceptance among American strategists that it is currently impossible to attain sufficient strategic superiority to yield political dividends. It is by no means certain, however, that their Soviet counterparts share this view. For years the Soviets have heard the claim that overwhelming American strategic power insured stability. They have devoted considerable time and resources to trying to bridge the missile gap. Moscow may well feel that there is a definite, if intangible, political advantage to strategic superiority and that this is attainable. If gained, it would in Soviet eyes, seriously erode the coupling of the American nuclear umbrella to the defense of Europe. In the light of the political advantages the Soviets apparently perceive, there would be no reason to expect that they would give up the chance of reaching superiority the moment the prospect appeared near.

SALT and Parity

Western analysts usually describe the present strategic balance between the superpowers as one of approaching parity. This concept generally entails a quantitative definition: approximate numerical equality of launchers, warheads, megatonnage, or whatever criteria were selected. Regardless of specific numbers, it is likely that a SALT agreement will be perceived in much of the world as the codification of parity. This could entail a variety of restrictions, including limitations on the number of launchers or on the scope of ballistic missile defense.

Whatever the precise provisions, the codification of parity through the SALT would signal the formal end of the period of American strategic superiority. It would militate against efforts by the United States to regain its privileged position. There is no consensus among the experts on the extent to which the Soviet Union might try to gain a measure of qualitative superiority. This would, moreover, depend on the scope of BMD restrictions the USSR would be prepared to accept. The politico-military threat from China against the USSR alone, however, would suggest that Soviet acceptance of BMD limitations may be remote. Probably the most that can be expected to develop from the SALT is, in the sobering words of one observer, an improved management of the arms race.[15]

Whether or not it is ratified in the SALT, the United States remains confronted with the emergence of strategic nuclear parity between the superpowers. In addition, the very real possibility continues to exist that the Soviets will try to achieve at least a technological lead in the strategic arena that can be exploited for political purposes. For the student of the Middle East the question arises whether the attainment of parity and the possible prospect of superiority will affect Soviet behavior in the Middle East. The translation of Soviet strategic nuclear gains into Soviet actions in the Middle East will depend not only on Soviet perceptions of the strategic equation and possible reactions by the United States and other interested powers, but also on Moscow's calculations of its interests and capabilities in the Middle East. Therefore, the role of this region in Soviet foreign policy needs to be examined before trying to estimate the effect, if any, of the constellation of strategic power on the Middle East.

The Importance of the Middle East in Soviet Policies

Since the days of Peter the Great the Russians have tried to extend their influence in the Middle East. The contiguous Middle East countries, notably Turkey and Iran, have served both as a buffer that protected Russia's southern flanks and as a barrier that prevented Russian encroachment southward. The Turkish Straits limited the accessibility of Black Sea ports. Expansion into the Middle East, particularly through pressure on Turkey and Iran, and access to warm-water ports have traditionally been Russian objectives. The presence of British and French forces in the Middle East was a major factor in preventing the realization of Russian goals.

The establishment of American power in the region during and after the Second World War further thwarted these age-old Russian aspirations. The undermining and eventual elimination of the American political and military presence, notably the U.S. naval presence, became Soviet goals.

Although of increasingly limited importance, the ideological dimension to Soviet policy has not yet completely disappeared. Partly to offset any attraction that Peking's brand of communism may have in the Middle East and partly to prove that the Soviet Union remains the leader of the Communist world, Moscow seeks to consolidate its influence in the Middle East. To the extent that ideology still helps to shape Soviet foreign policy, the Soviet thrust into the region is a matter of scoring ideological successes and prestige points.

The USSR has, further, very pragmatic interests in Middle Eastern oil. Present forecasts suggest that by 1980, if not before, Soviet consumption of oil is expected to outstrip domestic production. Furthermore, East European oil requirements, of which Moscow provides more than half (55 percent) at the present, are expected to triple by 1980. Equally important, 80 percent of the military and economic machine of NATO Europe runs on Middle East fuel. The prospects are, moreover, that within a few years the United States will also need to start importing oil from the Middle East. In addition to the Soviet Union's own needs, leverage over Mideast oil will give Moscow a very powerful weapon not only against the European NATO allies, but against Washington as well.

The Middle East is particularly important to the success of Soviet maritime strategy. The region comprises the shortest water passage between Europe and Asia and the fastest route from Black Sea and Baltic Sea ports to India and the Far East. The reopening of the Suez Canal would markedly facilitate Soviet access to the Persian Gulf and the Indian Ocean, where Moscow already deploys a limited naval force. The availability of the canal would considerably enhance the mobility of the Soviet Mediterranean fleet.

Soviet concern with the Middle East further derives from the region's place in Western policies. Soviet hegemony in the region would be the realization of some of the most fundamental objectives of Soviet foreign policy. It would mean outflanking NATO from the south. It would also provide the Soviet Union with the capability to deny the strategic and economic assets of the Middle East to the Western allies.

To be sure, since the development of the ICBM and Polaris the region has declined in strategic value for the United States. Geographically, the Middle East has also become less important; air transport does not require land bridges or crossroads. Even for the West European allies the region's transit and economic value has somewhat diminished. The Europeans have lost their Far Eastern empires. The development of supertankers and large bulk carriers increasingly erodes the commercial value of the Suez Canal.

Nevertheless, in spite of this limited devaluation in the region's role in Western policies, should the USSR succeed in drawing the Middle East into its sphere of influence, the overall balance of power in the world could be seriously upset. It would signify a major political and psychological defeat for the United States, with profound repercussions on its posture throughout the world. It would accelerate a political reorientation of Iran and other pro-Western countries in the region toward a more neutral foreign policy stance. Certainly Turkey, if not also Italy, would seek an accommodation with the Soviet Union, thereby precipitating the breakup of the NATO alliance. For the European NATO allies the region continues to have important assets. These factors go far to explain why the Middle East will continue to be of vital interest to both the United States and the Soviet Union.

Soviet Exploitation of Middle East Interactions

Given these interests and objectives, the Soviets have been ready to exploit every opportunity that has come along. They have skillfully used existing regional differences and conflicts. Soviet policies have helped to link the three levels of conflict and interaction in the Middle East: the intra-Arab split, the Arab-Israeli conflict, and the superpower confrontation.

By exploiting the split between the radical or revolutionary Arab leaders and the traditional and politically more conservative ones, the USSR has sought to make it increasingly difficult for the traditional Arab regimes to maintain their ties with the United States. Radical Arab regimes currently rule in Algeria, Libya, Egypt, Syria, Iraq, Yemen, Southern Yemen, and the Sudan. There are several expressions of Arab radicalism, notably Nasserism and the Baathist movement, and there are profound differences and rivalries within and among radical movements. They have in common, however, a bitter opposition to the traditional Arab regimes, and they demand revolutionary change in order to establish some form of Arab socialism. The radical Arabs also share a deep distrust of the West, particularly the United States, which they identify with imperialism and neocolonialism. The various versions of radicalism generally stress Arab nationalism. They call for the termination of Arab dependence on Western imperialism by eliminating all military and political ties with the West, closing all Western bases in the region, pursuing a neutralist foreign policy, and striving for Arab unity and solidarity.[16]

As is the case with their radical counterparts, there is little cohesion among the traditional Arab states. Their group comprises Morocco, Tunisia, Jordan, Saudi Arabia, Lebanon, Kuwait, and the Persian Gulf states. Although not an Arab state, Iran shares with the traditionalists their suspicion of the radical Arabs and a willingness to maintain close and friendly relations with the United States and its allies.

Both categories of Arab leaders have since the 1967 war sought to downgrade their own animosities. But on the whole, the suppression of the radical-traditional rift has had only limited success. The lack of Arab cohesion can be seen in Syria's intervention in the Jordanian civil war of September 1970, Arab reactions against Jordan's continued offensive against the Palestinian guerrillas, and Libya's vociferous approval of the efforts of Moroccan rebels to overthrow King Hassan.

The importance of the intra-Arab split lies not so much in the possibility of the eruption of an armed conflict; rather it derives from its political implications. The ideological bias of the radical Arabs causes them to find their allies in the East, where they can obtain the necessary support. Although the radicals are not necessarily pro-Communist, particularly not where domestic affairs are concerned, they are opposed to Western influences. The Soviet Union, on its part, has promptly taken advantage of the opportunities the radical Arabs offered. The receptivity of the radical Arabs to Soviet offers of military and economic aid and political support greatly contributed to the entrenchment of the USSR in the Middle East.[17] As such, the radical-traditional rift has been a major factor in American-Soviet competition for influence in the Middle East.

Prospects are that radical Arab forces will continue to work against Western interests in the region and that in their efforts they will continue to receive Soviet support. Moreover, the number of radical Arab states can be expected to grow. In much of the Arab world the traditional rulers are perceived as friends of Western imperialism and therefore also as friends of the allies of Israel. Radical leaders are bound to exploit this image of the traditional rulers in order to divert attention from their own failures and to enhance their own position. Radical agitation against traditional governments and domestic unrest combine to create a climate that will engender coup attempts against the remaining traditional rulers. In light of these possibilities, the intra-Arab split is likely to continue to work in favor of Soviet interests.

In the Arab-Israeli conflict the Soviet Union has championed the

Arab cause and has tried to polarize the situation by isolating the United States with Israel as its only ally in the Middle East. Partly because an acceptable settlement continues to escape the frustrated Arabs and partly because the Soviet Union is perceived as the only possible ally in radical Arab eyes, the Soviets have reaped substantial gains. The fundamentally opposed goals of Israel and its principal Arab adversary, Egypt, have contributed to the continuing stalemate. Israeli demands for a settlement that provides for maximum security through defensible borders are not compatible with Egyptian hopes for a political settlement that returns occupied Egyptian territories and accommodates in some fashion Jordanian and Syrian as well as Palestinian claims.

In spite of the massive Soviet arms deliveries to Egypt and the efforts of more than six thousand Soviet military instructors,[18] the Egyptian armed forces themselves are still no match for the highly trained and strongly motivated Israeli troops. Reports indicate that there is little improvement in the performance rate of Egyptian army officers.[19] They continue to lack the leadership qualities and the combat experience necessary for modern warfare. The effectiveness of the Egyptian navy remains doubtful vis-à-vis its Israeli counterpart. The capability of the Egyptian air force remains marginal because of the chronic shortage of combat pilots and its limited number of bombers with the range to reach Israel and return. In addition, it is unlikely that in case of war Egypt could depend on effective military support from other Arab powers. Without active Soviet support, therefore, another full-scale Arab-Israeli war appears remote, for the specter of a fourth Egyptian defeat would probably suffice to restrain Egypt from launching an all-out war. In the unlikely event of another round, much will depend, therefore, on Soviet reactions.

The Arab-Israeli conflict was a major factor that facilitated the consolidation of the Soviet position in the Middle East. The USSR benefited greatly from the widely held belief that Washington was honor bound to support Israeli interests. Arab antagonism to Israel, however, was by no means the only factor that permitted the Soviet Union to score its gains in the Middle East. It frequently had no bearing on the initial acceptance of Soviet arms aid by an Arab client. Most Soviet aid recipients had first tried unsuccessfully to obtain arms aid from the United States or another Western power in order to strengthen their domestic position or their position vis-à-vis a regional rival other than Israel; others sought Soviet arms in order to demonstrate their general defiance of Western cold war policies. However, once the arms aid relationship with the Soviets had been created, the belief that the donor was the only reliable ally of the Arabs against the Israelis paved the way for deeper entrenchment of the USSR and further erosion of the American position in the Middle East. By the time of the June 1967 war, the radical Arab states were so deeply committed to the defeat of Israel and so dependent on Soviet support that the Arab-Israeli issue dominated their relations with the Soviet Union and with the United States as well.

The years since the Six-Day War have demonstrated the rise of Soviet influence and the decline of that of the United States in the Middle East. Initially, the humiliating Arab defeat proved to be embarrassing for Moscow. In addition, Soviet unwillingness to intervene during the fighting undoubtedly disappointed many Arabs. But the hostility that the radical Arabs felt against the Anglo-American powers outweighed by far their disillusionment in the Russians. Nasser's accusations of Anglo-American complicity in the 1967 war inflamed anti-Western sentiments throughout the Arab world. Compounding these passions was the recognition that only Moscow could be depended upon to defend the Arab cause in diplomatic circles, and only Moscow was prepared to rebuild the smashed Arab armies. Thus the radical Arabs felt forced to rely increasingly on the Soviet Union for military and political support. In addition, even the traditional Arabs shared the perception of the radical Arab leaders that American policy-makers had unduly favored Israel. After the June war, therefore, Washington's stature had declined in all Arab states.

The prompt and vigorous Soviet military aid program was a key factor in regaining the political ground lost by the Soviets and in compensating the Arabs for their bitter humiliation. Within four months Moscow had replaced about 80 percent of Egyptian losses, and by 1969 the radical Arabs were quantitatively and qualitatively better off in terms of equipment than before the war. The introduction in 1970 of an impressive air defense screen in Egypt, manned by Soviet troops, and the subsequent dispatch of a number of Moscow's most sophisticated fighter planes complete with combat crews further tied the Egyptians to the Soviets. The establishment of the Soviet air defense network, together with the dispersal of Egyptian planes and the hardening of shelters, has made a repeat performance of the 1967 war highly unlikely for the Israelis. Inasmuch as Israel's defense is based on the option of resorting to a preemptive first strike, the local balance of forces was considerably affected.

Perhaps the most dramatic result of the 1967 war has been the expansion of the Soviet naval presence in the Mediterranean, coupled with the availability of Arab ports to Soviet ships for repairs, replenishment, and storage of supplies. The deployment of Soviet warships is designed partly to counter the Sixth Fleet and partly to deter Israel. Probably more important, however, is the political utility of the Soviet flotilla. The Soviet naval presence symbolizes Soviet political identification with the Arab cause. It is also directed at the southern NATO flank, notably at Turkey and Greece. It seeks to instill a perception of the decreasing value of the U.S. presence in the Mediterranean in order to undermine the credibility of the U.S. commitment to defend the NATO members against aggression. The belief that the Soviets have just about attained strategic nuclear parity has exacerbated these concerns. The close surveillance of the Sixth Fleet by Soviet ships and planes is not lost upon the southern NATO members, even though in numbers and capability American and allied naval forces are still considered superior to the Soviet squadron. But the visibility of Soviet ships constantly impresses the NATO nations along the coast with the warning that the USSR is present near their own shores.

The deployment of the Soviet fleet further implies a subtle political and psychological defeat for the United States and serves as a reminder to Washington that from now on it will be constrained in exercising its political and military options. The possibility of American intervention in the Mediterranean littoral, as for example in 1958 in Lebanon, would henceforth be much more risky.

Few would question the position of the Soviet Union as a major power in the Middle East. This does not mean that Moscow can manipulate the Arabs at will as the expulsion of Soviet military personnel from Egypt in July 1972 demonstrated. There are some fundamental inconsistencies in Soviet Mideast policies that reduce the influence the USSR may have in the Arab world. Soviet aid to Syria is basically incompatible with aid to Iraq; a similar contradiction exists in Soviet military support of other long-standing rivals, such as Iran and Egypt.

Paradoxically, the Arab-Israeli issue, which provided the USSR with its largest dividends, can also produce its most agonizing problem. In the volatile Middle East the possibility remains for a crisis to escalate into a full-fledged war. If the Arabs were again threatened with defeat, the Soviets would be under considerable pressure to intervene rather than risk losing their arduously built influence. With the presence of even small numbers of Soviet military personnel on the scene, it would also be politically more difficult to refrain from helping the Arabs. On the other hand, if the Arabs, with Soviet support, threatened to defeat Israel, the United States might feel forced to rally to Israel's support. The Soviets are unlikely to welcome the prospects of either scenario. Both would entail considerable risk of a Soviet-American confrontation. Unless parity has radically changed Soviet attitudes toward the use of force against the United States, Moscow will continue to try avoiding the risk of armed collision with Washington. The USSR can derive greater political advantage from the presence of Soviet forces in the Middle East in peacetime than from their use in wartime, particularly when war risks U.S. intervention and involves such a highly motivated combatant as Israel—hence Soviet refusal to provide Egypt with ground-to-ground missiles and aircraft with a range capable of striking targets in Israel. From a Soviet point of view, a continued state of tensions below the level of war holds the best promise for the achievement of Soviet objectives.

SALT and the Middle East

The sketch of Soviet objectives and activities in the Middle East does not augur well for Soviet cooperation in finding a political solution to the Arab-Israeli issue. Whether a SALT agreement would make the Soviets more amenable to a peaceful settlement in the Middle East or would affect the policies of other actors interested in the region depends largely on the confluence of other forces generated by the agreement in the SALT.

The absence of an agreement in the SALT would barely affect the pattern of relations in the Middle East. The Soviets may be even less inclined to encourage a political settlement, but the mere lack of a formal SALT accord would not be sufficient for the Soviets to assume greater risks than in the past; nor would it influence the behavior of other nations in the Middle East.

Perhaps the major result of an accord in the SALT, regardless of the meaningfulness of its content, will be to engender an upsurge of optimism in the Western world about *détente* and a relaxation of tensions. The conclusion of an agreement would have little direct effect on the Middle East, but it could eventually have politically important ramifications for that region.

If the Soviet Union genuinely sought to moderate the arms race and obtain ·recognition as the strategic equal of the United States, such motivations might also affect Soviet policy in other areas. The Soviets might be willing to pursue a less activist policy in the Middle East. Furthermore, the existence of sharp disagreement within the Soviet Union over the SALT has been discussed in Western circles.[20] An agreement in the SALT might strengthen the hand of those Soviet leaders who held out for negotiating with the Americans. They might well call for further improvement in U.S.-Soviet relations and argue to avoid jeopardizing the spirit of *détente* by encouraging crises elsewhere. They could counsel caution in other areas, particularly in a region as fraught with risks as the Middle East. For all these reasons, the possibility exists that the Soviets might be willing to relax their pressure on the Middle East and adopt a more flexible attitude. However, given their past record in the Middle East, such a course of action for the Soviets appears remote.

It is possible that the international recognition of Soviet-American equality may encourage the Soviets to be more adventurous in the Middle East and to take greater risks. If the SALT agreement would restrict BMD to Moscow and to a sufficient number of U.S. strategic missile bases to insure a U.S. second-strike capability, it would lock the superpowers into a mutual assured destruction posture. The Soviets might then feel that they had neutralized U.S. strategic power and could afford to be less restrained in their actions at the lower end of the conflict spectrum. Yet in spite of such Soviet perceptions, Russian activities in the Middle East may remain restrained and cautious. Western Europe continues to be a much more vital area in Soviet strategic calculations than the Middle East. The present *détente* climate in Europe, fueled by the SALT agreements, promises the achievement of some long-coveted Soviet goals. Any rash Soviet action in the Middle East would undoubtedly arouse Western European suspicions and might act as a catalyst to draw the NATO allies together again. It is unlikely that the Soviets would be prepared to jeopardize the possibility of winning their most treasured objectives on the European continent. An accord at the strategic arms control negotiations would not by itself generate much change in Soviet policies.

An agreement in the SALT could, however, affect the United States. The perception of a changed and much improved international climate —whether imagined or real—could create increased domestic pressures on the American government to continue negotiations with the Soviet Union toward further arms control agreements. Washington would probably be extremely reluctant to jeopardize the *détente* by trying to restrain Soviet probing or militancy in the Middle East. Domestic euphoria about the perceived possibility that the arms race could be significantly restricted could create a climate at home in which it would be increasingly difficult to obtain congressional approval of requested military appropriations. It is likely that in the opinion of some liberal leaders the utility of U.S. military forces, notably those stationed overseas, would progressively decline. The reduced military budget might affect the capabilities of the United States to support its policy in the Middle East with force, if necessary. At the same time, the domestic climate would make it more difficult to provide Israel with more aid.

If the SALT were to generate such pressures in the United States, then Israel may conclude that the U.S. government was trying to disassociate itself from the security of Israel. Compounding this concern may be the perception on the part of the Israelis that American strategic power had been neutralized by Soviet parity. These perceptions may motivate Israel to develop its own nuclear capability or to threaten to do so. Western observers generally concede that Israel has the potential to develop nuclear weapons in the near future. The Israelis may wish to realize this potential and exploit it as a bargaining instrument in the hope of precipitating a settlement.

The existence or possibility of an Israeli nuclear capability may well cause the Soviets to adopt a much more cautious policy. Under heightened pressures to protect their Arab clients, the Soviets may try to persuade their protégés to negotiate some type of compromise settlement.

The foreign policies of both Turkey and Iran are likely to be redirected to some extent as an eventual consequence of a SALT agreement. Turkey is bound to take note of the internal pressures in the United States generated by a strategic arms control agreement. In the Turkish point of view, NATO is primarily identified with the United States. Turkish concern about the credibility of American protection under NATO might cause Turkey to hedge its bet and seek further accommodation with the Soviet Union. Turkey might, for example, apply in a very liberal manner the restrictive provisions of the Montreux Convention to the transit of Soviet ships or it might eventually give in to Soviet pressures to revise the convention.

Iran may similarly conclude that U.S. readiness to defend Western interests in its area is declining. Neither Turkey nor Iran is likely to become a close Soviet collaborator. Existing suspicions reflecting traditional rivalry with the Soviet Union argue against such a development. But Iran, like Turkey, may try to take out insurance against a diminishing U.S. commitment and seek a diplomatic *détente* with the USSR. Greece will have few options but to stay closely allied to the United States, at least as long as the present junta remains in control. Should, however, another regime accede to power, Greece may well follow the example of Turkey and Iran.

In short, a strategic arms limitation agreement may help to erode what remains of the U.S. position and influence in the Middle East. Such a development, however, is by no means inevitable. For one thing, the Soviets may overplay their hand and alienate their Arab clients, who already resent the Russian presence in their midst. The Soviets, moreover, are likely to refrain from actions that may seriously upset the European NATO allies. Then, too, the American administration is likely to be especially careful to restrain undue optimism at home about the possibility of limiting the arms race.

From the standpoint of American interests, the most hopeful prospect appears to lie in keeping the Middle East crisis relatively dormant. Given sufficient time, the Arab-Israeli question is likely to solve itself, for a lasting settlement lies in the possibility that the protagonists learn to tolerate each other. Admittedly, this is a solution for the long run. But no imposed arrangement is likely to endure. This means that the United States should exercise restraint in trying to precipitate a settlement. It requires at the same time some evidence of a continued American commitment to retain a reasonable balance of forces in the Middle East, lest the Soviet Union attempt to exploit its newly won strategic parity.

NOTES

1. The possible implications of the difference in Soviet and American estimates of the utility of military power are suggested in a perceptive and thought-provoking analysis by Andrew J. Pierre, "America Down, Russia Up: The Changing Political Role of Military Power," *Foreign Policy,* no. 4 (Fall 1971), pp. 163–87.

2. An analysis of different sets of motivations that have driven the Soviets to the conference table can be found in Thomas W. Wolfe, "Soviet Approaches to SALT," *Problems of Communism,* 19 (September–October 1970), pp. 1–10.

3. See, for example, Marshall Schulman, "The Effect of ABM on U.S.-Soviet Relations," in *ABM: An Evaluation,* ed., Abram Chayes and Jerome B. Wiesner (New York: Harper & Row, 1969), pp. 155–56.

4. For studies of Soviet defense expenditure trends, see S. A. Anderson, W. T. Lee et al., *Probable Trend and Magnitude of Soviet Expenditures for National Security Purposes,* SSC-RM-54 (Stanford: Strategic Studies Center, Stanford Research Institute, February 1969), and W. T. Lee, I. M. Oakwood, and J. H. Alexander, *Production and Allocation of Hardward to Military, Space, and RDT&E Programs, 1955–65,* SSC-TN-76 (Stanford: Strategic Studies Center, March 1968).

5. For a commentary on Soviet concern with China and its relationship to the SALT, see Lawrence T. Caldwell, *Soviet Attitudes to SALT,* Adelphi Paper, no. 75 (London: Institute for Strategic Studies, 1971), p. 13.

6. The effect of the SALT on Europe is discussed in Wilhelm Grewe, "The Effect of Strategic Agreements on European-American Relations," in *Soviet-*

American Relations and World Order: Arms Limitations and Policy (London: Institute for Strategic Studies, 1970), pp. 16–24.

7. See for example the report by William Beecher, "Satellites Spot a Soviet Buildup for Atomic Arms," *New York Times* (October 11, 1971).

8. Wolfe, "Soviet Approaches to SALT," p. 3.

9. See the testimony of Dr. John S. Foster, Jr., Director of Defense Research and Engineering, before the Committee on Appropriations, U.S. Senate, on March 24, 1971, for an examination of the dangers inherent in current comparative U.S./Soviet military technological development trends.

10. A now well-nigh classical statement of this claim is found in Col. V. M. Bondarenko, "Military-Technical Superiority: The Most Important Factor in the Reliable Defense of the Country," in *The Nuclear Revolution in Soviet Military Affairs,* eds. William R. Kintner and Harriet Fast Scott (Norman: University of Oklahoma Press, 1968). See also Caldwell, *Soviet Attitudes to SALT,* p. 12.

11. For a discussion of the consistency between Soviet doctrine and force development, see William T. Lee, "The Rationale Underlying Soviet Strategic Forces," in *Safeguard: Why the ABM Makes Sense,* ed. William R. Kintner (New York: Hawthorn Books, 1969), pp. 160–78.

12. For example, see D. G. Hoag, "Ballistic Missile Guidance," in *Impact of New Technologies on the Arms Race: A Pugwash Monograph,* ed. Steven Weinberg et al. (Cambridge: The M.I.T. Press, 1971), pp. 102, 107–8.

13. The significance of qualitative improvements has been analyzed by R. B. Foster, "The Overall Balance of Power in the 1970s: Military, Economic, Moral," a paper presented at the conference, "Alternatives to Attrition: United States Policy and Wars of National Liberation," cosponsored by the National Strategy Information Center and the Airlie Institute for International Studies (March 11, 1971).

14. While Moscow is unlikely to attain in the near future a decisive strategic superiority over Washington—the United States would still retain its second-strike capability—a margin of superiority would enable the USSR to foreclose an increasing number of options to the United States. The difference between decisive and marginal superiority is analyzed in R. B. Foster, "Strategic Interactions: A New Mode," unpublished paper (Washington, D.C.: Stanford Research Institute, 1971).

15. Colin S. Gray, "The ABM and the Arms Race," *Aerospace Historian,* 18 (Spring, March 1971), p. 31.

16. For a more detailed discussion of Arab radicalism, see George Lenczowski, "Radical Regimes in Egypt, Syria, and Iraq," *Journal of Politics,* 28 (February 1966), pp. 29–56, and Robin Buss, *Wary Partners: The Soviet Union and Arab Socialism* (London: Institute for Strategic Studies, December 1970).

17. For a detailed discussion of Soviet military and economic aid, see Wynfred Joshua, *Soviet Penetration into the Middle East* (New York: National Strategy Information Center, 1971).

18. Soviet air defense troops and Soviet combat pilots are not included in the number of instructors.

19. *New York Times* (May 11, 1971).

20. Caldwell, *Soviet Attitudes to SALT,* pp. 12–19.

GEORGE H. QUESTER

Implications of SALT Outcome for Potential "Nth" Powers: Israel, India, and Others

Introduction

THE STRATEGIC ARMS LIMITATION TALKS (SALT) have assuredly been the most significant development in arms control since the United States and the Soviet Union presented their agreed text of the Nuclear Non-Proliferation Treaty (NPT). It is only natural, therefore, to expect some interrelationship between two consecutive arms control steps of major importance, all the more so when the success or failure of either venture is not yet determined and when success for one could contribute to success, or to failure, for the other.

Erecting a barrier to the spread of nuclear weapons has been discussed since the later 1950s. More serious comparisons of Soviet and American positions began after 1965, and final agreement on a treaty was reached between 1967 and June of 1968.[1] Although a number of significant "near-nuclear" states signed the treaty within the month after it was presented, the Soviet invasion of Czechoslovakia in August substantially delayed the accretion of signatures and ratifications thereafter, showing how much the symbolism and reality of great-power behavior can affect smaller nations in their willingness to commit themselves.

By 1970, enough signatures and ratifications had been collected to put the treaty into legal effect, but a number of the most significant "near-nuclear" states have not fully bound themselves. West Germany, Italy, Japan, Australia, and the United Arab Republic have signed, but have not yet ratified. Israel, India, Brazil, Pakistan, and South Africa have not even signed the NPT.

All along there has been an argument that arms limitations on the two superpowers, as envisaged in the SALT, would actually weaken the chances of the NPT. In this view, a continued arms race between the United States and the Soviet Union is required to reduce incentives for other states to enter the "nuclear club" and to reassure the neighbors

255

of such states. ABM and the latest missiles in the American and Soviet arsenals thus might make a Japanese nuclear program look more inappropriate, since it would be all the harder to catch up. The latest increments of the two great arsenals indeed cast doubt on the military efficacy of the British, French, and Chinese nuclear weapons programs, and even more so on that of India and Israel. If India wished to be assured that it could not be blackmailed by China, in this view, it would be better if the Soviet Union and the United States went ahead with ABM protection for their own cities, so that the threat of nuclear reprisal by either one of these states against China, on behalf of India, would remain credible.

By the same line of argument, any substantial great-power decision to go beyond a freeze, to reduce nuclear weapons arsenals, would simply be that much more of a temptation for an erstwhile "sixth" or "seventh" nuclear power to enter the "club" when the standards of admission and annual dues had just been lowered. Total nuclear disarmament by the five existing nuclear weapons states might seem the full moral equivalent of what the NPT is proposing for all the others; yet the chances of adherence to an NPT by all the others would seem considerably less than whatever chances we see today.

Yet there is, of course, a strong counterargument that successful SALT will help assure the success of the NPT, since Article VI of the NPT itself imposes an obligation on the great powers to "pursue negotiations in good faith on effective measures relating to cessation of the nuclear arms race at an early date and to nuclear disarmament, and on a treaty on general and complete disarmament under strict and effective international control." Many commentators on the NPT have questioned the apparent asymmetry and inequity of the treaty, tolerating the weapons prerogative forever for those five nations, the United States, the Soviet Union, Britain, France, and China, that were prudent enough to enter the "club" before 1967, denying the nuclear weapons prerogative to everyone else.[2] Some diplomats have even described it as the "first unequal treaty of the twentieth century." A failure to reach agreement might well be cited as an excuse to withhold ratifications in some countries, or even at the extreme to withdraw from the treaty where it had been ratified. Disarmament has perhaps too long been viewed as a moral question, portrayed as such by opposing sides in the Cold War, each trying to divert the world's accusations against the other. Yet as long as this moralistic interpretation of disarmament remains persuasive on much of our globe, a failure of the SALT may well be bitterly resented by the nations that are asked to renounce nuclear weapons, resented enough to upset full or final agreement on the NPT.[3]

It is argued in this chapter that neither argument sufficiently describes the impact of the SALT on nuclear proliferation, since more complicated linkages will have to be discussed after looking at the particular political or strategic problems of the countries we fear may become the "nth."

In terms of threatening to become the sixth nation with nuclear weapons, only two nations offer cause for immediate alarm, Israel and India. For these states the status of the formal Non-Proliferation Treaty makes less of a difference, since neither has signed, and neither has shown any willingness to sign. India has stated very clearly its objections, which intentionally or otherwise will be impossible to satisfy. Israel has been much more quiet about the NPT, but also has raised enough objections to suggest that it will make its rejection of the treaty permanent. If these two nations do not sign the NPT, they would of course still abide by its most important provision as long as they did not acquire nuclear weapons. The weapons procurement decisions of these states hence will still be of enormous significance in motivating those other "near-nuclear" states which have signed and ratified the treaty, or those which have signed but not yet ratified.

Israel

Why should Israel be suspected of seeking to produce nuclear weapons?[4] The answer may seem obvious, since the country is confronted with military engagements on all its frontiers, and since it has done the basic research that would be required to manufacture atomic bombs.[5] Yet Israel cannot be considering its nuclear options simply in terms of advantages these might offer over Arab enemies, since as elsewhere the great powers are also involved in the Middle East.

The United States is assuredly opposed to Israel's acquisition of nuclear weapons. The Soviet Union, aligned with the Arab states, is also opposed. The degree of U.S. anger at the Israelis if a bomb were produced may be difficult to gauge, but it is not yet expected to be trivial. It is also possible that an Israeli bomb would drive the Soviet Union to deepen its commitments to Egypt and other Arab states, lest these states frantically look elsewhere, perhaps to Peking, for support.

What purposes would an Israeli nuclear arsenal serve? Abstractly, one could all along have conjured up battlefield scenarios in which Israeli nuclear weapons would have made a significant difference. The classic Israeli fear used to be of an Arab conventional armored attack that somehow would succeed and would then sweep down on Tel Aviv and Haifa to push the Israelis into the sea. Such an attack has often seemed to be the Arab dream. The Israeli expansion of 1967 may have made such an eventuality seem less likely, but one can still speculate about it, if forty million Arabs ever become as technically and militarily competent as two or three million Israelis. To remove the Israeli nightmare or Arab dream, might one not add a small nuclear retaliatory force capable of destroying five or six Arab cities and the Aswan High Dam? Would this not force the Arabs once and for all to give up hopes of driving Israel into the sea? Would it not mean, in Pierre Gallois fashion, that the Arabs could never exploit any battlefield victory they might ever win, for fear of the intolerable last-gasp retaliation the Israeli nuclear force would inflict?

Apart from deterrence and specific strategic scenarios, Israelis tend to see even the rumors of their bomb program as having important psychological impact in intimidating the Arab states. The theories of strategic psychology propounded here are quite different from those used by Americans to describe their balance of terror with the USSR. Israelis are not so directly concerned with carrot-and-stick games of encouraging the Arabs to do this or deterring them from that. Rather than attributing a rational calculus of costs and gains to their Arab adversaries, Israeli planners impute a more visceral sense of power and weakness. By refusing to sign the NPT, therefore, while for the moment not openly detonating any bombs, the Israelis do not guide the Arabs, but rather hope to cow them with a vaguer sense of power, a sense that can be furthered by periodic rumors of bomb projects. Arab propaganda inevitably assists in this purpose by claiming that Israel is already manufacturing nuclear weapons; if enough Arabs come to believe this, it might be gratuitous to dispel their illusions.

What of a guarantee by one of the existing nuclear powers, specifically the United States, as an alternative to Israeli atomic bombs? The United States might very credibly be expected to retaliate for any nuclear attack on Israel, but such nuclear attacks are not the most pressing threat. Would the American "nuclear umbrella" extend to deterring Arab conventional attacks on Israel? The answer has hardly been certain to be "Yes." Washington would very probably escalate to the nuclear level in the defense of West Germany against Soviet armor, but very possibly might not in the defense of Israel against the identical model of Soviet tanks driven by Syrians or Egyptians.

Yet Arab defeats of Israeli forces in conventional battles are hardly imminent. By acquiring nuclear weapons, Israel might thus simply be changing a game when she has consistently been winning under the old rules. For the Arabs to sweep the battlefield in the foreseeable future, massive Soviet assistance and participation would be required. But Soviet intervention in the Middle East for the moment is not likely to include armored columns punching through the Sinai desert. Such intervention is constrained by the Soviet desire to avoid baiting the United States into a direct confrontation, and by the danger of neutral world condemnation following any combat operations directly involving Soviet fighting men. Moscow presumably would prefer to offer the kinds of military assistance that make overt hostilities generally less, rather than more, likely in the Middle East, as long as some pressure is maintained to get the Israelis eventually to withdraw. Risks of more serious escalation preclude the Soviet Union from indiscriminately making available the weapons and armed forces that suggest Cairo's taking the offensive.

But Soviet assistance to the Egyptian armed forces has not been merely a small inconvenience for the Israeli power position. The supplying of enormous artillery establishments allowed Egypt in 1969 and 1970 to impose a continual casualty cost on the Israeli forward positions along the Suez Canal. When Israel tried to counter this with over-flights of Cairo and bombings of the Egyptian artillery positions, the USSR supplied Egypt with an advanced air defense system that of necessity will include some participation by Russian pilots flying interceptors over Egyptian territory. Presumably this can be arranged so that no Soviet pilot ever has to parachute east of the Suez Canal into Israeli captivity, with the open escalation this would admit. Yet the stiffening of the Egyptian air defense makes any Israeli preemptive attack on the 1967 pattern far less plausible. Even retaliatory aerial bombardment of Cairo, or of Egyptian artillery positions, will be less easily undertaken now. If going nuclear would have changed the rules in the past, in a game that the Israelis were easily winning, Soviet assistance to Cairo has now itself changed the game, and the Israelis may now more willingly contemplate their nuclear option than before.

If increases in Soviet assistance to Egypt thus heighten Israeli interest in nuclear weaponry, other considerations are still relevant in the opposite direction. It is difficult to imagine a set of issues more difficult to resolve than those which divide Israel from the Arab states, but peace is never totally impossible; indeed, Moscow will argue that its assistance to the Arabs is intended to force Israel to consider more peaceful solutions. The resumption of the cease-fire between Egypt and Israel along the Suez Canal, and more importantly, the death of President Nasser, at least open possibilities that previously seemed very remote. Only the most optimistic observer would see such a settlement coming without the most prolonged and tortuous diplomatic maneuvering, but those seeking a "new way out" of Israel's defense problems for a time can fix their attentions on how best to exploit Nasser's departure rather than nuclear physics. To detonate or publicize a nuclear bomb would now seem to risk whatever chances might have existed for a peaceful settlement.

Israel will not bear all the blame for introducing nuclear possibilities into the Middle East. It is certainly plausible that the greatly expanded Soviet navy in the Mediterranean has some nuclear weapons on board, if only because its American opposite number has been widely advertised as possessing them. There is nothing in the Non-Proliferation Treaty to preclude this, or even to preclude the deployment of Soviet nuclear weapons ashore in Egypt, as long as they are not placed under non-Soviet control. Here the Israelis are correct in their statements that the NPT settles nothing for the Middle East.

The presence of the U.S. and Soviet navies thus brings nuclear umbrellas (as well as "nuclear rain") more visibly into the picture. Access by sea may be a blessing if it means that tactical nuclear weapons can be kept around without deploying them on someone's territory, surrounded by his troops. But this access can also generate some drawbacks, if it tempts the superpowers to intervene in ways that destabilize the region.

By the text of the NPT, the Soviet Union stands committed not to give the Arab states nuclear weapons, no matter what Israel does—even if Israel makes bombs. By the political liturgy that accompanied superpower efforts to sell the treaty, however, the USSR is morally obligated to provide extensive assistance to any nonnuclear state threatened by any nuclear-weapon state. An Israeli bomb can thus serve to deepen Soviet involvement on behalf of the Egyptians, perhaps with Soviet armored forces being deployed to Egypt and Syria. It is also possible that fears of Israel's going nuclear have in part deterred the Soviets from so explicit a deployment in the past. Undeployed Russian troops and unmanufactured Israeli bombs may thus deter each other.

The balance of trade-offs could instead rest at, or shift to, an entirely nuclear level. If Israel were tempted to announce itself as the sixth member of the "nuclear club," the Soviet Union might have to match this somehow; if the USSR decided to brandish its own nuclear weapons in any fashion, either by rocket-rattling from the Soviet Union itself, or by deploying visible nuclear capabilities in the Mediterranean or Egypt, the Israeli public would undertake a more serious discussion of its nuclear weapons option.

Egypt signed the NPT under apparent Soviet pressure, and would presumably be persuaded to ratify if Israel were to accept the treaty. There have been press reports that the Soviets rejected Egyptian requests for assistance on nuclear weapons, even requests for assistance contingent only on Israel first having gone nuclear.[6] It thus seems probable that Moscow still wants Egypt and the entire Middle East to remain nonnuclear.

If the immediate requirement for nuclear weapons is not yet overwhelming, there are other serious arguments against Israel's acquiring them. The alienation of the United States is clearly an important consideration, perhaps the most important. It would be one thing for Israel to refuse to sign the NPT, another to violate it. Such a move would shock and immobilize the American Jewish community and would generally antagonize other pro-Israeli opinion in America as well as in Britain and on the Continent. No one can definitively predict the U.S. governmental reaction. If an American administration were at all anxious to disengage from commitments to Israel, world resentment of Israel's nuclear weapons production might uniquely enable it to do so. If it conversely chose to remain responsible for peace in the Middle East, the United States might nonetheless decide that such nuclear activity required severe retaliation, as with a freezing of American private monetary transfers to Israel, perhaps until Israel canceled all nuclear weapons programs and submitted completely to IAEA inspection guaranteeing no resumption. If Israel were forced to submit in such a case, it would be worse off than when it began.

The logical place to draw the line against an Israeli bomb might thus seem to lie at the plutonium separation plant. Soon any advanced country may be able to make a commercial case for a plutonium plant, and the last plausible distinction between military and civilian production facilities will have been clouded. For the moment, however, Israel's commercial claim for such a facility can still be challenged. Israel, like India, could claim that this plant is already commercially necessary, if only to prepare fuel for fast breeder reactors of the future; but the suspicions of a move to weapons are strong in both cases.

American pressure has indeed been quietly applied against any Israeli construction of a plutonium plant, in both the Johnson and

Nixon Administrations. The United States has demanded and received the right to "visit" Dimona twice a year, although these are not to be labeled officially as inspections. Threats have not been made explicitly or publicly, but it has at least been hinted that the United States would treat this Israeli approach to the bomb as cause for some of the reprisals suggested above.

Yet if a clear barrier to nuclear weapons is Israel's lack of a plutonium reprocessing plant, it is possible that this barrier no longer remains. The plant is rumored to have existed already for several years in Beersheba rather than Dimona. Given the regular surveillance of the Middle East by American (and Soviet) reconnaissance satellites, as well as by U-2 overflights, it is likely that the United States would be fully aware of this plant, which enables Israel to prepare plutonium for use in bombs.

The United States may thus have been outflanked by the Israelis on the implicit sanctions for such a plant. As long as Israel does not publicize its existence, the United States does not have to take a stand, unless it elects to publicize the plutonium plant itself. The tennis ball, in effect, is in the American court. If the plant's existence is announced, the United States will be faced with an embarrassing need for choice, given the continued availability of Soviet military assistance to the Arab states. Most of the world does not understand so clearly what role a plutonium processing plant plays, or even what plutonium is. If Israel were to detonate a device under the Sinai desert, this indeed could transform American public opinion and world opinion so that the Nixon Administration could credibly withdraw from its Middle Eastern involvement, or alternatively impose financial or other sanctions on Israel. If the evidence, however, is simply U-2 photos of a plutonium plant, Zionist opinion in the United States will hardly be neutralized, and the world would wonder whether the United States had not simply seized an excuse to back out of the Middle East in the face of Soviet pressure.

If the plutonium processing facility is already in operation, whether or not Israel "has the bomb" becomes a semantic question. Israeli statements do not necessarily pledge that no bombs are in its arsenal. Premier Eshkol stated that his nation would not be the first to introduce nuclear weapons into the Middle East.[7] His pledge leaves ambiguities that hardly renounce all Israeli bomb programs, since nuclear weapons have already been introduced into the Middle East, on board ships of the American Sixth Fleet, and very possibly on board Soviet ships in the Mediterranean. Aside from this, bomb components can now be produced and accumulated in growing quantity without necessarily finally assembling them. Even American nuclear weapons are flown in configurations with enough of the rim missing so that they cannot explode accidentally. Is something that cannot explode a "bomb"? Perhaps American (as well as Israeli) assemblies would become bombs only in flight, when a crewman inserts the last component.

If one wanted to make a definitively clear announcement of one's stockpile in this world, an actual detonation might still be required. If Israel felt that it had to conduct a test detonation for any other reasons, it would conversely be saddled with the costs as well as advantages of such a definitive announcement. Perhaps there are still some generals around who would really refuse to accept an untested nuclear weapon. Israeli military officers, perhaps because of their lack of old traditions, have shown themselves to be generally more sophisticated than the average officer in other countries' military hierarchies. It surely would be possible for an Israeli physicist to convince an air force general that the bomb would be much more likely to explode than the "untested" bomb the United States dropped on Hiroshima. Computer simulations can test an explosive device. Whether or not this form of "testing" is fully equivalent to a real detonation in political terms is a different question.

Slightly less-sophisticated "world opinion" still believes that a nation must go out of its way to make nuclear weapons. It will also continue to believe that Israel must explode a bomb in order to have one. Any definitive condemnation of proliferation will thus be held in abeyance until a detonation occurs. No matter how conclusively our scientists tell us that the bombs must exist, detonations will be required to convince the public of the need for real sanctions against Israel.

India

Why should India be suspected of wishing to produce nuclear weapons? [8] Like Israel, India has long had hostile relations with some of its neighbors, most particularly with Pakistan and China; China, after all, has the bomb. Also, like Israel, India has done much of the basic preparatory work for the production of nuclear weapons, albeit somewhat more openly than in the Israeli case. [9]

Yet, as in the Israeli case, an Indian nuclear bomb decision would have to come in face of often-expressed Soviet and American opposition. India at the moment is not suffering nuclear attacks on its cities or undergoing invasions of its territories. Does it really therefore need the bomb? The answer assuredly will depend somewhat on the actions and postures of the two superpowers. Yet the linkages here are as complex and subtle as the domestic and international drives of Indian politics.

What use can India make of the bomb? There has never been a weapon that someone could not speculatively find a use for. As many Western as Indian strategic writers have set themselves to composing scenarios in which an Indian bomb would be of great military value. Memories of 1962 conjure up hordes of Chinese Communist troops crossing the Himalayas; perhaps "tactical" nuclear weapons could be used to repulse them. If the development of the small warheads for tactical situations were too costly (there is a great difference between a crude Nagasaki-type plutonium bomb and the warhead of a modern nuclear artillery shell), the cruder devices could still perhaps be planted as nuclear land mines in key valleys in the invasion routes, to be detonated when aggressor forces have filled the valleys.

Yet memories of 1962 are misleading. The Indian army was unprepared for the Chinese attack and was not nearly as strong in conventional terms as it is now. Furthermore, even in 1962, the Chinese chose to withdraw, in part because they would soon have been forced to. The logistic situation south of the Himalayas heavily favors India, just as the area to the north favors China; transporting supplies across the mountains is not easy. By "voluntarily withdrawing" in 1962, the Chinese may have caused the Indians and others to forget how defendable India was even then, by conventional arms alone.

In terms of capabilities, China may thus not be so threatening.[10] In terms of intentions, Peking has also not been noticeably aggressive since 1962. Yet hypothetical wars have a reality of their own, and Indians may still wish to seem stronger for any future outbreak that might occur. The Chinese might someday explicitly threaten to use their own nuclear weapons against Indian armed forces or Indian cities. Perhaps Indian bombs would then be valuable only to counter this threat, to make it clear from the start that any Himalayan war will have to remain conventional because both sides can make it nuclear.

When the final version of the Non-Proliferation Treaty was presented in 1968, spokesmen for the superpowers might have argued that China was already deterred from using nuclear weapons against India by the likely responses of the United States and the Soviet

Union. Indeed, as part of trying to sell the NPT, the United States and the Soviet Union said they would have immediate recourse to the procedures of the UN Security Council after any such use of nuclear weapons against a have-not state that signed and ratified the NPT. For that matter, China has over and over again sworn never to use nuclear weapons in combat unless someone else has used them first.

It is plausible that the possibility of a severe American response has indeed long sufficed to deter any Chinese use of nuclear weapons against New Delhi, as well as against Tokyo, Bangkok, or Sydney. Potential Soviet responses here also probably have deterred China. Even in response to a conventional attack, American and Soviet assistance for India has all along been extremely likely. Indeed, Indian defense plans could be rationalized as assuming a great probability of such moral and material support from the outside world in the event of a Chinese attack. Only the more polemical Indian statements would have denied this; yet only the more polemical Western statements claimed that this summed up the issue. The existence of even a rudimentary Indian bomb stockpile would inevitably change the expectations of both China and India about any new confrontation in the Himalayas, and the balance of this psychological change might yet favor India. If the introduction of a superpower's nuclear arsenal on behalf of India were not plausible and salient enough in the minds of all the publics that matter, Indian nuclear warheads would not be redundant. Any confrontation along a hostile frontier is rather a game of "chicken," a test of whose resolve will come into question first. A visible addition of weapons of mass destruction to one side will not be without effect.

If India had never had occasion to inquire about the specific extent of American or Soviet support, such support might always have seemed relatively obvious. Proposals such as the NPT, however, induce attempts at explication that can be quite upsetting. When the Indian government in 1967 sent high-level missions to sound out Moscow and Washington on the nature of future guarantees, both superpowers were far from definitive in the assurances offered. Since the likely enemy for India was still China, Moscow could hardly yet go as far as New Delhi would have desired; but the United States, even under President Johnson, had already become intent on "building bridges" to China and on avoiding new exacerbations of the allegedly basic Sino-American conflict, so that it was hardly the moment for a very explicit guarantee to India.

An American aversion to new commitments also had certainly

emerged in the wake of the Vietnam War; Secretary of State Rusk's testimony to the U.S. Senate on behalf of the NPT, already circumscribing the implicit American commitments, did not make the treaty any more attractive for New Delhi. The joint U.S.-USSR-Great Britain statement suggesting immediate recourse to the processes of the UN Security Council, however intended, served similarly to convince many Indians that great-power guarantees were somewhat deceptive; [11] Security Council action could indeed be vetoed by France and by China (the Republic of China in 1958, but by 1971 replaced by the People's Republic of China). The recourse to the Security Council in the event of aggression was already called for by the terms of the UN Charter; now the superpowers were suggesting that it would only come on behalf of nonnuclear parties to the NPT, a shrinkage of guarantees perhaps rather than an extension of them.

Great-power postures, even as of 1970, thus left India very unimpressed by the advantages of renouncing nuclear weapons and accepting the NPT. Two major changes occurred in 1971 to push India all the more toward a nuclear weapons program. There was the dramatic rapprochement between the United States and the People's Republic of China, at the same time that Peking won its seat in the United Nations. No one can predict how far this rapprochement will go in the wake of President Nixon's visit to Peking. Yet in the past, speculation about nuclear threats involving South Asia would always have expected American strategic forces (perhaps joined by the Soviets) to threaten China and shield India. Today such speculation already has had to be altered, with the United States remaining disengaged in its general withdrawal from the Far East or possibly, as part of its new alignment, even warning the Soviet Union not to attack China. This assuredly is the kind of change that can affect how decisions are made in India on nuclear weapons.

The second major event of 1971 was of course the secession in East Bengal that led to the Pakistani army's brutal campaign of repression, and that then saw the Indian army conquer all of East Pakistan, to be proclaimed as the independent state of Bangladesh. Even before the Indian conquest, the internal breakup of Pakistan might have been seen as easing India's defense problems, since fewer meaningful threats could any longer be directed at Kashmir. Yet the Indian government was motivated to do more than sit back on the defensive by the plight of the refugees from Bengal, by the opportunity to defeat Pakistan more decisively, or by both. The campaign into East Pakistan saw India draw closer to the USSR in a treaty of friendship, while being subjected to vocal Chinese attacks and to a thinly disguised American hostility. In the final stages of the Bengal hostilities, an American aircraft carrier task force even left Vietnam and entered the Bay of Bengal, quite obviously to deter India from exploiting its military victory over Pakistan to the very fullest.

Perhaps some enhanced Soviet influence will emerge in New Delhi from gratitude for the treaty, the arms shipments. and the timely vetoes of anti-Indian resolutions in the UN Security Council. Perhaps this influence will be channeled into persuading India not to make atomic bombs. More plausibly, the splitting of Pakistan has eliminated what was the major military threat to India: a Pakistani attack on two fronts, intended to liberate Kashmir and supported by China. Since Pakistan has been crippled, India has less of a real military need for nuclear weapons.

Yet considerations of military need will not by themselves settle Indian decisions on nuclear weapons. The experience of actual combat operations, and more particularly the recent specter of veiled threats by two nuclear-weapons states, can well have set up India emotionally to go ahead with the bomb.

Having achieved the dismemberment of Pakistan, India may not need Soviet aid as much any more, and Moscow's antiproliferation leverage may not amount to much. If the Nixon Administration's gestures in support of Pakistan seemed to demean Indian prestige, New Delhi's bomb appetite may have been whetted.

Indian sentiment for the bomb has all along been based somewhat on prestige. Few Americans or Europeans today know that India is capable of making nuclear weapons; educated persons should be aware of the scientific prowess that India has shown, but many are not. It is thus useless to deny that the explosion of a rudimentary Indian nuclear bomb or peaceful explosive would make editorial writers and citizens all around the world sit up and take notice. The reaction of Afro-Asian countries to the Chinese explosion of 1964 was not to condemn, but to show respect. Already we have had suggestions that India be offered some substitute form of prestige, such as permanent membership on the UN Security Council, thus presumably removing its psychological need for the bomb. Yet this all comes late; the lesson is clearly that if India had not moved this close to a bomb, such suggestions would never have been made. One can conversely ask how much importance the outside world would attach to China today if it had not entered the "nuclear club." Would we not have passed off Peking during the Cultural Revolution as an internationally insignificant conglomeration of feuding factions, its economic house not in order, greatly overrated as an international actor? Bombs do make a difference.

The question of India's future relationship with China quite interestingly brings out some of the interplay of these arguments. There are Indians who have long been advocating new approaches to China, in the expectation that Peking will become more rational and reasonable now that the Cultural Revolution has run its course. Yet such persons also tend to be strong advocates of an Indian nuclear bomb program, on the grounds that successful negotiations with a reasonable China must be negotiations among near equals, and that at least a nominal nuclear capacity will be required to endow India psychologically with this equality. Any Chinese reversion to greater bellicosity, as for example with new border incidents in the wake of the war in East Bengal, would also increase Indian pressures for a bomb from a different camp.

Too many outsiders have thought that India could be dissuaded from producing nuclear weapons simply by their economic cost. India, after all, is still a very poor country. Yet such arguments are losing strength. Already a number of very reputable Indian economists have begun telling the public that plutonium bombs will soon no longer be expensive. If any of their calculations were oversimplified for 1970, they may not be so for 1975.[12] As India very sensibly begins a large-scale exploitation of nuclear energy for production of electricity, supplies of plutonium will come into being. The separation plant for the enrichment of such plutonium to weapons-grade fissionable material already exists.

SALT and Israel or India

With regard to nuclear proliferation and Israel, it might seem easy to dismiss our first argument on the impact of the SALT: that a Soviet-American arms limitation would encourage acquisition of nuclear weapons simply because it was easier for an "nth" nation to match the superpowers. Israel will not be building an ABM system that Soviet MIRVs might be needed to penetrate, and it will not be building missiles as a delivery system to threaten an unprotected USSR. Israel is not threatened by any other nuclear power, moreover, so that the United States or the Soviet Union would have to acquire ABM to shield Israel with credibility.

With regard to India, there is again no possibility of New Delhi buying the latest ABM or missile system if and when it gets its bomb, and a superpower termination of the arms race does not therefore increase the temptations of nuclear weapons here either. It is more possible that the absence of ABM protection will cast some doubt on superpower willingness to retaliate against Peking in the event of a Chinese nuclear strike at India. Yet such protection for American and Soviet cities against Chinese attack has all along been somewhat questionable, since several Soviet cities are so close to China's borders and several American cities are exposed to submarine attack on the Pacific coast. Any American or Soviet nuclear umbrella protecting India has thus always been premised on a willingness to suffer some Chinese nuclear counterretaliation if war had broken out; a Soviet-American decision to freeze or eliminate ABM is thus not as crucial to changing this as events might be on the political front.

The second argument about the SALT impact on nuclear proliferation is essentially one of image, but it nonetheless may be more significant. If the superpowers show a willingness to deemphasize nuclear weapons and to forgo procuring more and more of them, it becomes harder for countries like Japan and Australia to delay ratifying the NPT. It will also make it more difficult for India or Israel openly to acquire nuclear weapons.

As noted, prestige plays a role in both nations' decisions on the bomb. Israel welcomes the reputation of being able to make the bomb, for the unconfirmed rumors that she is doing so are seen as demoralizing the Arab side. For reasons of American and Soviet pressure, or world reaction, this is probably as much of an open nuclear reputation as Israel will seek, so that a bomb will not be tested in a detonation. India has similarly welcomed whatever intimidating effect emerged in Pakistan as a result of rumors about Indian bomb projects, but the appetite for reputation and prestige is not as likely to be satisfied here. Many of the Indians that matter also want the developed nations to sit up and take notice of Indian scientific prowess, and for this an actual nuclear detonation might be required.

If serious strategic arms limitation negotiations occur, they will thus tend to diminish the prestige desirability of bombs in both countries. India might then have to think twice about how well an explicit entry into the nuclear club would be received abroad, when the Soviets and Americans had just set such an apparently fine example at Vienna and Helsinki. Both Israel and India would have to be more judicious about releasing rumors in their psychological warfare game.

Yet several more influences of the SALT on nuclear proliferation have to be discussed, besides the material worldwide strategic balance or the perceived legitimacy of nuclear weapons. It might seem obvious that if the two superpowers are serious about preventing further proliferation, their success will relate directly to how much they can coordinate their efforts. The SALT remain enormously important in their own terms; it would be worth pursuing a Soviet-American agreement even if there were no impact on proliferation. Yet a most important impact of the SALT may now well be to remind the two superpowers that the issues on which they can agree may be more important than those on which they compete, and to signal this to the outside world.

Successful SALT would elevate the status of the officials on each side who have staked their reputations on great-power cooperation, thereby preserving and enlarging conduits for agreement on other subjects. A successful experience in Helsinki and Vienna could be immensely valuable training for Soviet and American diplomats posted to South Asia or the Middle East. Concerted and coordinated action by the United States and the Soviet Union in these regions could slow down nuclear proliferation while also bolstering the "conventional warfare" peace. Ideally, each of the superpowers will carefully apply its leverage to deter a bomb decision, as much as it can muster up such leverage; each would also do what it could to keep India or Israel from fearing military or political disasters as a result of having foreclosed the nuclear weapons option.[13]

Yet this may only illustrate the difficulty of maintaining or exploiting the expected spinoff from the SALT, for the local issues in each theater are also real, with other portions of the Soviet and American bureaucracies committed to contesting them for a while longer. It is always difficult to predict whether a first step in détente will generate anything else. Will a successful strategic arms limitation agreement spill over into fuller Soviet-American coordination in the Middle East and South Asia, or will it simply free funds to expand the navies and conventional air forces that show the superpower flags in these areas? How large a fleet will the two powers deploy in the Mediterranean? And how large will the deliveries of tanks or jet aircraft be to the Arab states or to Israel? How clear will various pledges of support be in South Asia, and how will the arms deliveries compare here? Support by one of the great powers might make India or Israel feel more secure, so that it can forgo or at least postpone any decisions to go nuclear. But the provision of too full or decisive support can also remove whatever checks and leverage the superpower has in deterring proliferation, if the potentially "sixth" nuclear country is determined on actually becoming the "sixth."

Achieving fuller coordination between the United States and the Soviet Union will thus not be so easy. The SALT may fail; if they succeed, their spinoff may be outweighed by other events. The most spectacular international happenings of 1971, as noted, have not related directly to either strategic arms limitation negotiations or the spread of nuclear weapons, but rather to the war between India and Pakistan and the opening of summit-level contacts between the United States and China. The Kissinger and Nixon visits to Peking modify all predictions about whose side the United States would have to be on in the event of a war between China and the USSR, or even China and India. The secrecy and abruptness of the change obviously antagonized the Japanese government, and the revision of American economic and trade policies later in the summer considerably exacerbated this. The Indian government's shock at the change was reflected almost immediately in its treaty signed with the Soviet Union in August. The treaty also, of course, reflected Soviet annoyance at President Nixon's initiative.

How far will the Chinese and the Americans now go in wooing each other, and what will be the impact on the SALT or on the Soviet-American cooperation needed to head off nuclear proliferation? For the moment, the major issues of the SALT probably do not so much reflect any powers of China. Peking is not advanced enough in strategic weapons to have anything significant to forgo; its political posture has been moderated enough to deny either of the superpowers a China-oriented excuse to build ABM or a new round of offensive weaponry. If either the Soviet Union or the United States were now to achieve *détente* with Peking, it would presumably relate instead to issues such as conventional and subconventional warfare, boundaries and trade.

It is possible that the SALT will be upset by Soviet suspicions of the implications of the American dealings with China. Yet negotiations at Helsinki have gone ahead in as businesslike a manner as before. American seriousness about the talks indeed can serve as a most reassuring signal to the Soviets that the United States is not simply placing all its bets now on its dealings with Peking, to the exclusion of Moscow. The conclusion of a new arrangement on access to West Berlin similarly suggests that cooperation between the Soviet Union and the United States is still very possible.

Yet, even if the United States and the Soviet Union move ahead with a closer cooperation based on *détente* in Western Europe and real progress in the SALT, the format of such cooperation might become so menacing to Israel or India that these may yet decide to become "nth" countries. We therefore might just now have oversimplified the problem in contending that closer coordination between Moscow and Washington will be the most important impact of the SALT for the prevention of proliferation.

For example, the United States could obviously draw closer to the Soviet Union in the Middle East by giving greater support to Arab grievances and applying greater pressure to Israel to withdraw from the territories seized in 1967. Perhaps this could come as a by-product of the SALT and an American desire to deemphasize military commitments. Yet this certainly would not postpone an Israeli decision to produce the bomb. A closeness produced by Soviet moves in the opposite direction might have a much more beneficial effect, at least in terms of stopping nuclear proliferation. Will the Soviet Union soon resume formal diplomatic relations with Israel? The Russian decision obviously depends on a delicate balance between the gains of apparent solidarity with the Arabs and the gains of playing some of the middleman role that has now become an American monopoly. No Soviet decision is likely to be taken solely because diplomatic relations would help keep the Israelis from producing nuclear weapons. Yet this can have as much influence on the "nth" country problem here as any impact of the strategic arms limitation talks.

The United States, in opening contacts with the Peking regime, has declared that this is done with no hostile intent toward the USSR or anyone else. If the Soviet Union responds in spirit, it might be able to improve its own relations with China, and Soviet proposals for a broadening of the SALT to include Peking (as well as London and Paris, to bring in all the nuclear-weapons states) might have been a straightforward illustration of this. Perhaps this would again illustrate fuller coordination and less counterproduction between the two superpowers, or among all five of the nuclear powers. Yet it would hardly reassure India or make less likely Indian decisions to produce atomic bombs.

For the short run, Peking's rejection of the Soviet proposal thus made Indian nuclear weapons less likely. If Peking had canceled

President Nixon's visit and denounced the United States in the most vehement terms, it would have been a somewhat reassuring sign for New Delhi.

Thus India and Israel each have particular substantive defense problems. It would be a happy world if all forms of Soviet-American *détente,* or Chinese-Soviet-American *détente,* also served to ease the tensions of the Middle East and South Asia and to decrease the attractions of nuclear weaponry. Perhaps over the longer term some greater compatibility of goals here can be found. Over the short run, some conflicts will persist.

There may be disagreement about whether or not a Chinese-American rapprochement was always likely on the basis of American disengagement in Southeast Asia and President Nixon's Guam doctrine. Some could argue that Peking has reduced pressures on the American government before it is even certain that the United States is withdrawing completely from South Vietnam. Any American disengagement would have caused Indians to wonder whether the United States really was prepared to defend India against Chinese nuclear threats. Yet the suddenness of the Chinese-American opening, coming at the time of hostilities between India and Pakistan, does more than confirm Indian anticipations of diminished American commitment. It begins to suggest a reversal of commitments, at the least making it more difficult for the Soviet Union to make nuclear threats against Peking on India's behalf.

Whether or not Moscow chooses to coordinate with the United States in improved relations with Peking, all this does not bode well for the ultimate prevention of nuclear weapons spread. It suggests that new hypothetical nuclear warfare scenarios for the future will emerge to replace those of the late 1960s, nuclear wars in which the United States is not (in conjunction with the Soviet Union) defending India against China, but rather warning Moscow against striking at China. All of this may lack reality, but there is a political reality to what the imaginations of the world choose to dwell upon, and the script has been shifting from Chinese strikes against India to a Soviet preemptive strike at the nuclear facilities of China.

A successful strategic arms limitation agreement can lead to extensive Soviet-American coordination and consultation on nuclear weapons matters. But it might also lead to a considerable deemphasis on such weapons. What will be the impact here on the extent and functioning of the nuclear umbrella, the expectation (sometimes sanctified by treaty, sometimes not) that American or Soviet nuclear weapons would come into play on behalf of various nonnuclear countries if they should be attacked?

As the two superpowers limit their weapons acquisitions, and perhaps utilize some of their spare launch vehicles in a space program, a joint guarantee to India (or Japan) might seem less far-fetched than in the past. Yet what is somewhat more likely is that each superpower after the SALT will feel less disposed to make any reference to possible use of its nuclear weapons and that each will thus drift toward a de facto endorsement of Chinese proposals on "no first use" of nuclear weapons. The same kind of person who allows his imagination to conjure up desirable uses of weapons in protecting India is also typically an advocate of increased procurement of such weapons; if the SALT discourage the latter, they work similarly for the former.

In the abstract, the American and Soviet nuclear umbrellas were questioned even before Pierre Gallois explicated his doubts at length.[14] Frenchmen professed to fear that America would never retaliate against Moscow just because Europe had been invaded; hence an independent French retaliatory force would be needed. Americans in turn denied that their commitment had ever been in question. For any particular theater, several categories of questions are raised.

First, will one of the nuclear powers protect a nonnuclear state against nuclear attack, by meaningfully threatening to retaliate against the source of the attack? Will the United States or the Soviet Union drop a bomb on Peking after a Chinese attack on Tokyo, even if this may produce further Chinese attacks on Moscow or San Francisco? Second, does this "nuclear umbrella" extend also to deterring conventional attacks? Would nuclear weapons be made available to stop a horde of Chinese coming through a pass in the Himalayas or to stop a victorious Arab army from advancing on Tel Aviv? Third, can the "nuclear umbrella" be used to deter acquisitions of nuclear weapons by one's unfriendly neighbors? Can it assure Egypt that Israel will be deterred from manufacturing such bombs, or could it reassure Pakistan about India?

The last is clearly the least credible occasion for U.S. or Soviet intervention. The text of the NPT in fact forbade giving nuclear weapons to Egypt even if Israel manufactures them, or to Pakistan if India does. Whatever moral obligation the two superpowers accepted to protect nonnuclear countries against nuclear-equipped neighbors has been obscured by references to "Security Council procedures," wherein a Chinese Communist veto would now apply.

The nuclear threat as a deterrent to conventional attack is also less credible than in the past. If the United States withdraws from Vietnam without ever even threatening to escalate to the nuclear level, Indians and Israelis can have their doubts about the coverage someone else's nuclear umbrella will give them in such an instance. The net effect of the SALT will presumably be to discourage attempts to couple nuclear threats to nonnuclear situations.

The same deemphasis of nuclear retaliatory threats will probably also apply to the first case, as the SALT run their course; it may always seem reasonable that a nuclear warhead on New Delhi or Tel Aviv would leave some threat of nuclear retaliation against the source of attack, but the explication and likelihood of this will be less than in the past.

Yet the general delegitimization of nuclear-use threats that would emerge after the SALT would apply not only to American and Soviet warheads. If that had been so, the SALT would certainly be an encouragement for many nations to seek the bomb. The world euphoria that would greet successful SALT would also make it more costly for China ever to threaten any use of its nuclear weapons in the future, thus reducing the threat of nuclear rain on India, in addition to shrinking the Soviet-American nuclear umbrella. (It likewise would increase the world's disapproval of Indian procurement or threats of the use of nuclear weapons.) Chinese statements today do not hint at threats of using nuclear weapons. Yet such threats will be even more difficult to voice in the aftermath of successful SALT, if only again because that nebulous thing called "world opinion" would resent actions that spoiled the mood of Helsinki and Vienna.

As noted, the suddenness of the improvement in Chinese-American relations may be an obstacle to both the SALT and the NPT, and may have been particularly upsetting for the Indian and Japanese governments. Yet such a *détente* might still be applicable to stopping proliferation in the longer run, if the Peking regime can be induced to participate in any arms-control negotiations and agreements whatsoever. China, to be sure, has regularly denounced the Non-Proliferation Treaty. Yet Peking definitely has it own reasons to wish that Japan and India forgo acquiring nuclear weapons, and has shown no signs of being willing to give nuclear weapons to states such as Pakistan or Egypt.

China has expressed great skepticism on the SALT, and has declined feelers on participation in disarmament talks specifically involving the five nuclear powers; yet Peking is officially in favor of disarmament talks including all the world's nations, nuclear and non-nuclear, and it substantively supports a no-first-use agreement on nuclear weapons.

It seemingly will be far into the future before the Peking regime feels that it can specifically reverse itself on the Non-Proliferation Treaty. If we contemplate such a happy day of enhanced arms control consensus among the nuclear weapons states, a Chinese endorsement of the specific NPT might indeed be counterproductive to preventing an Indian bomb decision. Some elements of Indian opinion today see the treaty as leaving India defenseless against nuclear China. The fact that Peking has regularly denounced the NPT confuses their argument somewhat and weakens it. If China were suddenly to sign and endorse the NPT, the Indian fears would seemingly be confirmed.

If Chinese agreement on the prevention of nuclear proliferation came as part of a larger agreement and accommodation with the Soviet Union and the United States, however, the Indian reaction of course could be very different. Serious progress in the current Soviet-American talks would help to set the stage for this, but much would depend on Soviet-Chinese and American-Chinese *détente,* and ultimately on the international course Peking wishes to steer on the basis of its domestic ideological needs.

If China were to become much more bellicose vis-à-vis India, this could clearly drive India to make atomic bombs. If China becomes much more reasonable, there are still those within India who argue for nuclear weapons, merely to set the stage for negotiations on the basis of what will resemble nuclear equality. The prevention of an Indian nuclear bomb program may thus entail moderating the Chinese foreign policy stance while at the same time deemphasizing the relevance of nuclear weapons for international dealings. Successful SALT might yet supply what is needed here.

The Rest of the "Nths"

What of the SALT impact on the acceptance of the NPT elsewhere in the world? As noted, no countries seem on the verge of deciding to produce nuclear weapons except Israel and India. Yet a number of important nations are reluctant to give final approval to the NPT.

Countries like Australia and Italy are not imminently threatened by any hostile neighbor, or by a nuclear power standing behind that neighbor. In terms of functional application of nuclear weapons, there is no need for such countries to seek their own, or to question the coverage of the American "nuclear umbrella." Nuclear weapons options are thus more symbolic than operational, and arms limitations accepted by the Soviet Union and the United States will seem quite relevant to the parallel obligations accepted by smaller powers under the NPT. Public opinion on the treaty is quite significant to the ratification processes in most of these countries, including West Germany and Japan. Most publics are still a little more moralistic on disarmament questions than the professional foreign ministries that represent them; they will not seize on Soviet-American restraint simply as their own option for instant great-power status via entry into the "nuclear club." The situation becomes more complicated if the SALT produce much less great-power arms limitation than had been hoped for. This could show up in an open and acrimonious Soviet-American disagreement, but it might emerge even if there were a tacit arrangement between the superpowers to make some trivial arms control agreement sound very significant.

As noted, indignation at the moral unfairness of the superpowers in failing to disarm may be less crucial for India or Israel than whether superpower cooperation is maintained in forms relevant to regional disputes. An acrimonious dispute that sees each superpower directing propaganda barrages at the other will not be conducive to peace in the Middle East or South Asia, or to the continued denuclearization of these areas. Very different results could emerge from a tacit Soviet-American conspiracy to agree on only minor arms limitations, but to pretend that major agreement had been accomplished.

For countries beyond Israel and India, it might in places be more crucial that some real substance emerge from the SALT. The first review conference on the workings of the NPT will convene in 1975; an absence of serious arms limitations on the great powers can clearly be exploited by Japanese or Brazilian spokesmen to explain why the treaty was not yet acceptable. All of this will depend on whether the relevant public opinions have really sensed that the SALT have failed. If the Soviets and Americans are saying that it has failed, mutually accusing each other of bearing the blame, it will be quite easy for Italian and Australian public opinion to decide that the superpowers have not kept faith. If the Soviets and Americans are mutually pretending that great progress has been achieved at Helsinki and Vienna, however, it may be more difficult for nationalist opinionmakers in such countries to convince their public otherwise, for the details and issues of strategic weapons limitation are too complicated for the average person to digest readily. If the public is moderately prepared to be skeptical about the sincerity of superpower disarmament efforts, a government may be able to cite the inadequate output of the SALT as an excuse for its own rejection of the NPT. If the public has not reached this level of cynicism, the excuse may not be available.

The success of the NPT may depend on seeing to it that no nation ever becomes the "sixth" nuclear power, if every other near-nuclear state would use such an event as an excuse to leave or reject the treaty. If this is so, Israel and India will remain the centers of attention on nuclear proliferation.

Yet it is possible that proliferation can still be contained by decoupling the "sixth" from further entrants into the "nuclear club." As noted, Israel might never have to embarrass the great powers by publicly showing its nuclear arsenal. If India must detonate a bomb at some point to achieve its national purposes, seemingly successful SALT might still have put much of the rest of the world into the mood to remain bound by the NPT rather than to seize upon New Delhi's action as a reason to go nuclear themselves.

NOTES

1. The text of the Nuclear Non-Proliferation Treaty is to be found in the United States Arms Control and Disarmament Agency, *Documents on Disarmament, 1968* (Washington, D.C.: GPO, 1969), pp. 461–65.

2. For a view highly critical of the way the superpowers handled the treaty, see Elizabeth Young, "The Control of Proliferation: The 1968 Treaty in Hindsight and Forecast," *Adelphi Papers,* 56 (April 1969).

3. A fuller statement of this view can be found in Frank Barnaby, "Salting Down Non-Proliferation," *New Scientist,* V (March 4, 1971), pp. 476–77.

4. An earlier and fuller version of this author's views on Israel can be found in "Israel and the Non-Proliferation Treaty," *Bulletin of the Atomic Scientists,* XXV (June 1969), pp. 7–9, 44–45.

5. A concise description of the early evolution of the Israeli nuclear program and the facility at Dimona can be found in Leonard Beaton, *Must the Bomb Spread?* (Hammondsworth, Middlesex: Penguin, 1966), pp. 77–81.

6. *New York Times* (February 4, 1966), p. 1.

7. Statement of Prime Minister Eshkol as quoted in the *New York Times* (May 19, 1966), p. 14.

8. An earlier and fuller version of this author's views on India can be found in "India Contemplates the Bomb," *Bulletin of the Atomic Scientists,* XXVI (January 1970), pp. 13–16, 48.

9. A perceptive account of Indian policy on nonproliferation is presented in Shelton L. Williams, *The U.S., India, and the Bomb* (Baltimore: Johns Hopkins

Press, 1969). See G. G. Mirchandani, *India's Nuclear Dilemma* (New Delhi: Popular Book Services, 1968) for an Indian view of these questions. See also R. Rama Rao, "The Non-Proliferation Treaty," *The Institute for Defence Studies and Analyses Journal,* I (July 1968), pp. 12–29, and Ashok Kapur, "Peace and Power in India's Nuclear Policy," *Asian Survey,* X (September 1970), pp. 779–88.

10. Assessments of necessary Indian responses to the threat of China are argued in Dilip Mukerjee, "India's Defence Perspectives," *Survival,* XI (January 1969), pp. 2–8, and K. Subrahmanyam, *The Asian Balance of Power in the Seventies: An Indian View* (New Delhi: The Institute for Defence Studies and Analyses, 1968).

11. For the relevant portions of Secretary Rusk's testimony denying any new U.S. commitment as the result of the NPT, see U.S. Senate, Foreign Relations Committee, 90 Cong., 2 Sess., *Hearings on the Nonproliferation Treaty* (Washington, D.C.: GPO, 1968), pp. 15–16.

12. For surprisingly low estimates on bomb costs, see *Report of the Secretary-General on the Effects of the Possible Use of Nuclear Weapons and the Security and Economic Implications for States of the Acquisition and Further Development of These Weapons* (New York: United Nations, 1968).

13. A very useful cross section and analysis of Soviet public statements on proliferation can be found in Roman Kolkowicz, Matthew P. Gallagher, and Benjamin Lambeth et al., *The Soviet Union and Arms Control: A Superpower Dilemma* (Baltimore: Johns Hopkins Press, 1970), pp. 70–115. For an early Soviet discussion of the treaty specifically mentioning India and Japan, see the broadcast text reprinted in "Soviet Comments," *Survival,* IX (May 1967), pp. 150–51. For later comments similarly explicit, see A. Alexeev, "Non-Proliferation Treaty and Security," *International Affairs* (Moscow) (January 1969), pp. 10–14, and A. Alexeev, "Non-Proliferation Treaty and the Non-Nuclear States," *International Affairs* (Moscow) (March 1969), pp. 9–13.

14. Pierre Gallois, *The Balance of Terror* (Boston: Houghton Mifflin, 1961).

Japan's Choice

PRESIDENT NIXON'S DECISION to visit Peking had a serious impact on the Asian countries situated around China. The quickest to react was India, which has a long border with two hostile countries: Pakistan and China. New Delhi chose to strengthen its ties with the Soviet Union as a counter to China, and concluded a twenty-year Treaty of Nonaggression and Mutual Cooperation with Moscow.

No marked change has yet appeared in Japan's foreign policy in the wake of new Sino-American contacts, although Chou En-lai has invited Premier Tanaka to visit Peking. To a far greater extent than India, Japan has been subject to strong Russian pressure in the past. Therefore, the formation of an alliance with the Soviet Union in order to resist pressure from China would meet with unfavorable reaction in Japan. Yet sooner or later Japan will grant diplomatic recognition to Peking.* For the moment, the psychological shock that the Japanese have experienced from the U.S. rapprochement with Peking is masked by their diplomatic inactivity. Japan's military strength is less than one-tenth of China's in ground forces and less than half of the twenty-three Soviet divisions regularly deployed in the Far East. (According to Chou En-lai, the Soviet Union has deployed more than one million troops in the Far East.) Nor does Japan possess nuclear weapons. Still, the Japanese people have been told by successive governments during the past twenty years that they are fully protected by the American strategic umbrella against security threats from the Soviet Union and China.

America's gradual move toward the improvement of relations with China has been a source of constant anxiety to Japanese politicians in recent years. That the Japanese might awake one morning to find that the United States had granted diplomatic recognition to China, giving Japan no advance notification, was a recurring nightmare.

The nightmare has now come closer to reality. A number of columnists and commentators have compared the U.S. rapprochement with Peking to the "affair of 1939," when the Soviet Union and Germany unexpectedly signed a nonaggression treaty. At the time, Japan had just concluded the anti-Comintern pact with Germany.[1]

---

* EDITORS' NOTE: In September 1972, during a meeting in Peking between Premier Tanaka of Japan and Premier Chou En-lai of China, agreement for the restoration of full diplomatic relations was reached.

The economic clash between Japan and the United States has further intensified Japan's feeling of isolation. In Japan there is considerable pressure to improve relations with Peking, lest Japan become diplomatically isolated in Asia. Such pressure can be found among businessmen and politicians as well as among newspapers that wish more extensive representation in China. On the other hand, there is a broad consensus in Japan in support of a cautious policy toward Peking.

If Taiwan were to fall into the hands of China, the Philippines would be exposed to Chinese pressure. Peking's foreign policy is by no means adventurous, and its military power is rather defensive in character, a conclusion that has been reached by many scholars. This, however, does not prevent Peking from assisting Communist guerrilla groups in the Philippines. It may be easily imagined that Peking will attempt in the Philippines what it did in Indonesia and Brazil in 1965 and also what it has consistently done in some countries in Africa. If the shadow of Peking's power extends to the Philippines, China will obtain leverage over shipping lanes vital to Japan's economy. This scenario is extremely discomforting to many in Japan. Peking shows open animosity to the Japanese government and actively encourages the subversive activities of Japan's extremist students, with the result that many leading members of the Liberal Democratic party in Japan are adopting an attitude of caution toward Peking. Yet some politicians, ambitious to come into power at the next election, are altogether too ready to make political capital out of the China problem, and this makes the foreign policy of the Liberal Democratic party ambiguous.

There is growing sentiment in Japan that the strategic umbrella that the United States has extended in the past generation is about to be withdrawn. Moreover, it is difficult now to convince the government in Taiwan that the United States will protect it in all circumstances against an attack from Peking. Similarly, it is more difficult now than it was a decade ago to convince the Japanese that America will without fail support Japan against a challenge from China.

One, although by no means the only, way to maintain a nation's political position is military power. Although the Soviet Union gives evidence of its growing military power in the Mediterranean and the Pacific, Japan has no effective military capabilities. This military weakness persists despite the fact that Japan must exist in Asia with three heavily armed Communist neighbors: the Soviet Union, China, and the People's Democratic Republic of Korea (North Korea).

The shift in the U.S. policy toward Peking is already changing the structure of Asian international politics. Japan's attitude toward nuclear weapons must be considered in light of this new state of affairs. The fear felt by the Japanese is not that of an invasion by conventional means from China. It is not realistic to think that China would embark upon such a military expedition against Japan, and even if it should, Japanese defense capabilities would be adequate to cope with it. Similarly, Japan need not fear North Korea as long as the Republic of Korea remains stable and strong. Only the Soviet Union could pose a menace to Japan by conventional military force.

However, when it comes to the problem of nuclear weaponry, the situation differs greatly. China may lag in its schedule of developing the means to deliver nuclear weapons. Although many experts forecast in the middle of the 1960s that Peking would have completed an ICBM by around 1970, the attainment of that goal appears to have been delayed by several years. In any case, China may already be in a position to threaten Tokyo and eventually even cities in the United States. As one analyst of Indian security policy, S. Gopal, has suggested:

The major issue here, so far as India is concerned, is not one of first and second strike, but that of nuclear blackmail. Between peace and war there is a large territory—ultimatums, threats, retreats, compromises—and here nuclear weapons provide a powerful leverage. . . . It is not relevant to say that China would never use nuclear weapons. This may be so, but it would be an irresponsible government that acted on that assumption. . . .

Any answer to Chinese threats supported by nuclear weapons will have to be found by India out of her own resources. She must have sufficient political, military and diplomatic deterrence to resist, or she must yield.[2]

The menace to which Japan is being subjected in some ways resembles the case of India. For more than a generation India has maintained a basically neutralist policy, while Japan has relied on the American strategic umbrella. This point may be what differentiates the positions of the two countries. In his analysis, Gopal mentions the "credible guarantee" of other countries:

There is no such thing as a credible guarantee; it is, like ghosts and perfect love, something which people talk about but never see. No guarantee is credible because no guarantee given by one state to another to use nuclear weapons can be automatic. No nuclear power would be willing to embark on a nuclear war with somebody else's hand on the trigger.[3]

The vital question to present-day Japan is whether the American guarantee is more than words only and whether the American approach to Peking represents a fundamental shift in U.S. alignment in Asia.

Japan is already within range of Chinese nuclear bombs and missiles. According to reports of U.S. intelligence, China by mid-1972 possessed at least 50 and perhaps as many as 300 tactical nuclear warheads (10 to 30 kilotons). They could be delivered, it was reported, by 200 F-9 fighter-bombers, 15 to 30 MRBMs, 5 to 15 IRBMs, and 30 to 60 Tu-16s.[4] This is sufficient to place all of its neighboring countries within its attack radius. Countering this menace there is, of course, the American promise in the form of the Nixon Doctrine to "provide a shield, if a nuclear power threatens the freedom of a nation allied with us." [5] Yet the specific contents of U.S. policy behind the Nixon Doctrine remain ambiguous, and its thrust leaves doubts about America's ultimate intentions in Asia.

It is difficult to imagine what would occur should China launch a conventional attack on neighboring countries. The Soviet Union might regard this as an excellent opportunity to invade China. What the American response would be is, to say the least, uncertain. It is difficult to assess the extent to which the United States would be prepared to respond to conventional attack on Japan by a nuclear power.

Let us assume that the United States threatened Peking with direct retaliation by nuclear weapons. The response from a China equipped with MRBMs and IRBMs would be directed only against its neighboring states, rather than against the United States itself. The neighboring friendly states, to which the Nixon Doctrine has promised to provide a shield, would be "nuclear hostages." All neighboring states of China (except the Soviet Union) are extremely vulnerable to a Chinese nuclear attack.

Japan is also likely to be one of the "hostages." In Japan more than one-fourth of the population of one hundred million is concentrated in eight major cities. Even if the United States were to decide to retaliate against China with nuclear weapons, such actions would take place after a major part of the population of Japan had been killed. This is by no means a pleasant prospect to Japan.

Even if the United States were to deliver a first strike against China, Peking might protect some of its missiles against an American attack, at least later in the 1970s, by placing them on submarines. Submarines of the conventionally propelled type might be sufficient to retain for Peking a second-strike capability. An American threat of retaliation against China by way of nuclear weapons, even if translated into action, is a doubtful help to the states situated near

China. The American capability is huge, but the possibility exists that it will be neutralized in Asia by the smaller Chinese nuclear deterrent.

If China acquires an ICBM capability, Peking may thereby win one more target in addition to Asian "hostages," namely, mainland America. All-out nuclear confrontation between China and the United States would lay waste to China and inflict damage on the United States as well. In the event of a general war, twenty-five Chinese missiles might take a death toll of one million in the United States, and seventy-five missiles may take a toll of twenty-three million. Yet it is expected that the deployment of an ABM capability may reduce these figures to one million or less.

Discussing the effects that China may theoretically expect from its first-generation ICBMs, Prof. Harry G. Gelber suggests that:

The first would be the ability to destroy or use up enough American weaponry, including missiles, to leave the United States with too few deliverable warheads to maintain assured destruction against the Soviet Union. This may be the least important possibility. . . . The second possibility would be for China to threaten the destruction of vital parts of the American command and control machinery. . . . Insofar as it seems reasonable to envisage a limited Soviet strike, it would be in the interests of the Soviets themselves to spare much of the American command and control system, including Washington, if only to ensure that the exchange remained limited. In the case of an all-out Soviet attack, all that the United States would require would be a command system of sufficient capability to operate the mechanics of reprisal.[6]

Gelber remarks that if Peking were to deal a heavy blow to this command system, the balance of power between the United States and the Soviet Union would necessarily be affected.

But there is a third factor: the impact on the morale of American citizens. According to Gelber:

It is the third category which could be crucial: that of casualties and the associated intangibles of morale. . . . It is difficult to believe that, following a disaster such as the loss of ten to twenty million people, any American administration would be able to make the thought of another nuclear confrontation with a different enemy, the Soviet Union, bearable in any circumstances except those of a direct Soviet nuclear strike against the United States.[7]

A relationship of imperfect mutual deterrence exists between the United States and China. This may resemble the existing relationship between Western Europe and the Soviet Union. Both the retaliatory power of Western Europe against the Soviet Union and that of China

against the United States are insufficient. According to Gelber, however, Peking's retaliatory capability, even though inadequate, can
upset the balance of power between the United States and the Soviet
Union:

Whereas the United States and the Soviet Union required forces capable of
inflicting unacceptable damage on each other, the Chinese only need a force
which, in the event of a clash—and even its own elimination—would un-
acceptably weaken the United States or the USSR in their subsequent dealings with one another.[8]

In the event that China were laid waste as a result of an all-out
nuclear clash with the United States, the Soviet Union might take advantage of this opportunity to order conventional forces into China.
This contingency must be taken into account in Japan. This is what both
Peking and Washington may fear. If Peking were to possess, by the
mid-1970s, missiles powerful enough to threaten the lives of perhaps
ten- or twenty-million American citizens, it would be quite natural that
Washington should seek to restore communications with Peking before
these lives were lost and to enter into negotiations with the Chinese
leadership. It may not be unreasonable to imagine that such a consideration contributed to President Nixon's decision to visit Peking.

The change in Washington's China policy can be understood from
a global perspective. Yet this does not ease the anxiety of those
countries that are China's neighbors. By switching its Peking policy
from containment to negotiation, America has removed a large part
of the bulwark that has stabilized relations in Asia.

Some measure of imagination is essential to appreciate the feelings
of the people on the other side of the Pacific. All the states near
China are already, or will soon be, within range of Chinese missiles.
Although only ninety miles from Florida, Cuba is more than one
thousand miles away from Washington, D.C., yet President Kennedy
believed that missiles installed there threatened large parts of the
United States; land controlled by China lies only seven hundred miles
from Tokyo.

Americans may ask why their repeated reassurances do not quiet
Japanese apprehension about the U.S. security guarantee. The answer
is that political or military dynamics, not personal trust, play the
crucial role in international relationships. As S. Gopal writes, ". . . the
government of a nuclear power which acted without any consideration
of the merits of the specific issue, on a 'blind' guarantee given to
another state," should be regarded as having abdicated "its responsibility to its own people." [9]

There is fear in Japan that the political or military dynamics will leave the neighboring states as "hostages," left to their fate. In Japan, concern has risen that the mutual deterrence between the United States and the Soviet Union might cause Washington to hesitate in making an effective reprisal against China. Peking would be shrewd enough to see through these apprehensions on Japan's part. At the moment, international circumstances in the Far East present a far more basic challenge to the American "credibility gap" than circumstances in Western Europe. Moscow may expect that Peking would make the most of this "credibility gap."

The obstacle that may be anticipated by Peking for the present is the nuclear arming of India and Japan. Referring to Japan, Dr. Alice Langley Hsieh has suggested:

It is my conclusion that the Chinese are more sensitive to [nuclear] weapon systems developed in the region. . . . Any strengthening of Japan militarily, particularly as far as nuclear weapons are concerned . . . would be bound to make [the] Chinese even more cautious [concerning] military policies. . . . [Then] the present [nuclear] balance of power might be further complicated to China's disadvantage. . . . A Japanese regional nuclear capacity . . . may well have the effect of limiting China's political/psychological use of its emerging nuclear capability.[10]

If Japan should prove to be able to develop nuclear arms while maintaining internal political stability and its fundamental alliance with the United States, the restraints on China would surely be substantial.

Japan is not only limited in territory. Its population is excessively concentrated in a small land area, and its industrialization is much more advanced than that of China. Hence Japan is extremely vulnerable to nuclear attack. However, China is also heavily handicapped since it has to fear two other hostile superpowers and must be ever on the alert not to provide an opportunity for an invasion from the north.

The nuclear arming of Japan, if wisely effected, could contribute to the stability of Asia. However, this choice will by no means be easy for Japan to make. When viewing the future of Japan's nuclear policy, there are two basic questions that cannot be ignored. One is the nuclear policy of the United States and the other concerns the political and emotional conditions in present-day Japan. There is no need to trace the whole history of the development of the U.S. policy of nuclear nonproliferation. Suffice it to point to two decisions made during the past generation that were destined to have far-reaching effects on contemporary international politics: America's feud with

France and the stillborn program of a multilateral force (MLF).

Until the middle of the 1950s, the United States seemed to give priority to nuclear arms collaboration with NATO allies. Britain started to equip itself with nuclear weapons during this period. However, toward the end of the 1950s, and especially in the 1960s, Washington adopted with the Soviet Union a duopoly nuclear strategy, which eventually was challenged by France and China, both of which developed nuclear weapons.

The Kennedy Administration moved toward the formation of a nuclear force for Western Europe, and it seemed that West Germany would participate directly in the MLF. This would have given the West European countries an opportunity to express their views on nuclear strategy and to obtain a more direct control over nuclear capabilities. Yet the plan failed to materialize in the face of the U.S.-Soviet duopoly.

The Non-Proliferation Treaty (NPT) represents the embodiment of this duopoly strategy. This treaty, ratified by one of the two countries in Western Europe that have already created the *fait accompli* of nuclear armament, is ostensibly aimed at maintaining international security with these countries as pillars—apart from some ulterior motives that may exist. However, the NPT as the expression of this duopoly or, with Britain added, triopoly, makes nonnuclear nations feel uneasy on two points. One is the above-mentioned issue of the security guarantee and the other is the question of whether the NPT may not prevent a normal development in the field of national security. According to one analysis:

> The nuclear Powers are surrendering nothing, but the non-nuclear countries are being asked to mortgage their future development and to trust in promises of nuclear assistance which may never materialise. While the backward countries have virtually no reasons, aside from political ones, for not signing the NPT, . . . the potential nuclear Powers, Brazil included, must not be expected to accept the prospect of becoming the proletariat of the nuclear age by refraining from developing nuclear explosives for peaceful purposes.[11]

Another writer, summarizing the conditions created by the NPT, has suggested:

> Washington's assurances notwithstanding, the Federal Republic [of Germany] expressed grave concern about the future supply of nuclear fuel under "reasonable" conditions. Any agreement, it was argued, could make basic research as well as the actual production of plutonium even more subject to control by the nuclear states. Some also suggested that the "haves"

could then effectively strangle the German reactor industry by refusing to share their technology or by supplying only those states which purchase equipment from reliable (read American) manufacturers. . . . Just as do India, Italy, Israel, Japan and Sweden, the Federal Republic sees all the sacrifices and risks being required of the nuclear "have nots." The oligopoly of the "Nuclear Five" will submit to no corresponding restrictions, will lock in their present superiority, and will be increasingly able to make life-and-death decisions regarding all other states.[12]

It would be unreasonable to think that countries with a semblance of national pride would gladly accept such a unilateral restriction. When China continues to exploit its nuclear weaponry, when Washington seems to give a green light to Peking's intentions against Asian countries, why must Japan be kept bound hand and foot?

It must be recognized that there is a strong aversion to nuclear weapons in Japan. The feeling of what is generally called "nuclear allergy" is, however, not simply a product of the calamities of Hiroshima and Nagasaki, as is usually believed. At the time the bombs were dropped on these two cities, a high percentage of the people of Japan accepted this fate as an unavoidable consequence of the war. A public poll conducted by *Mainichi Shimbun* in 1970 shows the reaction of the people with regard to the use of atomic bombs against Japan (see table 1). (It must be noted that this poll was taken twenty-five years after the tragic events.)

Table 1
REACTIONS TO USE OF ATOMIC BOMBS AGAINST JAPAN

When I Got to Know the Calamities Caused by the Dropping of A-Bombs, My Impression Was[a]	*Adults (over 20)*	*Youth (16–19)*
"This is war"	32%	50%
Astonishment at immense destructive power	45	30
Misery	29	35
Indignation against the country that dropped them	36	28
Indignation against the Japanese Government, which invited this	19	22
"No more war, never!"	52	39

a. Plural answers have been omitted.

The Japanese "nuclear allergy" was formulated in the postwar anti–atom bomb and antiwar movements. The Russian-inspired worldwide campaign for "peace," which started in 1948, was especially successful in Japan.

In 1947 and 1948 the Soviet Union deployed massive military forces in Eastern Europe: one need only think of the Berlin blockade, the Communist coup d'état in Czechoslovakia, the Communist uprising in Greece. During this period the Soviet Union was conducting an International Congress for Peace in Warsaw, where it successfully gathered a large number of intellectuals. This "peace movement" was aimed at binding the hands of the United States. It was indeed the masterpiece of Soviet diplomacy since the close of World War II. It was more than enough to convince a considerable number of the world's intellectuals that peace was threatened by the United States and not by the Soviet Union, even though the Soviets had concentrated more than one hundred divisions of ground forces in Eastern Europe.

The impact of the Soviet propaganda campaign was especially great in Japan. The sudden change of the policy of the United States at this time helped to confuse the Japanese. The U.S. forces occupying Japan under General MacArthur had intended to build a demilitarized nation and had forced through a "peaceful constitution," which contained Article 9.[13] To be sure, it was understood, both by the occupation authorities and by the Japanese government at the time of promulgation, that Japan did not and could not lose the inherent and universal right of national self-defense, a right that had just been confirmed a year before in the newly established Charter of the United Nations. Yet by what effective measures could Japan exercise the inherent right of self-defense without being allowed recourse to "armed forces" in the ordinary meaning of the word?

Only three years later, General MacArthur requested Prime Minister Shigeru Yoshida to organize an army under the name of a Police Reserve Force. Such a drastic change in policy was undoubtedly based on changes in international politics (such as the war in Korea), yet it could only create confusion in Japan. Was the constitution with its nonbelligerent ideas not considered to be an ideal one after all? It was quite understandable that people began to question whether all this had not been done for the convenience of the United States. Leftist elements were quick to seize this opportunity to denounce the United States as a belligerent nation, betraying its self-proclaimed ideals.

In 1951 Japan concluded a peace treaty with the Allied nations, excluding Communist countries; the treaty came into effect the following year. Press control by the Occupation Forces was abolished, and gradually the actual pictures of the Hiroshima and Nagasaki disasters were shown to the public. The leaders of the Soviet-inspired "peace movement" could not forgo such a great opportunity. At the same time, the Korean War still raged.

It was during this period that the so-called "nuclear allergy" emerged in Japan. To this day the allergy exists, and leftist groups continue to make use of it according to their convenience. Whenever U.S. nuclear submarines and aircraft carriers such as the *Enterprise* arrive in Japanese ports, protest demonstrations are organized, although they seem to be becoming smaller in scale.

It can thus be seen that the negative Japanese reaction to nuclear weapons was, to a considerable degree, politically motivated. In other words, these feelings may change according to shifts in the political climate. Table 2 shows Japanese reactions to China's nuclear armament from a poll conducted by *Mainichi Shimbun*. This table indicates that close to 80 percent of the Japanese people are fearful of nuclear armament by China in some way. Table 3 sets forth views on Japanese nuclear armament.

Table 2
REACTIONS TO THE NUCLEAR ARMAMENT OF CHINA

Armament Is	April 1969	March 1970
Very dreadful	43%	46%
Rather dreadful	35	32
Not too dreadful	15	14
Not dreadful at all	3	3

Table 3
VIEWS ON JAPANESE NUCLEAR ARMAMENT

	Japan Should Have Nuclear Armament				Should
	Right Now	Near Future	Sooner or Later	Total	Not
1968	—	—	—	21%	66%
1969	2%	16%	27%	45	46

Sources: The Asahi (December 1968); *The Mainichi Shimbun* (May 12 and 29, 1969).

China has begun to raise its voice against "Japan's revival of militarism" in order to block the development of Japan's military power. Peking has persisted with this vicious propaganda while at the same time inviting Japanese businessmen to visit Peking and holding out the bait of increased Sino-Japanese trade.

Because of China's diplomacy of smiles, if opinion surveys on the issue of China's nuclear armament were taken at this time in Japan, they might indicate a decline in the degree of fear of the possibility of attack from Peking. Even if this were so, it would be a temporary phenomenon. The fact remains that China is a country whose government has often said it would not shirk a third world war and that possesses a population of eight hundred million and a growing nuclear capability.

Japan has essentially three choices on the nuclear question: the first is to arm itself unilaterally with nuclear weapons. The Japanese people are aware that Japan would irritate the United States in this case and would thus face the risk of being isolated from the three leading powers—the United States, the Soviet Union, and China.

When France under General de Gaulle decided to acquire nuclear weapons, it was noted in Japan that no one in the United States suspected France of really being America's enemy. Unlike France, Japan was America's enemy in the past and is not a member of the white community. It might, therefore, be natural for the Americans to suspect the motives of the Japanese. Indeed, it appears that the United States, while wanting to make Japan a strong power, also desires to keep it weak. In other words, the United States urges Japan to expand its conventional military power but wishes to restrain its nuclear armament. Japan has had in the past the bitter experience of being sandwiched between the United States and the Soviet Union, and is mindful at present that its nuclear armament, if not supported by the United States, would place it once more in a similar position.

Objections to Japan's nuclear armament are heard in Asian countries. In this regard it is instructive to look at a poll conducted by *Yomiuri* in September and October 1970 among university students in several East Asian countries (see table 4).

China's propaganda against "Japan's revival of militarism" is quite intensive in Asian countries, but there is no indication that Asian public opinion is absolutely opposed to Japan going nuclear. Should there be some guarantee from the United States, their anxiety might be greatly eased, and it might not be difficult to obtain greater acceptance of the development of nuclear weapons by Japan. This choice, therefore, depends on the attitude of the United States.

The second choice is for Japan and the United States to evolve a joint cooperative basis for security in Asia. The aim would be to build some kind of subsystem of regional balance of power in the Far East, a balance that is a common and vital concern both for Japan and the United States. Japan would develop nuclear capabilities supported by the United States. The military personnel of both nations would man missile-equipped submarines. To adjust the differences caused by the differing positions of the two countries, a mutual veto right could be established.

This method, however, may have its difficulties. Such a plan based on mutual deterence is unlikely to satisfy either party. Apart from

Table 4
FURTHER VIEWS ON JAPANESE NUCLEAR ARMAMENT

Should Japan Go Nuclear When American Nuclear Arms Are Withdrawn from Okinawa?	Indonesia	Korea	Malaysia	Singapore
Yes	56.3%	36.9%	58.0%	53.5%
No	41.3	40.4	40.4	44.8
No answer	2.5	1.6	1.6	1.7

	Hong Kong	South Vietnam	Philippines
Yes	31.5%	45.0%	55.3%
No	67.3	53.0	43.3
No answer	1.2	2.0	1.4

nationalist feelings on the Japanese side, the United States might hesitate to become involved to that extent. There are American analysts who recommend that it would be better in the long run to keep Japan unarmed. Yet if Japan remains unarmed it is certain that the leadership of Asia will definitely fall to China.

If the United States should desire to keep the hands of Japan tightly bound, Japan may have to make a third choice—to ratify the NPT. To do that, however, Japan would have to insist, as a minimum condition, that Peking also become a signatory. In this case, there is the definite danger that the pent-up emotions of the Japanese would explode.

Japan is also concerned with the problem of industrial uses of nuclear energy. A defense policy and foreign policy that preclude maximum efforts to explore and harness the potential of nuclear energy for peaceful purposes may restrict Japan's ability to meet its energy needs. The imposition of restrictive measures to Japanese development of energy resources can only lead to the eruption of repressed sentiments. Instead, other free nations should make effective use of the capabilities of Japan. Who would rejoice if Japan, as a result of misguided policy, unwittingly took a course that did not accord with the interests of the United States?

NOTES

1. The Hitler-Stalin nonaggression pact of 1939 was a special shock to Japan. The anti-Comintern pact between Japan and Germany was then in force, and negotiations were under way for a military alliance between the two countries. This alliance was being debated when the German-Soviet pact was signed, precipitating a governmental crisis in Japan and the resignation of the cabinet.

2. S. Gopal, "The Choice," *Seminar,* no. 96 (August 1967), pp. 25–26.

3. Ibid., p. 26.

4. William Beecher, "Shift in Strategy by Peking is Seen," the *New York Times,* July 25, 1972, p. 1.

5. Richard Nixon, *U.S. Foreign Policy for the 1970's,* a Report to the Congress (February 25, 1971), p. 13.

6. Harry G. Gelber, "The Impact of Chinese ICBM's on Strategic Deterrence," *Orbis,* 13 (Summer 1969), pp. 411–12.

7. Ibid., p. 412.

8. Ibid., p. 414.

9. Gopal, "The Choice," p. 26.

10. Alice Langley Hsieh, "China's Nuclear Strategy and a U.S. Anti-China ABM," Statement before the Subcommittee on Arms Control, International Law and Organization of the Senate Foreign Relations Committee, 91 Cong., 2 Sess., in *The ABM, MIRV, SALT and the Nuclear Arms Race* (Washington, D.C.: GPO, 1970), pp. 135–36.

11. H. Jon Rosenbaum and Glenn M. Cooper, "Brazil and the Nuclear Non-Proliferation Treaty," *International Affairs* (London), 46 (January 1970), p. 82.

12. Catherine M. Kelleher, "The Issue of German Nuclear Armament," in "The Atlantic Community Reappraised," *Proceedings of the Academy of Political Science,* 29 (November 1968), pp. 102–03.

13. Article 9 of the Japanese Constitution states:

Aspiring sincerely to an international peace based on justice and order, the Japanese people forever renounce war as a sovereign right of the nation and the threat or use of force as means of settling international disputes.

In order to accomplish the aim of the preceding paragraph, land, sea, and air forces, as well as other war potential, will never be maintained. The right of belligerency of the state will not be recognized.

SALT, Proliferation, and International Security

THIS SESSION PROVIDED an opportunity to assess the implications of the rationale for superpower arms control, the emergence of a more multipolar world, the decline of an American imperial will, and changing technologies of offensive and defensive weapons systems. In the next decade each may affect the prospects for nuclear proliferation. Five issues provided the focus for discussion:

1. superpower motivations and the SALT,
2. the concept of parity and the SALT,
3. the possible effects of success or failure at the SALT,
4. Western European security and the SALT, and
5. nuclear proliferation, superpower guarantees, and the SALT.

Superpower Motivations and the SALT

The following remarks on superpower motivations within the context of the SALT extended the analysis made in the first plenary session of the symposium. Two explanations of Soviet motivations were suggested. One view optimistically suggested that the Soviet Union is basically sincere in its intent to stabilize the strategic environment through an agreement at the SALT. This view assumed, to a certain extent, that the whole panoply of Soviet signals on *détente* and disarmament originated from the Soviet belief that certain possible advantages may evolve from the acceptance of a position of rough strategic equality with the United States. Such a choice would serve to limit increases in the Soviet military budget, thus freeing funds for domestic and consumer purposes. Another possible advantage would be an enhanced opportunity to promote a continued relaxation of world tensions; this is seen particularly within the context of Western Europe. Moreover, while it is difficult to measure

---

In addition to those persons presenting papers, the following participated as discussants: Waldo Dubberstein, Marc Geneste, and Andrew Pierre. Yuan-Li Wu served as chairman for this panel.

or validate, the implied acceptance of Soviet equality by the United States could serve to satisfy Soviet needs for prestige.

The alternative view of Soviet intentions was more pessimistic and, many said, more realistic. This assessment held that the Soviet Union is interested in the SALT, first, as a means of obtaining certain objectives and immediate benefits and, second, as a screen to seek a margin of superiority that would confer a *political* advantage. The most immediate advantage that the Soviet Union could attain from the SALT would be the alleviation of concern that the United States would seek to develop a counterforce strategy, one that would make credible a first-strike option for the United States. The SALT might present the Soviets with a unique opportunity for preventing the development of such a strategic posture by the United States. A second immediate advantage that the Soviet Union might derive from the SALT would be the freeing of resources for other activities. A reallocation of the Soviet defense budget in favor of conventional arms would allow Moscow to accept greater risks in the promotion of its interests in areas where an increased conventional capability may be the deciding factor. A similar reordering of priorities might permit an acceleration of the Soviet naval buildup in the Mediterranean and the Indian Ocean as well as the development of Soviet capabilities to counter the Chinese threat.

In the longer term, it is conceivable that the Soviet leadership might view the SALT as providing a temporary period of consolidation in a continuing Soviet drive to gain a margin of strategic superiority over the United States. It was noted several times throughout the symposium that the two superpowers have differing conceptions of the political advantage of military capabilities, especially strategic nuclear forces. If this contention proves to be correct, then one could make a strong case that superiority rather than parity has been Moscow's long-range objective. Several participants suggested that they found no evidence that the Soviet Union even has a conceptual equivalent to the Western view of parity. Rather, Soviet military writers repeatedly state that the objective of the Soviet Union should be to gain a quantitative and qualitative military superiority over the United States. The Soviets might interpret this emerging superiority as one more indication of the declining stature of the United States. Soviet strategic superiority would also make the American nuclear umbrella less credible in the defense of both Western Europe and Japan.

In this interpretation of Soviet motives, the SALT could also give the Soviet Union needed time to eliminate certain inequalities with the West in various areas of military technology, such as MIRV and strategic underwater systems. The hiatus in U.S. spending for strategic weapons could also enable the Soviet Union to pursue more actively the development of a credible counterforce capability—assuming that the United States would not react positively to indications that the Soviet Union was using the SALT to screen its attempts to gain such a capability.

A caveat was offered in regard to placing too much confidence in discrete measures of superiority or parity in Soviet-American relationships. Asymmetry between Washington and Moscow concerning the political uses of nuclear weapons does not stem from the simple explanation of quantitative or qualitative superiority. Rather, it is determined by a complex of factors such as (1) perceived values of the prizes at stake as well as (2) each participant's conception of its political role within the nation-state system. The political utility of nuclear weapons does not emerge directly or solely from quantitative measurements of nuclear force.

A fairly widely held opinion among the participants in this discussion and the symposium as a whole was that Soviet motivations at the SALT are based more on objective, realistic considerations than on any desire to bring greater security to the world. If this is the case, then, as was pointed out by several discussants, a more sober appraisal of Soviet interests in the SALT should be the guide for Western policymakers.

In the discussion about U.S. motivations, several points were emphasized. Foremost was the view that, because of domestic pressures and a certain disenchantment with overseas commitments, not only in Vietnam but also in Europe, the United States is seeking to alter the nature of its involvement in the world. The United States is losing confidence in its ability to achieve the goals that have guided U.S. foreign policy over the past generation. The implications of such a development were considered to be obvious.

Besides the problem of domestic pressures and disillusionment, several other explanations were proffered for the U.S. desire for a lower profile in the world. By adopting a strategic posture emphasizing sufficiency, the United States might be signaling that it no longer believes it possible to attain a politically significant strategic superiority. Thus a growing desire for strategic stability and the existing concern over the risks and economic burdens of the arms race could be the main reasons that the United States has sought a SALT agreement. It was pointed out that one danger of the negotiations is that Soviet motives may be entirely different. The United States, in its anxiety to achieve an agreement, may be willing to accept less than a *quid pro quo* arrangement at the SALT. Such a result could destabilize U.S. relations with allies and client states.

On the other hand, as one European participant pointed out, an agreement initially requiring the United States to give more than it gets might be acceptable if, in the immediate future, another agreement providing the United States with an acceptable *quid pro quo* could be reached. However, one would not know if the second agreement would be possible until it actually occurred. Thus it might be difficult to justify the first agreement by arguing that inequalities would be rectified in a future agreement.

Another explanation for the declining U.S. desire to maintain its vast foreign commitments has to do with the unique nature of the U.S. alliances with Western Europe and Japan. It was pointed out that this association is not really an alliance in the classical sense, but rather a unique agreement by the United States to perform the security function for all the nations concerned, especially in nuclear matters. An additional unique feature of these relationships has been the relative acquiescence on the part of Washington's allies in allowing the United States to control not only the nuclear weapons but also the strategy and the decision-making processes that would determine where, when, and for what purpose the weapons would be used. It is this unique pattern of relationships that the United States is possibly seeking to change. A partial explanation of the Nixon Doctrine might be that it is preparing the way for a return to a classical conception of alliances, in which member states are more clearly responsible for their own defense than has been the case since World War II. United States participation in the SALT might be viewed as an attempt to make the transitional period less dangerous. However, from the viewpoint of U.S. allies, the SALT could engender an acute sense of insecurity and a search for an answer to the question: What can a nation do when its superpower ally appears no longer willing to provide nuclear security?

It was apparent from the discussion of Soviet and U.S. motivations at the SALT that certain critical asymmetries are believed to exist in superpower motivations for participating in the SALT. As a result, there is concern both in the United States and in Western Europe about the implications of the SALT for international security.

The Concept of Parity and the SALT

Two general ways of looking at parity at the superpower level were seen to exist. The first is that of objective calculations reflected in the following kind of question: What are the quantitative factors that determine whether or not actual parity exists? Several possible determinants in this context were mentioned. If megatonnage is used as the quantitative measurement, then the Soviet Union has a clear superiority. On the other hand, if deliverable warheads are seen as the key variable, the balance shifts to the United States. Finally, if launch vehicles are the chief consideration (and this seems to be the current focus), then the United States possesses a marginal edge that will probably disappear within two years. Using this last indicator, one could claim that actual parity would be achieved shortly by the Soviet Union, assuming no rapid shift in American strategic programs in the next two years.

If the launch vehicle variable is employed, it might—as was indicated in the discussion—emerge that the Soviet Union rather than the United States would have to accept the codification of parity at the SALT. This would be the case because it is the Soviets who are engaged in a dynamic program of expanding their number of launch vehicles. They, rather than the United States, would be required to scale down their program, since the United States is not currently involved in this dramatic buildup of launch vehicles.

Several participants suggested that parity in the objective sense was achieved almost a decade ago, when mutual assured destruction became operable as the United States became vulnerable to nuclear devastation from a possible Soviet attack. However, the question was asked: Why, if parity has existed for a decade, should anyone holding this viewpoint be concerned whether or not a strategic arms limitation agreement occurs?

A possible answer exists in a second way of looking at superpower parity. The "codification of parity" argument sees such a development at the SALT as being at least as important symbolically as it is as an indicator of an objective fact. The point was stressed that parity is not only a question of weapons but also a political phenomenon. And in the political sense it is the perception of parity rather than parity itself that is the dominant factor. Consequently, the case could be made that parity is being achieved through its codification at the SALT. If this is the case, then one might ask: What would be its impact on the international system? First and foremost, it would signal the formal end of American strategic superiority. This, in turn, could substantially affect alliances, superpower guarantees, Soviet-American rivalries in sensitive areas like the Middle East, and the debates on nuclear power now taking place in potential Nth countries. In fact, it is conceivable that the codification of parity would serve to unhinge the Western international security system, founded initially on a U.S. nuclear monopoly, then on an American offensive superiority, and most recently on the belief that the United States is correct when it emphasizes that its superiority in nuclear warheads guarantees the security of allies. The United States, by accepting parity with the Soviet Union, would erode the psychological framework that has served to maintain a relatively high degree of credibility in the U.S. strategic guarantee. Moscow may perceive this to be the case and may seek an agreement at the SALT that would lead to a decoupling of U.S. strategic nuclear forces from the defense of vital areas, such as Western Europe.

Other participants suggested that it would be a mistake to over-emphasize the importance and inevitability of negative consequences arising from a SALT agreement that codified parity. An alternative to deterministic thinking emphasizes certain factors affecting the impact of parity on the United States that are not predetermined. Among these are: (1) the economic strength of the United States; (2) the social stability of the country; (3) the prevalent public attitudes and beliefs; (4) the ability of the United States to maintain an "internationalist" foreign policy, including the fulfillment of vital commitments; and (5) a continued American capacity and will to intervene in the world when deemed necessary. The extent to which Washington is free to influence the impact of parity depends on the evolution of these and other factors.

The Possible Effects of Success or Failure at the SALT

One of the questions of concern during all of the symposium sessions was: What will be the general effects of either success or failure at the SALT? Also important in this area was the question: What kind of agreement will evolve and what will be its timing? The scenario that developed in the second plenary session, positing a freeze on new starts of land-based ICBMs, no freeze on SLBM development or deployment, and a roughly symmetrical ABM limitation at low levels, was an attempt to answer at least one part of this latter question. Several participants in this session addressed themselves to the task of providing some possible answers to these questions.

There were two general appraisals of the impact of a strategic arms limitation agreement. Some participants proposed that the impact of success or failure at the SALT is likely to be much less than is generally believed. Failure might cause some uneasiness but no drastic changes in policy for either superpower or for other nations. Success would not be viewed as indicative of a safer world. It was suggested that superpower agreements and United Nations declarations will not induce most of the nations in the world to believe that their security will be safeguarded.

From this perspective, the international system will continue to be dominated by the need for each nation to do all it can individually to insure its own security.

Little significance was attached to the content of the SALT, whether interpreted as a codification of parity or as a Soviet opportunity to gain superiority that could affect adversely the relationship of the United States with its allies. Both the negotiations and possible agreements were seen as likely to be secondary in importance to the overall system of relationships that exist first at the political level and then at subordinate levels, including quantitative measurements of armed forces. An agreement at the SALT or the lack of one will be only one of many inputs that will shape these overall relationships.

An opposing viewpoint stressed that agreement or nonagreement, as well as the form of agreement, involves serious implications not only for the superpowers but also for the international security of other nations, particularly Western European countries, and for the problem of proliferation.

In the United States, an agreement could lead to an increase in domestic pressures for further negotiations of a character that could restrict U.S. involvement in foreign affairs. Several participants alluded to the problems that might be caused by euphoria in the United States stemming from a SALT agreement. Congressional appropriations in support of foreign policies might be further curtailed, greater pressures might be exerted to decouple U.S. interests from the security concerns of *de jure* (Western Europe) or *de facto* (Israel) allies or client states, and, most importantly of all, there might be generated such an intense desire among the general public for further agreement that the government's ability to bargain from a position of equality at any subsequent negotiations would be limited.

The domestic euphoria thesis mentioned above was challenged as a dangerous oversimplification. Several discussants thought it much more likely that the "gut" issues of security would be decoupled from the negative effects of any euphoria over an agreement at the SALT. In fact, it was pointed out that though a possibility of euphoria might exist in the United States, there is also the opposite penchant of Americans to react violently if there are indications that the Soviet Union is using an agreement in a suspect manner.

In respect to the effects of nonagreement on the United States, two hypothetical alternatives were outlined. First, Washington might accept the fact that a Soviet buildup is likely to continue without substantially altering U.S. policies. Such a position would probably be politically dangerous in the short run and possibly dangerous militarily in the long run. A second alternative would be for the United States to try to match or exceed the Soviet buildup. Under present conditions in the United States, this would be a difficult policy to implement politically unless the Soviets were to become more bellicose.

Given the difficulties inherent in these two alternatives, an agreement at the SALT is probably the best alternative facing the United States at the present time. It was decided to avoid the dilemma of a choice between the other two alternatives. Both the possible acceptance of parity by the Soviet Union, with the resultant scaling down of its arms buildup, and the chance to curtail the arms race in general were held to be sufficient justifications for the United States to seek an agreement.

Discussion then centered on the effects of the form of agreement. The view was expressed that an agreement such as that envisaged in the hypothetical scenario presented during the discussion of technology (see p. 122) would be destabilizing from the American viewpoint. It would leave room for extensive qualitative improvements in offensive forces by the Soviet Union for which the United States could not compensate by anything but extensive deployment of new sea-based systems. Thus, under the scenario agreement, the United States would be forced to rely more and more on such systems. This would negate the confidence engendered in the United States by the viability of its strategic force triad. A few participants concluded that it is certainly possible to see an agreement at the SALT as extremely destabilizing, whereas nonagreement, by allowing the United States greater freedom to respond to provocative Soviet initiatives, could very well be more stabilizing over time.

As in other sessions of the symposium, a wide range of views concerning the implications of agreement or nonagreement at the SALT was evidenced in this discussion. Such a divergence of views seems to be a further indication that no generally acceptable conceptual milieu for evaluating the SALT exists either between the United States and the Soviet Union or among experts from the United States and its allies.

Western European Security and the SALT

Extensive attention was given to Western Europe during this session of the symposium. The basic security problem currently confronting Western Europe was tackled in a discussion that focused on the nature of the Soviet threat. It was suggested that there is almost no likelihood of a massive Soviet strategic or conventional attack upon Western Europe in the foreseeable future, even though a great imbalance will continue to exist between Soviet missiles targeted upon Europe and the limited European nuclear capacity targeted upon the Soviet Union. It was emphasized that this imbalance has both political and military implications.

The real security problem for Western Europe posed by the Soviet Union is how to counteract the tremendous Soviet mobilization capability. One alternative is to return to the sizable armies of the early twentieth century and World War II. However, this alternative was dismissed as being impossible because of economic and political constraints and the changes wrought by the advent of nuclear weapons.

The alternative favored by several of the Europeans was that Europe could rely on tactical weapons to deter the Soviet Union from attempting to coerce Western Europe into becoming another "Finland." It was emphasized that reliance upon a strategy based on the European possession of an extensive tactical nuclear capability is important more for deterrent value than for possible operational use except in the unlikely event that a conventional clash would occur at some time in the future. A European tactical nuclear force would be designed so as to make the Soviet Union hesitant to initiate aggressive movements, since the costs would promise to outweigh any possible gains from a Soviet conventional thrust into Western Europe.

At a higher strategic level of analysis, the problem was seen as one of determining what alternatives are open to a Western Europe threatened by the possibility that its superpower ally may be preparing to decouple its extended nuclear guarantee from Europe. Decoupling could occur from a "codification of parity" at the SALT and/or a return to some form of U.S. isolationism arising from disenchantment with extensive military commitments. Posing the question in these terms provided a further indication that in Western Europe the belief in the U.S. will to maintain its commitment to the military security of Europe has been eroded in recent years.

The declining efficacy of the U.S. strategic umbrella is having several effects on Western Europe. First, there is the danger that a European euphoria will develop as a result of a seeming U.S. belief in the sincerity of Soviet interest in making acceptable sacrifices to promote a relaxation of tensions. It was suggested that the only way a beneficial agreement with the Soviet Union can be reached is to insure that the West, and especially the United States, bargains from a position of strength. If, however, it is perceived that in the negotiations with the Soviet Union, the United States is willing to make an agreement at a seeming disadvantage to itself, there might be the tendency in Western

Europe to believe that a new era of peace is just around the corner. From the implications of the remarks of several of the Europeans in the audience, it was clear that the development of such sentiment would be potentially dangerous for European security.

A second, more positive effect of the folding of the "umbrella" might be to shock the Western European nations into making greater and more rapid strides toward unity, especially in the field of strategic doctrine and defense cooperation. It was pointed out, however, that this type of unity will remain difficult to achieve because of the lack of a sense of urgency about the security problem in Europe and the continuing dearth of political cohesion among the European nations.

Several participants suggested that even though impediments to cooperation exist, pressures for greater European defense collaboration might eventually lead to positive results. The most likely form of such collaboration would be Anglo-French nuclear cooperation. If this assumption is correct, the issues and topics discussed by Kemp and Smart in their paper at the symposium will become especially crucial. They made three main assumptions that, if true, would determine the essential nature of the nuclear debate in Europe. These assumptions are: (1) Western European nations will continue to desire some credible strategic nuclear capability of their own. (2) The primary purpose of a European nuclear force would be to deter the Soviet Union from taking any military or political initiatives detrimental to the vital interests of Western European nations. This type of strategy would emphasize a countervalue civilian-oriented targeting posture, since any counterforce first-strike capability would be out of the question for the Western Europeans. (3) The design of the deterrence system itself would be based upon a submarine-launched ballistic missile (SLBM) capability. Deterrence under these assumptions would be achieved through a certain probability of survivability, strength of will, effectiveness of command and control, reliability and penetration capabilities of the systems, and the probability that the targets threatened will be perceived as so valuable by the Soviet Union that the threat of their loss will achieve effective deterrence.

From this strategic framework, several comments were made regarding the political implications of a European nuclear force based on the Anglo-French nuclear capability. It is questionable, according to many observers, that the British and French would be able to resolve the difficulties inherent in collaboration on such a highly sensitive issue. Moreover, there is the formidable problem of how to include the German Federal Republic in a nuclear arrangement, while at the same time ensuring that Bonn does not gain possession of such weapons. A third problem of such a collaboration would be the necessity to find some way to circumvent the restrictions of the McMahon Act on Britain's sharing of nuclear weapons information. However, once Britain and France were to make the political decision to enter into nuclear collaboration, the declining influence of the United States as it disengaged from Europe would probably be insufficient to prevent such cooperation. In fact, it was pointed out that should the United States seek to inhibit the transfer of nuclear information between the two countries, there might be greater impetus toward such cooperation.

Given the uncertainty over the U.S. nuclear guarantee and Europe's potential need to find sources of security, the implications of the SALT for Western Europe are quite important. Three levels of impact of the SALT on European attitudes were postulated: (1) the impact of the agreement by the superpowers to enter negotiations with each other, (2) the impact of the negotiating process itself, and, finally, (3) the possible impact of an agreement coming out of the SALT. In relation to the first two levels of impact, it was posited that the SALT are important not because they have generated novel pressures and attitudes, but rather because they reinforce already developing perceptions in Europe about U.S. attitudes and policies. This point was emphasized several times throughout the symposium.

In the discussion of the possible impact of the SALT on Western Europe, it was emphasized that the two basic considerations for Western Europe are an agreement on ABM deployment and the issue of antisubmarine warfare (ASW) capabilities. If the SALT should result in an agreement allowing an extensive deployment of ABMs, the credibility of existing national nuclear forces in Western Europe as deterrent systems would be seriously weakened. Such a development would also call into serious question the possibility of developing a credible European nuclear capability in the future.

The absence of any attempts at the SALT to limit ASW development seriously affects the prospects of a Western European deterrent force based on submarines. If the Soviet Union were to make major advances in its ASW capabilities, it would be necessary for the Western Europeans to revise upward their requirements for a SLBM force that could pose a credible deterrent threat to the Soviet Union.

Nuclear Proliferation, Superpower Guarantees, and the SALT

During this session the proliferation issue was approached from two perspectives. The first emphasized some of the implications that the SALT might have for proliferation and the issue of superpower guarantees to potential nuclear countries. The second emphasized the pressures being exerted on India, Israel, and Japan to decide whether to opt for a nuclear posture.

Several attempts were made to outline possible effects of the SALT on the Non-Proliferation Treaty (NPT). George Quester remarked that speculation has centered on two contrary efforts. First, the SALT could possibly jeopardize the success of the NPT by providing the nonnuclear powers with an opportunity to gain a more credible nuclear capacity vis-à-vis the superpowers. Second, the SALT could, conversely, promote the general chances of success of the NPT by indicating superpower sincerity in fulfilling the obligation under Article VI of the NPT to reach an agreement on strategic arms limitations. On this point it was suggested that superpower fulfillment of obligations under the NPT would make it more difficult for nations to delay ratification of the treaty or to seek openly to acquire nuclear weapons. Dr. Quester remarked that neither of these linkages is sufficient to explain the complex nature of the issue of proliferation in regard to possible Nth country decisions to "go nuclear."

Following Quester's statements, some attempts were made to establish a linkage between the parity question and proliferation. It was contended that parity might lead defense planners in potential nuclear states to shift their emphasis from nuclear weapons to conventional arms. This would be the case if the condition of parity between the superpowers was seen to inhibit their ability to offer security guarantees to other nations.

The reference to the effect of parity on superpower guarantees evoked an extended response. There was a general consensus that a simple linkage between parity and the question of guarantees does not exist. Rather, one must look at the effects of certain technical considerations on the interlocked issues of guarantees, parity, and proliferation. In this context a question regarding the effect of extensive deployment of ballistic missile defense on superpower guarantees and proliferation was posed: Would a heavy deployment of Ballistic Missile Defense (BMD) as a result of success or failure to reach an agreement at the SALT make more efficacious the superpower guarantees designed to inhibit proliferation that were made to potential Nth countries? It was suggested that it might be necessary to maintain a posture of mutual assured destruction capability at the same time heavy investments were being made in BMD. This might be necessary because the superpowers would probably not have sufficient confidence in defensive capabilities to rely upon such weapons as the prime component of a guarantee designed to inhibit proliferation pressures in another nation.

Several participants questioned the assumption that BMD deployment is linked to the U.S. security guarantee to allies. In the extreme case that both superpowers would develop a high degree of confidence in their respective BMD capabilities, the credibility of any guarantee would be negligible. Even if one assumed the possibility of extensive BMD deployment with a moderate superpower confidence in its reliability, it would still be difficult to inspire a great degree of confidence in Nth countries regarding a guarantee proffered by a superpower. Under these conditions it would be very difficult for a superpower to wage a controlled and limited nuclear war in defense of an ally's interests. The need to overcome the other side's extensive BMD would probably necessitate a saturation attack that would probably involve the use of a large amount of a superpower's second-strike capability. It would be very unlikely that a superpower would be willing to expend its second-strike reserves on behalf of an ally. Hence, a credible guarantee by a superpower under conditions of large-scale BMD deployment would be difficult to sustain.

However, the question of guarantees, especially the automatic ones, might be irrelevant because such guarantees are so dangerous that a nation seldom enters into them with an intention to abide by them if conditions should require it not to do so. This point was qualified by the comment that the key variable in assessing whether or not a guarantee will be upheld is not the "fine print" but rather the nature of the political will of the parties concerned with the guarantee.

The focus of the discussion shifted to the general effect of BMD deployment on proliferation. If both superpowers decided to adopt a defensive emphasis, would proliferation become a far less significant problem? One response suggested that international peace would be assured when the defense gained complete ascendancy over the offense. Nuclear firepower might give the world a unique opportunity to achieve this situation. In a more realistic sense it was pointed out that this question assumes that the only neutralization of possible systems of proliferation will be undertaken by the Soviet Union or the United States. However, if one looks at the pressures being exerted on individual potential Nth countries, it is apparent that other considerations—besides reactions to the superpowers—would be involved in any decision to go nuclear. Thus, the issue is intrinsically complex.

Attempts were then made to discuss the possible relationship of BMD deployment to proliferation, even with the above caveat in mind. A decision to go nuclear is not likely to be deterred by any American or Soviet deployment of an active defense system. It appears unlikely that any strengthening of U.S. guarantees by BMD deployment would inhibit the decision to acquire nuclear weapons. However, extensive BMD deployment by the superpowers might very well determine the extent and size of the strategic system an Nth country might attempt to erect. For instance, the Chinese decision to acquire nuclear weapons was not influenced by American or Soviet deployment or possible deployment of active or passive defense systems. However, the Chinese decision on the size and sophistication of their nuclear configuration might very well be influenced by superpower deployment of defensive systems.

Another aspect of the proliferation problem as it relates to superpower BMD deployment is concerned with limiting the danger of an accidental or catalytic missile-firing at one of the superpowers by an unidentifiable source. This problem would become especially acute if there were a proliferation of SLBM systems. The point was made that the dangerous instabilities that could arise from this situation could be somewhat mitigated by even a light deployment of an active missile defense system by the superpowers. If an incoming missile from an unidentified source could be destroyed with a high degree of reliability, the dangers of proliferation could be somewhat diminished.

INDIA, ISRAEL, AND JAPAN

In the analysis of national considerations, there was widespread agreement among discussants that India, Israel, and Japan, for different reasons, might seek to acquire nuclear capabilities. The growing belief in these countries that neither the United States, the Soviet Union, nor the United Nations could be depended upon to guarantee their security was seen as a prime factor in the impetus toward nuclear proliferation. However, several participants suggested that domestic and regional considerations, rather than relationships with superpowers, might be the determining factors in the decision. No clear consensus emerged on this issue.

Within the last decade, the nuclear debate within India has gained prominence. As do other nonnuclear nations, many Indians view superpower guarantees as vague and unlikely to insure their country's security in time of need. Hence, in order to counter the Chinese threat and to maintain a superiority over Pakistan, India may feel compelled to go nuclear. Nuclear weapons are also seen as a means of acquiring prestige, not only in the sense of a "ticket to the top table" but also as a way of augmenting its prestige among Afro-Asian countries. These factors might very well be perceived in India as outweighing the economic and psychological problems that might arise from a decision to acquire nuclear weapons.

An Israeli decision to procure nuclear weapons would be based on different considerations from those which are of primary importance to India and Japan. Israeli possession of nuclear weapons, it was pointed out, might preclude the possibility of an Arab victory on the battlefield or even deter the Arabs from initiating another round in the conflict.

Next came a challenge to the view that Israeli interest in nuclear weapons was based on deterring the Arab states rather than the Soviet Union. If nuclear weapons were developed by Israel, it could be for the purpose of persuading the Soviets to avoid steps that would be seen by Israel as direct threats to its vital interests. Several participants disagreed vehemently with this viewpoint, stating that the only conceivable use of nuclear weapons by Israel would be against the Arabs, since Israeli delivery systems are insufficient to threaten the Soviet Union. The successful test of the Jericho missile (its range is estimated at three hundred miles) does nothing to alter this view. This point, in turn, was countered by the observation that there is evidence that the F-4s that Israel has in its inventory might very well have sufficient range to pose some form of deliverable threat to the Soviet Union. However, the essential point in regard to the Israeli use of nuclear weapons as a deterrent to the Soviet Union is that even a minimal nuclear capacity might be sufficient to influence the Soviets to recalculate the costs of provocative coercive actions against Israel. Thus, Israeli thinking on the subject might be moving along the lines of the proportional deterrence theory advocated by many strategists in Europe.

Potential negative effects of an Israeli decision to go nuclear were mentioned. Such a decision would probably decrease American interest in continuing its *de facto* alliance with Israel. It might also increase the possibility of a Soviet preemptive strike against Israeli nuclear installations. Israeli acquisition of nuclear weapons might also lead the Soviet Union, despite its reversals in Egypt, to station nuclear weapons there under its own control, if Egypt so requested. These possibilities make the Israeli decision more complicated than that faced by India or Japan.

In a discussion of the proliferation question as it affects Japan, the issue of domestic factionalism was emphasized. Those discussants believing that Japan will decide to acquire nuclear weapons considered domestic considerations to be highly unstable and subject to abrupt change. Therefore, the current "nuclear allergy" in Japan, it was argued, is not a permanent phenomenon. If the extended nuclear guarantee of the United States were eroded or withdrawn and the menace of a nuclear China were to become more apparent to the Japanese, domestic inhibitions would probably recede.

Several participants were reluctant, however, to dismiss the impact of Japanese domestic considerations on the proliferation issue. Nuclear allergy and other inhibitions, including constitutional ones, were considered to be much more important and lasting than had been assumed by those who suggested that Japan will eventually build a nuclear capability.

Moreover, considerations other than domestic ones are important in assessing the nature of Japanese interest in nuclear weapons. Japan's dependency on outside sources for raw materials and trade, as well as the decreasing credibility of the U.S. nuclear guarantee, will push Japan toward the acquisition of nuclear weapons. Nevertheless, a Japanese decision to opt for a nuclear capability in the near future would virtually require the approval of the United States. It was felt that such approval would be highly unlikely, not only because of American reluctance to help Japan abrogate the NPT but also because of the continued belief in Washington that proliferation should be strongly resisted in areas of instability where nuclear weapons might transform a local conflict into a global one.

Summary

While it is clear that the SALT, proliferation, and international security have an impact on each other, the results of that interaction are far from clear. Nevertheless, the following points emerge: (1) the important asymmetry in superpower motivations concerning involvement in the SALT determines in part how other nations perceive the implications of the SALT for their security needs; (2) the concept of parity and its possible codification at the SALT have a direct linkage to superpower motivations and intentions, not only in the negotiations but also in superpower interactions with allies and potential Nth countries; (3) success or failure at the SALT is important, not only for the qualitative effect it will have on the arms race but also for its symbolic effect on security for the international system in general; (4) the impact of the SALT on Western Europe will be determined by what the negotiating process communicates about U.S. resolve in maintaining its extended commitment; and (5) nuclear proliferation is not a problem to be assessed by generalizations but requires an intensive analysis of each individual national case.

PART V

WILLIAM R. VAN CLEAVE

Implications of Success
or Failure of SALT

THE ONLY CLEAR ANSWER to the question "What are the implications of success or failure of SALT?" is that we do not know. In the first place, we cannot yet foresee the outcome of the SALT, either over the long run or the near future. In the second place, in no precise or realistic terms has any clear standard for judging success or failure been set forth. As the discussion at the Fifth International Arms Control Symposium demonstrated, there is some variance among specialists as to the proper standards. Objectively, the plain truth is that, despite some two years' experience in SALT, our lack of knowledge about the crucial questions relevant to success or failure remains far greater than our knowledge.

There are other problems as well: The standards for success or failure seem to change with time; a strategic arms limitation agreement may be far less effective and make much less of a contribution than is commonly supposed; and an agreement may well have effects unintended or unforeseen. Although we can discuss possibilities, we cannot really discern the effects of an agreement, or of the talks themselves, on our long-range security, on strategic stability, or on the security and politics of our alliances.

In view of the dynamic strategic situation since the SALT began, it is fair to ask whether the basis for the SALT, derived in 1968 and 1969, remains valid, and whether the outcomes and positions contemplated during that time are still relevant. We have not been told that these have been boldly adjusted or reconsidered. Yet the environment of the SALT, prospects and expectations for a SALT agreement, and the SALT themselves all appear to have changed in significant ways since the preparation for and beginning of the SALT. And, comparing the early optimism about the SALT with what seem to be the expectations at present, one might more judiciously and skeptically question the degree of "success" represented by the conclusion of an agreement.

The reaching of an agreement, per se, whatever its purported symbolic value, is not an adequate standard for success. Success and failure cannot be judged devoid of the content of the agreement. The terms of an agreement do indeed matter. The terms may contain seeds of destabilization and insecurity. That agreement may be the only one concluded, even if it is represented as a "first step." If there is a follow-on agreement, it may build on the terms of the first, exacerbating its defects.

On the other hand, it is entirely possible that an agreement may do very little or nothing at all. There are many indications that we have attributed too much importance to concluding a strategic arms limitation agreement and have expected too much from it. One gathers from official public utterances and the news media that the SALT are about the last chance there is to *do* something about strategic arms limitation and that the penalty for failing to do this something or other will be high. The putative benefits of "successful" SALT (in terms of concluding a strategic arms limitation agreement) and the warnings of dire consequences in the event of SALT "failure," as usually encountered, are respectively grand and terrible indeed. It is very doubtful that either is true. Success or failure will probably rest more with factors extraneous to a strategic arms limitation agreement than with any agreement itself.

Do we really know what consequences will result from an agreement limiting strategic arms? That also is very doubtful. Henry Kissinger once wrote concerning arms control: "We are in no position to know whether a given plan enhances security, detracts from it, or is simply irrelevant."[1] Discussion of strategic arms control generally focuses on how an agreement would enhance national security and strategic stability or would promote *détente* and arms control. There has been very little consideration of an agreement that is irrelevant in terms of its contribution to security and stability. Yet, in terms of any presently likely strategic arms limitation agreement, that may well be the case. The direct and indirect consequences from the SALT will depend much more on what we do or fail to do than on the outcome of the SALT themselves.

The test of time has demonstrated that there are mixed blessings, at best, from international arms control and security agreements. Advantages and disadvantages must be weighed together in any evaluation of such agreements. Many expected advantages have been set forth for a strategic arms limitation agreement. Some may be realized. But disadvantages may emerge as well. The balance sheet will ultimately be determined by the interplay of U.S. and Soviet decisions and actions outside the terms of an agreement.

In terms of a balance sheet of probable advantages and disadvantages from the SALT, I find myself more concerned about the potential disadvantages than expectant about possible benefits. This is partly because the very serious strategic problems facing the United States over the next decade are not very sensitive to probable SALT outcomes in any helpful way. These problems have come from the astounding buildup of Soviet strategic forces and the disparity in the recent respective efforts of the United States and the USSR in this area. With or without a strategic arms limitation agreement, success or failure in strategic terms will rest with whether or not the United States can successfully deal with these problems. With or without a strategic arms limitation agreement, technological development and competition in strategic forces (hopefully less one-sided) will continue.

In these terms, as far as the SALT are concerned, my answer to the corollary question of what we should expect from the SALT is: Do not expect very much. Neither the inherently limited potential for strategic arms control, per se, nor the history of the SALT and of Soviet strategic behavior permits us to expect very much "success" from the SALT. Unless a strategic arms limitation agreement reduces the threat, or stringently constrains it, and does so more than it limits our own ability to cope with the threat, we will have to concern ourselves even more than in the past with the quality and adequacy of our strategic forces.

It is possible that the United States and the Soviet Union will eventually agree to certain limitations on particular strategic systems. It is questionable, however, whether the agreement will make a clear contribution to national security, to strategic stability, or to the moderation of future competition in strategic armaments. It is distinctly possible that a strategic arms limitation agreement will have little bearing on future strategic relationships and strategic force competition. In practical terms, strategic arms limitation agreements may do very little—if anything at all—to change the rate of strategic force spending or the rate of technological change and competition. Whatever is limited, deployment will undoubtedly take place in systems and technologies not limited, and modernization and qualitative improvements will continue. Whatever quantitative limitations may result from an agreement, Soviet strategic forces will undoubtedly continue to be modernized and improved, probably toward counterforce and damage-limiting capabilities. The need for continuing effort on the part of the United States to adjust its strategic forces to a changing threat will not be lessened. What we must be concerned about is that failure on our part to look after our strategic objectives and requirements, with or without an agreement, may give the Soviets a historic opportunity to seize an important, perhaps irreversible, advantage.

Already an enormous change has taken place in the strategic balance, continuing during the two years we have been engaged in the SALT to the point that numerical limitations at existing levels of Soviet forces will be of little help strategically, and alone will not reduce the need for further U.S. countermeasures. The change that has taken place during the past two years of the SALT has already changed many of the conditions and possibilities for arms control that may have existed in 1969.

Take one example of the implications of this change for 1972 as compared with 1968–69: A freeze on new starts of ICBM launchers today would be of very little help, if any at all, in easing our major strategic problems or furthering arms control objectives. The numbers and throw weight of Soviet ICBMs, and the buildup of the Soviet SLBM force, are sufficient today to provide a first-strike disarming capability against U.S. land-based strategic forces through normal qualitative improvement. Consequently, an agreement at this point of time freezing ICBMs might make no contribution to stability. If it also left our ICBM force vulnerable, it certainly would not.[2] This raises the unavoidable question of whether we should bend our primary efforts to improving the technology necessary for a more stable situation in terms of force survivability and flexibility, including the ability to limit damage, before looking to a strategic arms limitation agreement to stabilize the strategic situation. Perhaps doing so would improve the long-term chances for an advantageous and durable agreement limiting strategic armaments.

One might suggest that a freeze on new starts of ICBM and SLBM launchers would be preferable to continued Soviet deployments. We would unavoidably have to either respond to these deployments with new strategic programs or accept an undeniably great Soviet superiority. Such a case is reasonably arguable, and if an interim agreement is concluded it must be expected that this will be the case argued by the administration, along with the promise of a follow-on agreement that will make a greater contribution to arms control and stability. This view ignores, of course, the changes that have taken place since the inception of the SALT. In a curious reversal of previous perennial predictions that Soviet ICBM and SLBM deployments would soon level off and stop, the hypothetical alternative of an ever continuing buildup is contrasted with an agreement that "prevents" such a buildup.

The problem, however, is that the present level of Soviet strategic offensive forces is sufficient to establish strategic superiority and to present the United States with the most serious security problems it has ever faced, unless adequate compensatory measures are taken. The expected strategic arms limitation agreement will not change that.

This unpromising forecast should not come as a surprise to anyone who has followed the course of the SALT as indicated by official public statements. The expectations expressed for a SALT agreement have become increasingly modest, and in public discussions the scope of an agreement has steadily decreased. Henry David Thoreau wrote of the young man gathering materials for a bridge to the moon, from which the elderly man, grown mature, eventually builds a woodshed. Apparently the young SALT man has become elderly.

As the SALT were about to begin in November 1969, the U.S. Secretary of State declared that the United States hoped to "negotiate an arms limitation agreement that will keep us in the same relative position that we are now." [3] At that time, the Soviet Union had about the same number of ICBMs as the United States (some 1,050) and had just begun deploying Polaris-type SLBMs (Y-class submarines). By midyear 1971, the Soviets reportedly had some 1,500 ICBMs and some 400 Polaris-type SLBMs.[4] According to recent reports, the Soviet ICBM total now exceeds 1,600, there are some 100 large but differently configured silo-launchers for new ICBMs under construction, and the Soviets have 41 Y-class submarines operational or under construction—the size of the U.S. Polaris force.[5] The throw weight (i.e., payload, which affords the Soviet Union far greater flexibility than the United States in terms of yields, numbers of warheads, and mission capability) of the Soviet strategic offensive missile force shows an even more striking differential. The probable throw weight of 300 SS-9s alone is approximately double that of the entire U.S. Minuteman and Polaris force combined. In addition, the Soviet Union has conducted a vigorous R&D program directed to the improvement of the forces that have been or are being deployed—MIRVs, penetration aids, improved accuracy, new ABM radars, and interceptors.[6]

What is clear from this incomplete summary is: (1) the Soviet strategic offensive missile force has approximately doubled during the two years of the SALT, and the objective expressed in November 1969 by the Secretary of State is clearly unobtainable, a thing of the past; (2) the Soviet momentum has been and continues to be tremendous and has resulted in a current and projected threat that will necessitate offsetting U.S. measures, whether or not there is a SALT agreement along the lines now being suggested; and (3) our crystal ball is at best quite cloudy when guessing Soviet strategy and force objectives.

On the last point, it is instructive that Secretary of Defense McNamara, in a 1965 interview, proclaimed perpetual superiority for U.S. strategic forces: "The Soviets have decided that they have lost the quantitative race, and they are not seeking to engage us in that contest. It means that there is no indication that the Soviets are seeking to develop a strategic force as large as ours." [7] In 1967, again, he predicted that in the early 1970s "we still expect to have a significant lead over the Soviet Union in terms of numbers." [8] Such statements are reminiscent of the congressional hearings over the Limited Test Ban Treaty in 1963 when administration spokesmen, including Secretary McNamara and Secretary Rusk, extolled continued U.S. strategic superiority as the *sine qua non* of security and international stability—and argued that it would be maintained and perhaps even improved by that treaty.

To contribute to a SALT environment a policy of superiority has been eschewed by the United States. Indeed, since the logic of SALT was based upon rough equality in strategic forces, many regarded the drawing abreast of the Soviet Union in 1969 as necessary to the success of the SALT, as the opportunity for a stable strategic arms limitation agreement based upon parity and mutual assured destruction.[9] It is a fair question whether U.S. relaxation after 1965 deliberately provided the Soviet Union with the opportunity to achieve strategic force equality with the United States and whether continued relaxation has encouraged a Soviet drive for superiority.

In April 1970, the Secretary of Defense told the public: "For the past five years the United States has been in neutral gear in the deployment of strategic offensive forces, while the Soviet Union has moved into high gear in both deployment and development of strategic nuclear weapons." He went on to state that this situation has come to the point where we are now "literally at the edge of prudent risk." Why has this situation been allowed to develop? Why such U.S. passivity? According to the Secretary of Defense, the United States "did not respond in past years because the United States deliberately chose to assume that the Soviet buildup at most was aimed at achieving a deterrent posture comparable to that of the U.S. . . . [and we] have not responded this year because we hope that SALT can render response unnecessary." [10]

Are we imprudently continuing to relax in order to keep the SALT going? If we were "literally at the edge of prudent risk" in the spring of 1970 and the Soviet buildup has continued (Secretary Laird announced in September 1971 that "there has been tremendous momentum" continuing in the Soviet buildup during 1971, which has made previous estimates "if anything . . . too conservative" [11]), how do we stand now with continued relaxation? The administration has demonstrated remarkable restraint in order to give the SALT every chance to succeed. In view of the drawn-out lack of success in reaching an agreement limiting strategic arms, and in view of the type of agreement apparently now expected, is further relaxation in order to keep the SALT going a wise and safe policy?

It might be useful at this point to review the course of the SALT. After preliminary talks in Helsinki late in 1969, SALT II got under way in Vienna in April 1970. According to the President's report to Congress on foreign policy, at Vienna the United States began to move to a discussion of concrete measures of limitation. The United States delegation, according to the report, initially suggested both quantitative and qualitative limitations on both offensive and defensive forces, including a MIRV limitation, and also suggested an alternative agreement that would actually reduce strategic offensive forces. When it was seen in Vienna that the Soviets were not responsive to these approaches and progress could not be made, the U.S. delegation was authorized to move to a modified approach taking account of Soviet objections. All along, the Soviet approach to the SALT was very general and unspecific ("Soviet suggestions . . . lacked the specificity and detail to permit firm conclusions about their overall impact. . . . The Soviet position has not been presented in the detail that ours has"), and apparently based upon a definition of "strategic" systems that enabled them to focus on limitations of U.S. forward-based tactical systems rather than giving priority to the core strategic offensive systems that they were busily building up.[12]

On May 20, 1971, the President acknowledged a deadlock in the SALT; in an attempt to break this deadlock, we agreed to "concentrate this year on working out an agreement for the limitation of deployment of antiballistic missile systems." This announcement, which took place simultaneously in Washington and Moscow, seemed to maintain some link between defensive and offensive limitations in the understanding that such a defensive agreement would be accompanied in some unspecified way by "certain measures with respect to the limitation of offensive strategic weapons." At a subsequent press conference, the President explained that there might be separate agreements taking different forms, for example, a treaty covering ABM limitations and an understanding or less-formal agreement on offensive limitations. Some newsmen have interpreted this to mean that ABM limitations are now first priority, in and of themselves, while the corollary "certain measures" limiting offensive forces is, in the words of one of them, "a rather thin cover." [13]

Whatever its specific terms, we are now apparently attempting to conclude a very limited agreement,[14] one that Dr. Kissinger has referred to (hopefully) as an "interim" agreement, and that is already being celebrated for its symbolic and promotional value more than for its contribution to security and stability. That is to say, such an agreement, if it comes, will be supported not chiefly on its own merits but primarily for its promise to lead to a better, follow-on agreement.[15] This appears to be a change in the U.S. position, inasmuch as the President's February 1971 foreign policy statement implied rejection of symbolic agreements: "If all the effort that has gone into SALT were to produce only a token agreement, it could be counterproductive. *There would be no reason to be confident that this could serve as a bridge to a more significant agreement"* (emphasis added).

If SALT Agreement No. 1 does not produce the desired outcome from the SALT, what evidence is there that SALT Agreement No. 2 will? Paradoxically, if there is to be a more valuable future agreement, is it not necessary for the United States to do what it would in the absence of the SALT; that is, demonstrate its capability to solve its major strategic problems through its own efforts and show that it will not permit the Soviet Union to acquire meaningful strategic superiority?

Whatever the nature of the SALT Agreement No. 1,[16] we are not in a position to assess the success or failure of the SALT or to discern its implications. In early 1972 it was not possible with full confidence even to predict the conclusion of an initial or interim agreement limiting strategic armaments, much less a more significant follow-on agreement. We did not yet know whether the Soviets wanted either agreement, although if there were to be an agreement along the lines indicated by the press speculation noted, it is difficult to imagine why the Soviet Union would turn it down.

To elaborate on what has already been said, the point here is that an agreement of that nature would essentially mean that the U.S. Safeguard program would be stopped, apparently along with U.S. freedom to defend its retaliatory ICBM force, while the Soviet threat in terms of strategic offensive missile launchers would have approximately *doubled* since the start of the SALT in November 1969. The flexibility afforded the Soviet Union by the throw weight of such a force would permit it to develop a clear counterforce capability at the same time that options for U.S. force survivability were being restricted. In other words, such an agreement would freeze and guarantee Soviet superiority and thus contribute to instability.

It would also of course abandon defense of population against the Chinese nuclear threat and against accidental attacks, a defense about which the President in March 1969 said: "No President with the responsibility for the lives and security of the American people could fail to provide this protection." [17]

If the benefits of such a strategic arms limitation agreement are so questionable, are there other compensatory benefits from the SALT? Usually, much is made of arms control dialogue in terms of its contribution to mutual understanding of concepts and objectives and—through U.S. pedagogy—to the eventual merger of strategic concepts (in the direction of those of the United States, of course). Some profess to see such a dialogue produce an agreement on the strategic concepts necessary to a strategic arms limitation agreement; others argue that talk on strategic arms limitation is beneficial in itself and constitutes a useful interaction whether or not an effective agreement is produced.

Unless the other side is using the SALT "dialogue" as a political weapon aimed, for example, at U.S. alliance relationships or at slowing down U.S. strategic weapons development, the discussions are harmless, cost little, and should be educational. Peripheral agreements, such as the Hot Line and Accident Measures Agreements, may result. And, of course, a central agreement limiting strategic arms may be produced, although most probably without explicit agreement on strategic concepts and objectives, perhaps even without any real dialogue concerning them. Strategic concepts do not emerge from a dialectic or from the intellectualizing of a dialogue between two contending powers, much less from an interchange that is more negotiation and staking out of positions than it is a dialogue. They are the product of the interaction for each side of its own objectives, geopolitical situation, opportunities, constraints, resources, technology, and institutional characteristics. Strategic concepts—and political or strategic objectives—are therefore likely to be dissimilar and continue to remain so. As Robert R. Bowie has noted: "Given the differences in history, geography, and commitments, it is hardly likely that the US and USSR would be able to agree on strategic doctrine or even on relative importance of different weapons for stable deterrence. But it is not necessary that they should do so in order to agree to limit or regulate specific weapons systems or activities." [18]

Professor Bowie's last point is also well taken. The necessity and productiveness of discussion and attempted prior agreement on strategic concepts are generally assumed in most arms control literature but are actually quite questionable. As another student of arms negotiations observed: "It may be argued that arms control agreements have been arrived at in the past essentially by a process of bargaining, in which the rationale of the positions adopted, if not actually an obstruction, has been irrelevant to the outcome." [19]

The likelihood of the SALT producing a strategic arms limitation agreement based upon agreed mutual understanding of concepts and an agreed common framework to which our respective force postures will conform is scant. In fact, the more we try to produce such a situation—the more we, in effect, try to get involved in joint strategic force planning—the more chimerical arms control becomes and the less likely is any significant agreement. Yet the logic of those who look to the SALT to establish and codify an agreed relationship of mutual assured destruction requires this.

If the SALT are to be in some sense productive, this will come from demonstrating that we will not tolerate inferiority or instability and from tough bargaining, rather than from any seminarlike approach to arms control and strategic concepts. In other words, as it used to be said when the power aspects of negotiations were more explicitly acknowledged than they seem to be today, ultimately it is not principle but bargaining power that counts.

What is suggested here is that too much is made of the presumed dialogue that takes place in U.S.-Soviet arms limitation negotiations. Too much is expected in terms of the establishment of mutual understanding and the setting of common concepts. Essentially, such an approach is little more than a modern expression of the naïve nineteenth-century liberal-rational conception of international politics, wherein it was assumed that communication or dialogue produced understanding, which necessarily decreased hostility and resulted in détente and the absence of conflict.

This fifth symposium has been unusually refreshing in the extent to which so many participants questioned the dialogue aspects of the SALT, the coincidence of strategic concepts and objectives, and the validity of U.S. concepts themselves. Many expressed doubt that parallel strategic concepts guide the two parties in the SALT. Others wondered whether the dialogue is principally a monologue with ourselves ("auto-negotiating," as Amrom Katz put it). Some expressed the view that stability based upon mutual assured destruction is probably not a common goal—and also not a preferable strategic relationship.

Despite two years of talk about strategic arms limitation, we do not know that we are pursuing similar, or even compatible, strategic force concepts and objectives. To the contrary, the weight of available evidence—and, I believe, the views of most who expressed themselves at the symposium—suggests that we are not.

For some time in the United States it has been commonly believed that there are certain absolute and immutable truths about strategic stability and the optimum strategic relationship, which only need to be learned and understood by all. Little thought has been given to the fact that these truths or concepts were formulated in a different world than we now face in the 1970s. The development of hardened silo-launchers for ICBMs and submarines for subsurface launching of SLBMs, together with an early stage in the development of missile accuracies and ASW capabilities, guaranteed the survivability of second-strike retaliatory forces. ABM was undeveloped. There were few good prospects for damage-limiting, for counterforce, or for flexible rapid targeting. United States superiority, or at least equality, was presupposed. The only threat was the USSR, and stability could be defined in bipolar terms alone. All of this led to the sanctity and sufficiency of "assured destruction" retaliatory forces, which—if only the Soviet Union would follow the rules of the game—would lead to a stable situation based upon mutual assured destruction. As Senator Edward W. Brooke of Massachusetts described such stability: "Mutual deterrence depends on mutual vulnerability. It is in neither side's interest to threaten the other side's retaliatory forces." [20]

Yet developing a counterforce threat is precisely what the Soviet Union is doing, and the evidence that the USSR is not playing the game by our rules is overwhelming. Unable to cope with this evidence, we stick with stereotyped arms control principles and prolong the half-life of our strategic concepts and suppositions. We overintellectualize arms control and stability in an apolitical and abstract fashion that is highly ethnocentric and mirror-imaging. And we persuade ourselves that it is only a matter of time until Soviet leaders understand, appreciate, and adopt our intellectualizing.

American theorists have persuaded themselves of the theory of a Soviet doctrinal lag of approximately five years. . . . The conclusion that the Soviet Union rejects the American strategic enlightenment has been steadfastly rejected. . . . The arms control miscalculation of the late 1960s was the belief that the Soviet leaders, reasoning like American strategic logicians, would appreciate the folly of a bid for superiority. Hence, strategic arms limitation should be possible once the Soviet Union attained its definition of parity.[21]

Pondering these problems, the course of the SALT, and the continued buildup of the threat, one must consider the possibility that our greatest failure so far associated with strategic arms limitations endeavors may be an intellectual one.

Another part of this intellectual problem might be seen in what seem to be different approaches to the SALT and perhaps different motivations—possibilities that seem insufficiently taken into account in arms control discussions.

Leonard Beaton has speculated: "In SALT, as in so many things, it is possible to suspect that the American objective is essentially technical and the Soviet objective political." [22]

Do these differences exist, and if so what are their implications for success or failure? It seems clear that the United States looks to the SALT to solve or ease strategic force problems technically—and given the present mood of Congress and the country toward defense expenditures and major weapons programs, the SALT may seem like the only solution. The U.S. approach to the SALT, as described in the President's foreign policy statement, is technical and analytical. It seems equally clear that whatever the Soviet desire for arms limitation, the Soviet approach, by contrast, is highly political.

The political approach of the Soviet Union was suggested in the first issue of *USA,* the journal of the Institute of the United States, under the Soviet Academy of Sciences. G. A. Arbatov in both the editorial and the lead article emphasized the primarily political Soviet approach to the SALT, as contrasted with a purported primarily technical approach of the United States. Arbatov suggested that the central strategic force issues, as the major questions of the U.S. foreign policy, would be decided by domestic strains within the United States. In discussing these domestic strains, Arbatov stated frankly, "In this case, only one of its aspects interests us—the effect which the aggravation of internal problems has on Washington's foreign policy." The U.S. strategic position and the outcome of the talks, therefore, depend "on the struggle among supporters and adversaries of the agreement in the United States." The articles suggested strongly that such domestic factors would take care of the central strategic relationship and that the USSR at the SALT could focus on peripheral and partial measures in line with current Soviet objectives, including political ones. In view of the fact that only two partial agreements have emerged, concerning the Hot Line and accident measures, and of the apparent Soviet focus on U.S. tactical theater (alliance) systems and a separate ABM agreement,[23] the Arbatov suggestion seems to be borne out.

If the SALT are primarily political exercises to the Soviet Union, stabilization of strategic relations and abatement of competition in strategic arms may not be the major Soviet objectives, as they are of the United States. Negotiations may be seen as an opportunity to play on those domestic vulnerabilities identified by Arbatov, to inhibit U.S. strategic arms programs, and to raise problems within U.S. alliances. It may be seen, at least, as a demonstration of the new Soviet position of strategic equal, at a mimimum based on a kind of duopoly of international power—wherein, however, the United States is in a stage of withdrawal, and the Soviet Union a stage of expansion.

If this is so, and the United States approaches SALT as the means of solving pressing strategic problems, the relative advantage in negotiation is clear. "Much as arms control may be desired, it must not be approached with the attitude that without it all is lost. The consequence of such a conviction must be to encourage the Communists to seek to use arms control negotiations primarily for psychological warfare." [24]

Negotiations can clearly be used as a political weapon. One study of a decade ago concluded that arms control and disarmament negotiations characteristically have had the goal of "the attainment of political objectives not immediately associated with disarmament as such." [25] This hardly is descriptive of the U.S. approach, but concern that it may be of the Soviet approach is warranted. Historically,

> not all of the negotiations entered into by the Soviet government are intended to eventuate in settlements. Negotiations may be begun, or agreed to, by the Soviets, not as a means of promoting agreement on an issue, but of delaying it, pending the clarification of problems in other areas. . . . They may be started out of mere speculation, as a means of eliciting the views, defining the interests, of testing the tenacity of the parties of the other side. They may be designed for purely propagandistic purposes.[26]

Since differences do exist between the United States and the Soviet Union, and the situations they face, it is understandable that we may not approach strategic arms control in the same manner. That Soviet motivation and behavior are mirror-images of our own seems most improbable. The political differences between the two are important to their relations and to arms control, and need to be taken seriously into account.

This may be an unfashionable view of international relations in general and arms control in particular. Nevertheless, strategic or arms control theories that do not recognize the political differences suffer from a serious weakness. Trying to understand international relations in terms of an international "system" with abstract "actors" X-Y-Z, who behave, *mutatis mutandis,* in mirror-image symmetry, may have a place in academic model-building, but it is stercoraceous when it comes to the real world of policy.

At this symposium, more commentators than usual seemed to agree with this. Some pointed out that, at least, we cannot assume that both the United States and the Soviet Union want the same world and have the same political and strategic objectives. A contrast was made between an introverted United States and an active, opportunistic Soviet Union guided by an "imperial will." The United States is a status quo power, the USSR is not. As discussed in Robert Pfaltzgraff's chapter the policies and approaches of status quo and imperialist powers differ in ways that are important for stability. It makes an enormous difference between a status quo power and an imperialist power which possesses a strategic advantage, which holds superiority, which has a first-strike capability. In the past, the United States has had rather clear strategic force superiority over the Soviet Union. It was not used in a first strike, and there is no evidence that anyone really feared that it would be except in a last-ditch defense of vital interests. It was used politically very seldom and then only to support international stability. It was, in short, a stabilizing, not a destabilizing factor. Will the United States and the rest of the world be able to regard Soviet strategic superiority in the same way?

A growing recognition that the Soviets would realize and exploit a political advantage from some form of strategic superiority, or from the stalemate of U.S. strategic power, is itself a reversal of the long prevailing notion in the United States that strategic forces confer no political benefits and have no political utility. The recognition is belated, but perhaps not so much that it is not useful to the formulation of U.S. and Allied policies. The realization that strategic superiority of the type the Soviet Union now seems to be seeking might also be usable militarily absorbs a good deal of the energies of the Department of Defense; one can only express the hope that the general recognition of this possibility is not too late.[27]

There are as well other significant differences, which should be borne in mind in addressing the SALT. One is in decision-making concerning the SALT and the strategic forces relevant to the SALT. The SALT are subject to greater emotional and political influences in the United States than they are in the Soviet Union. Therefore, the U.S. position is subjected to pressures and vicissitudes that the Soviet leaders do not encounter, at least to the same extent. Our strategic programs are affected by these pressures during negotiations, while the Soviet programs obviously are not. Thus the effects of the SALT on the respective strategic programs differ with or without an agreement.

If there is a strategic arms limitation agreement, there will be a tendency to euphoria in the United States, which might well result in a paralysis of strategic force programs well beyond the actual terms of the agreement. Similarly, one should expect there to be a disproportionate conformity to the "spirit" of the agreement, as contrasted to its literal provisions. For a specific example, if there is an agreement banning or limiting ABM to low levels, but not prohibiting R&D and/or modernization, we must expect that the Soviet R&D program in missile defense will continue vigorously while our own will suffer. A zero ABM agreement would probably mean zero over the long term for the United States but not for the Soviet Union—not only because, given the Soviet radar and interceptor base, it is difficult to conceive a true zero for the USSR, but also because strong Soviet air defense and ABM development programs would likely continue. As a general proposition, it will be very difficult to get money for R&D in the United States for any system banned or limited by a strategic arms limitation agreement.

One other difference in decision-making concerning strategic forces relevant to the SALT is that the concepts generally held in the United States concerning stability influence U.S. decisions. The United States government has held a mutual assured destruction view in making its strategic force decisions, and, further, has tended to base them on an action-reaction view of arms competition. Such concepts have been included in our decisions and probably will continue to be. There is no evidence that this is true for the Soviet Union.

With this background, how can we evaluate success or failure as a consequence of the SALT? Partly, it depends upon the expectations or standards one sets. If one regards the conclusion of a strategic arms limitation agreement as the mark of success, perhaps because of its expected symbolic or promotional value if not because of its specific terms, then this constitutes a modest but narrow standard, which might well be met. If one expects an agreement to reduce arms competition, stabilize the U.S.-Soviet strategic relationship without destabilizing third-country relations, solve our basic strategic problems, and usher in a period of constructive *détente* between the superpowers, he will be sadly disappointed.

The view has already been expressed that success or failure cannot be determined by the conclusion of an agreement, regardless of its terms, and that the goals popularly expressed for strategic arms limitations are not likely to be achieved. It is possible that we will get a limited agreement, but most unlikely that we will get a broader or more comprehensive agreement that will produce what we initially hoped to obtain. The limited agreement may be termed "interim," but no one can say whether there will be a second agreement or whether a second agreement will be any better than the first. Any agreement entered must be judged by its overall impact on U.S. political relations and strategic objectives or requirements. Further, the effects of the SALT, with or without an agreement, will depend upon what we ourselves do about our strategic problems, for the need to make difficult decisions about requirements to cope with the threat is going to remain with us.

It may be old-fashioned to suggest it, but in approaching the SALT and strategic force planning, words written a quarter of a century ago by Walter Lippmann seem appropriate: "I do not find much ground for reasonable confidence in a policy which can be successful only if the most optimistic prediction should prove to be true. Surely a sound policy must be addressed to the worst and hardest that may be judged to be probable, and not to the best and easiest that may be possible." [28]

How then do we attempt to evaluate success or failure, realizing that we will not be able at this time, or at the time of any eventual agreement, to see all of the effects and implications? Should the SALT be evaluated by the way the strategic balance has changed during the talks? By the strategic balance accepted or established, explicitly or implicitly, in an agreement? Should we ask if the agreement demonstrably "curbs the arms race" or reduces defense expenditures? If it does neither, should we ask if it enhances stability and eases specific strategic problems? What if it does not; do we then optimistically regard it as a first step to an eventual agreement that will? If the agreement itself does little along these lines, does it restrict U.S. strategic options? If it does not, for example, provide for the survivability of our retaliatory forces, does it require that we leave them vulnerable?

These are some of the questions that should be raised in evaluating the SALT or a strategic arms limitation agreement. There are others that may be more difficult to answer due to their indirect or long-term effects. What effect is there on the security interests of our allies and on the viability of our alliances? Is our ability, or that of our allies, to meet alliance security requirements affected? Some of the European participants at the symposium voiced concern that some inhibition, explicit or implicit, on U.S. military and technical support of allies might accompany an agreement.

What will be the effect of the SALT on third-world stability, including the incentives of other nations to obtain national nuclear capabilities? Perhaps it will have no influence. Some at the symposium felt that, far from furthering the arms control obligations promised in the Non-Proliferation Treaty, the SALT might encourage proliferation.

Answers to questions of this nature are obviously speculative. As maintained at the outset of this chapter, we simply do not know the answers at this time. The answers, again, will depend more upon what we do or do not do as a matter of policy than upon the terms of a strategic arms limitation agreement.

There are also doctrinal questions, and questions concerning preferable future strategic postures that are even more unanswerable. What, for example, are the long-term implications of an agreement that directly or indirectly paints us into a corner on strategic systems and concepts? Do we really want to freeze current systems and a posture of assured destruction, and exclude other options? The President has emphatically said "No" ("I must not be—and my successors must not be—limited to the indiscriminate mass destruction of enemy civilians as the sole possible response to challenges"); [29] yet the SALT seem inexorably headed in that direction. Would such an agreement constitute success or failure?

Most students, and apparently policy-makers, follow the statement by Senator Brooke quoted earlier in this chapter. They view arms control and stability in terms of mutual assured destruction (vulnerability), where both sides eschew damage-limiting objectives and deliberately forgo counterforce and active defense (which the Soviets do not). A minority—to some extent apparently supported by President Nixon—does not regard assured destruction only as the preferable posture. This group would argue that mutual assured destruction may be the current state of affairs, but is not a goal we should work toward (and is not a relationship to which the Soviet Union will agree anyway); that "success" is not reached by making rigid a system in which responses are directed to large-scale destruction of civilian life and property ("especially so when that response involves the likelihood of triggering nuclear attacks on our own population," according to President Nixon).[30] This group would also argue that one of the most unfortunate outcomes would be an agreement that sealed off other strategic options.

Doctrinal questions of this nature are a matter of view and are not susceptible of resolution, but they do illustrate the uncertainty associated with SALT outcomes and the definition of success or failure. My own view is that of the minority. The logic of the SALT, from the U.S. viewpoint, is clearly that of the majority, and a strategic arms limitation agreement embodying the minority view is presently inconceivable.

However, a more modest and measurable standard might be suggested for the SALT. The administration has announced a strategic policy of "sufficiency" and has, moreover, established specific criteria for strategic sufficiency that go beyond assured destruction only.

Should a strategic arms limitation agreement be evaluated by the standard of the four criteria for strategic sufficiency? Whatever one thinks of the "sufficiency" criteria, they do represent national security policy; therefore, it is not unreasonable that they be used as a standard for evaluating the terms of a strategic arms limitation agreement. Yet, curiously, SALT success or failure has not been discussed here in terms of this standard. The criteria, as set forth in the 1971 defense report, are as follows:

(1) Maintaining an adequate second-strike capability to deter an all-out surprise attack on our strategic forces.
(2) Providing no incentive for the Soviet Union to strike the United States first in a crisis.
(3) Preventing the Soviet Union from gaining the ability to cause considerably greater urban-industrial destruction than the United States could inflict on the Soviets in a nuclear war.
(4) Defending against damage from small attacks or accidental launches.

Should an agreement be evaluated in terms of its contribution to these criteria? Should an agreement that undermines, or does not contribute, to the aims of these criteria be rejected? Of course, to be realistic, our ability to meet these criteria depends upon our own forces and upon the forces of the Soviet Union, and a feasible arms control agreement may be able to do nothing at all about the existing strategic situation. Moreover, it can be argued persuasively that the criteria are objectives, all of which we may not be able to accomplish. It may be necessary to make trade-offs among them, for example, forgoing the fourth by dropping Safeguard in order to promote an agreement that would strengthen the first and second, which after all constitute the *sine qua non* of American security.

The question then becomes, Does the agreement do this? Is the gain in increased reliability of retaliatory forces and in crisis stability worth what may be given up (light area defense and the ability to reduce damage)?

We have as yet no agreement by which to judge these questions. An agreement along the lines speculated by the press would not contribute to holding to the third and fourth criteria. It would seem to abandon the fourth and, inasmuch as it would freeze a situation of substantial Soviet superiority in numbers and throw weight of strategic offensive missile launchers, would seem at least to weaken the third. If these two criteria were, in effect, traded to help preserve our ability to meet the first two, does the agreement effectively accomplish that?

The requirements of the first criterion—an "adequate second-strike capability to deter"—are not clear. Some apparently—and mistakenly—feel that this exists rather automatically as a state of nature. It is not at all clear what is required to deter, whether it is some level of urban-industrial destruction or the ability to fight a war and in some sense win it. The President also said in his 1971 foreign policy report that it is inconsistent with sufficiency to base our planning "solely on some finite—and theoretical—capacity to inflict casualties presumed to be unacceptable to the other side." In any case, there must be a sufficient, survivable capability for an effective response, however measured, and the Soviet Union would have to be persuaded of the reality and the effectiveness of the response. It would have to be a credible threat in the accepted jargon. In the words of the 1971 report by the Secretary of Defense, this requires that we "maintain a reliable retaliatory force, placing primary emphasis on measures that both reduce vulnerability to attack and assure defense penetration."[31] To what extent does the agreement contribute to the maintenance of such a reliable retaliatory force?

This provides a link also to the second criterion, which most specialists regard as a necessary corollary to the first. For example, a staff member of the Senate Sub-Committee on National Security and International Operations recently argued that "crisis stability should be the acid test for both strategic force planning and arms control proposals" and that, while arms control agreements that promote crisis stability should be welcomed, those that tend to weaken it should be rejected.[32] The criterion requires that our force posture give the Soviet Union no incentive to preempt, that the Soviets could gain nothing through a first strike over what they could expect from a second strike, that there be no significant absolute or relative advantage to be gained from preemption. This requires that *all* of our strategic force components be survivable, do not tempt by their vulnerability to a first strike, and be capable of carrying out their mission as well in a second strike as in a first strike.

If an agreement does not promote this survivability, it may contribute nothing of strategic significance. If it leads toward vulnerability by restricting our own survivability options without reducing the threat, if it does not "narrow the difference between striking first and second," it promotes instability and, according to the view cited above, should be rejected.

What does the agreement accomplish in real terms, rather than in vague promises of betterment of relations and promotion of arms control? That is the question we must all ask ourselves seriously and specifically when we are able to see the terms of any agreement.

Ideally, a strategic arms limitation agreement should preserve or enhance U.S. security, hopefully at lower levels of cost and effort, but certainly at no increase in cost or effort. It should do so without significantly reducing our ability to promote the security interests of our allies and without contributing to regional instability. In addition, it goes without saying, the other side must in fact be as effectively limited as the United States (the controls should be equally applied and equally effective); there must be confidence in verification of conformance with the agreement; and if the other side abrogates or otherwise nullifies the agreement, the time and effort needed for him to degrade U.S. security must not be less than that for U.S. compensatory measures.

Above all, an agreement should reduce or limit the threat more than it limits our means of coping with it, or it is contrary to the interests of stability and of U.S. security. If the threat left by the agreement is sufficient now or in the future to call into question the reliability of our retaliatory capability, in the sense of the first criterion, or to be destabilizing, in the sense of the second criterion, the agreement should not limit or reduce our means of countering the threat. We must be able continually to assure the survivability, penetrability, and adequacy of our second-strike forces, or an agreement in the name of arms control will promote instability and insecurity. If it does so at the expense of other values, as well, for example, the ability to defend against light attacks or to provide assistance to allies, it would be doubly counterproductive.

Is it possible to have an agreement that neither promotes the above objectives nor seriously runs counter to them? Certainly. Its worth would be justified in terms of its promise to lead to further, more significant agreements, or to a bettering of political relations. Since such payoffs are impossible of demonstration at the time of the agreement, it must rest on a certain optimism. The promissory nature of the agreement must be weighed against its indirect effects, which may be politically important. These effects may be felt within the United States and in U.S. relations with other countries.

The strategic risk run with such an agreement is that it could produce false comfort and a sense of euphoria about our strategic problems and requirements. We are facing present and future strategic problems of enormous magnitude, which will remain even in the presence of a strategic arms limitation agreement. If, either to promote or to follow the "spirit" of an agreement, we unduly restrict our ability to help ourselves, if we give up more than the agreement is worth or fail to support the necessary R&D and force improvement, these problems will be seriously worsened.

None of this can we foresee now with any certainty. We must await the agreement, along with any tacit corollaries; we must wait to see its effects on U.S. programs and strategic decisions; we must wait to see its effects on our relations with others. More than two difficult years of negotiation have gone into producing an agreement. The difficulty of negotiation is of relatively little interest to the public. We must now see the product before we can judge whether the effort has been worthwhile. As Johnny Sain is reported to be fond of saying: "The world doesn't want to hear about labor pains. It only wants to see the baby." [33]

NOTES

1. Henry A. Kissinger, *The Necessity for Choice* (Garden City, N.Y.: Doubleday, 1962), Anchor Books edition, p. 4.

2. For a discussion of this problem in terms of crisis stability, see Richard Perle, "Superpower Postures in SALT: The Language of Arms Control," An Occasional Paper of the Center for Policy Study, University of Chicago (1971).

3. An agreement would also, according to the Secretary, enhance international security by maintaining a stable U.S.-Soviet strategic relationship, halt the "upward spiral" of strategic arms, and reduce the likelihood of a nuclear war through a fruitful dialogue about issues!

4. These 1969 and 1971 figures are from the Secretary of Defense, Defense Reports, for Fiscal Year 1971 and Fiscal Year 1972 Defense Programs and Budgets.

5. William Beecher, "Satellites Spot a Soviet Build-Up for Atomic Arms," *New York Times* (October 11, 1971). Subsequently Senator Henry Jackson announced that the Soviets were building their 42nd Y-class submarine ("Meet the Press," November 21, 1971).

6. For more detailed information on Soviet forces and strategic programs, there are numerous public statements by Secretary Laird and by Dr. John Foster. Also see, e.g., Brigadier General Harry N. Cordes, "The Strategic Threat," *Air Force & Space Digest* (July 1971), and the five-part series "The Growing Threat," *Aviation Week & Space Technology* (starting Oct. 4, 1971, and ending Nov. 8, 1971).

7. "Is Russia Slowing Down in Arms Race—Interview with Robert McNamara, Secretary of Defense," *U.S. New and World Report* (April 13, 1965), p. 52.

8. Secretary of Defense Posture Statement for FY 1968–1973.

9. President Nixon reported subsequently, referring to the preparation for the SALT in 1969, the expectation at that time: "The approaching strategic parity provided an opportunity to achieve an overall agreement that would yield no unilateral advantage and could contribute to a more stable strategic environment. For the first time it was possible to conceive of agreements reflecting a genuine balance" (*U.S. Foreign Policy for the 1970's (III): a Report to Congress by Richard Nixon, February 9, 1972*).

10. Address by the Honorable Melvin R. Laird at the Annual Luncheon of the Associated Press, New York (April 20, 1970). (Office of the Assistant Secretary of Defense, Public Affairs.)

11. Statement by Melvin Laird at Airlie House, Warrenton, Virginia, September 18, 1970, *New York Times* (September 20, 1970), p. 24.

12. All of the above information, including the quotations, is from Richard M. Nixon, *United States Foreign Policy for the 1970s,* A Report to Congress (February 25, 1971).

13. Don Cook, "SALT Talks: After Two Years, A Clear Objective," *Los Angeles Times* (June 6, 1971)'.

14. Newsmen seemed generally to interpret the May 20, 1971, agreement specifically as pointing toward a SALT agreement limiting Soviet ABMs to the Moscow area defense and U.S. ABMs to one or two ICBM sites, along with at least an understanding prohibiting new ICBM starts and perhaps new SLBM submarine starts. See, e.g., Chalmers M. Roberts, "A SALT Agreement Near at Hand?," *Washington Post* (October 6, 1971). At the Fifth International Arms Control Symposium William Beecher of the *New York Times* suggested that discussion center on a hypothetical agreement restricting the two sides to no more than two ABM sites, freezing new ICBM starts, but *not* limiting SLBMs.

15. That this is the case subsequently became clear with the issuance of President Nixon's foreign policy report for 1972. In contrast with the optimistic statements of 1969 and 1970 about the clear benefits expected of a SAL Agreement, the President stated that "there will be *no disadvantage* for the U.S." in the expected agreement [emphasis added]. Instead of arguing that the anticipated agreement will make a major contribution to strategic and arms control objectives, it was portrayed as an interim step that will symbolize "Soviet willingness to limit the size of its offensive forces" and lead to an agreement that will eventually make such a contribution (*U.S. Foreign Policy for the 1970's (III): February 9, 1972*).

16. As the SALT reopened in November 1971 in Vienna, Ambassador Smith expressed the hope, reminiscent of the previous year, that a specific agreement would be reached by the end of the year and "trust" that one would be reached at least "not long after the beginning" of next year. Minister Semenov more cautiously referred to the "possibility for achieving positive results" with the qualifying admonition that "of course, the realization of the available possibilities depends not only on one side but both" (*Los Angeles Times* [November 15, 1971]). Such a contrast has been characteristic of opening statements since the beginning of the SALT.

17. President Nixon's Safeguard announcement (March 14, 1969).

18. Robert R. Bowie, "The Bargaining Aspects of Arms Control: The SALT Experience," paper given at the Fifth International Arms Control Symposium.

19. Hedley Bull, "Strategic Arms Limitation: The Precedent of the Washington and London Naval Treaties," An Occasional Paper of the Center for Policy Study, University of Chicago (1971).

20. Letter, Senator Edward W. Brooke to the Honorable Melvin R. Laird, Secretary of Defense (October 27, 1970).

21. Colin S. Gray, "What RAND Hath Wrought," *Foreign Policy,* 4 (Fall 1971), pp. 111–29.

22. "Secondary and Almost-Nuclear Powers: How Do They Affect Strategic Arms Limitations?" An Occasional Paper of the Center for Policy Study, University of Chicago (1970).

23. On the U.S. theater systems, the President said: "The USSR has broadly defined 'strategic' offensive weapons . . . [to] include our theatre nuclear delivery systems, including those on aircraft carriers. . . . On the other hand, the Soviet approach would not include limitations on its own theatre nuclear forces, including their own medium or intermediate range missiles" (Richard M. Nixon, *United States Foreign Policy for the 1970s,* A Report to Congress [February 25, 1971]).

24. Kissinger, *The Necessity for Choice,* p. 285.

25. John Spanier and Joseph Nogee, *The Politics of Disarmament* (New York: Praeger, 1962).

26. Gordon Craig, "Totalitarian Diplomacy" in *Diplomacy in Modern European History,* ed. Laurence Martin (New York: Macmillan, 1966). Fred C. Ikle has also touched on such matters in his book, *How Nations Negotiate* (New York: Harper & Row, 1964), and in his essay for the Subcommittee on National Security and International Operations, "American Shortcomings in Negotiating with Communist Powers" (Washington, D.C.: GPO, 1970).

27. Few seemed to recognize this as a real problem at the Fifth International Arms Control Symposium, possibly due to a residual conviction that deterrence will continue to exist and render a first strike irrational. Yet Soviet strategic force development points clearly toward the capability for a partially but significantly disarming first-strike capability with a fraction of the total force, enabling an overwhelming assured destruction capability to be held in reserve. Even if U.S. calculations "show" that surviving U.S. forces would retain some magical assured destruction capability (20–25 percent fatalities?), the question remains whether the U.S. would respond in such fashion, given its reduced force, and only call down greater retaliatory destruction on itself. In other words, instead of the simple model of aggressive Soviet first strike and U.S. retaliation, we now face a situation where the Soviets could strike first and still retain their own assured

336 · WILLIAM R. VAN CLEAVE

destruction retaliatory force, leaving the U.S. in the position of being the *initiator* of nuclear war against civilian populace and the Soviet Union in the position of being the retaliator. This is what the President referred to when he asked in his 1970 foreign policy statement if a President should "in the event of a nuclear attack, be left with the single option of ordering the mass destruction of enemy civilians, in the face of the certainty that it would be followed by the mass slaughter of Americans." In his 1971 foreign policy statement, he emphatically rejected this—yet it is precisely the situation we seem headed toward, and one that our apparent SALT approach would seek to freeze.

28. Walter Lippmann, *The Cold War: A Study in U.S. Foreign Policy* (New York: Harper & Bros., 1947).

29. *United States Foreign Policy for the 1970s,* 1971 Report (Washington, D.C.: Dept. of State Publication, 1972), p. 170.

30. It is ironic that a traditional objective of arms control—cited as one of its two objectives in the Arms Control & Disarmament Agency handbook on arms control contained in a SALT packet for newsmen (*Arms Control and National Security,* 2nd ed.)—is to limit damage in the event a war occurs; yet the major approach encountered in discussing strategic arms control ignores this objective entirely.

31. 1971 Defense Report. *Statement of Secretary of Defense Melvin R. Laird on the Fiscal Year 1972 Defense Program and Budget.*

32. Perle, "Superpower Postures in SALT," pp. 5, 2–3.

33. Quoted by Jim Bouton, *Ball Four* (New York: Dell, 1970), p. 158.

JAMES E. DOUGHERTY

SALT and the Future of International Politics

ON NOVEMBER 18, 1944, a committee of seven scientists submitted to Arthur H. Compton a statement entitled "Prospectus on Nucleonics," better known as the Jeffries Report, which contained the following conclusion:

We believe that the inevitability of the development of nucleonics by some if not all nations shows compellingly, because of its potential military consequences, the necessity for all nations to make every effort to cooperate now in setting up an international administration with police powers which can effectively control at least the means of nucleonic warfare.[1]

Seven months later, on June 11, 1945, the famous Franck Report, when delivered to Secretary of War Henry L. Stimson, carried a similar warning paragraph:

In the past, science has often been able to provide also new methods of protection against new weapons of aggression it made possible, but it cannot promise such efficient protection against the destructive use of nuclear power. This protection can come only from the political organization of the world. Among all the arguments calling for an efficient international organization for peace, the existence of nuclear weapons is the most compelling one. *In the absence of an international authority which would make all resort to force in international conflicts impossible, nations could still be diverted from a path which must lead to total mutual destruction, by a specific international agreement barring a nuclear armaments race.*[2]

There has always been a note of urgency in the warnings of the scientists and in the public political rhetoric of presidents, premiers, and diplomatic representatives who have reminded us over and over that we are confronted by "a choice between the quick and the dead." Yet as Mason Willrich trenchantly points out in his recently published book, *Global Politics of Nuclear Energy,* despite the fact that the advent of nuclear weapons technology in 1945 created an imperative challenge to the international political system, no dramatic fundamental changes have occurred in that system after more than twenty-five years. The nation-state remains the basic unit of political organization and

337

seems if anything to have been strengthened rather than weakened by scientific-technological developments.[3]

Despite considerable speculation five years ago concerning *le renversement des alliances,* the two alliance systems of the super-powers in Europe scarcely appear on the verge of sudden collapse, despite—or perhaps because of—the fact that Europe is the only region in the world where nationalism shows some signs of abating in favor of a broader functional unity based on economic, social, and political factors. On the other hand, it is impossible to conclude that the impetus toward strong universal organization (in the United Nations) is more pronounced today than it was in the late 1940s. In fact, it is much weaker.

No effective supranational peace-keeping machinery has yet emerged or appears likely to emerge during the decade of the 1970s. Moreover, there is every reason to expect that as the "peaceful atom" becomes more common throughout the world as a source of energy, the "military atom" will become more difficult than ever to control, and the strains upon the Non-Proliferation Treaty and the philosophy of restraint that underlies it will grow inexorably greater— perhaps not necessarily unbearable, but certainly greater. The prospect that man will tame the technology of mass destruction and bring it under reliable political control is one that can only give pause to thoughtful minds.

Nuclear weapons have made a paradoxical contribution to the international system, as John H. Herz has noted from two different vantage points. Back in 1957, he argued that the advent of nuclear weapons had put an end to the "hard shell" defense of the state, which had historically enabled the government to claim that the state was impenetrable and could provide security to its population. Writing twelve years later, however, Herz admitted that his earlier diagnosis concerning the "demise of the territorial state" had probably been premature. The very same nuclear developments that in theory had rendered modern industrial states so vulnerable to the threat of physical annihilation had also, in practice, rendered all military force, including conventional force, "unavailable" in the direct relations between major nuclear powers and their allies.[4] Governments have been forced to become more cautious than ever in their efforts to avoid such confrontations as might lead to uncontrollable military embroilment. There have, of course, been scores of international and internal conflicts in various less industrialized regions of the world. But slowly and gradually, the condition of mutual nuclear deterrence, which has prevailed for several years between the two superpowers, is being extended to provide security against attack for larger numbers of political communities, as non-nuclear-weapon states are drawn into the circle of deterrence and commitment of the nuclear weapon states. Perhaps five or ten years from now we shall look back and interpret some of the ambiguous developments of the past year or so in Southeast Asia, the Middle East, and the Indian subcontinent in the light of this general concept of what is happening in the international system.

Let me put it in more Hobbesian terms: Even though the nation-states have not been able during the past twenty-five years to covenant among themselves to create a strong international sovereign capable of taking them out of the state of war and of imposing his peace upon them, nevertheless the dreadful power of the atom itself has served as a kind of surrogate sovereign to hold men and governments in awe, reminding them that there do exist certain bounds, however unclear, that governments must restrain themselves from crossing in their behavior toward one another.

In all honesty, perhaps we must admit that the world has been rather fortunate in the past twenty-five years, not in its ability to prevent or control all forms of large-scale social conflict and war and to reduce substantially their economic, psychological, sociological, and political causes, but rather insofar as the international system has managed in one way or another to avoid the catastrophe of nuclear war. We can wonder whether, if the United States had never used the two atomic bombs against Hiroshima and Nagasaki in 1945, if the world had never become aware, from those tragic experiences and their aftermath, of the terrible implications of these weapons for mankind, and if a few nations had begun to manufacture and stockpile such weapons (as they almost certainly would have under the circumstances), if we might not have blundered our way into a much more widespread nuclear catastrophe between 1945 and 1971, involving perhaps two hundred cities instead of two. Japan suffered much, but when we consider how much worse off the world might have been if nuclear weapons had been used for the first time at the beginning rather than at the end of a later war, perhaps we can all better realize what a great human debt the world may owe to the Japanese people.

During the past twenty-five years we have had some narrow escapes in the international system—exactly how narrow we shall never know for sure. But it is easy now to forget that tensions were rather high at times as the great powers have become committed to a degree in localized conflicts (Korea, Southeast Asia, the Middle East) or areas of tense confrontation (Berlin, Cuba). Almost anything might have happened in some of those crises. No doubt the two superpowers have up to the present time demonstrated a certain facility in crisis management and in averting a frontal collision. But the following caveat is well worth quoting: "There is a danger that previous successes in avoiding head-on encounters may breed an unwarranted overconfidence in the ability of the United States and the Soviet Union to manage future crises and always to act with mutual restraint." [5]

A central question confronting us is whether the international system will be able to continue to avoid a large-scale nuclear war during the next decade, when total nuclear stockpiles will be at higher levels than in the past. This no one can predict with certitude. From a strictly scientific standpoint, it simply is not possible to assign a precise probability to such a "discrete" event as the occurrence or nonoccurrence of nuclear war within a specified period of time.[6] We can, of course, make an assumption that there will be no nuclear war, thereby removing the single most significant variable from our attempted prevision of the future. This is a hopeful and not unreasonable assumption. At least so far as the deliberate political decision-making process goes, there is no compelling reason to think that any one of the five existing nuclear weapon states would expect to achieve a definable political purpose by initiating large-scale nuclear war within the next decade.[7]

Rationality in political decision-making dictates that as stockpiles and capabilities of assured destruction go up, the risks of a deliberate political choice for nuclear war go down. (We might ask whether this is a universal proposition, applicable in Peking as well as in Moscow and Washington. The author is inclined to think it is.) Thus so far as *deliberate* action is concerned, the normal prospect is for the circle of deterrence to widen steadily, as larger numbers of states are drawn into the ambit of one or other of the nuclear protector states (whichever these may be). Beyond the realm of deliberate choice, the greater danger probably lies in the unknown possibility of the unintended or the uncontrollable (accident, miscalculation, escalation, and other situations in which "rationality" may break down), which we mention frequently but, in the nature of things, can understand but little, for the simple reason that we want the empirical evidence to remain as scarce as possible.

There are advantages and disadvantages in making an assumption like the foregoing one. One of the principal advantages is that it can help to create a perspective conducive to the attenuation of suspicion and the facilitation of compromise agreements. On the debit side, it can lead to the development of an unwarranted sense of security—to a vague impression that we really need not worry about the occurrence of nuclear war in an environment of mutual deterrence, regardless of what may happen or fail to happen. Perhaps better questions for us to ask are not whether nuclear war will occur within the next ten years but what developments within that time frame are likely to have an effect upon the stability and relative peace of an international system in which some forms of conflict are bound to recur, and what can the great powers do to make sure that the international system in the early 1980s will be more secure than it is today against the danger of nuclear war, whether intended or unintended.

During the past twenty-five years, several proposals have emanated from various quarters for the ostensible purpose of enhancing the safety of the international environment against the dangers posed by nuclear armaments. Some were nobly if naïvely utopian; some bordered on the absurd; some were cynically propagandistic; some embodied to a greater or lesser degree an intelligent and moderately realistic vision appropriate to the *modus operandi* of governments. Let me list the principal models that have been advanced, and then comment very briefly on a few of them:

1. The Baruch Plan of 1946 for the creation of an International Atomic Development Authority (IADA).[8]

2. The Soviet proposal of the late 1940s to "ban the bomb."

3. The Soviet and U.S. proposals of 1959 and 1961, respectively, for general and complete disarmament.

4. Various proposals for "disengagement," "thinning out," or reduction of forces in Europe, with or without the creation of denuclearized zones—from the ideas suggested in the mid-1950s or thereafter by Anthony Eden, George F. Kennan, and Adam Rapacki down to current proposals for negotiated mutual and balanced force reductions (MBFR).

5. Unilateral tension reduction and disarmament initiatives designed to reverse the arms spiral and create a wholly different climate of international relations.[9]

6. Negotiated arms control agreements of a limited-risk, limited-cost character, including the Nuclear Test Ban Treaty, the Hot Line,

the Outer Space Treaty, the Non-Proliferation Treaty, the Seabed Treaty, and the Agreement to Reduce the Risk of Accidental Outbreak of Nuclear War, all leading up to the SALT. These have been supplemented, of course, by a variety of unilateral national arms control policies designed to enhance the safety of the environment through weapons design, deployment patterns, command and control systems, contingency planning, and so forth.

The Baruch Plan seemed bold and generous enough at a time when the United States possessed an atomic monopoly. Today we can see that it was unrealistic of us to expect the Soviets to accept it, if indeed we did. In the Soviet view, the IADA would have been established on American terms. The United States was then so far ahead of the USSR in nuclear technology that the former would have been able to dominate the international control system and prevent its rival from ever obtaining independent ownership of nuclear weapons. This was at least in part what the Soviets meant when they said that the Baruch Plan would infringe upon the sovereign rights of the USSR. Both superpowers must for several years to come recognize a similar negative disposition on the part of China to enter any international control system on analogously disadvantageous terms.

We need devote no time either to the "ban the bomb" campaign or the proposals for unilateral disarmament, except to say that they were as irrelevant to the political realities of the international system as are most of the disembodied schemes of the contemporary radical antiwar movement. One of the most hopeful long-term trends in Soviet-American relations has been the slowly growing recognition by the two governments that the organization of a stable international peace requires the highest application of political intelligence; that this is a task that will be furthered less by the politics of alienation, demonstrative rejection, and reduction to absurdity than by policies of intergovernmental negotiation based upon objective humanist and scientific analysis, the ethics of politico-military fairness, and the formulation of prudent diplomatic strategies of mutual restraint.

As for some form of zonal arms limitation, or "disarmament on the geographical installment plan," we can say that ten or fifteen years ago, when we referred to it as "disengagement," it had no chance at all, whereas today what we call MBFR is well worth pursuing provided that we do so for the correct pragmatic reasons, within an assumed framework of limited interalliance cooperation that will neither raise false hopes among publics nor provoke genuine misgivings among knowledgeable policy-makers.

General and complete disarmament (GCD) merits a fuller comment because the United States and the Soviet Union are still on record as being officially committed to it as a goal, because it represents an ideal that exerts a powerful appeal to certain basic religious-philosophical-psychological instincts in men, and because if achieved it would mark a profound change in the international political system, including the end of nation-state security communities as we have historically known them in recent centuries. A basic dilemma of the superpowers' own making is that, for reasons of ideology, political rivalry, international propaganda objectives, and the placation of elitist public opinion, the two governments have adopted a public rhetorical posture which, regardless of whether or not it may conform with the internal value-motivational structures of individual policy-makers, definitely lies beyond the realm of the possible within the next decade for the bureaucratic decision-making structures and processes of the principal national governments in the world today.

Paradoxically, despite all the terrors that inhere in contemporary advanced weapons technology, not one of the five nuclear powers has acted consistently during the past decade as if she looks upon complete nuclear disarmament as the only way, or necessarily the best way, of safeguarding national security. Every one of the five assigns higher priorities to objectives other than GCD. The same technology that makes total disarmament appear more imperative than ever also makes it more difficult to attain.

As to the technical, strategic, and political obstacles to GCD, we need mention only a few of the most obvious: (1) Among the nuclear weapon states, serious asymmetries of statistically measurable symbolic power obtain, which greatly complicate the prospect for "pentagonal" negotiations. (2) Given the discrepancies in geostrategic requirements among the five, it is difficult to determine in which weapons sectors the process of limitation should begin, in what ratios the reductions should be made, at what pace we should move, and how far down the scale reductions should be carried before the beneficent condition of mutual deterrence might give way to renascent incentives for surprise attack. (A decade ago this was regarded as the central strategic problem in all planning for nuclear disarmament.[10] It was never fully resolved.) (3) The problems of "inspection," "access," and "control" at the levels of intensity required by GCD and as viewed by the disparate Soviet and American political systems were never really overcome.[11] (4) The two principal parties could not reach agreement on the development of an effective international peace-keeping organization in lieu of national military establishments for safeguarding external security. This leads to the further question (which has been "shoved under the rug," as it were) as to whether the objective of disarmament planning is to ban all existing nuclear weapons from the entire face of the earth (i.e., "to put the nuclear genie back in the bottle") or to reorganize existing national nuclear arsenals by internationalizing them (i.e., placing them at the disposal of a world authority, which would then be vested with an insuperable monopoly of military power adequate to the task of preventing national rearmament and aggression. Here we come face to face with the anomaly that the United States has called for an international military "peace force" under suitable civilian political control at a time when no intelligent analyst seriously argues that there exists an adequate international political consensus for the underpinnings of such an instrument. Soviet analysts may actually have been horrified by the premature "world federalism" of American policy elites.[12]

Governments are among the most conservative and cautious of all institutions known to social scientists. When issues of national security are at stake, all governmental bureaucracies act slowly and warily. No government will opt for sudden, sweeping changes in the environment in which it operates (it has a hard enough time adjusting to changes over which it exercises no control). Governments prefer to slice up their problems into digestible proportions, and this holds particularly true of proposals that have implications for national security. Thus governments almost by a law of their inner nature shun those far-reaching proposals which, if accepted, would usher in a radical transformation of the international politico-strategic environment with which they are familiar.

Of all the models suggested above for dealing with the dangers and dilemmas of nuclear armaments, the path of negotiated arms agreement on limited risk-limited liability is really the only method suited to the nature of the existing nation-state system. The arms control school is convinced that, given the dangerous condition in which the world finds itself and the current impossibility of any radical transformation of the international political system, the most important task of the moment is to keep staving off catastrophe by persuading governments to pursue rational policies based upon a realistic understanding of the politico-military environment. The SALT, because of the total context in which they are conceived, are the most important efforts yet to be made to achieve agreement on the international distribution of power at the level of crude parity between the superpowers. Conceptually, therefore, they are potentially the kind of arms control effort fraught with the greatest consequence for the future of the international political system.

II

At the Fifth International Arms Control Symposium we examined the rationale for superpower arms control negotiations. We analyzed strategic arms competition in the light of current and pending technological changes. We looked into the dynamics of the bargaining process as well as the connection between the SALT and the problems of future nuclear weapons proliferation. We tried to assess the implications of the success or failure of the SALT for international peace and security. Obviously we perceived the present situation from different perspectives, and thus were unable to reach complete agreement concerning the prospects for the future. What follows in the remainder of this chapter is a summary of one analyst's reflections on U.S.-Soviet negotiations toward strategic arms limitations.

There is always a spectrum of possible interpretations for every international politico-strategic development. Whatever trend some look upon as desirably stabilizing, others are bound to regard as disastrously destabilizing. Whether or not a specific arms control agreement that freezes or otherwise limits a particular military-technological sector will contribute toward stability or instability depends more upon the political motives and intentions of the parties than upon "neutral" or "objective" scientific facts. In the final analysis, the motives and intentions of governments are largely impenetrable to accurate investigation and evaluation from outside—and sometimes even from inside. It is the task of statesmanship to ponder all the data, all the contradictory interpretations of the data, and all the competing demands and requirements of the national and the international common good, and then to make the best practical judgment as to what is to be done at the time, without the comfort of absolute certitude concerning the future. It is no longer possible, in terms of sheer human morality, to force every security decision into the restricted framework of "national interest." We must realize that fact, and so must the Soviets, or there can be no really rational arms negotiations in the age of nuclear missiles. If there are intolerable asymmetries in the degree to which the two superpowers perceive the need to balance national interest with international interest today, then it means that the more responsible superpower must educate the less responsible one, for there can be no doubt that such an asymmetry of perception is itself highly dangerous, not only to any given nation, but to the world.

Why have the Soviet Union and the United States carried on the Helsinki-Vienna negotiations? There is a variety of reasons, some better and some worse, but not necessarily similar or of equal intensity on both sides. It makes sense that both Washington and Moscow would wish to reduce uncertainty about each other's future weapons deployment plans, slow the development of potentially destabilizing weapons systems (which would make the international environment less familiar to and more dangerous for both governments), avoid the economic futility of a mutually canceling arms competition, and divert resources from arms expenditures to other social purposes. Both nations are beset by uncertainties. Decision-makers in each country cannot help wondering at times whether things are really going as well as they might, domestically and abroad. They are also aware that the simplistic assumptions of cold war bipolarity have been in the process of dissolution for several years and are now giving way to the much more subtle and complex requirements of conducting foreign and defense policies in an emerging "pentagonal" world of the United States, the Soviet Union, Western Europe, China, and Japan.

First, let us compare the domestic problems, which in the past few years have been more serious for the United States than for the Soviet Union. As a nation, the United States has become frustrated by the Vietnam War and by her effort to establish some sort of equilibrium in Asia (despite a degree of success). She has experienced internal social disorders arising from urban crises, racial conflicts, and campus unrest, as well as a pervading inflation, which has contributed to general discontent with the existing institutional structure. The intelligentsia and youth have fed on one another's alienation from the nation's political, economic, and technical culture. All of these factors have generated a demand, led by youth and responded to by some politicians, for a reordering of national priorities from defense and outer space to the environment and the inner city.[13]

The Soviets, too, have experienced the beginnings of protest against their own political system. They have their own counterparts to America's disaffected intelligentsia and minorities, although on a smaller scale as far as political activity is concerned. The Sakharovs, Medvedevs, and Solzhenitsyns, who probably reflect the sentiments of many scientists, writers, artists, and intellectuals, apparently do embarrass the Communist leaders with their criticisms. They cannot organize demonstrations. They have no access to the technical communications media. But they circulate "underground" newsletters (*samizdat*) and have charged that mentally stable persons have been sent to psychiatric hospitals for treatment because of their dissident beliefs.[14] Moreover, thousands of Soviet Jews, unable to appreciate the distinction Soviet leaders often draw between anti-Zionism and old-fashioned Czarist anti-Semitism, have made known their desire to depart from the socialist fatherland, thus prompting unflattering comparisons between the USSR and Nazi Germany. Thus far the Soviets have managed without too much difficulty to keep the internal dissent under control. But perhaps there lurks in the back of their minds the historic fear of all Russian leaders, czarist and Communist alike, of an uprising by unsatisfied national minorities against Russian rule. This fear may now be heightened by misgivings over a future "countercultural" rebellion by youth.

When we shift our attention from the domestic to the international dilemmas of the two superpowers, the picture becomes even more ambiguous. On the one hand, the United States has felt itself under growing pressure within recent years to lower its international profile and reduce its global commitments, undertaken in the era of containment, to act as "policeman of the world." One can discern at least an adumbrative response to such pressures within the "Nixon Doctrine"—however vague it may be—especially with respect to Asia. In other words, it is possible to look upon the U.S. involvement in Vietnam as a kind of holding operation until the fuller emergence of China and Japan as active players upon the world scene would contribute to the inevitable enhancement of stability in a multipolar international system. For having played this role, the United States has paid a price in political popularity. But that is a price that probably had to be paid before the international system constructed during the cold war, with all its old rigidities, could become "unstuck," as it certainly has since President Nixon made the startling announcement in July 1971 that the United States was adopting a dramatic new diplomatic stance toward the People's Republic of China.

Geographically, the Soviet Union is closer than the United States to Western Europe and to China, and it has also shown itself during the past decade to be more apprehensive about developments in both regions, with implications for national security. In the early 1960s, the Soviets exhibited considerable concern over a possible German *revanchism* aiming at a forceful change in Europe's postwar boundaries. The Russians certainly seemed fearful that West Germany might some day either drag NATO into an anti-Soviet war to recover East Germany or acquire an independent nuclear capability of its own. Those fears were not well founded: The German Federal Republic could not possibly have posed a military threat to the Soviet Union, nor did it ever exercise as much control over U.S. and NATO strategy as the Russians seemed to suppose. But the fears were present, nevertheless, reaching paranoic proportions when the Soviets projected the potential consequences of a NATO multilateral force (MLF) into the future, until the MLF proposal was finally scrapped during the course of the negotiations for the Non-Proliferation Treaty.

During the ensuing *détente* in Europe, the Federal Republic of Germany was able to intensify its *Ostpolitik*. But when the European political atmosphere relaxes too suddenly, the Soviets find that they must occasionally resort to a show of massive force in order to maintain control in East Europe—as in Hungary in 1956, in Berlin with the Wall in 1961, and in Czechoslovakia in 1968. The Soviet leaders are aware that the Common Market exercises a powerful attraction upon East Europeans who are anxious for increased trade. But whereas the East Europeans have generally favored British entry because of its expected loosening effects in the economic order, the Soviets are looking ahead to the long-range political and strategic implications of British membership in the European Economic Community, including the possibility of a joint European nuclear deterrent, about which Moscow is understandably unenthusiastic. The Soviet leaders realize, of course, that the sobering lessons of the invasion of Czechoslovakia may eventually wear off in Eastern Europe, as they did long ago in the West. If a conference on European security should come about, and if the East Europeans should once again mistakenly act as if a new day of freedom is dawning for them, or if they should seek to exploit for their own benefit the tensions that have developed between the Soviet Union and China along the Amur-Ussuri Rivers, the Soviets can be expected to apply the Brezhnev Doctrine once again (despite Brezhnev's denial while visiting Yugoslavia in September 1971 that such a doctrine exists). The point to be made here is that the Soviets cannot assume that all their problems in Europe have been solved; "fraternal assistance" to suppress "counterrevolutionaries" may yet prove necessary. The conduct of the SALT helps to make whatever problems may arise a bit more manageable than they might otherwise be. (This suggests the possibility, not to be discounted, that merely carrying on negotiations can sometimes be more useful than actually reaching agreements.)

There has been a widespread assumption among Western analysts during the past decade that the Soviets perceive a significant interest in promoting *détente* in Europe in order to "safeguard their western rear" while they are involved in a serious dispute with China over national interests, interpretations of Marxist ideology, and leadership and strategies of the world revolutionary movement. Such an assumption is quite compatible with the classic Russian-Soviet strategy of avoiding conflict on opposite fronts simultaneously. But it might be just as logical, as a French analyst has suggested, to argue that the Soviets have adopted a militant posture toward a nuclear-weak China in order to "safeguard their eastern rear" and to free themselves for the conduct of a more dynamic diplomacy in Europe.[15] In either case, no one would deny that Sino-Soviet relations and U.S.-Chinese relations comprise an important part of the background of the SALT. The Washington-Moscow-Peking "triangular relationship," comparable in some respects to the insoluble "three body" problem in Newtonian physics, will undoubtedly add a new dimension of complexity to the arms control picture in the 1970s.[16]

Within the foreseeable future, the Soviets will have greater reason than the United States, because of geographical factors, to worry about the growth of China's nuclear capability. We cannot discount the possibility that Soviet apprehensions over China (as over Germany) may have been exaggerated in the past by Soviet policy-makers, or by Western commentators, or by both. The Peking leadership must recognize its country's strategic vulnerability in this nascent nuclear phase of its history, as well as the necessity of avoiding strategic adventurism.[17]

The Soviets are well aware that they now enjoy a vast margin of nuclear superiority over China. But they cannot ignore the problems that might conceivably arise in the years ahead along the forty-five-hundred-mile Sino-Soviet border, as China develops her capability to threaten Soviet cities, industrial complexes, and even missile sites with a surprise nuclear attack. (Even granted that a Chinese nuclear attack may be a very remote possibility, the Soviets cannot afford to ignore it.) In late 1969 and early 1970, some Western analysts suggested that the Soviet military forces were preparing to mount a preventive attack on the Chinese nuclear installations at Lop Nor.[18] We may now never know the full story of what happened at that time. Perhaps the U.S. move into Cambodia in the spring of 1970 prompted Moscow and Peking to attenuate their animosity, lest the United States try to exploit the Sino-Soviet dispute even further to its own advantage. Perhaps it became apparent to the Soviet leaders that a Soviet attack on China might irreparably weaken communism as a world political force, give rise to internal upheavals within the Soviet empire, and benefit the Western imperialist camp. If this kind of analysis was performed in the minds of the Soviet leaders, then it would not be inaccurate to conclude that the United States, without communicating any warnings or threats, helped to deter a Soviet attack upon China.

As Peking's nuclear arsenal grows, it will become increasingly difficult for the Soviet politico-military leadership to entertain the idea of a preventive attack upon China. Historical-psychological factors rooted in the Russian character and culture, as well as the rationalist dictates of communist ideology, already militate in favor of caution and nonviolent resolution of conflict. Perhaps the Soviets realize that, as a sheer matter of coldly calculated *Machtpolitik,* they have passed the point where they could deliberately opt for war with China, and that they must look forward to the inevitable development of conditions of mutual deterrence in Asia. Moreover, to the extent that the United States, in view of modifications envisaged in the Nixon Doctrine, reduces its military commitments in Asia, the Soviet Union will find itself constrained to develop its own quasicontainment policy vis-à-vis China. We must, therefore, recognize the essential ambiguity of the part that China plays in Soviet thinking about the SALT. On the one hand, the dispute with China apparently motivates the USSR to negotiate with the United States. But on the other hand, the fear of a future danger emanating from China sets limits to what the Soviets are willing to negotiate. As the Soviets contemplate China's growing nuclear capability and the great population imbalance between the two nations, they are probably motivated to strive to maintain a comfortable margin of strategic superiority over China as long as possible. The Soviet Union, in working out its policy for the SALT, might be willing to accept and observe a certain type of freeze agreement with the United States for as long as the Chinese can be safely expected to behave discreetly, like an inferior nuclear power. But it will be extremely difficult for the Soviet leaders, given their traditional defense-mindedness, to put their country on the "down escalator" while the Chinese are on the "up escalator." Thus it is probably unrealistic to expect substantial strategic force reductions in stage 2 of the SALT.

It would be highly misleading to imply that China poses dilemmas only for the Soviet Union and not for the United States. To be sure, the emergence of China as a quasi-superpower creates the conditions for a new type of equilibrium politics in Asia and makes it easier for the United States to reduce its military commitment to Southeast Asia. But the United States has to be concerned about the possible effects of a more activist Chinese international policy upon such countries as Japan, Australia, and the Philippines, especially if China were to begin developing a substantial naval capability. The Soviets and the Americans, too, assuming that they are interested in limiting their strategic rivalry in the Middle East, may find that the Chinese are determined to exacerbate rather than attenuate conflict in that region.[19]

Furthermore, the United States confronts a long-run danger that cannot be ignored. At the present time, virtually everyone assumes that the Sino-Soviet dispute arises out of the fact that either the centrifugal forces of Soviet and Chinese nationalism in interaction have proved stronger than the centripetal forces of Communist ideology or else that the differences in ideological outlook which reflect different stages of historical development have become so great themselves as to divide the two principal Communist powers. But the question is whether the indefinite prolongation of the Sino-Soviet dispute is inevitable. Must we rule out the possibility of a future rapprochement between the Soviet Union and China, and on what basis do we do so? If we glance retrospectively over the past fifteen or twenty years, we see that China has been much more vehement in her denunciation of American than of Soviet foreign policy and nuclear weapons policy. To be sure, within recent years the Chinese have expressed fears of Soviet attack, and shortly after Peking's entry into the United Nations the USSR and China found themselves on opposite sides of the politico-rhetorical fence in the Indo-Pakistani conflict. But only a few years ago the worst accusation the Maoist regime could hurl against the Soviet Union was not that it endangered peace but that it was in "collusion" with the leader of the imperialist camp—that is, the United States. Peking frequently criticized Moscow for being more interested in seeking *détente* and arms control agreement than in lending militant support to the world revolutionary movement. The United States would be unwise to discount entirely the possibility that if the Soviet Union should gain a politically useful margin of strategic weapons superiority—sufficient to enable her to "lean harder" in future crises (e.g., in the Middle East)—the People's Republic of China may begin to praise the leadership in Moscow for abandoning the errors of Khrushchevist revisionism. This would hardly be the most incredible *volte-face* of the twentieth century. Thus it would be highly imprudent of U.S. policy-makers to entertain any suggestion that the Soviets need a strategic force equal to that of the United States and China combined—a spurious argument that we can expect will be made eventually.

As the United States and the Soviet Union try to envisage the future world scene, they probably perceive another important set of shared motives for negotiating strategic arms limitations. These arise out of the connection between the SALT and the Non-Proliferation Treaty. The superpowers definitely prefer a world of five nuclear powers to a world of ten or fifteen. Hence they must take into account the implications of the outcome of the SALT for the viability of the Non-Proliferation Treaty. Although this is not the central issue in the minds of the Vienna-Helsinki negotiators, still it is by no means negligible. Participants at the Fifth International Arms Control Symposium disagreed as to whether a simple phase 1 SALT agreement would stimulate or discourage proliferation of nuclear weapons to additional countries. It is generally recognized, of course, that the nuclear superpowers cannot prevent proliferation. The most that they can do is to discourage it, by providing disincentives and compensations (i.e., by giving or withholding economic-technological assistance, conventional arms aid, defense guarantees, etc.). The shipment of conventional arms by the superpowers into regions of local conflict, such as between the Arabs and Israel or between India and Pakistan, may under some circumstances decrease pressures—and under other circumstances increase pressures—to acquire nuclear weapons for deterrence or defense. It is at this point that the behavior of the superpowers in support of friendly states involved in local or regional conflicts becomes relevant to the SALT, inasmuch as conflict control on a global scale is now integrally related to international arms control. If a power acts in such a way as to initiate, support, expand, prolong, or obstruct the settlement of violent conflict anywhere in the world, then its motives for negotiating strategic arms limitations in Helsinki or Vienna can never be entirely above suspicion. It will become increasingly necessary for the United States and the Soviet Union to avoid exacerbating situations of local conflict by overcommitting themselves to third parties outside of Europe, which is an area of familiar and nonhostile confrontation.

The decision of a nation to acquire nuclear weapons has never yet proved to be by itself a *casus belli*. It probably will not prove so in the future, but there will always be a possibility that such a decision might precipitate a decision for preventive war. For years the United States has sought to persuade aspirants to the nuclear club that the game is not worth the candle because small deterrents are costly, provocative, accident-prone, noncredible, subject to rapid obsolescence, and highly dangerous, since young nuclear powers are peculiarly vulnerable to preemptive attack. None of these arguments has proved overwhelmingly convincing, and some have seemed irrelevant to countries worried about deterring or neutralizing not the superpowers but their immediate neighbors.

In the final analysis, the outcome of the SALT alone will not determine whether the decision to go nuclear is taken in such capitals as New Delhi, Toyko, and Tel Aviv. The failure of the SALT would supply not so much reasons for acquisition as an additional moral-political justification. Some of the participants at the fifth symposium reflected the view that if India, Japan, and Israel were to acquire nuclear forces, this would not be a cause for alarm but might even produce greater stability in the multipolar international system that is now emerging. At the present time, however, it is natural for the two superpowers to be wary of proliferation. The breakdown of the Non-Proliferation Treaty would be certain to complicate the foreign policy problems of the superpowers. If India should obtain nuclear weapons, Pakistan would desperately seek nuclear weapons or firm defense guarantees, either from the United States or China. If Israel should obtain nuclear weapons (and divulge that fact to the world), the Soviets would face the uncomfortable dilemma of having to bestow a token nuclear capability upon the Arabs (something that Moscow probably has no desire to do) or else of forfeiting her coveted title of "protector of the Arabs." Moreover, if the Non-Proliferation Treaty breaks down anywhere, this will in all probability lead eventually to the nuclearization of Japan and the Federal Republic of Germany, and neither the United States nor the Soviet Union can predict where the pressures for proliferation would be felt after that, nor can they regard with equanimity the prospect of conducting foreign policy in a world of more than five nuclear powers.[20]

In summing up the Fourth International Arms Control Symposium in October 1969, just a few weeks before the announcement concerning the start of the SALT in Helsinki, the author tried very roughly to adumbrate the shape of a strategic arms agreement between the

United States and the Soviet Union. At that time the following points seemed relatively clear:

1. The SALT had to be considered broadly—not merely as a diplomatic-dialectical exercise in numerical and technological gamesmanship, but as a more comprehensive effort to understand and manipulate the relationship between strategic armaments and the outstanding problems of international politics.

2. The first phase of the SALT would last for a year or two and would focus on U.S.-Soviet communication with a view toward structuring the total international problem on which we wish to negotiate.

3. Each side must speak frankly about what it finds most worrisome in the political and military-technological postures of the other.

4. Both sides should recognize the possibility that local conflicts in which we are involved could flare out of control and force us against all will and reason into a disastrous confrontation. (This is especially true in the Middle East.)

5. Progress in the SALT need not wait for the achievement of final and satisfactory solutions to outstanding U.S.-Soviet political differences in all the critical areas of the world. But on the other hand, we cannot really expect the SALT to proceed serenely at the level of technical negotiations without any reference to the world political climate.

6. We and the Soviets are presently talking about a freeze, not about reductions.

7. Europe and the alliance systems of the two superpowers must be fully taken into account in working out the SALT equations.

8. Whatever arms limitations may be agreed upon, they must lie within the unilateral verification capability of the nations involved.

9. Thus the initial agreement would have to exclude multiple warheads (MIRV and MRV), since these cannot be detected by satellite reconnaissance.

10. Probably submarine-launched missiles could not be included in the first-phase agreement. (This prediction was ill-founded.)

11. Probably ABM cannot be totally proscribed at the start, but there should be a slow and low deployment of ABM.

12. Land-based launchers represent the logical starting place for SALT, since an agreement in this sector is most readily verifiable and also because it would reduce pressures for the continued deployment of ABM.[21]

Although the likely conditions and characteristics of a SALT agreement appeared rather obvious in 1971, there still has lingered a good deal of apprehensiveness over and opposition to a simple first-stage agreement that would limit only a few basic variables in the strategic weapons equation. Some fear that there is an inverse dialectical relationship between arms control negotiations and armaments competition, not only insofar as one side or the other may strive to gain the greatest possible quantitative advantage before the freeze goes into effect, but also insofar as advanced weapons competition can be expected to intensify once the quantitative ceiling is fixed. In such an environment, it is inevitable that on both sides some analysts fear the element of the unknown in a first-stage agreement, with its potentially unilateral adverse effects upon security.

It is not unreasonable to proceed on the assumption that the existing strategic equilibrium—looked at in strictly military terms—is a highly stable one, and that it will not be easily destabilized. Neither the Soviet Union nor the United States appears seriously worried today about a deliberately planned surprise attack by the other. Neither side needs to be greatly concerned over mild disturbances in the prevailing equilibrium of mutual deterrence caused by fluctuating, marginal differences in particular weapons sectors. Most policy-makers are probably convinced that, for all practical decision-making purposes, there has existed for the past two years or so a temporary, crude parity based on compensating and fluctuating offensive and defensive asymmetries. These asymmetries involve different numbers of bombers, land-based missiles, and sea-based missiles, all of differing ranges; different numbers of deliverable warheads of varying yields; different total throw weights (measured in megatons); differences in hardening and dispersal (which affect vulnerability), firing reliability, guidance accuracy, reentry speeds, penetration aids, detonation altitudes, and other weapons-design characteristics; and differences in warning systems, intelligence, strategic doctrines, offensive and defensive weapons mixes, command and control systems, and so forth.

Given the present levels in numbers of strategic launchers (with growing numbers carrying multiple warheads), one can argue that the uncertainties inherent in the calculus of a nuclear exchange are, on the whole, more stabilizing than destabilizing. Military strategists may continue to worry, as they must, about the numbers game, about the possibility of decisive technological breakthroughs, and about the "worst possible case" in which *our* systems fail to perform well while *theirs* work perfectly. But the political leaders in Washington and

Moscow cannot under existing circumstances conceive of any rational purpose to be served by a deliberately planned first strike, simply because the risks of retaliation are too frightful.

The widespread assumption of a U.S.-USSR crude parity of assured sufficiency is important because this is the first time in the history of the nuclear era that such a condition has been thought to exist. One might infer that American decision-makers have been virtually "marking time" for nearly a decade and refraining from deploying strategic launcher capabilities, as if waiting for the Soviets to "catch up" to the point where serious arms negotiations could begin. But the Soviets have been "coming abreast" at a disturbingly rapid rate on land and sea during the past three years. They have surpassed the United States in the number of land-based launchers by more than 50 percent and they have approached parity with the U.S. in respect to submarine-launched missiles.[22] The United States has sought to reinsure its own security position by scheduling the deployment of the Safeguard system (around a pair of missile sites) and by arming half its land-based Minuteman missiles and three-quarters of its submarine missiles with multiple-warhead weapons.[23]

Ever since the SALT got under way, a central focus of debate has been the question whether the United States should be willing to negotiate a separate agreement to ban ABM, as demanded by the Soviets, or hold out for an agreement encompassing both offensive and defensive missiles. Advocates of the separate agreement argued that a ban on ABM would help to pave the way for a subsequent limitation on offensive deployments. The Nixon Administration, in my opinion, was well advised to take the position that the offense-defense problem is a single problem and should be negotiated as such. First of all, it is the Soviet deployment of large numbers of SS-9s and the threat of possibly deploying other large ICBMs, capable of hurling three to six warheads at Minuteman silos, that has reduced the invulnerability of the U.S. land-based missile force and increased the U.S. motivation to deploy a Safeguard system around selected Minuteman sites. Second, an ABM-only agreement would be more likely to diminish than to augment the Soviet incentive to negotiate a limitation on offensive missile systems. Third, a combined defense-offense agreement would be, compared with an agreement covering ABMs only, both strategically more significant (because it would halt both ongoing and planned deployments) and politically more viable (because it would reduce apprehensions in the United States as well as in the Soviet Union). Thus the fact of the offense-defense linkage that was announced in Washington and Moscow on May 20, 1971, was more important than the precise form of the ABM limit.

The crucial question prior to the Moscow Summit was how long strategic planners in the United States could assume that "crude parity" exists, given recent Soviet deployment rates. The third edition of *Jane's Weapons Systems,* published in late 1971, carried this conclusion: "Russia now has the initiative in weapons technology. Whereas for a long time it was assumed—with considerable justification—that the NATO countries had a clear lead in the development of sophisticated weapons, it is now clear that the USSR has extinguished that lead and is now outstripping the west." [24] For two years or more, U.S. defense and arms control planners have wondered whether the Soviets would be content to level off at crude parity, or whether they might try to sustain and increase their recent momentum in an effort to achieve the kind of strategic superiority that the United States has, for all practical purposes, renounced. Such superiority, even if not intended for surprise-attack purposes, could be exploited to the Soviets' advantage in critical politico-military confrontations, especially in the sensitive NATO area. We should not forget that even when the United States enjoyed a reputation as the possessor of superiority, some NATO countries exhibited strong currents of neutralist opinion.

Those who are skeptical of the SALT's prospects of success often contend that although American writers frequently speak of "parity," no such concept can be found in Soviet strategic literature. But it is precisely the central U.S. purpose in the SALT to find out whether the Soviet political leaders are ready to accept the notion of parity and to impose it upon the Soviet military. The SALT will not put an end to technological competition in strategic weaponry. Both sides recognize the growing importance of sea-based deterrence, and they will replace some of their land-based missiles with SLBMs. The United States has little choice but to maintain an R&D effort along a broad front in order to ensure the prolongation of parity. Walter Slocombe has noted that one of the principal advantages to be derived from a SALT agreement is that it would reduce the danger that "parity is merely a prelude to substantial American inferiority"—an inferiority with "great potential for creating continued and politically disturbing anxiety." [25]

If the Soviets now have it within their power to achieve a politically advantageous margin of strategic weapons superiority, why should we expect them to observe a SALT agreement? This is an important question, and it merits an answer. We have already noted the ambiguous effects of their relationship with China upon the SALT. Other aspects of the situation are equally conjectural. First, they would probably like to use the SALT to inhibit the deployment of an operational ABM system in the United States. They still respect the total productive capabilities of the American economic-technological system, and they know that once the Safeguard ABM and radar technology has been developed for a few sites, it could be extended nationwide rather quickly. They are probably also concerned over the superior U.S. ability to upgrade the quality of strategic weapons by rapidly equipping them with MIRVs. They must ponder at times the "economics of futility," which involves the indefinite expansion of nuclear missile capabilities and investment in costly new weapons systems throughout the 1970s, with the result at the end of the decade that such programs have had a reciprocal canceling effect. They must also realize that if the SALT were to collapse, competition in military research, development, and deployment might well be stepped up. The familiar action-reaction process, marked by occasional overreactions, might end the existing condition of crude parity, creating new military-technological imbalances that could lead to imprudent decision-making in a future international crisis.

Soviet leaders undoubtedly feel economic pressures to limit spending for strategic arms—pressures to increase investment in agriculture and consumer industries, to increase imports, to narrow the "technological gap" with the West in nondefense sectors, and to reallocate defense resources to the army and navy. The Soviet Union may experience splits of opinion, too, among party leaders, diplomats, the military, and the R&D scientists.[26] Yet the Soviet Union is not under as much domestic political pressure to reallocate national budgetary resources to nondefense purposes as U.S. political leaders are.

Are the Soviet leaders really afraid that the United States, given its present mood, will resume a vigorous defense policy even if the USSR should move toward a fundamental alteration of the strategic equation to the disadvantage of the United States? Perhaps they think that the United States, preoccupied with domestic problems, would be content to allow the USSR to take a commanding lead. Certainly in recent years U.S. defense policies have encountered a rising chorus of criticism, and a majority of the members of the Senate are inclined to evaluate new weapons programs less on the basis of national security requirements that on the basis of their estimated likely impact on the SALT. In the last analysis, however, the Soviet leaders cannot be sure how the American political system would react if the USSR were to push on toward a psychopolitically impressive missile superiority. The

American people, with some internal strains, have been persuaded to abandon the quest for strategic superiority and to think of national security in terms of balance, mutual restraint, equitableness, and negotiated settlements advantageous to both parties. These concepts are not inconsistent with the American ethos or the American national character. But never in their history have the American people shown themselves willing to accept a subordinate role to an external dominant power, particularly one disposed to exhibit any political hostility. It might therefore be unwise for Soviet policy-makers to expect that the USSR, having moved abreast of the United States in strategic military power, could substantially surpass her and achieve such a strategic preponderance as to pose a continuing psychopolitical threat. That development *might* not be tolerated by the American political system. Realizing this, the Soviets, while striving to put themselves in the most favorable possible military position in advance of an arms agreement, may be unwilling to press so hard for an advantage as to jeopardize arms negotiations and provoke an intensified competitive reaction from the United States.

The United States now finds itself in an uncertain pause, wondering whether to accelerate its defense effort. It is obvious that there is a widespread reluctance in the United States to start a new round, and there may be some reluctance in the Soviet Union to slow down. Thus the force of psychopolitical inertia exerts somewhat opposite effects in the two countries, and opposite kinds of decisions are being called for in the two capitals by those who want a change of course. This may reflect a discrepancy of "imperial will" referred to frequently throughout the Fifth International Arms Control Symposium.[27]

At the risk of being misinterpreted, I would use a bold analogy from animal behavior, and compare the long period of strategic weapons competition between the two superpowers to a struggle between two wolves. (This does not mean that my philosophy is based on the maxim *homo lupus hominis,* but I choose this analogy because, despite its undeniably chilling aspect, it contains a hopeful element.) We have now arrived at that dramatic moment in the contest when one of the wolves, not at all beaten yet feeling that he has had enough, temporarily and tenuously bares his neck while the adversary moves menacingly as if to overpower him. Those who study the behavior of wolves tell us that in such circumstances the onrusher, instead of moving in for the kill, can be expected to hesitate in a species-survival response that assures continued life to both.

The United States and the Soviet Union at this juncture have no choice but to watch each other carefully. They are still rivals, each seeking foreign policy goals that are not perceived as compatible with those of the other. There are still profound differences between liberal democracy and Soviet Marxism, and in their conceptions of the basis on which society should be organized. What is more, these differences are certain to endure for decades. But the two superpowers can no longer be preoccupied with each other in the same way as they were in the days of the cold war. The international system is becoming more complex as it undergoes transition from bipolarity to multi-polarity. Important new actors are appearing on the world stage. The entry of Peking to the United Nations has already changed that organization. The entry of Britain will change the European Economic Community. Japan is now assessing her new quadrilateral relation-ship with the United States, the USSR, and China. The Third World will continue to seek "liberation" through fundamental structural changes in the international economic system. Peaceful nuclear tech-nology will continue to spread throughout the globe, making the mili-tary atom harder than ever to keep under control, unless the super-powers can convincingly extend the umbrella of deterrence to threatened nations that will otherwise be tempted to go the nuclear route. (Perhaps the Soviet treaties of 1971 with Egypt and India will in the long run prove regionally stabilizing, perhaps not, once the India-Pakistan conflict of late 1971 subsides; only time will tell.) The two superpowers must adjust their mutual relationship to the increasing danger and complexity of the international environment. We might even anticipate a growing concern for human ecology to provide a motive for international cooperation between the two superpowers, but this will come slowly.

Both nations can find good reasons for observing a SALT agree-ment, if they decide politically that they want one. By making the SALT a persistent theme in their diplomacy, the United States and the Soviet Union have already created a certain set of expectations within the international system. They cannot allow the SALT to collapse ignominiously unless they are prepared to reverse a decade of cautious arms control cooperation. Our European allies are more likely to be shaken by the failure than by the success of the SALT. Superpower agreements need not cause nervousness among our allies, provided that we carry on adequate consultation in advance of and during the negotiations. Our NATO allies are quite sophisticated enough to realize that the world will need more arms control rather than less in the remainder of this century.

Up to now, the SALT has been bilateral. It is difficult enough for the two leading powers to work out a formula defining stable strategic parity between them. But that is where the process of controlling the arms problem on a world scale must begin. Eventually the negotiations will have to be gradually expanded on a selective basis, both as to parties involved and as to subject matter discussed. Naturally, this will complicate the negotiations even further. It would be unwise to burden the early stages of the SALT by prematurely interjecting the issues of later stages. But it is not too soon for us to start thinking about how to structure the extension of the SALT, especially in respect to Europe and China.

Europe is a region whose peace has hitherto depended on intricate and subtle linkages. Nuclear weapons in Europe are related to conventional force levels in Europe, and both are related to strategic nuclear weapons outside Europe. The SALT forms a major backdrop for that developing pattern of negotiations in Europe (including the Bonn-Moscow and Bonn-Warsaw treaties, as well as the quadripartite agreement on the status of Berlin) that may signal, more than twenty-five years after the end of World War II, the beginning of an intricate and durable peace settlement in the West. At some point in the relatively near future, a connection will have to be drawn between the SALT and continued mutual stable deterrence in Europe, including the mutual and balanced force reductions (MBFR) to be discussed by NATO and the Warsaw Pact, or at least by some of their members, perhaps in parallel with a European Security Conference.

As for China, most of the participants at the Fifth International Arms Control Symposium seemed to take it for granted that the Peking government must eventually enter the arms control club, now that it is in the United Nations. The question is when and how to phase the entry. It is probably a case of "the sooner, the better." The longer China stays outside, and the greater the number of specific agreements in existence, the more difficult it may be to arrange admission. (Here the analogy of arranging the British entry into the European Economic Community is apt.) The logical place for China to come into the arms control club is through the door of the Partial Test Ban Treaty. China has been in recent years the major nuclear polluter of the atmosphere, and she has been developing her underground testing capabilities. Adhering to the Test Ban Treaty would, of course, constitute a form of "collusion" by the PRC with "American and socialist imperialists," but this would be politically easier to accept than signing the Non-Proliferation Treaty. The latter would pose political problems within the China-India-Japan triangle. (Japan, for example, has signed the NPT but probably will not ratify unless China signs and ratifies it. Yet if China does sign it, India would be almost certain to regard this as an affront.) In the past China has publicly expressed the conviction that the cause of peace would be strengthened if more socialist states possessed nuclear weapons to hold the imperialists at bay, but in practice China has shown herself no more willing to proliferate nuclear weapons than France which, although a nonsignatory, has given assurances that she will act as if she had signed the Non-Proliferation Treaty.[28]

Actually, Chinese restraint in Asia will be more important than Chinese adherence or nonadherence to the NPT in helping to determine whether India and Japan continue to forgo nuclear weapons. India and Japan can also be expected to watch carefully to see whether China's status within the international system is enhanced as her nuclear stockpiles grow, and whether the possession of nuclear weapons guarantees her access to diplomatic summits closed to New Delhi and Tokyo. If this should be the case, the temptation in the latter capitals to acquire nuclear weapons will probably grow. Here is an implication of the proposed Five-Power Nuclear Disarmament Conference that should be pondered carefully. Meanwhile, it is in the joint interest of the superpowers to cooperate for the purpose of imparting an "arms-control-mindedness" to Chinese policy and of transmitting technical arms control information to China.

In summation, then, I see more positives than negatives in a SALT agreement. Both the United States and the Soviet Union are endowed with a wealth of politico-diplomatic and scientific-technological talent. It should not be impossible for intelligent planners, analysts, and negotiators in the two countries to devise an initial freeze measure that would be simple rather than complex, represent a logical place to start, be fair on its face in keeping with the McCloy-Zorin principle of 1961 that no arms agreement should place either party at an unfair military advantage, and be limited to such items as will enable governments to feel satisfied concerning their unilateral ability to verify compliance with the agreement. We could argue long and hard as to whether uncertainty varies proportionately or inversely with the number of variables we are trying to control. Undoubtedly any SALT agreement, however simple, will be fraught with uncertainties. We can never predict with confidence just what stage 1 might lead to in stage 2. But the Soviets, too, have to worry about uncertainty, unless they have mastered the mathematics and psychology of uncertainty better than we have—a point I am not prepared to concede. If we should conclude that any SALT agreement involving a fairly small number of definitional and quantitative variables is too fraught with unknowns and unknowables to be acceptable, then the world's outlook for ever achieving any kind of rational, negotiated control over nuclear weapons and the dangers they pose to mankind is bleak indeed.

We should be careful not to place upon the SALT accords of May 26, 1972, the burden of too much immediate significance. It is clear that they are not the keys to the kingdom of heaven and perpetual peace. But the Helsinki-Vienna negotiations furnished the governments of the two superpowers with a unique opportunity for the longer range to review a quarter century of policy attitudes toward the applied science of massive destructiveness. Both we and the Soviets have placed too much faith in technology and in our own righteousness. There has been something inevitable about it all, given the deepest impulses of modern civilization. Neither we nor the Soviets can afford any longer to pass moral judgment upon each other, and no other nation has had the total existential experience that would warrant their passing moral judgment upon either the Soviets or ourselves. But as Goethe wrote: "No nation acquires the power of judgment unless it can pass judgment upon itself." Only two judges must we heed—God and ourselves.

Strategic nuclear deterrence has worked up to now. In my opinion it will probably continue to be effective for a long time, so long as rational decision-making prevails in the capitals of the nuclear powers. But the longer that man relies for his peace and security upon a purely mechanistic equilibrium, founded on the fear of expanding arsenals of nuclear-tipped missiles, the greater will become the danger that his mind and thought processes, his values and psychological attitudes will become warped, until that very rationality on which mutual deterrence rests will begin to dissolve under the pressure of internal and external forces that man no longer understands and to which he can no longer readily adjust. As responsible superpowers, the United States and the Soviet Union cannot entirely rule out the possibility that if they fail to attenuate their natural proclivity to "get the better of each other," they will be drawn irresistibly along a path leading eventually to that encountering place which both dread most.

In the final analysis, we and the Soviets cannot make crucial decisions for other countries or compel them to adopt our preferred solutions. But we can decide for ourselves. The fact that we are so far advanced in weapons technology over all other countries gives us an unparalleled freedom of judgment and choice for at least this decade. We are in a position to teach others a useful lesson if we pause, step back, and reflectively ask ourselves toward what kind of human future we are rushing. It is still not too late for the United States and the Soviet Union to retreat a safe distance from the precipice of the unpredictable, where—to use the ominous words of Thucydides—we would have to abide the outcome of events in the dark.

NOTES

1. See Appendix A in Alice Kimball Smith, *A Peril and a Hope: The Scientists' Movement in America 1945–47* (Chicago: University of Chicago Press, 1965), p. 554 (italics in original).

2. For the text, see Appendix B in ibid., p. 561 (italics in original).

3. Mason Willrich, *Global Politics of Nuclear Energy* (New York: Praeger, 1971), esp. chs. 1 and 11.

4. See John H. Herz, "The Rise and Demise of the Territorial State," *World Politics* IX (April 1957), pp. 473–93, and "The Territorial State Revisited: Reflections on the Future of the Nation-State," in *International Politics and Foreign Policy: A Reader in Research and Theory,* ed. James N. Rosenau (New York: The Free Press, rev. ed., 1969), pp. 76–89.

5. Report of discussion group on "U.S.-USSR Relations in the Seventies," Twelfth Strategy for Peace Conference, Airlie House, Warrenton, Va. (September 30–October 3, 1971), p. 2.

6. Bruce M. Russett, "The Ecology of Future International Politics," *International Studies Quarterly,* XI (March 1967), pp. 12–13.

7. See James E. Dougherty, "Introduction," in *Arms Control for the Late Sixties,* ed. James E. Dougherty and J. F. Lehman, Jr. (Princeton: Van Nostrand, 1967), p. xxii, and "Arms Control in the 1970's," *Orbis,* XV (Spring 1971), p. 195.

8. The IADA was to have an operational monopoly in the conduct of all intrinsically dangerous activities in the nuclear field; own and control all materials and installations; carry on research; license all national and private activities; reserve the right of inspection without warning; and be responsible to the political organs of the United Nations without being subject to any nation's veto. See the Statement by the United States Representative to the United Nations Atomic Energy Commission, June 14, 1946 and United States Memoranda on the Proposed Atomic Development Authority, in *Documents on Disarmament 1945–1959,* Department of State Publication 7008 (Washington, D.C.: GPO, 1960), vol. I, pp. 7–16, 25–42.

9. See, e.g., Arthur I. Waskow, *The Limits of Defense* (Garden City, N.Y.: Doubleday, 1962); Charles E. Osgood, *An Alternative to War or Surrender* (Urbana: University of Illinois Press, 1962); Mulford Sibley, *Unilateral Initiatives and Disarmament* (Philadelphia: American Friends Service Committee, 1962);

Eric Fromm, "The Case for Unilateral Disarmament," in *Arms Control, Disarmament and National Security,* Donald G. Brennan ed. (New York: George Braziller, 1961), pp. 187–97.

10. See Thomas C. Schelling, *The Strategy of Conflict* (New York: Oxford University Press, 1963), ch. 10, esp. pp. 235–36; Henry A. Kissinger, "Arms Control, Inspection and Surprise Attack," *Foreign Affairs,* 38 (July 1960), pp. 559–61; Hedley Bull, *The Control of the Arms Race* (New York: Praeger, 1961), pp. 168–69; Glenn H. Snyder, *Deterrence and Defense* (Princeton: Princeton University Press, 1961), pp. 97–103.

11. In the early 1960s American analysts demonstrated a creative imagination in devising a variety of physical and nonphysical inspection and control schemes to insure either compliance with the disarmament agreement or effective sanctions in case of violation. But that intellectual exercise remained rather theoretical. Virtually all the proposed schemes were vulnerable to serious criticism: They could be circumvented; they were politically obnoxious to the Soviets; or they were so bizarre that they would be unacceptable even in the more permissive framework of American politics. One crucial inspection problem—that of "hidden stockpiles" sufficiently large to threaten a disarmed power's survival—was never overcome.

The author has dealt in detail with these technical problems—see James E. Dougherty, "The Disarmament Debate: A Review of Current Literature" (Parts One and Two), *Orbis,* 5 (Fall 1961 and Winter 1962); "Nuclear Weapons Control," *Current History,* 47 (July 1964); "The Status of the Arms Negotiations," *Orbis,* 9 (Spring 1965); and *Arms Control and Disarmament: The Critical Issues* (Washington, D.C.: Center for Strategic Studies, Special Report Series, 1966), esp. Chs. 6 and 7.

12. See Lincoln P. Bloomfield, "Arms Control and World Government," *World Politics,* XIV (July 1962) and "The Politics of Administering Disarmament" in *Security in Disarmament,* eds. Richard J. Barnet and Richard A. Falk (Princeton: Princeton University Press, 1965); Arthur J. Waskow, "Alternative Models of a Disarmed World," *Disarmament and Arms Control,* II (Winter 1963–64); Arnold Wolfers, Robert E. Osgood et al., *The United States in a Disarmed World* (Baltimore: Johns Hopkins Press, 1966).

13. A national survey in mid-1971 showed that 47 percent of the American people were not only concerned over national unity and political stability but feared that current unrest is likely to lead to a "real breakdown" in the United States. *New York Times* (June 26, 1971).

14. *New York Times* (October 24, 1971). See also Walter C. Clemens, Jr., "Sakharov: A Man for Our Times," *Bulletin of the Atomic Scientists,* XXVII (December 1971), pp. 4–6, 51–56.

15. Michel Tatu, *The Great Power Triangle: Washington-Moscow-Peking,* Atlantic Papers, no. 3 (Paris: The Atlantic Institute, 1970).

16. For a discussion of the complexities of this relationship, see Pierre Maillard, "The Effect of China on Soviet-American Relations," in *Soviet-American Relations and World Order: The Two and the Many,* Adelphi Papers, no. 66 (London: Institute for Strategic Studies, March 1970). See also, of course, the excellent analysis by Robert A. Scalapino in this volume.

17. For an analysis of Chinese attitudes toward arms control, see A. Doak

Barnett, "A Nuclear China and U.S. Arms Policy," *Foreign Affairs,* 48 (April 1970). During the India-Pakistan War over Bangladesh in the fall of 1971, China certainly behaved with the cautious restraint of an inferior nuclear power.

18. The reader is referred to the following articles by Victor Zorza in *Manchester Guardian Weekly:* "Is Russia Planning War on China?" (October 4, 1969); "Chinese War Buildup Worries Kremlin" (December 13, 1969); "Polemics on a Powder Keg" (January 17, 1970); and "Spectre of War on Two Fronts" (January 24, 1970). In the last article Zorza presented the following analysis of Moscow's concern: "The United States does not expect to be bothered by China's nuclear capability until the mid-seventies, if then, and not seriously at that. But the threat to Russia from missiles with a much shorter range, from much cruder nuclear weapons, which might even be carried by aircraft, could materialize much earlier. There is some reason to believe that the threat exists already. Of course, the Soviet Union would be able to respond to a Chinese strike, however small, with a massive salvo that would lay the whole country waste. But even a small Chinese strike is obviously more than the Soviet Union is now prepared to accept, and its policy is to prevent it, rather than to retaliate."

19. This was the interpretation that several UN diplomats placed upon Chinese Delegate Chiao Kuan-hua's references to the "connivance of the superpowers" and "political deals" behind the backs of the Arabs in his maiden speech to the General Assembly. See the *New York Times* (November 16 and 17, 1971).

20. Some years ago a Soviet mathematician expressed the danger of nuclear weapons proliferation in the formula $R = N^2$, in which R stands for the risk of nuclear war and N for the number of nuclear powers, thus implying a geometric progression in the chance of nuclear war with every increase in the number of nuclear weapon states. The formula was deficient in that it ignored certain political realities, including the kind of governments involved and the aggressiveness or restraint of their foreign policies. Nonetheless, most arms control analysts have taken it for granted that a world of twelve or fifteen nuclear powers would be less stable than a world of five, because it would pose a greater statistical probability of technical accident, unauthorized use, or uncontrolled escalation from a limited to a general conflict. It took the United States several years to persuade the Soviet government of the validity of various arms control concepts. It took the Soviets quite a while to overcome their suspicion and to perceive the element of mutual interest in negotiated arms control agreements. They were able to do so because of their scientific intelligence and their innately cautious character. As the number of nuclear weapon states increases, the "culture lag" and lead time from sophisticated arms control analysis to a political decision by governments to embrace arms control policies might prove to be of catastrophic proportions.

21. All of the foregoing points can be found spelled out in James E. Dougherty, "A Nuclear Arms Agreement: What Shape Might It Take?" *War/Peace Report,* IX (December 1969), pp. 8–11, 16–18.

22. Cf. *SIPRI Yearbook of World Armaments and Disarmament 1969/70,* Stockholm International Peace Research Institute (Stockholm: Almqvist and Wiksell, 1970), pp. 36–58; *The Military Balance 1971–1972* (London: International Institute for Strategic Studies, September 1971), pp. 1–2.

23. *New York Times* (February 27, 1971, and October 3, 1971).

24. *New York Times* (November 21, 1971). Just a few weeks earlier, U.S.

satellite reconnaissance produced evidence that the Soviets were continuing to build new classes of silos, or emplacements, for large missiles, and were doubling the production facilities for missile submarines. *New York Times* (October 11 and 20, 1971).

25. Walter Slocombe, *The Political Implications of Strategic Parity*, Adelphi Papers, no. 37 (London: Institute for Strategic Studies, May 1971), p. 18.

26. For analyses of the conflicting economic, technological, strategic, and political pressures upon Soviet decision-makers, see the chapter by Thomas W. Wolfe in this volume and his earlier "Soviet Approaches to SALT," *Problems of Communism*, 19 (September/October 1970). Cf. also Lawrence T. Caldwell, *Soviet Attitudes to SALT*, Adelphi Papers, no. 75 (London: Institute for Strategic Studies, February 1971). Caldwell describes the pressures in terms of "modernist" versus "orthodox" positions with respect to the SALT in the USSR.

27. The fact is that the international self-confidence of the United States is declining while that of the Soviets is growing. See Peter Wiles, "Declining Self-Confidence," *International Affairs* (London) (April 1971), reprinted in *Survival*, XVIII (August 1971), pp. 256–63.

28. Statement by the French Representative, Pierre de Chevigny, to the First Committee of the General Assembly, November 24, 1969, *Documents on Disarmament 1969*, U.S. Arms Control & Disarmament Agency Publication, no. 55 (Washington, D.C.: GPO, 1970), p. 579.

Implications of Success or Failure
of SALT for International Security

THE PAPERS PRESENTED at the final session, together with ideas developed in the earlier sessions, provoked a lively discussion that focused on:

1. success or failure at the SALT: the problem of evaluation,
2. international security, the international system, and the SALT,
3. alliance relations and the SALT,
4. the SALT and the future, and
5. gaps and follow-on research.

The general mood of the discussion was influenced by the pervasive realization (as one participant put it) that "we just don't know with any degree of clarity what the implications of success or failure of the SALT will be."

Success or Failure of the SALT: The Problem of Evaluation

In his prepared remarks, William Van Cleave noted that no real foundation of reciprocity between the superpowers exists in the SALT. Consequently, the United States may be engaging in a monologue with itself rather than in a dialogue with the Soviet Union. An evaluation of success or failure of the SALT under these conditions is a very difficult and speculative task.

THE POINT OF DEPARTURE: SUPERPOWER ASYMMETRIES

A popular tenet of many participants at the symposium was that the success or failure of the SALT could not be examined outside the context of the basic asymmetries between American and Soviet motivations, objectives, and expectations as well as situational conditions. Asymmetries between the superpowers exist at several levels. First,

---

In addition to those presenting papers, the following participated as discussants: Morton A. Kaplan, Evgeny Kutovoj, and Pierre Hassner. William R. Kintner served as chairman of this session.

there is the problem of situational asymmetry. Several participants continually emphasized the fact that the Soviet Union's strategic buildup has achieved a high level of momentum not only in the sense of the imperial will thesis propounded during the symposium but also in the qualitative and quantitative development of strategic arms. It was noted that domestic pressures in the Soviet Union cannot prevent the continuation of this many-faceted momentum. A different situation was believed to exist in the United States. Domestic pressures, characterized by an unwillingness to tolerate a continued dynamism in the foreign involvements of the United States or in the future augmentation of defense capabilities, were seen to have led to a general diminution of the will of the United States to maintain its global position.

A second level of asymmetry concerns the different motivations of the two sides for engaging in the SALT. Whereas the United States may be looking to the SALT to provide a solution to important strategic problems, the Soviet Union may have fundamentally different, if not incompatible, reasons for participating. For example, Soviet literature on strategic doctrine does not accept the concept of strategic parity, but rather emphasizes the need for the Soviet Union to gain both qualitative and quantitative superiority over the United States. This ambition could obviously influence Soviet approaches to the SALT.

A third area of asymmetry lies in the differing approaches of the superpowers to negotiations. For example, the United States likes to use negotiations for conducting a strategic dialogue. Frequently, American negotiators attempt to tell the Soviets how they ought to think regarding strategic issues so as to induce them to accept the American strategic calculus. Thus, the United States has attempted to tell Soviet policy-makers that the SS-9 is completely unnecessary in a condition of mutual assured destruction capability and mutual crisis stability. If the Soviets are not convinced that these conditions exist, American efforts to "teach" their Soviet colleagues may prove more irritating than successful.

A second example of the asymmetry in approaches was posited to exist in the area of differing views on the concept of an action-reaction syndrome in the development of strategic forces. It was stated that the United States builds into its defense calculation certain propositions about this syndrome that enter into its decision-making process regarding strategic forces. It was suggested that no evidence exists that the Soviet Union makes a similar calculation of the impact of the action-reaction syndrome, but tends to make its strategic decisions on the basis of unilateral calculations. Finally, it was emphasized that the

Soviet Union, as in past negotiations, focuses heavily on the political aspects of its participation in the SALT. Thus, political objectives beyond the area of the immediate negotiations influence the Soviet negotiating approach. A recent article by Arbatov in the Soviet journal entitled *USA,* in which the author emphasized the primarily political approach of the Soviet Union to the negotiations as opposed to what he perceived to be a predominantly technical approach on the part of the United States, was noted as an example of this type of asymmetry.[1]

A fourth possible asymmetrical condition was posited to exist in the long-term effect that an agreement (such as that put forth in the second session of the symposium: a freeze on new ICBM starts, no freeze on SLBM development or deployment, and a roughly symmetrical ABM limitation at low levels) would have on the subsequent strategic positions of the two superpowers. Some participants projected that the scenario agreement would freeze or codify equality. However, others claimed that it was difficult to see how such an agreement would result in a freeze. The Soviets possess 1,600 or more ICBMs with a vast throw-weight advantage, an unlimited opportunity for SLBM development, and an acceptance by the United States of the existing Moscow Ballistic Missile Defense (BMD) complex. On the other hand, such an agreement would tend to be restrictive for the United States. It would stop or greatly inhibit the development of the presently conceived Safeguard program as well as destroy any possibility of deploying a light area-defense capability in the United States. Such an agreement would thus imply that the United States would give up its fourth criterion for sufficiency, that is, the defense against damage from small attacks or accidental launches. This type of agreement would also make difficult the fulfillment of the third criterion, that is, "preventing the Soviet Union from gaining the ability to cause considerably greater urban/industrial destruction than the United States could inflict on the Soviet Union in a nuclear war." Finally, such an agreement could call into question the fulfillment of the second criterion, that is, "providing no incentive for the Soviet Union to strike the United States first in a crisis," under conditions of tension between the two nations such as that which occurred at the time of the Cuban missile crisis.[2]

CRITERIA FOR ASSESSING A STRATEGIC ARMS LIMITATION AGREEMENT

The criteria that should be used in assessing a strategic arms limitation agreement were then discussed. Several ancillary questions were also formulated. In judging the SALT, do we first weigh how the strategic balance might be affected by an agreement? To what extent would a specific agreement codify a particular strategic concept or rule out "freedom of action" in adopting different concepts? The difficulty in answering these questions was highlighted by reference to the questionable nature of an agreement that would codify "mutual assured destruction" doctrines directed to civilian life and property rather than to traditional military objectives. Would such an agreement be a success or a failure? This problem arises from the unique nature of arms control under contemporary conditions. Historically, a traditional objective of arms control has been the limitation of damage in the event of war. Can the SALT be successful in fulfilling this objective? A positive answer is by no means certain.

The difficulty of determining success or failure at the SALT implicit in these observations is compounded by the fact that the SALT will not succeed or fail in a vacuum. The impact of the SALT will transcend the narrow technical limits of an agreement. It was reiterated that the type of strategic arms limitation agreement that may emerge from the negotiations could be evaluated in accordance with the criterion: To what extent will such an agreement promote the achievement of strategic sufficiency?

Certain other criteria that had also been emphasized during the symposium were then recalled. These included the effect of an agreement on alliance structures, the security interests of allies and Third World countries, and, in particular, the implications of the SALT for the proliferation of nuclear capabilities. A useful contribution to the literature on the SALT would be an extensive inventory of the criteria that could be used to judge success or failure of the negotiations.

ANALYZING AN AGREEMENT: ITS SUCCESS OR FAILURE

Several pertinent comments were made as to what specifically would constitute success or failure of the SALT under the criteria mentioned above. In the overall sense success or failure was seen as a function of what the parties would do with or without an agreement. In this sense a warning was given that the United States might fail to make necessary strategic decisions with or without an agreement, thus conferring an advantage upon the Soviet Union.

Two patterns of thought concerning what would constitute success or failure emerged from the discussion. The more optimistic viewpoint, reflected initially in James Dougherty's prepared remarks to the session, emphasizes the belief that it should be possible to conclude a fair initial agreement in keeping with the McCloy-Zorin principle that no arms accord should place either superpower at an unfair military disadvantage. The logical starting place for such an agreement would be with ICBMs. From this point of departure, the agreement should be limited to those items on which each government could unilaterally verify compliance. In this area the technical experts should provide the necessary information as to whether: (1) the agreement should encompass the total number of offensive and defensive delivery vehicles; (2) limiting the agreement to land-based ICBMs would make any sense; (3) zero ABMs or a low-level of deployment of ABMs would cause any serious problems for stable security; and (4) sea-based systems and multiple independently targeted re-entry vehicles (MIRVs) would have to be included or excluded from an initial agreement.

Attention would have to be given to the problem of uncertainty as it relates to the stability of such an agreement. On this point it would be important to limit the number of variables of a first-stage agreement. The more variables included, the more difficult it is likely to be to reach an accord. A case can also be made that uncertainty may vary proportionally with the number of variables included in both the negotiations and the final agreement. Because any strategic arms limitation treaty will certainly evoke many uncertainties, it is necessary that the items included in the initial accord be limited.

If sufficient attention is paid to the above requirements, then an agreement at the SALT might codify parity and contribute to a permanent strategic dialogue between the superpowers. Whether this will be the case depends not only upon the agreement itself but also on diplomatic, social, psychological, and economic trends in international politics.

A more pessimistic viewpoint stressed the need of the United States to come out of the SALT with as little damage to its strategic position as possible. The minimum U.S. requirement, if the SALT are to be viewed as desirable as a long-term process, is to insure that the United States minimizes the chances that its interests would be affected adversely by the first-stage agreement. In this perspective, a limited agreement now would be preferable to an extensive one because so little is known about the aftereffects of an agreement. Such a development could be productive (if not successful) if the U.S. negotiators at the SALT demonstrate that they will not give the other side the opportunity for strategic advantage and certainly not for meaningful superiority. If this is to be accomplished, it will take bargaining power at the negotiations rather than the promotion of principles.

On the other hand, failure at the SALT would mean that the Soviet

Union might have the opportunity to attain strategic superiority. Grand failure would occur if at the same time the United States failed to counter the Soviet buildup. To avoid this type of failure, an agreement should limit or reduce the threat of Soviet strategic superiority. If this threat cannot be materially reduced, but an accord is still considered desirable for other reasons, the agreement should not greatly restrict U.S. flexibility to respond to Soviet initiatives; nor should it limit U.S. ability to achieve the objectives of strategic sufficiency.

At the symbolic level, an agreement at the SALT should not cost more in terms of political security than it is worth. In other words, the United States should avoid an agreement that would undermine the credibility, both at home and abroad, of extended U.S. security guarantees.

The Significance of the SALT

Common to all the varied viewpoints expressed on the SALT during the symposium was the general belief that the SALT, in and of themselves, were not of major significance in contributing to international stability. Very few participants credited the SALT with a fundamental importance in determining the future of the strategic milieu or of the world in general. The prevalent view was that the SALT, although an important contemporary fact of the international environment, could not be assumed to be a dominant factor in the current strategic calculus. Paraphrasing Walter Lippmann, William Van Cleave suggested that it was hardly logical to believe fervently in a policy that had, as its prime requirement for success, the most optimistic predictions for its fulfillment. A sound policy must rather be addressed to the worst and the hardest that may be judged probable, not to the best and easiest that may be possible. It is hardly conceivable that the SALT will produce in the near future an agreement that will solve any of the basic strategic problems confronting the world or will stabilize the superpower relationship without undermining relations between the United States and its allies.

Several participants addressed themselves to the implications of failure to reach an agreement. Such an event would not have a disastrous effect. Some suggested that failure to reach an agreement would increase the pressure toward nuclear proliferation. Whether such would be the case remained a moot question throughout the symposium.

The opinion was expressed that failure to reach an agreement at the SALT might lead U.S. allies to conclude that the United States no longer has the ability to manage effectively a strategic relationship with its superpower adversary. In this respect it is the *process* of the

SALT rather than the agreement itself that is important. One participant stated that in evaluating the SALT it is important not to concentrate on the specific *form* of agreement but rather to realize that since the *process* is the message, success should be measured in terms of the effectiveness of the negotiating performance.

The emphasis by some on the importance of the process evoked a caveat from one participant. He pointed out that the terms of an initial strategic arms control agreement are important because the first-stage agreement may be the only accord that will be achieved. Then, too, it may be the basic building block to future agreements. Therefore, to emphasize the process and ignore the substance of an agreement would be misleading and possibly dangerous.

Although there was a general hesitancy to forecast the outcome of the SALT, there was a relatively broad consensus that some form of agreement would be reached. Two reasons were given in support of this belief. First, the superpowers, having invested so much time and effort in bringing these negotiations about, must arrive at some agreement in order to fulfill the expectations that the very fact of the negotiations has aroused. Second, a direct linkage between the viability of the NPT and the SALT requires some form of agreement from the SALT if the NPT is to be successful.

Certain incentives for agreement were then mentioned. In the United States, impetus for an accord stems from the fear that the country will be in a worse domestic position in the future if it does not sign an agreement. In fact, the view was expressed that one reason for support for a strategic arms limitation agreement is that U.S. public opinion is moving against continued high levels of defense spending. Hence, an agreement at the SALT, along the lines of the scenario outlined during the symposium, would be preferable to a completely uninhibited Soviet strategic buildup. The Soviet incentive to sign an agreement at this time was seen to be prompted by the fear that the psychological milieu in the United States might change, creating an American willingness to engage in a renewed strategic arms race, which, because of superior U.S. industrial and technological capacity, the United would win. In addition, the Soviet Union cannot be sure that American leaders will resist U.S. domestic pressures and initiate a new strategic buildup to prevent the Soviet Union from attaining strategic superiority.

President Nixon's statement in early 1972 is relevant to this point:

Achieving initial agreements to limit both offensive and defensive strategic programs will be a major step in constraining the strategic arms race without compromising the security of either side. On the other hand, if negotiations are protracted while the Soviets continue offensive missile deployments and development of new systems, the U.S. has no choice but to proceed with major new strategic programs. This is a reality of our competitive relationship. The SALT negotiations offer a constructive alternative to unlimited competition.[3]

Some participants held that even if an agreement does not result, in spite of the aforementioned pressures, benefit will have still been derived from the negotiations. The United States and the Soviet Union will have had an opportunity to review a quarter century of development of nuclear strategies and attitudes toward technology and nuclear weapons. Such a review might have a sobering effect on both nations.

International Security, the International System, and the SALT

The structure of the international system and the parameters it sets for the security issue are two fundamental determinants of the SALT. The impact of a SALT agreement will be very different, depending on whether it occurs in a predominantly bipolar world dominated by the United States and Soviet Union or whether it occurs in an international system increasingly gravitating in the direction of multipolarity.

The discussion during the final session of the nature of the international system was more general than the conversation that took place at the beginning of the symposium. Many participants believed, contrary to expectations in the 1940s, that the development of nuclear weapons has not caused an extensive reorganization of the international system and that it is unlikely to occur in the future. Although armed conflict has been avoided at the strategic level, the system was seen as more prone to conflict than cooperation.

At the same time, nuclear weapons have introduced certain unique features into the global system. The nuclear balance of power cannot be described in the same terms as a classical balance system. The factors that give stability to the classical diplomatic balance of power may destabilize a nuclear one. The beginnings of a dialogue between the superpowers and the transformation of the bipolar system into a more unpredictable multipolar configuration may erode existing strategic stability.

The question of why the SALT have come into existence was reopened in the light of considerations about the nature of the international system. A consensus appeared to exist among symposium participants that the shifting strategic balance makes inevitable some form of negotiations. The need for the SALT arose once both superpowers realized that neither would use its nuclear forces except in conditions in which it perceived its existence or status to be in jeopardy. From a condition of relative nuclear sufficiency on both sides came the desire to limit the possibility of direct confrontation between the two superpowers, the aspiration to lessen the possibility of accidental nuclear war, and, finally, the need to seek some means of controlling the economic costs of an increasingly sophisticated arms race.

This optimistic view of the reason for the SALT was challenged as being too simplistic. Some thought that it took insufficient account of the asymmetries between the two superpowers that had been discussed throughout the symposium. Because of such asymmetries, it *does* matter which superpower obtains a first-strike capability, if such is possible. Several participants argued that the SALT, in the current international system and strategic milieu, should be examined from this perspective.

Alliance Relations and the SALT

The effect of the SALT on U.S. relationships with its allies, especially its European allies, received much attention in the concluding session. It was generally accepted that success or failure at the SALT, in and of itself, is not likely to have a dramatic effect. One discussant defined "success" from a European standpoint as an agreement along the lines of the one that had been outlined during the symposium. Such an accord would not include forward bases in Europe or consideration of the medium-range ballistic missile (MRBM) problem. Nor would it be a principal impediment to further technological developments in strategic weaponry, nor would it upset the present strategic balance.

"Failure" was defined as a total and final breakdown of the SALT, which was viewed as a highly unlikely development. Because of the superpowers' wish to appear to comply with their obligations implicit in the Non-Proliferation Treaty, one can expect prolonged negotiations and delayed decisions.

European-American Relationship

Within this framework of success or failure, the implications of the SALT for European-American security relations were addressed. In Europe some argue that a successful agreement would probably diminish the credibility of the extended American nuclear guarantee. Failure to reach an agreement, however, would probably jeopardize the NPT and lead to an acceleration of the arms race. Failure, as has been mentioned, could also serve to signal that the United States is losing its will to engage in a continuing global competition with the Soviet Union. Thus, failure to reach an agreement could be more serious than success. It is probable that because the United States has made a consistent effort to keep its NATO allies fully informed about the developments at the SALT, any successful agreement will have had the prior acquiescence, if not approval, of the Western Europeans. From the viewpoint of most Europeans, an agreement is preferable to no agreement, although the effects of either outcome are not likely, in and of themselves, to jeopardize the European-American relationship.

Although a consensus existed that the SALT, when isolated, have but a small significance, it was emphasized again that the SALT gain in importance for the Atlantic relationship when they are linked to other possible international developments. For instance, if increasing tensions in the alliance are assumed to exist because of the possibility of unpredictable Gaullist-type diplomatic initiatives and because of increasing economic conflicts among the allies, then developments at the SALT may very well have extensive political and psychological effects on NATO. In the situation that is developing today, a measure of nuclear balance and a certain degree of cooperation between the superpowers (perhaps an inevitable development) could become coupled with a U.S. military withdrawal from Europe, thus giving tacit recognition to the Soviet claim that Europe should be within its military sphere of influence. If an agreement at the SALT is seen as enhancing such a possibility, the short-term viability of the alliance could be eroded. An agreement could also accelerate a move to develop a European nuclear capability. Thus, a strategic arms control agreement, when considered in the light of possible developments, has importance both for the Western Europeans and for the United States.

THE SALT AND EUROPEAN DEFENSE EFFORTS

A second concern for Western Europe is the impact of the SALT on existing and potential European defense efforts. Western Europe presently needs to begin the transition from overdependence on the United States for security to greater self-reliance. While Europe is in the process of increasing its capacity for deterrence and defense, the United States should maintain its troops and tactical weapons in Europe, as well as the credibility of the U.S. strategic guarantee.

These considerations provide another context in which success or failure of the SALT should be viewed. Success might create some doubt in Europe as to the ability of the United States to extend a nuclear guarantee to Europe. Moreover, even a sharp decline in the credibility of the U.S. nuclear deterrent would be unlikely to stimulate a dramatic move to strengthen European defenses. The Soviet invasion of Czechoslovakia in 1968, a more dramatic event than the SALT, did not provoke such a response on the part of the Europeans. Finally, failure at the SALT was seen as unlikely to spur European interest in increasing defense capabilities, since failure would be seen as essentially no change in the current situation.

THE SALT AND *Détente*

Regarding the possible relationship between the SALT and the European version of *détente,* it was postulated that failure at the SALT would not halt European efforts to develop a more acceptable *modus vivendi* with the Soviet Union. Yet, success at the SALT would be likely to enhance European efforts to promote an East-West reconciliation and might even increase momentum for a conference on European security and for negotiations on mutual and balanced force reductions (MBFR). The impact of the 1972 Moscow Summit between Secretary Brezhnev and President Nixon was along precisely these lines.

It was remarked that a close connection exists between the MBFR issue and the SALT; success at the latter is likely to have a spillover effect on the former. If the SALT should fail, then the prospects for any form of MBFR agreement would be slight. If the SALT succeed, both the Europeans and Americans would be encouraged to pursue MBFR further, even though such negotiations would probably be much more difficult than any first-stage strategic arms limitation agreement that is achieved.

The SALT and the Future

The comments made during the session about the future in general and the SALT in particular were circumspect and limited. There was a consensus that general conditions over the short term are not likely to change. At the strategic level a limited relationship between superpower adversaries will probably continue within a framework of avoidance of general war. A superpower condominium was viewed as unlikely. Soviet problems with China will continue to be acute, especially as the Chinese attain a stronger strategic position. However, war between the two nations was deemed to be unlikely. If the United States continues to reduce its direct involvement in the world, anxieties in both Western Europe and Japan about the U.S. defense commitment will be intensified. As a result, several nations will be subject to mounting pressures to acquire nuclear weapons. There was little agreement among participants regarding the implications of proliferation for international stability.

Several participants expressed the belief that the SALT will be an ongoing process in international relations. Both the United States and the Soviet Union have created certain expectations that will encourage the continuation of the negotiations. The present bilateral nature of the negotiations will probably be expanded on a selective basis to include additional participating nations and to broaden the subjects discussed. As more variables are introduced into the process, greater complications will arise. At least three specific considerations that will command the attention of future SALT negotiators can presently be envisaged:

1. It is likely that the next specific concern of the SALT after the initial agreement will be some form of arms limitation in Europe. The attempt will probably be made to link the strategic and conventional weapons levels through some agreement on tactical nuclear weapons and MBFR. It is also likely that an attempt will be made to lessen the imbalance between Soviet strategic weapons targeted on Europe (about 700 MRBMs) and those of Western European origin targeted on the Soviet Union (the British Polaris fleet and the small force of French IRBMs and SLBMs).

2. Future stages of the SALT will be designed to develop more concretely the now implicit linkages between present negotiations and the NPT.

3. Future negotiations will probably consider how to "phase in" China's participation in the SALT. It is unlikely that this can be done in one step. Rather, the process will probably be evolutionary, with Chinese agreement to sign the Nuclear Test Ban Treaty as a logical starting point *after* Peking has developed sufficient confidence in its nuclear capacity to participate in arms control discussions as an equal.

This discussion of the future prospects for the SALT stressed the likelihood that the SALT process will be tedious, difficult, and unspectacular.

The hope was expressed, and it was seen as possible, that the process could be extended indefinitely into the future so that the cumulative effects might lead to a less dangerous world.

Gaps and Follow-on Research

Although the symposium provided for a comprehensive discussion of many topics, there was agreement that several problems merited greater consideration than was possible at that time. These included:

a. political factors inhibiting nuclear proliferation by Japan,

b. possible political uses of strategic nuclear superiority and the assumption that strategic superiority could not bestow military advantages,

c. the assumption that mutual deterrence based on mutual assured destruction capability is, in actuality, assured,

d. the implications of the dramatic change in the strategic force balance in the world over the past several years,

e. domestic problems in the Soviet system and their effects on Soviet policy, and

f. humanistic considerations that affect (or should affect) arms control deliberations.

A second category of comments focused on the areas in which additional basic research was believed to be needed, in many cases related to the above gaps. Topics meriting further research include:

a. The means by which arms control can be used as a political instrument.

b. Development of an adequate strategic calculus to understand the relationship between type of weaponry and the strategies that underlie their development. In this area a relevant question was posed: Can certain strategies for the employment of strategic nuclear weapons give one side such an advantage that the other side would be well inclined not to use its forces in retaliation?

c. The reliability of superpower second-strike capability.

d. The linkage between proliferation and the strategic arms race. It is possible that limited proliferation might dampen the uncertainties of the arms race that feed the race itself.

e. The formulation of an adequate theory of arms control. The development of such a theory becomes increasingly important as the gap between technology and theory continues to widen.

f. The refinement of the concept of uncertainty and its integration into general theories on international politics and the specific theory on arms control.

g. The development of a theory on restraint that would be applicable to the current negotiations and capable of providing a means to begin working toward a philosophy of restraint that could be built into the future structure of negotiation.

h. The examination of the possible role international organizations might play in arms control.

NOTES

1. G. A. Arbatov, "American Foreign Policy on the Threshold of the 1970's," *USA: Economics, Politics, Ideology* (January 1970), translated in *Soviet Law and Government* (Summer 1970) and reprinted in *Orbis* (Spring 1971).

2. *Statement of Melvin Laird on FY 1972–1976 Defense Program*, p. 62.

3. *U.S. Foreign Policy for the 1970's: The Emerging Structure of Peace*, A Report to the Congress by Richard Nixon, President of the United States (February 9, 1972), p. 176.

PART VI

WILLIAM R. KINTNER

ROBERT L. PFALTZGRAFF, JR.

The Strategic Arms Limitation Agreements of 1972: Implications for International Security

THE NEGOTIATIONS DISCUSSED at the Fifth International Arms Control Symposium culminated in the signing of the ABM Treaty and the Interim Agreement on Offensive Missiles by President Nixon and General Secretary Brezhnev on May 26, 1972 (see the Appendix for the full texts of the treaty and interim agreement). Since the symposium was addressed to many of the issues contained in the U.S.-Soviet Accords, it is useful to review the outcome of phase I of the SALT.

During the last decade, advocates of arms control generally have advanced four basic rationales to justify arms-control negotiations between the United States and the Soviet Union:

1. An agreement for the control of arms would lessen the likelihood of nuclear war by halting the nuclear arms race between the superpowers without lessening security.

2. The proliferation of nuclear weapons to other powers could be prevented if the United States and the Soviet Union would demonstrate that national security could be safeguarded more adequately by arms restraint and limitation, thus impeding proliferation by example.

3. An arms agreement between the Soviet Union and the United States would contribute to the reduction of hostility, leading to a *détente*.

4. The resources devoted to the arms race could be diverted to the resolution of other problems, especially at the domestic level.

In the light of these objectives, do the agreements signed by the United States and the Soviet Union in Moscow contribute to international security and to U.S. security or at least not detract from existing security? Do they, in fact, restrict proliferation? Do they lead to superpower *détente* or at least improve the prospects? Do they facilitate the

385

reduction of military spending? The Fifth International Arms Control Symposium provided an opportunity for an appraisal of each of these questions.

The Treaty and the Executive Agreement

In phase I of the SALT, the United States and the Soviet Union signed a treaty and an executive agreement; the former is unlimited, while the latter will terminate after five years unless renewed. The Treaty on Anti-Ballistic Missiles limits these systems to the protection of the respective national command centers and offensive missiles at a distant location. Both the United States and the Soviet Union are permitted two ABM sites, each of which is limited to one hundred interceptor missiles. Existing ABMs are to be deployed to protect the capacity, respectively, of the United States and the Soviet Union to act in a crisis and to supply minimal protection of land-based ICBMs. The treaty applies only to the current state-of-the-art ABM, namely, phased-array radars and short-range and long-range interception. Innovations in missile defense, for example, those based on a new principle such as the laser, are not proscribed. The transfer of ABM systems or their components by either the United States or the Soviet Union to other states is prohibited. Each state is to use national technical means of verification, and each agrees not to engage in "deliberate concealment measures" that impede verification by the other signatory. Although the ABM Treaty is of unlimited duration, it is subject to review every five years. Each state reserves the right to withdraw after giving six months' notice if it concludes that "extraordinary events" have jeopardized its national interests. As Professor Bowie points out in his chapter, the circumstances in which a signatory might be compelled to withdraw from a strategic arms limitation agreement include suspicion that the other party is violating the accord, that new weapons have changed the impact of the restrictions, or that the agreement has simply not functioned in the manner originally contemplated.

The executive agreement, made for five years, freezes the numbers of fixed land-based launchers and prohibits all but marginal increases in the size of the silos. According to this document, no new silo starts are permitted after July 1, 1972. The Soviets are not allowed to turn their old and lighter missiles into heavy missiles—SS-9s—and there is a prohibition against the significant enlargement of missile silos defined as greater than 15 percent of the diameter of the land-based ICBM silo. These restrictions are also applicable to the United States. There appears, however, to be some ambiguity about the definition of a heavy missile. The United States, after formally regretting that the Soviet Union had not agreed on a common definition of "heavy" ICBMs into which "light" ICBMs may not be converted, made a unilateral declaration that the agreement prohibits conversion of light ICBMs into missiles "having a volume significantly greater than the largest light ICBM now in operation."

The construction and deployment of fixed, land-based ICBMs are limited to those already being built before July 1, 1972: 1,054 for the United States and approximately 1,618 for the Soviet Union.[1] Because the Soviet Union never disclosed the number of ICBMs at its disposal, the United States concluded the agreement on the assumption, derived from intelligence, that the Soviet arsenal included 1,618 ICBMs. Although the interim agreement contains no prohibition on mobile, land-based launchers, the United States issued a unilateral declaration that it would regard deployment of such missiles as inconsistent with the goals of the agreement.

The agreement also provides for limitations on the deployment of submarine-launched ballistic missiles (SLBMs), which are restricted to 710 for the United States and 950 for the Soviet Union. The United States is limited to 44 modern ballistic-missile-carrying submarines and the Soviet Union to 62 such submarines. According to the agreement, older ICBM launchers can be replaced by SLBM launchers; it is likely that the Soviet Union, at least, will exercise this option. For example, the United States could trade its 54 Titan missiles for three modern new submarines, each armed with 18 missiles, while the Soviet Union could replace 210 of its pre-1964 land-based missiles with an equal number of more advanced SLBMs on 20 additional submarines not yet operational or under construction. The Soviets may also convert 30 older sea-launched missiles into an equal number of modern SLBMs. Because the agreement prohibits new construction of fixed ICBMs rather than specifying a maximum allowable number of ICBMs, the parties may not build up to their previous ICBM strength after converting older ICBMs into SLBMs. Thus, if the Soviets convert 210 older missiles into an equal number of SLBMs, their total ICBM strength will fall from 1,618 to 1,408 as their SLBMs rise from 740 to 950.

If all options are taken, through exchange of obsolete ICBMs for submarines and completion of present programs, the Soviets will achieve numerical superiority in ICBMs (1,408 to 1,000) and SLBMs (950 to 710). The willingness of the United States to accept numerical inferiority suggests its confidence in some qualitative advantage that will offset Soviet numerical superiority over the next five years.

The Soviet Union issued a unilateral declaration, rejected by the United States, that it would reserve the right to increase the number of its SLBM submarines if the United States and its NATO allies were to build more than a combined total of fifty such submarines with 800 SLBMs. Since together the British and French have a total of nine submarines in operation or under construction, the United States can increase the number of its submarines from forty-one to the forty-four permitted by the agreement only at the risk of leading the Soviet Union to make commensurate increases in Soviet SLBM strength. Hence, if the United States exercises a mutually agreed-upon option to exchange its old Titan missiles for modern SLBMs, it faces an expansion of the Soviet missile armed submarine fleet beyond the numbers set in the interim agreement. A similar Soviet expansion will probably result if the British and French build additional submarines to strengthen their strategic deterrents.

A Net Assessment of the Agreements

The gains and losses resulting from the Soviet-American agreements to limit some offensive and defensive missile systems may be calculated in the following terms:

1. mutual gains for both the United States and the Soviet Union,
2. net Soviet gains,
3. net U.S. gains,
4. mutual losses for both the United States and the Soviet Union, and
5. the unknown impact factor.

Mutual Gains for Both the United States and the Soviet Union

1. A limited step has been taken to curtail the arms race by restricting deployment of certain categories of weapons, thereby possibly reducing the danger of nuclear war. But the development of new weapons has not been halted.

2. For the short term at least, mutual confidence between Soviet and U.S. leaders may increase as a result of a SALT accord. But goodwill atmospherics may also obscure important political differences between the United States and the Soviet Union. The effect of this situation is greater for the United States than for the Soviet Union because of the fundamentally different role played by public opinion in the two countries. As suggested in the final session of the symposium, a major danger

of this asymmetry between the two superpowers is that domestic pressures may restrict the options available to the U.S. government, whereas the Soviet leadership has greater latitude in pursuing its aims within the loose framework of a SALT agreement.

3. The influence of Soviet "hard liners," who have stressed the possibility of winning a strategic nuclear war against critics who have advocated arms-control measures, may have been restricted. Soviet analysts who see a nuclear war with the United States as unwinnable may enjoy enhanced influence. Only the passage of time will tell if this is in fact the outcome. Such a development, it was suggested in the symposium, might possibly be promoted if the United States began to think of bargaining on the basis of what U.S. goals could best support groups in the Soviet Union most favorable to developments compatible with U.S. policies. This might be appropriate not only in future phases of the SALT, but in other Soviet-American bargaining situations as well.

It is risky, however, to impute such differences to members of the Soviet policy community. Even if such differences exist, their implications for Soviet strategy may be questionable. The Soviet Union may continue a large-scale R&D effort and the deployment of weapons in areas excluded from the SALT in order to gain political and psychological advantages in its overall strategy. As was pointed out during the symposium, the two superpowers may have reached agreement in the SALT while aiming at quite different objectives. If such were the case, the Soviet Union might seek to use the SALT as a device for increasing its capabilities in areas not included in the Agreement.

NET SOVIET GAINS

1. The SALT agreement freezes the arms race in fixed, land-based ICBM and SLBM launchers in a condition of U.S. inferiority in numbers of launchers and, more importantly, in throw weight. At the same time, it keeps the United States from undertaking further measures to improve the survivability of its land-based forces through defense. The freeze comes at the best time for the Soviets, who are at or just over the peak of their strategic buildup and who have developed a far more comprehensive civil-defense program than the United States. It comes at the worst time for the United States, which has not yet taken the decision to respond to that buildup. So while the freeze may halt Soviet "momentum," it does so at that very time when the United States must decide whether it will develop programs like ULMS (Undersea Long-range Missile System) to offset Soviet superiority in numbers of launchers.

2. The agreement cannot freeze the psychological dynamics of the arms race. Because of the Soviet strategic buildup over the last five years, the impression has been created that the Soviet Union has seized the initiative from the United States and has achieved important elements of strategic superiority. Thus, the agreement tends to enhance the belief abroad that the United States has been overtaken by the Soviet Union. And Soviet leaders can now derive greater confidence from dealing with the United States as peers or superiors.

3. American technological superiority in MIRVs is *not* frozen, nor is the Soviet capacity to develop similar capabilities restricted. As suggested during the symposium, sophisticated technical problems such as guidance, thrust termination, and adjustments for atmospheric variations become increasingly salient as greater accuracy and reliability are sought in delivery systems. It can be expected that the Soviets will continue their strategic arms buildup by transferring resources previously committed to achieving superiority in numbers of launchers to MIRV development and production. Qualitative gains in the Soviet strategic arsenal will not be susceptible to effective U.S. monitoring. And although SALT II will probably try to grapple with means of limiting MIRV development, Soviet reluctance to permit on-site inspection will cause those talks to drag on for months, if not years (SALT I, without dealing with this troublesome issue, required two years of negotiation, during which the Soviet buildup proceeded apace). During SALT II, intense pressure will be placed on the U.S. government to make agreement possible by such conciliatory gestures as slowing down or halting its MIRV program. At the same time, the Soviet leaders, being largely immune from similar domestic political pressure, will be able to embark on a crash MIRV program if they so decide.

4. The U.S. technological lead in ABM development is frozen effectively by the limit on ABMs to be deployed. Under the ABM Treaty, the United States forfeits the option of deploying on a national scale an antiballistic missile defense that would be technologically superior to its Soviet counterpart. The Soviet Union has already deployed a national capital area (NCA) defense system, but deployment of an ABM around Washington depends upon congressional appropriations and support. In the event an ABM system *is* erected around Washington, the Soviets will retain an edge over the United States since the Moscow area is far more heavily industrialized than Washington and is the scientific center of the Soviet Union. In these respects Moscow is the equivalent of Washington and New York combined.

5. The Soviet Union will achieve superiority in submarine-launched

ballistic missiles by taking full advantage of the options provided by the executive agreement to convert obsolete ICBMs (SS-7s and SS-8s) and obsolete SLBMs (G- and H-class submarines) into Polaris-type SLBMs. An expanded Soviet SLBM capability will require substantial increases in the U.S. budget for antisubmarine warfare (ASW), since SLBMs can be fired from the seas south of the U.S. border—a direction from which the United States lacks adequate warning. The United States has striven to avoid this contingency, from the Cuban missile crisis of 1962 to the understandings worked out in 1970 with the Soviet Union to prevent the stationing of Soviet submarines armed with strategic missiles in the Caribbean.

6. Both the United States and the Soviet Union may feel compelled to allocate new resources to develop an alternative to the ABM that is new "in principle." The need for such a new principle is already recognized in Moscow, and if the Soviet leaders should devote new resources to the problem while the United States does not, a direct loss may result for the United States. The U.S. government, in contrast to the Soviet Union, is likely to find it difficult to pursue a vigorous R&D program, even though research for ABMs is not prohibited by the treaty. If congressional sentiment opposes the development of such new defense programs, a net Soviet gain may materialize. According to several symposium participants, this could especially be the case given the problem of extended lead times which require decisions on weapons development to be made five to ten years before their actual production and deployment.

7. Large ruble appropriations previously consumed by the Soviet strategic buildup may be freed for domestic programs serving to strengthen the USSR's domestic political and economic base. Newly freed resources can be used to modernize and expand production of heavy industry (including conventional arms) and to increase consumer goods production. With greater resources available, the Soviet leaders will also be in a better position to overcome some of their country's perennial problems of agricultural production.

NET U.S. GAINS

1. The agreement leaves the United States with leads in strategic bombers and MIRV technology. In this respect the agreement cuts both ways. While it allows the Soviets to reallocate resources to areas of U.S. strength, it also permits the United States to continue to develop its advantages *if we have the political will to do so*. The agreement may prove disadvantageous, however, if the United States pauses in its R&D program and production while the Soviet Union plunges full steam ahead.

2. The Soviet numerical buildup in strategic offensive weapons is slowed, but the buildup is not halted unless the Soviets fail to take advantage of their options to convert obsolete missiles into SLBMs. As suggested above, the Interim Agreement on Offensive Missiles prohibits the construction of new launchers rather than prescribing a limit on numbers of launchers. The figures utilized in the SALT by the United States were our own, since no Soviet data were made available—this fact in itself reflecting a worrisome asymmetry between the superpowers. If the United States finds a new concentration of Soviet ICBMs, the question will arise as to when it was installed—before or after the agreement.[2] Thus, the agreement introduces an important ambiguity into the U.S.-Soviet arms-control relationship and leaves potentially unanswered important questions. Do we really know how many "operational" land-based ICBMs the Soviet Union possessed or had under construction as of July 1, 1972? Is disagreement likely to arise between Moscow and Washington as to when construction of a particular missile site began? Can we monitor other aspects of the SALT for violations of prohibited activities, including upgrading surface-to-air missiles and giving them an ABM capability, increasing the size of land-based ICBM silo launchers by more than 15 percent, or deploying ABM launchers with a capability for launching multiple interceptors?

3. The agreement might provide impetus in Europe toward the assumption of a larger role in European security. This would be a net gain for the United States if we seek, over time, to delegate greater local security responsibilities to the Europeans. Western Europe would have more incentive to maintain national nuclear forces and perhaps even collaborate technologically to build a new generation of strategic forces for the needs of deterrence in the 1980s. This is so because the accord freezes Soviet strategic defenses that European nuclear forces must be able to penetrate. As Geoffrey Kemp and Ian Smart point out in their symposium paper, the limitation of the Soviet ABM system leaves ample targets of value for European deterrent forces. An effective limitation on ABMs would have the effect of increasing, or at least not diminishing, the credibility of the offensive forces of nonsignatories. At the same time, however, the agreement creates an atmosphere of *détente,* real or perceived, that could make European nuclear forces appear less necessary to European publics eager to reduce defense spending.

MUTUAL LOSSES FOR BOTH THE UNITED STATES AND THE SOVIET UNION

1. The credibility of the future Chinese nuclear capability is increased since, like the European forces, China will not have to cope with large-

scale ABM defenses in either the Soviet Union or the United States. Both superpowers lose the advantage that a "thin"-area ABM might have provided against an accidental launch of an ICBM or an attack by a smaller nuclear power. If we assume that the Soviet Union, to a greater extent than the United States, has potential conflicts of interest with smaller nuclear powers, present and emergent, the loss of ABM, for this reason at least, may be greater for the Soviet Union than for the United States. In the absence of a comprehensive Soviet ABM, the result should be enhanced Chinese politico-military influence vis-à-vis the Soviet Union in the next decade. For this reason, however, the Soviet Union may have an incentive to engage in intensive R&D to produce a new-principle ABM designed to counter potential "Nth country" nuclear forces in a more multipolar world of the 1980s.

THE UNKNOWN IMPACT FACTOR

1. Often the most important impact of an international agreement is not known for years and cannot be anticipated by analysis at the time a decision is made. The history of past disarmament agreements cautions against euphoric interpretations of this most recent accord. Frequently, the impact of such agreements is (a) to rechannel military spending from one area to another; (b) to give one signatory a false sense of confidence; and/or (c) to ultimately arouse the antagonism of one power, which finally decides that the prohibitions to which it has agreed are asymmetrical. In the last case, the decision to rearm in contravention of an earlier agreement may gravely aggravate international tensions—even beyond what they would have been had no agreement been reached in the first place.

Several possible results of a "false sense of confidence" on the part of the United States were mentioned during the symposium. Congressional appropriations for defense and foreign policy initiatives might be further curtailed; greater pressures for the decoupling of American security guarantees, not only from Europe or Japan but also from *de facto* allies like Israel, might arise; and domestic pressure for further agreements might become so great as to limit seriously the government's ability to bargain from a position of "equality" at later negotiations.

2. The impact of the agreement upon the proliferation question is uncertain—as are the consequences of proliferation *and* nonproliferation in the face of the recent Soviet offensive buildup. The SALT limit on offensive weapons may halt the trend toward proliferation, since the Soviet threat may appear to some governments to have been scaled down. On the other hand, to the extent that the treaty limitations on defense make

nascent offensive systems more credible, they may encourage proliferation. Under conditions of strategic parity and Soviet equality symbolized by the SALT, the extended deterrent of the United States rests increasingly on uncertainty. The result could be to give impetus to the acquisition of nuclear weapons by other states fearful that the U.S. strategic deterrent has been, or will be, "decoupled" from their defense.

SALT, the Strategic Balance, and International Security

Even though the Soviet Union is permitted, under the terms of the SALT agreements, to maintain greater numbers of launchers with greater throw weight than needed for a countercity mutual assured destruction (MAD) strategy and to improve the accuracy of MIRV, some interpretations of the agreements suggest that a balance of terror has been recognized officially by both governments. This balance is to be sustained by preventing ABM deployment for area defense, which might make feasible a counterforce, first-strike strategy. Since the United States, with its advanced MIRVed missiles and smaller warheads, possesses a nuclear force largely but not exclusively designed for countercity targets, it is reasonable to allow the Soviet Union some numerical advantage to compensate for its less accurate and less advanced MIRVed weapons. Hence, the Soviets might be expected to have little incentive to exceed the quantitative limits of the agreements, already highly advantageous to the Soviet Union, because their own MIRV development or SLBMs will make up the difference. With its heavier missiles resulting in a four-to-one advantage in payload, the Soviet Union possesses a capability with impressive counterforce characteristics. Under the SALT, the Soviet Union is permitted greater numbers of launchers with greater throw weight than needed for a countercity strategy.

If the Soviet government has come to accept prevailing strategic thought in the United States, namely, that neither side could survive a nuclear war, has there been a major revision in Soviet strategic doctrine? It is difficult at this stage in the U.S.-Soviet strategic dialogue to discern whether or not a fundamental change in Soviet military doctrine has occurred. The answer to this question depends upon future Soviet arms-control initiatives as well as Soviet R&D trends and deployments of weapons systems now under development. As was pointed out in the final session of the symposium, an accurate answer depends on divining the strategic calculus of the opponent, which has not always been achieved by U.S. strategic analysts in the past. But the Agreement on Offensive Missiles is for five years only. For example, it is possible, as suggested earlier in this chapter, that a new-principle Soviet ABM will be developed. While researching and developing a new ABM system, the Soviets can deploy and place MIRVs on the maximum ICBM or SLBM forces permitted by the SALT accord. If the Soviets show marked restraint in such deployment, and in R&D, we will obviously have greater reason for optimism about a change in their strategic outlook than is now possible. It is conceivable, as critics of the SALT have contended, that the Soviet Union seeks to utilize the accords to ratify Soviet-American strategic parity, to freeze U.S. quantitative inferiority in those areas where it presently exists, and to allow the Soviet Union to maximize its potential in *qualitative* dimensions of strategic armaments.

The transfer from competition through deployment to competition through R&D does not necessarily end the Soviet quest for strategic superiority. Indeed, the SALT agreement increases the likelihood of the Soviet Union catching up in ABM and MIRV technologies, areas in which it currently lags behind the United States. The United States, on the other hand, is hampered from developing a counterforce strategy, since American megatonnage and weapons systems are largely counter-city and the agreement forecloses the upgrading of silos and weights of a new generation of offensive missiles.

In sum, then, the treaty and executive agreement delay the deployment of a complete Soviet counterforce, first-strike arsenal with ABM for at least five years, pending new-principle qualitative improvements in their numerically superior counterforce-weight missiles. If the Soviet Union chose to make such qualitative improvements, the United States would be without any recourse save by rapid application of its R&D in new ABM and ASW systems, provided the United States could overcome lead-time barriers. But will the United States maintain a strong R&D program in a period of expectation of further arms-control negotiations with the Soviet Union? Moreover, can the United States in future arms-control negotiations influence the evolution of Soviet strategic posture toward a more stable and secure balance at lower levels of effort?

Implicit in much thought about arms control is the assumption that nonproliferation is good in itself. Especially in the changing international system of the 1970s, this is not self-evident, as several of the papers in this volume illustrate, nor is it fully within the capacity of the superpowers to prevent the acquisition of nuclear weapons by "Nth countries." Will agreements which retard the deployment of nuclear weapons by the superpowers, in fact, retard the further development of nuclear weapons by existing nuclear powers and their acquisition by other states? This question concerns seven states in particular: China, India, Japan,

Israel, Egypt, France, and the United Kingdom. China has its own reasons—prestige and defense—to continue construction of its arsenal, especially against the Soviet Union.

As the Chinese arsenal grows, the nearby states of India and Japan may not maintain their faith in superpower protection. Hence, such countries cannot look to the SALT agreement as an argument against proliferation, unless the Chinese also agree to limit their arms. The prospects for such agreement by Peking are slim. As Robert Scalapino suggests in his paper, China will probably eschew strategic arms controls, while continuing to develop its military capacities as rapidly as possible, and—without neglecting selective conventional weapons—will develop a nuclear force oriented toward a regional capability.

Both Israel and Egypt see the deployment of nuclear weapons as the last resort, although there is some evidence, as suggested in George Quester's paper, that Israel has gone far toward the development of an atomic capability. So long as neither finds itself alone against the other in alliance with a superpower (e.g., Israel against Egypt and the Soviet Union), nuclear weapons have little military utility. But the superpowers can do little to affect this prospect through the SALT, unless the effect of the SALT is clearly to decouple the nuclear deterrent of one superpower, but not the other, from the defense of its erstwhile ally.

Finally, there is the European question. Here the result of the SALT is ambiguous. The agreements signed in Moscow contain no reference to NATO; both the Soviet Union and the United States issued unilateral interpretations of the arms pact. In addition to the unilateral Soviet statement claiming the right of the Soviet Union to increase the number of submarines if NATO, or the European countries, deployed additional submarines, the United States issued a statement of interpretation of Article IX of the treaty to limit ABMs. According to this article, both sides agree not to transfer to other states or to deploy outside their national territory, antiballistic missiles or their components. Although this forecloses one option available to the United States, namely, to assist Western Europe in acquiring an ABM, the United States issued a statement to the effect that the No-Transfer Article of the ABM Treaty did not establish a precedent for any future offensive-weapons treaty. According to the unilateral U.S. interpretation: "The question of transfer of strategic offensive arms is a far more complex issue, which may require a different solution." [3]

The question arises as to whether Article IX adds to the prohibitions contained in the Non-Proliferation Treaty, which does not prevent the transfer of nuclear technology to existing nuclear powers, such as Britain and France. Here again the potential for U.S.-Soviet disagreement arises if the Soviets seek to use such a no-transfer article to prevent U.S. technological assistance to nuclear allies by arguing that any transfer of information about, for example, nuclear warhead design and construction, violates Article IX of the SALT because such data form a vital component of an ABM.

Agreements—tacit or formal—between the United States and the Soviet Union on the transfer-of-technology issue will have important implications for European security. Since the British-French missile forces are not restricted by the SALT, these capabilities could be linked to form the core for a new European nuclear deterrent. In this process, the United States might play a crucial role either by agreeing to Britain's sharing of nuclear technology jointly developed under the 1958 amendment to the McMahon Act or by more actively assisting Britain and France in the development of a new-generation nuclear capability. This could improve NATO protection against Soviet MRBMs and IRBMs and Warsaw Pact conventional superiority, and possibly remove some of the uncertainty about the extent to which the U.S. deterrent continues to underwrite Western Europe. Preservation of the U.S. option to grant such assistance to Britain and France could increase the U.S. leverage over the Soviet Union to achieve a limitation of Soviet MRBMs and IRBMs targeted against Western Europe. This issue will be increased in importance in phase II of the SALT if NATO forward-based systems are included in the negotiations.

Under conditions of parity, U.S. strategic forces are offset by Soviet strategic capabilities, and the security of Western Europe is governed by the uncertainty of a U.S. nuclear response. Except for the British and French nuclear forces, the West European states currently have no capability comparable to the 600 to 700 Soviet MRBMs and IRBMs targeted on Western Europe. Because of this situation and because of a tendency toward a psychological decoupling of the United States from world affairs, there is growing doubt in Western Europe about the credibility of the U.S. nuclear commitment. Comments during the symposium emphasized that European fears of American strategic decoupling were much more a function of perceived intentions than of specific quantitative calculations of size of forces or nuclear megatonnage. The psychological problem would be intensified by prospects of large-scale unilateral U.S. troop withdrawals, since the deployment of U.S. forces on European soil provides tangible evidence of the U.S. military commitment to Western Europe. Hence, it becomes more important that West Europeans attain an active defense capability of their own. While the SALT agreement does not preclude such a development, there may be little public support for the necessary political and financial measures to create a more adequate nuclear force under European control. The SALT and the German treaties give impetus to a Conference on Security and Cooperation in Europe. Whatever the benefits from such a Conference, it may slow progress toward the development of a more cohesive West European defense grouping.

Will the Strategic Arms Agreement provide a sufficient foundation for U.S.-Soviet *détente?* Both the SALT and previous arms-control agreements between the United States and the Soviet Union have reflected an emphasis on their symbolic importance. They are likely to give impetus to further agreements in arms control and other fields. The Moscow Summit Conference of 1972 produced a Declaration of Principles providing for the conduct of relations on the basis of "peaceful coexistence" and recognition that neither superpower should seek to obtain "unilateral advantage at the expense of the other, directly or indirectly." The question facing the United States is the extent to which such general principles will be applied to the outstanding issues between the superpowers in the regions of Southeast Asia, South Asia, the Middle East, the Mediterranean, and Latin America.

Both the Soviet Union and the United States have claimed at one time or another that (1) regional tensions should not lead to superpower confrontation, and (2) short-term gains by one superpower may jeopardize the general superpower relationship. "Linkage" politics consist of determining where a regional dispute, aggravated by the superpowers, threatens the global balance of power and the prestige of one of the superpowers, and whether meeting this challenge requires military confrontation. Under nuclear parity, however, a state can hardly compensate for conventional disadvantage by recourse to nuclear confrontation. The strategic arms-control agreements emphasize anew the importance of the local conventional balance of power in coping with regional disputes. These agreements do not assure the local balance, nor do they promise superpower cooperation to achieve it. They simply confirm that nuclear weapons provide no last resort for the superpowers to redress a conventional or regional defeat.

The resolution of such problems depends instead on the strength and will of such allies, as well as the assistance provided by one or the other superpower. The question which remains unanswered at this stage is the extent to which agreement in the SALT will be conducive to superpower efforts to collaborate in the reduction of tensions in such regions as Europe, Southeast Asia, and the Middle East.

Finally, the strategic agreements and the circumstances of their signing acknowledge U.S. acceptance of the Soviet Union as a political and psychological equal. Thus, the Soviet Union has attained a long-sought goal. Just as the SALT codifies strategic parity, and in some areas Soviet superiority, the agreements between the German Federal Republic and the Soviet Union contribute to the attainment of another long-term goal of Moscow: international acceptance of the status quo in East Central Europe. These two achievements in themselves more than compensated for the embarrassment which Soviet leaders suffered as a result of the U.S. blockade of North Vietnamese harbors prior to and during President Nixon's visit to the Soviet Union.

Contrary to popular expectations, the arms agreements represent no real prospect for major reductions in military spending. This is because they retard only the *quantity* of certain weapons, restrict the *quality* of none, and even provide an incentive to both sides to continue major R&D programs especially in offensive weapons systems, and emphasize the value of regional conventional forces. The United States must probably increase its spending for R&D and for deployment of an ABM around Washington. Failure of the United States to complete certain of its existing programs, such as the B-1 bomber and MIRV development, would reduce the U.S. bargaining position in future SALT negotiations and might even affect adversely the U.S. strategic posture vis-à-vis the Soviet Union. Moreover, in the absence of congressional approval of the ABM protection for Washington, the United States will end up with only one ABM system as opposed to two for the Soviet Union, unless the Soviet Union decides to forgo deployment of one of its ABM complexes. Meanwhile, maximum reductions in other defense programs have already been made, and the cost of the U.S. Volunteer Army alone would easily consume any contemplated savings from the SALT. In the end, the conduct of research may not prove cheaper than deployment. Hence, the SALT may have the principal effect of shifting the concentration of military spending rather than reducing such expenditures.

In discussions of strategic "superiority," "sufficiency," "parity," and "inferiority," U.S. analysts have played a kind of numbers game. Some have minimized Soviet numerical superiority in launchers, throw weight, and warhead size, while suggesting that the United States retains an advantage in numbers of warheads and deliverable megatonnage, missile accuracy and new technology, for example, in MIRV. The United States, it is suggested, has a *qualitative* advantage which compensates for the Soviet quantitative gains of recent years. However, other strategic analysts, fearful of the implications of the Soviet strategic buildup, have emphasized the political and psychological advantages that may accrue to the Soviet Union from a growing perception around the world of the increased strength of Soviet strategic forces. As a result, the question has been asked as to whether the Soviet Union seeks "the numbers and types of forces needed to attack and destroy vital elements of our own strategic forces" by developing "strategic capabilities beyond a level which by any reasonable standard already seems sufficient." [4]

If the numbers of weapons available respectively to the Soviet Union and the United States do not matter, since the strategic balance allegedly is stable under conditions of sufficiency, the question remains as to why the Soviet Union has devoted major resources to the development of strategic systems. Do the Soviets share U.S. conceptions about the numbers and quality of weapons necessary to assure a strategic balance? If not, a destabilizing element is introduced into the U.S.-Soviet strategic relationship, especially if the Soviet Union seeks to extract political gain from the development and deployment of its strategic forces.[5]

Such questions may never be answerable. However, the goal of the United States in the SALT should be to produce a web of interlocking accords with the Soviet Union, in the preservation and extension of which each side has a stake. Under such circumstances the U.S.-Soviet relationship might be transformed from confrontation to less acrimonious competition and eventually to collaboration in certain fields.

Although both sides sought, and made concessions to achieve, agreement in the SALT, the United States appears to have had an even greater stake than the Soviet Union in the successful outcome of the negotiations. Because the United States was reluctant to embark on a major new armaments program to match the Soviet strategic buildup, it strove for a limited agreement to prevent a worsening in the U.S. position over the next five years. This situation prompted the various quantitative limitations on ICBMs and SLBMs set forth in the agreements. Moreover, for the most part, the protocols which accompanied the treaty and interim agreement were inserted unilaterally by the United States in order to set forth definitions and interpretations upon which agreement had eluded the negotiators in Helsinki and Vienna.

Even if both the Soviet Union and the United States observe to the letter the provisions of the SALT, the Soviets can improve their relative strategic position during the next five years, and the constraints upon them to do so are fewer than those upon the United States. For the United States, more than for the Soviet Union, however, the outcome of SALT I can best be justified by the successful conclusion, from the U.S. perspective, of the next phase. In this respect, the Soviet Union has created for the United States a major incentive to engage in a new round of SALT negotiations. The problem arises, then, of just what the United States can offer to induce the Soviet Union to scale down its offensive forces in such negotiations without jeopardizing U.S. relations with allies. The Soviet Union has suggested the inclusion of forward-based systems in the SALT, while the United States has sought to avoid discussion of a topic fraught with divisive implications for the Atlantic Alliance. In addition to the importance of forward-based systems for NATO, the presence of such capabilities outside the United States reduces the likelihood that the Soviet Union could contemplate a first-strike attack against the United States. The unwillingness of the United States to pay whatever price is sought by the Soviet Union might not only jeopardize the outcome of SALT II, but also cast into doubt the existing agreements. The question arises as to the degree of Soviet commitment to both the preservation of the agreements concluded thus far and the development of new SALT accords. In the absence of such a *shared* commitment by the superpowers, the interlocking nature of the SALT will be highly disadvantageous to the United States.

Conclusions

Several major factors are crucial to an evaluation of the implications of the SALT for international security and especially for the United States:

1. The arms agreement may provide a greater measure of security *if* the United States maintains a strong R&D program in areas vital to the strategic deterrent and at the same time monitors as closely as possible the Soviet R&D effort. An understanding of the nature of Soviet efforts, both as to strategy and goals, becomes even more essential for the period ahead. The arms race is retarded in certain categories of deployment for the next five years. But the agreements will not necessarily deter the Soviet Union from an R&D effort designed to enhance its position at the end of the time period or to enable the Soviet Union to eliminate its gap with the United States in such areas as MIRV and warhead accuracy. The absence of a major U.S. R&D program would place the United States at a distinctive disadvantage in all subsequent SALT negotiations.

2. Public pressure against military spending could hamper defense programs both in the United States and Western Europe. While the U.S. deterrent becomes less certain for NATO, the credibility of European deterrents against a fixed Soviet defense capability is preserved in the absence of a large-scale Soviet ABM. The agreements, by limiting a

Soviet ABM, make the Chinese arsenal more credible, and the arguments for Indian and Japanese nuclear accession gain strength. Inherent in the concept of multipolarity, as suggested in papers by the editors of this volume, is the problem of nuclear proliferation.

3. The outcome of the next phase of the SALT is of crucial importance. Although the Fifth International Arms Control Symposium dealt principally with the probable outcome of SALT I, participants referred to other aspects of the SALT that are likely to be considered in coming years. These include forward-based systems, the transfer of technology to allies, such as Western European countries, the reduction of numbers of strategic offensive systems, the redeployment of capabilities, and possibly the development of certain categories of future strategic systems.

4. The "linkage" problem remains. That is, the arms agreements suggest but do not compel greater U.S.-Soviet cooperation in regional disputes. Instead, the delicate relationship between regional competition and great power prestige remains, and the local conventional balance of power grows in significance. Under strategic parity, nuclear confrontation becomes more difficult, especially if the side initiating confrontation is inferior at the theater and battlefield levels. If one cannot deter his opponent at the strategic nuclear level, the latter is free to press whatever advantage he possesses at other levels of confrontation. The SALT contributes to the emergence of a more delicate form of competition between the superpowers, centering on R&D and regional balances of power that may include both nuclear and general purpose forces.

It is possible to attach alternative interpretations to the SALT accords. Whatever the Soviet motivation, the goal of U.S. national security policy, and especially arms-control negotiations, should be to encourage a shift in the U.S.-Soviet confrontation from the military to the political arena. Crucial to such a shift is the abandonment by the Soviet Union of the notion that it can ever contemplate a nuclear first strike.

In order to assure a U.S.-Soviet strategic relationship in which neither superpower possesses a first-strike capability, the United States should take several steps designed to maintain its present strategic forces, including:

a. completion of the ABM for the ICBM missile defense field, and construction of an ABM for the national capital to protect the U.S. command center in time of crisis;

b. improvements in MIRV reliability and accuracy; and

c. development of both ULMS and a bomber such as the B-1.

Unless we relate R&D to such specific tasks, we will risk the possibility of falling behind the Soviet Union and jeopardizing parity conceived as mutual incapacity to initiate a first strike.

If the SALT help to neutralize nuclear weapons at the global level under conditions of strategic parity, they enhance competition at the theater level, as suggested above. The task of U.S. national security policy must be to render theater aggression improbable. Especially in the case of Europe, this requires the preservation of a linkage between the U.S. strategic force and European security, at least while Western Europe acquires a more credible defense capability of its own. In the Third World, local insurgency conflicts, unless supported on a large scale by one of the major Communist powers, should not provoke massive U.S. military intervention.

In their explanations of the ABM Treaty and Interim Agreement on Offensive Missiles, U.S. spokesmen have stressed the importance of the accords in slowing the development by the Soviet Union over the next several years of a strategic posture increasingly disadvantageous to the United States. Without the SALT and in the absence of a vast new U.S. weapons program, a strategic gap of potentially destabilizing proportions would have developed between the United States and the Soviet Union. The willingness of the United States to accept the agreements resulting from SALT I reflects both a U.S. desire to dampen the arms race as well as a realization that the alternative would have been a weapons program that most Americans seek to avoid. Hence, a limitation on ICBMs and sea-based systems is in the U.S. interest to the extent that it will permit the United States to conclude more far-reaching and permanent agreements with the Soviet Union, while building national support for whatever strategic posture may be essential to provide for the defense of U.S. and allied interests in the late 1970s.

In several of the discussions at the Fifth International Arms Control Symposium, the question of political will arose. Ultimately, the political will of a nation is reflected both in its strategic posture and in the diplomacy conducted by its leaders. Arms-control agreements, like other forms of international diplomacy, reflect the level of national will of a state, especially as perceived by those with whom it negotiates. The emergence of a disadvantageous strategic balance can be postponed, but not necessarily prevented, by the conclusion of arms-control agreements, such as those in the SALT.

The goal of the United States should be to shift the focus of U.S.-Soviet conflict from military confrontation to political competition and eventually broadened cooperation in an international system in transition from bipolarity to multipolarity. In the aftermath of the Vietnam War, perhaps the United States can develop a national security policy adequate to compete effectively with the Soviet Union in the latter part of the 1970s. Provided they are viewed as part of a broader U.S. national security policy, backed by an adequate political will, the SALT accords can contribute to the building of a world in which large powers and small nations can gain a greater measure of security and the incentive of states to seek to use strategic capabilities to extract political gain can be minimized.

NOTES

1. According to public estimates, the Soviet Union already possesses an advantage of about 60 percent in ICBMs (U.S. = 1,054; USSR = 1,618) and under the SALT agreement could gain a similar advantage in missile-launching submarines (62–44), if it were willing to reduce its ICBM force to 1,408. By taking this option, the Soviet Union could acquire one-third more submarine-launched ballistic missiles (950–710) and a more than threefold advantage in megatonnage of total missile payload. See *The Military Balance 1971–1972* (London: International Institute for Strategic Studies, 1971), esp. pp. 3–5; see also the *New York Times,* June 5, 1972.

2. For an examination of this point, see Donald G. Brennan, "When the SALT Hit the Fan," *National Review,* June 23, 1972, p. 685.

3. Texts of Agreed Interpretations and Unilateral Statements with Arms Pacts, *New York Times,* June 14, 1972, p. 18.

4. *U.S. Foreign Policy: The Emerging Structure of Peace,* A Report to the Congress by President Richard Nixon, February 9, 1972 (Washington, D.C.: U.S. Government Printing Office, 1972), p. 159.

5. For an analysis of this problem, see Uri Ra'anan, *The Changing American-Soviet Strategic Balance: Some Political Implications,* U.S. Senate Committee on Government Operations, Subcommittee on National Security and International Operations (Washington, D.C.: U.S. Government Printing Office, 1972). See also William R. Kintner and Robert L. Pfaltzgraff, Jr., *Soviet Military Trends: Implications for U.S. Security,* special analysis by the American Enterprise Institute for Public Policy Research and the Foreign Policy Research Institute, 1971.

APPENDIX
LIST OF ABBREVIATIONS
GLOSSARY
BIOGRAPHICAL NOTES
INDEX

Appendix

92D CONGRESS 2d Session	HOUSE OF REPRESENTATIVES	DOCUMENT No. 92–311

SALT AGREEMENTS

COMMUNICATION

FROM

THE PRESIDENT OF THE UNITED STATES

TRANSMITTING

COPIES OF THE TREATY ON THE LIMITATION OF ANTI-BALLISTIC MISSILE SYSTEMS AND THE INTERIM AGREEMENT ON CERTAIN MEASURES WITH RESPECT TO THE LIMITATION OF STRATEGIC OFFENSIVE ARMS SIGNED IN MOSCOW ON MAY 26, 1972

JUNE 13, 1972.—Referred to the Committee on Foreign Affairs and ordered to be printed

---

In addition to the SALT Agreements, which are included here, Document No. 92–311 contains President Nixon's communications of June 13, 1972, to the speaker of the House of Representatives and to the Senate that accompanied the treaties. It also includes Secretary of State William A. Roger's outline of the treaties that he submitted along with the treaties to the president on June 10, 1972.

Treaty Between the United States of America and the Union
of Soviet Socialist Republics on the Limitation of Anti-
Ballistic Missile Systems

The United States of America and the Union of Soviet Socialist
Republics, hereinafter referred to as the Parties,

Proceeding from the premise that nuclear war would have
devastating consequences for all mankind,

Considering that effective measures to limit anti-ballistic missile
systems would be a substantial factor in curbing the race in strategic
offensive arms and would lead to a decrease in the risk of outbreak of
war involving nuclear weapons,

Proceeding from the premise that the limitation of anti-ballistic
missile systems, as well as certain agreed measures with respect to
the limitation of strategic offensive arms, would contribute to the
creation of more favorable conditions for further negotiations on
limiting strategic arms,

Mindful of their obligations under Article VI of the Treaty on the
Non-Proliferation of Nuclear Weapons,

Declaring their intention to achieve at the earliest possible date
the cessation of the nuclear arms race and to take effective measures
toward reductions in strategic arms, nuclear disarmament, and general
and complete disarmament,

Desiring to contribute to the relaxation of international tension and
the strengthening of trust between States,

Have agreed as follows:

ARTICLE I

1. Each Party undertakes to limit anti-ballistic missile (ABM)
systems and to adopt other measures in accordance with the provisions
of this Treaty.

2. Each Party undertakes not to deploy ABM systems for a defense
of the territory of its country and not to provide a base for such a
defense, and not to deploy ABM systems for defense of an individual
region except as provided for in Article III of this Treaty.

ARTICLE II

1. For the purposes of this Treaty an ABM system is a system to
counter strategic ballistic missiles or their elements in flight trajectory,
currently consisting of:

(a) ABM interceptor missiles, which are interceptor missiles constructed and deployed for an ABM role, or of a type tested in an ABM
mode;

(b) ABM launchers, which are launchers constructed and deployed
for launching ABM interceptor missiles; and

(c) ABM radars, which are radars constructed and deployed for
an ABM role, or of a type tested in an ABM mode.

2. The ABM system components listed in paragraph 1 of this Article include those which are:
    (a) operational;
    (b) under construction;
    (c) undergoing testing;
    (d) undergoing overhaul, repair or conversion; or
    (e) mothballed.

ARTICLE III

Each Party undertakes not to deploy ABM systems or their components except that:

(a) within one ABM system deployment area having a radius of one hundred and fifty kilometers and centered on the Party's national capital, a Party may deploy: (1) no more than one hundred ABM launchers and no more than one hundred ABM interceptor missiles at launch sites, and (2) ABM radars within no more than six ABM radar complexes, the area of each complex being circular and having a diameter of no more than three kilometers; and

(b) within one ABM system deployment area having a radius of one hundred and fifty kilometers and containing ICBM silo launchers, a Party may deploy: (1) no more than one hundred ABM launchers and no more than one hundred ABM interceptor missiles at launch sites, (2) two large phased-array ABM radars comparable in potential to corresponding ABM radars operational or under construction on the date of signature of the Treaty in an ABM system deployment area containing ICBM silo launchers, and (3) no more than eighteen ABM radars each having a potential less than the potential of the smaller of the above-mentioned two large phased-array ABM radars.

ARTICLE IV

The limitations provided for in Article III shall not apply to ABM systems or their components used for development or testing, and located within current or additionally agreed test ranges. Each Party may have no more than a total of fifteen ABM launchers at test ranges.

ARTICLE V

1. Each Party undertakes not to develop, test, or deploy ABM systems or components which are sea-based, air-based, space-based, or mobile land-based.

2. Each Party undertakes not to develop, test, or deploy ABM launchers for launching more than one ABM interceptor missile at a time from each launcher, nor to modify deployed launchers to provide them with such a capability, nor to develop, test, or deploy automatic or semi-automatic or other similar systems for rapid reload of ABM launchers.

ARTICLE VI

To enhance assurance of the effectiveness of the limitations on ABM systems and their components provided by this Treaty each Party undertakes:

(a) not to give missiles, launchers, or radars, other than ABM interceptor missiles, ABM launchers, or ABM radars, capabilities to counter strategic ballistic missiles or their elements in flight trajectory, and not to test them in an ABM mode; and

(b) not to deploy in the future radars for early warning of strategic ballistic missile attack except at locations along the periphery of its national territory and oriented outward.

ARTICLE VII

Subject to the provisions of this Treaty, modernization and replacement of ABM systems or their components may be carried out.

ARTICLE VIII

ABM systems or their components in excess of the numbers or outside the areas specified in this Treaty, as well as ABM systems or their components prohibited by this Treaty, shall be destroyed or dismantled under agreed procedures within the shortest possible agreed period of time.

ARTICLE IX

To assure the viability and effectiveness of this Treaty, each Party undertakes not to transfer to other States, and not to deploy outside its national territory, ABM systems or their components limited by this Treaty.

ARTICLE X

Each Party undertakes not to assume any international obligations which would conflict with this Treaty.

ARTICLE XI

The Parties undertake to continue active negotiations for limitations on strategic offensive arms.

ARTICLE XII

1. For the purpose of providing assurance of compliance with the provisions of this Treaty, each Party shall use national technical means of verification at its disposal in a manner consistent with generally recognized principles of international law.

2. Each Party undertakes not to interfere with the national technical means of verification of the other Party operating in accordance with paragraph 1 of this Article.

3. Each Party undertakes not to use deliberate concealment measures which impede verification by national technical means of compliance with the provisions of this Treaty. This obligation shall not require changes in current construction, assembly, conversion, or overhaul practices.

ARTICLE XIII

1. To promote the objectives and implementation of the provisions of this Treaty, the Parties shall establish promptly a Standing Consultative Commission, within the framework of which they will:

(a) consider questions concerning compliance with the obligations assumed and related situations which may be considered ambiguous;

(b) provide on a voluntary basis such information as either Party considers necessary to assure confidence in compliance with the obligations assumed;

(c) consider questions involving unintended interference with national technical means of verification;

(d) consider possible changes in the strategic situation which have a bearing on the provisions of this Treaty;

(e) agree upon procedures and dates for destruction or dismantling of ABM systems or their components in cases provided for by the provisions of this Treaty;

(f) consider, as appropriate, possible proposals for further increasing the viability of this Treaty, including proposals for amendments in accordance with the provisions of this Treaty;

(g) consider, as appropriate, proposals for further measures aimed at limiting strategic arms.

2. The Parties through consultation shall establish, and may amend as appropriate, Regulations for the Standing Consultative Commission governing procedures, composition and other relevant matters.

ARTICLE XIV

1. Each Party may propose amendments to this Treaty. Agreed amendments shall enter into force in accordance with the procedures governing the entry into force of this Treaty.

2. Five years after entry into force of this Treaty, and at five year intervals thereafter, the Parties shall together conduct a review of this Treaty.

ARTICLE XV

1. This Treaty shall be of unlimited duration.

2. Each Party shall, in exercising its national sovereignty, have the right to withdraw from this Treaty if it decides that extraordinary events related to the subject matter of this Treaty have jeopardized its supreme interests. It shall give notice of its decision to the other Party six months prior to withdrawal from the Treaty. Such notice shall include a statement of the extraordinary events the notifying Party regards as having jeopardized its supreme interests.

ARTICLE XVI

1. This Treaty shall be subject to ratification in accordance with the constitutional procedures of each Party. The Treaty shall enter into force on the day of the exchange of instruments of ratification.

2. This Treaty shall be registered pursuant to Article 102 of the Charter of the United Nations.

Done at Moscow on May 26, 1972, in two copies, each in the English and Russian languages, both texts being equally authentic.

For the United States of America:

RICHARD NIXON,
President of the United States of America.

For the Union of Soviet Socialist Republics:

L. I. BREZHNEV,
General Secretary of the Central Committee of the CPSU.

INTERIM AGREEMENT BETWEEN THE UNITED STATES OF AMERICA AND THE UNION OF SOVIET SOCIALIST REPUBLICS ON CERTAIN MEASURES WITH RESPECT TO THE LIMITATION OF STRATEGIC OFFENSIVE ARMS

The United States of America and the Union of Soviet Socialist Republics, hereinafter referred to as the Parties,

Convinced that the Treaty on the Limitation of Anti-Ballistic Missile Systems and this Interim Agreement on Certain Measures with Respect to the Limitation of Strategic Offensive Arms will contribute to the creation of more favorable conditions for active negotiations on limiting strategic arms as well as to the relaxation of international tension and the strengthening of trust between States,

Taking into account the relationship between strategic offensive and defensive arms,

Mindful of their obligations under Article VI of the Treaty on the Non-Proliferation of Nuclear Weapons,

Have agreed as follows:

ARTICLE I

The Parties undertake not to start construction of additional fixed land-based intercontinental ballistic missile (ICBM) launchers after July 1, 1972.

ARTICLE II

The Parties undertake not to convert land-based launchers for light ICBMs, or for ICBMs of older types deployed prior to 1964, into land-based launchers for heavy ICBMs of types deployed after that time.

ARTICLE III

The Parties undertake to limit submarine-launched ballistic missile (SLBM) launchers and modern ballistic missile submarines to the numbers operational and under construction on the date of signature of this Interim Agreement, and in addition to launchers and submarines constructed under procedures established by the Parties as replacements for an equal number of ICBM launchers of older types deployed prior to 1964 or for launchers on older submarines.

ARTICLE IV

Subject to the provisions of this Interim Agreement, modernization and replacement of strategic offensive ballistic missiles and launchers covered by this Interim Agreement may be undertaken.

ARTICLE V

1. For the purpose of providing assurance of compliance with the provisions of this Interim Agreement, each Party shall use national technical means of verification at its disposal in a manner consistent with generally recognized principles of international law.

2. Each Party undertakes not to interfere with the national technical means of verification of the other Party operating in accordance with paragraph 1 of this Article.

3. Each Party undertakes not to use deliberate concealment measures which impede verification by national technical means of compliance with the provisions of this Interim Agreement. This obligation shall not require changes in current construction, assembly, conversion, or overhaul practices.

ARTICLE VI

To promote the objectives and implementation of the provisions of this Interim Agreement, the Parties shall use the Standing Consultative Commission established under Article XIII of the Treaty on the Limitation of Anti-Ballistic Missile Systems in accordance with the provisions of that Article.

ARTICLE VII

The Parties undertake to continue active negotiations for limitations on strategic offensive arms. The obligations provided for in this Interim Agreement shall not prejudice the scope or terms of the limitations on strategic offensive arms which may be worked out in the course of further negotiations.

ARTICLE VIII

1. This Interim Agreement shall enter into force upon exchange of written notices of acceptance by each Party, which exchange shall take place simultaneously with the exchange of instruments of ratification of the Treaty on the Limitation of Anti-Ballistic Missile Systems.

2. This Interim Agreement shall remain in force for a period of five years unless replaced earlier by an agreement on more complete measures limiting strategic offensive arms. It is the objective of the Parties to conduct active follow-on negotiations with the aim of concluding such an agreement as soon as possible.

3. Each Party shall, in exercising its national soverignty, have the right to withdraw from this Interim Agreement if it decides that extraordinary events related to the subject matter of this Interim Agreement have jeopardized its supreme interests. It shall give notice of its decision to the other Party six months prior to withdrawal from this Interim Agreement. Such notice shall include a statement of the extraordinary events the notifying Party regards as having jeopardized its supreme interests.

Done at Moscow on May 26, 1972, in two copies, each in the English and Russian languages, both texts being equally authentic.

For the United States of America:

RICHARD NIXON,
President of the United States of America.

For the Union of Soviet Socialist Republics:

L. I. BREZHNEV,
General Secretary of the Central Committee of the CPSU.

PROTOCOL TO THE INTERIM AGREEMENT BETWEEN THE UNITED STATES OF AMERICA AND THE UNION OF SOVIET SOCIALIST REPUBLICS ON CERTAIN MEASURES WITH RESPECT TO THE LIMITATION OF STRATEGIC OFFENSIVE ARMS

The United States of America and the Union of Soviet Socialist Republics, hereinafter referred to as the Parties,

Having agreed on certain limitations relating to submarine-launched ballistic missile launchers and modern ballistic missile submarines, and to replacement procedures, in the Interim Agreement,

Have agreed as follows:

The Parties understand that, under Article III of the Interim Agreement, for the period during which that Agreement remains in force:

The US may have no more than 710 ballistic missile launchers on submarines (SLBMs) and no more than 44 modern ballistic missile submarines. The Soviet Union may have no more than 950 ballistic missile launchers on submarines and no more than 62 modern ballistic missile submarines.

Additional ballistic missile launchers on submarines up to the above-mentioned levels, in the U.S.—over 656 ballistic missile launchers on nuclear-powered submarines, and in the U.S.S.R.—over 740 ballistic missile launchers on nuclear-powered submarines, operational and under construction, may become operational as replacements for equal numbers of ballistic missile launchers of older types deployed prior to 1964 or of ballistic missile launchers on older submarines.

The deployment of modern SLBMs on any submarine, regardless of type, will be counted against the total level of SLBMs permitted for the U.S. and the U.S.S.R.

This Protocol shall be considered an integral part of the Interim Agreement.

Done at Moscow this 26th day of May, 1972.

For the United States of America:

RICHARD NIXON,
President of the United States of America.

For the Union of Soviet Socialist Republics:

L. I. BREZHNEV,
General Secretary of the Central Committee of the CPSU.

[Enclosure 3]

1. AGREED INTERPRETATIONS.

(a) *Initialed Statements.*

The texts of the statements set out below were agreed upon and initialed by the Heads of the Delegations on May 26, 1972.

ABM TREATY

[A]

The Parties understand that, in addition to the ABM radars which may be deployed in accordance with subparagraph (a) of Article III of the Treaty, those non-phased-array ABM radars operational on the date of signature of the Treaty within the ABM system deployment area for defense of the national capital may be retained.

[B]

The Parties understand that the potential (the product of mean emitted power in watts and antenna area in square meters) of the smaller of the two large phased-array ABM radars referred to in subparagraph (b) of Article III of the Treaty is considered for purposes of the Treaty to be three million.

[C]

The Parties understand that the center of the ABM system deployment area centered on the national capital and the center of the ABM system deployment area containing ICBM silo launchers for each Party shall be separated by no less than thirteen hundred kilometers.

[D]

The Parties agree not to deploy phased-array radars having a potential (the product of mean emitted power in watts and antenna area in square meters) exceeding three million, except as provided for in Articles III, IV, and VI of the Treaty, or except for the purposes of tracking objects in outer space or for use as national technical means of verification.

[E]

In order to insure fulfillment of the obligation not to deploy ABM systems and their components except as provided in Article III of the Treaty, the Parties agree that in the event ABM systems based on other physical principles and including components capable of substituting for ABM interceptor missiles, ABM launchers, or ABM radars are created in the future, specific limitations on such systems and their components would be subject to discussion in accordance with Article XIII and agreement in accordance with Article XIV of the Treaty.

[F]

The Parties understand that Article V of the Treaty includes obligations not to develop, test or deploy ABM interceptor missiles for the delivery by each ABM interceptor missile or more than one independently guided warhead.

[G]

The Parties understand that Article IX of the Treaty includes the obligation of the US and the USSR not to provide to other States technical descriptions or blueprints specially worked out for the construction of ABM systems and their components limited by the Treaty.

INTERIM AGREEMENT

[H]

The Parties understand that land-based ICBM launchers referred to in the Interim Agreement are understood to be launchers for strategic ballistic missiles capable of ranges in excess of the shortest distance between the northeastern border of the continental U.S. and the northwestern border of the continental USSR.

[I]

The Parties understand that fixed land-based ICBM launchers under active construction as of the date of signature of the Interim Agreement may be completed.

[J]

The Parties understand that in the process of modernization and replacement the dimensions of land-based ICBM silo launchers will not be significantly increased.

[K]

The Parties understand that dismantling or destruction of ICBM launchers of older types deployed prior to 1964 and ballistic missile launchers on older submarines being replaced by new SLBM launchers on modern submarines will be initiated at the time of the beginning of sea trials of a replacement submarine, and will be completed in the shortest possible agreed period of time. Such dismantling or destruction, and timely notification thereof, will be accomplished under procedures to be agreed in the Standing Consultative Commission.

[L]

The Parties understand that during the period of the Interim Agreement there shall be no significant increase in the number of ICBM or SLBM test and training launchers, or in the number of such launchers for modern land-based heavy ICBMs. The Parties further understand that construction or conversion of ICBM launchers at test ranges shall be undertaken only for purposes of testing and training.

(b) *Common Understandings.*

Common understanding of the Parties on the following matters was reached during the negotiations:

A. *Increase in ICBM Silo Dimensions.*—Ambassador Smith made the following statement on May 26, 1972: "The Parties agree that the term 'significantly increased' means that an increase will not be greater than 10–15 percent of the present dimensions of land-based ICBM silo launchers".

Minister Semenov replied that this statement corresponded to the Soviet understanding.

B. *Location of ICBM Defenses.*—The U.S. Delegation made the following statement on May 26, 1972: "Article III of the ABM Treaty provides for each side one ABM system deployment area centered on its national capital and one ABM system deployment area containing ICBM silo launchers. The two sides have registered agreement on the following statement: 'The Parties understand that the center of the ABM system deployment area centered on the national capital and the center of the ABM system deployment area containing ICBM silo launchers for each Party shall be separated by no less than thirteen hundred kilometers.' In this connection, the U.S. side notes that its ABM system deployment area for defense of ICBM silo launchers, located west of the Mississippi River, will be centered in the Grand Forks ICBM silo launcher deployment area." (See Initialed Statement [C].)

C. *ABM Test Ranges.*—The U.S. Delegation made the following statement on April 26, 1972: "Article IV of the ABM Treaty provides that 'the limitations provided for in Article III shall not apply to ABM systems or their components used for development or testing, and located within current or additionally agreed test ranges.' We believe it would be useful to assure that there is no misunderstanding as to current ABM test ranges. It is our understanding that ABM test ranges encompass the area within which ABM components are located for test purposes. The current U.S. ABM test ranges are at White Sands, New Mexico, and at Kwajalein Atoll, and the current Soviet ABM test range is near Sary Shagan in Kazakhstan. We consider that non-phased array radars of types used for range safety or instrumentation purposes may be located outside of ABM test ranges. We interpret the reference in Article IV to 'additionally agreed test ranges' to mean that ABM components will not be located at any other test ranges without prior agreement between our Governments that there will be such additional ABM test ranges."

On May 5, 1972, the Soviet Delegation stated that there was a common understanding on what ABM test ranges were, that the use of the types of non-ABM radars for range safety or instrumentation was not limited under the Treaty, that the reference in Article IV to "additionally agreed" test ranges was sufficiently clear, and that national means permitted identifying current test ranges.

D. *Mobile ABM Systems.*—On January 28, 1972, the U.S. Delegation made the following statement: "Article V(1) of the Joint Draft Text of the ABM Treaty includes an undertaking not to develop, test, or deploy mobile land-based ABM systems and their components. On May 5, 1971, the U.S. side indicated that, in its view, a prohibition on deployment of mobile ABM systems and components would rule out the deployment of ABM launchers and radars which were not permanent fixed types. At that time, we asked for the Soviet view of this interpretation. Does the Soviet side agree with the U.S. side's interpretation put forward on May 5, 1971?"

On April 13, 1972, the Soviet Delegation said there is a general common understanding on this matter.

E. *Standing Consultative Commission.*—Ambassador Smith made the following statement on May 23, 1972: "The United States proposes that the sides agree that, with regard to initial implementation of the ABM Treaty's Article XIII on the Standing Consultative Commission (SCC) and of the consultation Articles to the Interim Agreement on offensive arms and the Accidents Agreement,* agreement establishing the SCC will be worked out early in the follow-on SALT negotiations; until that is completed, the following arrangements will prevail: when SALT is in session, any consultation desired by either side under

---

* See Article 7 of Agreement to Reduce the Risk of Outbreak of Nuclear War Between the United States of America and the Union of Soviet Socialist Republics, signed September 30, 1971.

these Articles can be carried out by the two SALT Delegations; when SALT is not in session, *ad hoc* arrangements for any desired consultations under these Articles may be made through diplomatic channels."

Minister Semenov replied that, on an *ad referendum* basis, he could agree that the U.S. statement corresponded to the Soviet understanding.

F. *Standstill.*—On May 6, 1972, Minister Semenov made the following statement: "In an effort to accommodate the wishes of the U.S. side, the Soviet Delegation is prepared to proceed on the basis that the two sides will in fact observe the obligations of both the Interim Agreement and the ABM Treaty beginning from the date of signature of these two documents."

In reply, the U.S. Delegation made the following statement on May 20, 1972: "The U.S. agrees in principle with the Soviet statement made on May 6 concerning observance of obligations beginning from date of signature but we would like to make clear our understanding that this means that, pending ratification and acceptance, neither side would take any action prohibited by the agreements after they had entered into force. This understanding would continue to apply in the absence of notification by either signatory of its intention not to proceed with ratification or approval."

The Soviet Delegation indicated agreement with the U.S. statement.

2. UNILATERAL STATEMENTS

(a) The following noteworthy unilateral statements were made during the negotiations by the United States Delegation:—

A. *Withdrawal from the ABM Treaty*

On May 9, 1972, Ambassador Smith made the following statement: "The U.S. Delegation has stressed the importance the U.S. Government attaches to achieving agreement on more complete limitations on strategic offensive arms, following agreement on an ABM Treaty and on an Interim Agreement on certain measures with respect to the limitation of strategic offensive arms. The U.S. Delegation believes than an objective of the follow-on negotiations should be to constrain and reduce on a long-term basis threats to the survivability of our respective strategic retaliatory forces. The USSR Delegation has also indicated that the objectives of SALT would remain unfulfilled without the achievement of an agreement providing for more complete limitations on strategic offensive arms. Both sides recognize that the initial agreements would be steps toward the achievement of more complete limitations on strategic arms. If an agreement providing for more complete strategic offensive arms limitations were not achieved within five years, U.S. supreme interests could be jeopardized. Should that occur, it would constitute a basis for withdrawal from the ABM Treaty. The U.S. does not wish to see such a situation occur, nor do we believe that the USSR does. It is because we wish to prevent such a situation that we emphasize the importance the U.S. Government attaches to achievement of more complete limitations on strategic offensive arms. The U.S. Executive will inform the Congress, in connection with Congressional consideration of the ABM Treaty and the Interim Agreement, of this statement of the U.S. position."

B. Land-Mobile ICBM Launchers

The U.S. Delegation made the following statement on May 20, 1972: "In connection with the important subject of land-mobile ICBM launchers, in the interest of concluding the Interim Agreement the U.S. Delegation now withdraws its proposal that Article I or an agreed statement explicitly prohibit the deployment of mobile land-based ICBM launchers. I have been instructed to inform you that, while agreeing to defer the question of limitation of operational land-mobile ICBM launchers to the subsequent negotiations on more complete limitations on strategic offensive arms, the U.S. would consider the deployment of operational land-mobile ICBM launchers during the period of the Interim Agreement as inconsistent with the objectives of that Agreement."

C. Covered Facilities

The U.S. Delegation made the following statement on May 20, 1972: "I wish to emphasize the importance that the United States attaches to the provisions of Article V, including in particular their application to fitting out or berthing submarines."

D. "Heavy" ICBM's

The U.S. Delegation made the following statement on May 26, 1972: "The U.S. Delegation regrets that the Soviet Delegation has not been willing to agree on a common definition of a heavy missile. Under these circumstances, the U.S. Delegation believes it necessary to state the following: The United States would consider any ICBM having a volume significantly greater than that of the largest light ICBM now operational on either side to be a heavy ICBM. The U.S. proceeds on the premise that the Soviet side will give due account to this consideration."

E. Tested in ABM Mode

On April 7, 1972, the U.S. Delegation made the following statement: "Article II of the Joint Draft Text uses the term 'tested in an ABM mode,' in defining ABM components, and Article VI includes certain obligations concerning such testing. We believe that the side should have a common understanding of this phrase. First, we would note that the testing provisions of the ABM Treaty are intended to apply to testing which occurs after the date of signature of the Treaty, and not to any testing which may have occurred in the past. Next, we would amplify the remarks we have made on this subject during the previous Helsinki phase by setting forth the objectives which govern the U.S. view on the subject, namely, while prohibiting testing of non-ABM components for ABM purposes: not to prevent testing of ABM components, and not to prevent testing of non-ABM components for non-ABM purposes. To clarify our interpretation of 'tested in an ABM mode,' we note that we would consider a launcher, missile or radar to be 'tested in an ABM mode' if, for example, any of the following events occur: (1) a launcher is used to launch an ABM interceptor missile, (2) an interceptor missile is flight tested against a target vehicle which has a flight trajectory with characteristics of a strategic ballistic missile flight trajectory, or is flight tested in conjunction with the test of an ABM interceptor missile or an ABM radar at the same test range, or is flight tested to an altitude inconsistent with interception of targets against which air defenses are deployed, (3) a radar makes measurements on a cooperative target vehicle of the kind referred to in item (2) above during the reentry portion of its trajectory or makes measurements in conjunction with the test of an ABM interceptor missile or an ABM radar at the same test range. Radars used for purposes such as range safety or instrumentation would be exempt from application of these criteria."

F. No-Transfer Article of ABM Treaty

On April 18, 1972, the U.S. Delegation made the following statement: "In regard to this Article [IX], I have a brief and I believe self-explanatory statement to make. The U.S. side wishes to make clear that the provisions of this Article do not set a precedent for whatever provision may be considered for a Treaty on Limiting Strategic Offensive Arms. The question of transfer of strategic offensive arms is a far more complex issue, which may require a different solution."

G. No Increase in Defense of Early Warning Radars

On July 28, 1970, the U.S. Delegation made the following statement: "Since Hen House radars [Soviet ballistic missile early warning radars] can detect and track ballistic missile warheads at great distances, they have a significant ABM potential. Accordingly, the U.S. would regard any increase in the defenses of such radars by surface-to-air missiles as inconsistent with an agreement."

*   *   *   *   *   *   *

(b) The following noteworthy unilateral statement was made by the Delegation of the U.S.S.R. and is shown here with the U.S. reply:

On May 17, 1972, Minister Semenov made the following unilateral "Statement of the Soviet Side:" "Taking into account that modern ballistic missile submarines are presently in the possession of not only the U.S., but also of its NATO allies, the Soviet Union agrees that for the period of effectiveness of the Interim 'Freeze' Agreement the U.S. and its NATO allies have up to 50 such submarines with a total of up to 800 ballistic missile launchers thereon (including 41 U.S. submarines with 656 ballistic missile launchers). However, if during the period of effectiveness of the Agreement U.S. allies in NATO should increase the number of their modern submarines to exceed the numbers of submarines they would have operational or under construction on the date of signature of the Agreement, the Soviet Union will have the right to a corresponding increase in the number of its submarines. In the opinion of the Soviet side, the solution of the question of modern ballistic missile submarines provided for in the Interim Agreement only partially compensates for the strategic imbalance in the deployment of the nuclear-powered missile submarines of the USSR and the U.S. Therefore, the Soviet side believes that this whole question, and above all the questions of liquidating the American missile submarine bases outside the U.S., will be appropriately resolved in the course of follow-on negotiations."

On May 24, Ambassador Smith made the following reply to Minister Semenov: "The United States side has studied the 'statement made by the Soviet side' of May 17 concerning compensation for submarine basing and SLBM submarines belonging to third countries. The United States does not accept the validity of the considerations in that statement."

On May 26 Minister Semenov repeated the unilateral statement made on May 24. Ambassador Smith also repeated the U.S. rejection on May 26.

Commonly Used Abbreviations
in Arms Control Literature

ABM	Antiballistic missile
ASW	Antisubmarine warfare
BMD	Ballistic Missile Defense
CC	Command and control
C³	Command, control, and communications
CD	Civil defense
CEP	Circular error probable
FBS	Forward-based Systems
FD	Finite deterrence
FOBS	Fractional Orbital Bombardment System
ICBM	Intercontinental ballistic missile
IRBM	Intermediate-range ballistic missile
KT	Kiloton
MBFR	Mutual and balanced force reductions
MIRV	Multiple independently targeted re-entry vehicle
MRBM	Medium-range ballistic missile
MRV	Multiple re-entry vehicle
MT	Megaton
NDV	Nuclear delivery vehicle
NPT	Nuclear Non-Proliferation Treaty
PSI	Pounds per square inch overpressure
R&D	Research and development
RES	Re-entry system
REV	Re-entry vehicle
SAC	Strategic Air Command
SALT	Strategic Arms Limitation Talks
SAM	Surface-to-air missile
SLBM	Submarine-launched ballistic missile
ULMS	Undersea Long-range Missile System
VRBM	Variable-range ballistic missile

Glossary of Terms Used
in Arms Control Literature

ACTIVE DEFENSE. The type of defense that seeks, by use of defensive missiles or airplanes, to intercept an offensive missile strike before it reaches its targets.

ACTIVE SENSOR. Devices designed to gather evidence concerning incoming missiles by the emission of energy impulses that reflect back from objects in the air. The most obvious example is the radar.

AIR-TO-SURFACE MISSILE. A missile fired from a vehicle in flight against a target on the ground.

ANTIBALLISTIC MISSILE (ABM). A defensive missile fired to intercept an offensive ballistic missile at either an endoatmospheric or exoatmospheric level.

ANTISUBMARINE WARFARE (ASW). The type of "defensive" warfare whereby an attempt is made to combat the unique advantages of the submarine. There are five basic steps in antisubmarine warfare: (1) detection—the ability to determine that a submarine actually exists in the area under observation; (2) classification—the ability to identify friendly from hostile submarines, real from false targets like schools of fish, and types of hostile submarines; (3) localization—determining the accurate position of the detected hostile submarine; (4) attack—the use of weapons capable of reaching the submarine at varying depths; and (5) destruction—the actual ability to render the submarine inoperable. All five of these steps require a high degree of technical sophistication. At present, antisubmarine warfare capabilities lag behind the mobile offensive capabilities of submarines.

AREA TYPE OF DEFENSE. Defense systems that seek a capability to defend valued property over a fairly widespread geographical area.

ASSURED DESTRUCTION. The ability to inflict an "unacceptable" degree of damage upon an aggressor, even after absorbing his surprise first strike. The degree of unacceptable damage is a function, in part, of target selection, value preferences, and economic considerations. Mutual assured destruction is a condition in which this capability is possessed by opposing sides, resulting in deterrence by "mutual terror."

BALLISTIC MISSILE. A missile fired from land or sea sites against surface targets. Such a missile reaches, at the apex of its flight, an altitude out-

423

side of the earth's atmosphere before falling back toward its target under the influence of gravity.

BALLISTIC MISSILE DEFENSE (BMD). A system designed to destroy offensive ballistic missiles before they reach their targets. The system is composed of antiballistic missiles, radars, and control equipment.

BIPOLARITY. The model of the international system that is characterized by two opposed primary actors whose strength clearly outclasses that of the other participants in the system.

BUS. The portion of a multiple warhead missile containing the warhead packages and from which the individual packages are launched at their targets.

CATALYTIC WAR. Nuclear war between the superpowers triggered by the nuclear attack on one or the other by a third nuclear power.

CIRCULAR ERROR PROBABLE (CEP). The measure of accuracy of an offensive missile's warhead package against a target. CEP is the radius of a circle centered on the target within which 50 percent of the warheads can be expected to fall. The accuracy figure is usually given in nautical miles (NM) (one NM = 1.152 statute miles). A missile system with an accuracy of 0.5 NM CEP is therefore one that can be expected to deliver 50 percent of its warheads within a radius of one-half a nautical mile around the target.

CIVIL DEFENSE. See Passive defense.

COUNTERFORCE FIRST STRIKE. An initiatory attack aimed at an adversary's strategic weapons.

COUNTERFORCE WEAPONS. Weapons aimed at an opponent's strategic weapons—missiles or bombers—while they are still in prelaunch status.

COUNTERVALUE SECOND STRIKE. A retaliatory attack aimed at an opponent's cities or industries.

COUNTERVALUE WEAPONS. Weapons aimed at civilian targets. They are termed *countervalue* because their targets are the economic and human resources of the opponent state. (They are sometimes termed *counter-city weapons*.)

CRUISE MISSILE. A missile fired from sites on land or at sea against surface targets. Such a missile remains in the earth's atmosphere during its flight.

DAMAGE DENIAL. The capability of precluding any significant damage from an opponent's nuclear attack.

DAMAGE-LIMITING CAPABILITY. The ability to minimize the injury that a nuclear attack could cause within "acceptable" bounds, if deterrence were to fail.

DEPRESSED-TRAJECTORY MISSILE. A ballistic missile fired at a much lower angle than normal. Consequently, such a missile rises above the line-of-sight radar horizon at a later stage of flight, thus making detection and interception more difficult.

DETERRENCE. The strategy which seeks to persuade an opponent that in his own interest he should avoid certain courses of action, or in a nuclear sense that the costs and risks attendant to nuclear aggression clearly outweigh any calculable gains to be drawn from such aggression.

ENDOATMOSPHERIC DEFENSIVE MISSILE. A defensive missile designed to carry out interception of an offensive missile *after* the latter has *re-entered* the earth's atmosphere. The interception thus is designed to take place in the terminal phase of the offensive missile's flight.

EXOATMOSPHERIC DEFENSIVE MISSILE. A defensive missile designed to carry out interception of an offensive missile *while* the latter is still *outside* the earth's atmosphere. Interception is thus designed to take place during the mid-course phase of the offensive missile's flight.

FINITE DETERRENCE (FD). A deterrent strategy designed to create credibility by exclusive emphasis on countervalue targeting, that is, targets such as enemy cities.

FIRST STRIKE. The launching of an initial nuclear attack before the opponent attacked has used any strategic nuclear weapons himself.

FORWARD-BASED SYSTEMS (FBS). Aircraft and other capabilities that could strike the Soviet Union, at least in one-way missions, although such systems are designed primarily for missions in Western and Central Europe in support of NATO ground forces.

FRACTIONAL ORBITAL BOMBARDMENT SYSTEM (FOBS). A missile that achieves an orbited velocity but fires a set of retro-rockets before the completion of one revolution in order to slow down its re-entry system and to drop the warhead that it carries into a normal ballistic trajectory toward a target on the earth's surface.

HARDENING. The process by which land-based missiles or bombers are made less vulnerable to the blast effects of a nuclear attack through protective structures such as missile silos.

HARD-POINT DEFENSE. Defenses designed to protect ICBM sites or other key facilities that possess a relatively high degree of ability to withstand a high level of psi overpressure (also known as hard-site defense).

INERTIAL GUIDANCE SYSTEM. The basic guidance system for ballistic missiles consisting generally of an encased mechanism capable of detecting and correcting for deviation from planned trajectory and/or velocity.

INTERCONTINENTAL BALLISTIC MISSILE (ICBM). A ballistic missile launched from land with an approximate range of 4,000+ miles.

INTERMEDIATE-RANGE BALLISTIC MISSILE (IRBM). A ballistic missile launched from land with an approximate range of 1,500 to 3,000 miles.

INVULNERABILITY. The condition in which a nuclear force is protected from destruction by an enemy counterforce attack. Invulnerability is sought in several ways: (1) *dispersal,* whereby nuclear forces are positioned at multiple staging areas; (2) development of preattack *warning systems,* such as the U.S. Ballistic Missile Early Warning System (BMEWS); (3) development of *mobility* and *concealment* capabilities, the Polaris system being an example; and (4) *hardening.*

KILOTON (KT). The energy of a nuclear explosion that is equivalent to that produced by the explosion of 1,000 tons of TNT. The Hiroshima bomb had an approximate yield of 20 kilotons.

MEDIUM-RANGE BALLISTIC MISSILE (MRBM). A ballistic missile launched from land with an approximate maximum range of 1,500 miles.

MEGATON (MT). The energy of a nuclear explosion having a yield equivalent to one million tons of TNT. Equivalent of 1,000 kilotons.

MULTIPLE INDEPENDENTLY TARGETED RE-ENTRY VEHICLE (MIRV). A re-entry vehicle containing several warhead packages capable of wide separation and independent targeting. MIRV capability will be incorporated into Minuteman III and Poseidon missiles.

MULTIPLE RE-ENTRY VEHICLE (MRV). A re-entry vehicle containing several warhead packages of limited separation capability.

MULTIPOLARITY. The model of the international system in which several states exist whose individual power capabilities and/or potential, although not equal in all respects, are nevertheless comparable.

MUTUAL AND BALANCED FORCE REDUCTIONS (MBFR). Arms-control concepts for Europe that would provide for reduction in the military forces of NATO and the Warsaw Pact.

MUTUAL ASSURED DESTRUCTION. *See* Assured destruction.

NUCLEAR DELIVERY VEHICLE (NDV). The component of a delivery system designed to carry nuclear weapons to their target.

NUCLEAR NON-PROLIFERATION TREATY. Treaty negotiated by the United States and the Soviet Union and subsequently adhered to by many other states that seeks to inhibit the spread of nuclear weapons by requiring that signatory nonnuclear states agree not to acquire nuclear weapons and existing nuclear powers agree not to assist nonnuclear powers in acquiring such weapons.

NUCLEAR PROLIFERATION (NTH COUNTRY PROBLEM). Designation given to the problem of the possible spread of nuclear weapons to an indeterminate or "N" number of countries by national development of nuclear capability or procurement of nuclear weapons from existing nuclear powers.

OFFENSIVE MISSILE PHASES. An offensive missile can be postulated to go through three phases in its flight. The first is the *boost phase,* in which the missile is thrust upward from its launching pad by the rocket motors of the propulsion system. For an ICBM this phase lasts approximately from three to five minutes. The second phase is the *midcourse* one, which begins when the booster rockets have burned out.

The remainder of the missile continues upward without power until the force of gravity overcomes the impetus provided initially by the rocket motors. After reaching its zenith, the missile, reacting to the pull of the earth's gravitational field, begins to descend toward the target. The end of the mid-course phase occurs when the downward course of the missile approaches the upper limits of the earth's atmosphere. For an ICBM this mid-course phase lasts approximately twenty-five minutes. The last phase, the *terminal phase,* begins with the re-entry of the missile into the earth's atmosphere and ends with its impact on the target. In the case of the normal ICBM this phase lasts approximately one to two minutes.

PASSIVE DEFENSE. A defense against a nuclear strike whose objective is to gain the ability to absorb an attack by either removing the targets in question from offensive reach or protecting them against the effects of nuclear explosions. This latter objective usually involves the building of protective shelters, hardening, etc.

PASSIVE SENSOR. An information gathering and processing device that receives and identifies phenomena produced by an offensive missile itself. An example would be an infrared sensor capable of detecting and distinguishing the infrared radiation of a missile.

PAYLOAD. The weight that the rockets of a missile are required to lift. This includes both the weight of the booster stage of the missile and the re-entry vehicle with its warhead package.

PENETRATION AIDS (PEN-AIDS). Capabilities designed to neutralize the effect of ABM and to assure that a missile reaches its target.

POUNDS PER SQUARE INCH OVERPRESSURE (PSI). The measure commonly used to determine the capability of an object to withstand the pressure exerted by a nuclear blast. Current Minuteman silos in the United States are estimated to be hardened to approximately 300 PSI overpressure.

PREEMPTIVE STRIKE. A nuclear attack launched in anticipation of the opponent's decision to resort to nuclear war.

PREVENTIVE WAR. War initiated in order to forestall an opponent's acquisition of military preponderance.

RE-ENTRY SYSTEM (RES). Those parts of the missile, including the warhead, intended to fall back into the earth's atmosphere under the influence of gravity and to deliver the warhead to its target.

RE-ENTRY VEHICLE (REV). Each separate package of a multipackage re-entry system, designed to fall back through the atmosphere separately.

SECOND STRIKE. A missile attack launched in retaliation against an initial attack by an opponent.

SECOND-STRIKE FORCE. A force capable of extensive retaliation after absorbing an opponent's first strike.

SOFT FACILITIES. Missile sites, command and control centers, and other potential targets that have not been hardened to a degree sufficient to protect against the effects of nearby nuclear blasts.

STABLE STRATEGIC DETERRENCE. A situation in which both opposing nuclear powers have available weapons systems so numerous and diversified that neither side can hope to upset the balance either through war or through technological innovation.

STRATEGIC NUCLEAR FORCES. Those forces defined as having the capability of delivering nuclear weapons against countervalue or counterforce targets; also defensive forces designed to defend against such attacks. In the superpower context such forces are commonly thought to include those having intercontinental capabilities, such as long-range bombers, ICBMs, missile-launching submarines, and defenses built to counteract such offensive capabilities.

STRATEGIC NUCLEAR PARITY. A relationship between opposing nuclear military forces wherein such forces are roughly equal to one another in military capacity. Nuclear parity usually is measured in terms of megatonnage, numbers of launch vehicles, or deliverable nuclear warheads.

STRATEGIC NUCLEAR SUFFICIENCY. A term used by U.S. strategic security planners to denote a situation in which the United States possesses a nuclear capability able to: (1) maintain an adequate second-strike capability to deter an all-out surprise attack on U.S. strategic forces; (2) provide no incentive for the Soviet Union to strike the United States first in a crisis; and (3) prevent the Soviet Union from gaining the ability to cause considerably greater urban/industrial destruction than the United States could inflict on the USSR in a nuclear war.

STRATEGIC NUCLEAR SUPERIORITY. The possession by one power of a decided advantage in nuclear weaponry measured in terms of megatonnage, launch vehicles, and deliverable warheads. In addition to quantitative and qualitative factors, strategic superiority includes a psychological component. The impression by Power A that Power B has attained a condition of strategic superiority may confer on the latter a *political* advantage in its international relationships.

SUBMARINE-LAUNCHED BALLISTIC MISSILE (SLBM). A ballistic missile launched from an underwater-capable vehicle. The missile is capable of being fired while the vehicle is either on the surface or submerged.

SURFACE-TO-AIR MISSILE (SAM). A missile launched from the surface and designed to intercept a target in the air.

TERMINAL DEFENSE. The type of ballistic missile defense that seeks to intercept incoming missiles in the terminal phase of flight.

THEATER NUCLEAR FORCES. Those nuclear forces designated for use in a limited "battlefield" situation where conditions inhibit the use of weapons capable of causing extensive damage through actual nuclear explosion or fallout.

THROW WEIGHT. The weight of the re-entry vehicle with its warhead package. In contrast with payload, the weight of the booster stage of the missile is not included in the calculation of throw weight.

TRIAD. The term used in referring to the basic structure of the U.S. strategic deterrent force. It is comprised of land-based ICBMs, the Strategic Air Command (SAC) bomber force, and the Polaris/Poseidon submarine fleet.

UNDERSEA LONG-RANGE MISSILE SYSTEM (ULMS). The proposed successor to the U.S. Polaris submarine fleet. It will consist of submarines capable of extended periods at sea and requiring less time in port for overhaul. There will be an increase in on-board missiles in comparison to Polaris. (Current unclassified estimates are twenty-four as compared to sixteen on Polaris.) The expected range of the missile will be approximately 6,000 nautical miles, allowing the submarines, in their deterrent capacity, to be on station much closer to their home bases than is the case with Polaris. The missile is expected to have a sophisticated MIRV capability.

VARIABLE-RANGE BALLISTIC MISSILE (VRBM). Missiles located in the Soviet Union capable of intercontinental range but able to be targeted also on Western Europe.

WARHEAD. The explosive charge, nuclear or conventional, to be delivered by a missile.

YIELD. The force of a nuclear explosion expressed in terms of the number of tons of TNT that would have to be exploded to produce the same energy. The effects of the yield are caused by nuclear radiation, thermal radiation, blast, and shock. The extent of destruction is primarily a function of the medium in which the explosion takes place. The type of nuclear weapon and the time after detonation are also important factors in determining the extent of anticipated destruction.

Biographical Notes

Editors

WILLIAM R. KINTNER is Director of the Foreign Policy Research Institute, Philadelphia, and Professor of Political Science, University of Pennsylvania. For many years, he has concentrated on the analysis of American national security policy with special emphasis on the U.S.-Soviet strategic relationship. In addition, he has studied extensively the problems of deterrence and arms control, the evolution of NATO strategy and contemporary European security problems, the prospects for Western science and technology, and the role of the Third World in American national security policy. Dr. Kintner's books include *Atomic Weapons in Land Combat* (co-author, 1953), *Forging a New Sword* (co-author, 1958), *Protracted Conflict* (co-author, 1959), *The Haphazard Years* (co-author, 1960), *A Forward Strategy for America* (co-author, 1961), *Building the Atlantic World* (co-author, 1963), *Peace and the Strategy Conflict* (1967), *The Nuclear Revolution in Soviet Military Affairs* (co-author, 1969), and *Safeguard: Why the ABM Makes Sense* (editor and contributor, 1969). He is currently a member of several groups, some of which are the Council on Foreign Relations; the Civilian Faculty Advisory Committee of the National War College; the Board of Contributing Editors, *Freedom at Issue,* published by Freedom House; the International Institute for Strategic Studies, London; and the Board of Foreign Scholarship.

ROBERT L. PFALTZGRAFF, JR., is Deputy Director of the Foreign Policy Research Institute, Philadelphia, and Associate Professor of International Politics at The Fletcher School of Law and Diplomacy, Tufts University. Dr. Pfaltzgraff has long been interested in questions of international strategic affairs, U.S.-European technological relationships, West European regional integration, and the political, military, and technological problems of NATO. His books on these subjects include *Britain Faces Europe, 1957–1967* (1969); *Politics and the International System* (2nd ed., 1972); *The Atlantic Community: A Complex Imbalance* (1969); and *Contending Theories of International Relations* (co-author, 1971). Dr. Pfaltzgraff was instrumental in organizing both the Fourth and Fifth International Arms Control Symposia, and lectures frequently on issues of international security and arms control. He is currently a member of the Advisory Board on European Affairs, Department of State.

Contributors

ROBERT R. BOWIE is Director of the Center for International Affairs and Clarence Dillon Professor of International Affairs at Harvard University. He has served as Director of the Policy Planning Staff, Assistant Secretary of State for Policy Planning, and Counselor in the Department of State. Mr. Bowie's works include *Shaping the Future* (1963) and articles on international affairs, particularly on Atlantic relations and strategy.

J. I. COFFEY is Professor and Associate Dean of the Graduate School of Public and International Affairs at the University of Pittsburgh. Dr. Coffey is currently a consultant to the Arms Control and Disarmament Agency, the Department of Defense, and several research organizations. He is the author of *Strategic Power and National Security* (1971) as well as articles on arms control and disarmament.

JAMES E. DOUGHERTY is Executive Vice President and Professor of Politics and International Relations at Saint Joseph's College. He lectures frequently to governmental and other groups on arms control topics. Dr. Dougherty's works include *Arms Control for the Late Sixties* (co-editor, 1967), *Arms Control and Disarmament: The Critical Issues* (1966), and *Contending Theories of International Relations* (co-author, 1971). He has also contributed articles on international affairs to many leading journals.

WYNFRED JOSHUA is a Senior Political Scientist and Assistant Director at the Strategic Studies Center of the Stanford Research Institute, Washington, D.C. She specializes in NATO and Middle Eastern politico-military affairs. Dr. Joshua's works include *Soviet Penetration into the Middle East* (1971) and *Arms for the Third World: Soviet Military Aid Diplomacy* (co-author, 1969) as well as articles on many other topics.

GEOFFREY KEMP is Associate Professor of International Politics at The Fletcher School of Law and Diplomacy, Tufts University, and Research Associate at the Center for International Studies, The Massachusetts Institute of Technology. Dr. Kemp's works include *Arms and Security: The Egypt-Israel Case* (1969); *Arms Traffic and Third World Conflicts* (1970); "The International Arms Trade: Supplier, Recipient, and Arms Control Perspectives," *Political Quarterly* (October 1971); and "Dilemmas of the Arms Traffic," *Foreign Affairs* (January 1970).

TAKESHI MURAMATSU is Professor at Kyoto Industrial University, Tokyo, Japan. He has served as a correspondent on several Japanese newspapers, including *Mainichi, Yomiuri,* and *Sankei,* and as such has covered the Algerian War, the Six Days' War of June 1967, and the Suez conflict of 1956. Dr. Muramatsu's publications include books on de Gaulle, Paul Valery, and a history of the Jews.

GEORGE H. QUESTER is Associate Professor of Government and Director of the Program on Peace Studies at Cornell University. Dr. Quester has served as a Research Associate of the Center for International Affairs, Harvard University; a Consultant to The RAND Corporation; and Rapporteur for the Harvard–M.I.T. Arms Control Seminar. His works include *Deterrence Before Hiroshima* (1966), *Nuclear Diplomacy: The First Twenty-Five Years* (1970), and *Power, Action and Interaction: Readings on International Politics* (editor, 1971) in addition to numerous articles in leading journals.

W. W. ROSTOW is Professor of Economics at the University of Texas. He has held numerous positions in the U.S. government, including Deputy Special Assistant to the President for National Security Affairs in the Kennedy Administration and Special Assistant to the President for National Security Affairs from 1966 to 1969 in the Johnson Administration. Dr. Rostow's publications include *The United States in the World Arena* (1960), *The Stages of Economic Growth* (1960), *View from the Seventh Floor* (1964), *A Design for Asian Development* (1965), and *Politics and the Stages of Growth* (1971).

ROBERT A. SCALAPINO is Professor of Political Science at the University of California, Berkeley. He is also the Editor of *Asian Survey* and has written extensively on Japan, American-Far Eastern policy, and other topics dealing with Asian politics. Dr. Scalapino's works include *Parties and Politics in Contemporary Japan* (co-author, 1962); "Patterns of Asian Communism," *Problems of Communism* (1971); "The United States and Asia," in *U.S. Foreign Policy: Perspective and Proposals for the 1970s* (1969); and *Communism in Korea* (co-author, 1972).

IAN SMART is Assistant Director of the International Institute for Strategic Studies, a post which he has occupied since leaving the British Diplomatic Service in 1969. In addition to articles on the SALT and arms control, he has written two Adelphi papers: *Advanced Strategic Missiles: A Short Guide* (1969) and *Future Conditional: The Prospect for Anglo-French Nuclear Co-operation* (1971).

WILLIAM R. VAN CLEAVE is Associate Professor for Strategic and Defense Studies at the University of Southern California. On leave of absence from the university from 1969 to 1971, he served as Special Assistant, Office of the Assistant Secretary of Defense (ISA), and as an advisor on the U.S. delegation to the SALT. His articles have appeared in several journals. Dr. Van Cleave is currently a consultant to The RAND Corporation, the Stanford Research Institute, and several governmental agencies.

THOMAS W. WOLFE is Senior Staff Member of The RAND Corporation and a member of the faculty of the Institute for Sino-Soviet Studies, The George Washington University. Among his works are *Soviet Strategy at the Crossroads* (1964) and *Soviet Power and Europe: 1945–1970* (1970). Dr. Wolfe's career includes service as Air Attaché at the U.S. Embassy in Moscow and participation in arms control negotiations with the Soviet Union.

Discussants

BENSON D. ADAMS is a Staff Associate in the Bureau of Politico-Military Affairs, Department of State. He is also currently an Assistant Professorial Lecturer in Political Science at The George Washington University. Dr. Adams is the author of *Ballistic Missile Defense* (1971).

HAROLD M. AGNEW is Director of the Los Alamos Scientific Laboratory, University of California. He is also a member of the U.S. Army Scientific Advisory Panel, of which he was formerly Panel Chairman. Dr. Agnew has been a member of the U.S. Air Force Scientific Advisory Board, the Defense Science Board, and several Presidential Scientific Advisory Committee Panels. He received the Atomic Energy Commission's E. O. Lawrence Award for his contributions in nuclear weapons design and command and control.

WILLIAM BEECHER is the military correspondent for the *New York Times,* assigned to its Washington Bureau. A graduate of Harvard and Columbia Universities, he has written extensively on the strategic balance in the *Times* and in various military journals.

LINCOLN P. BLOOMFIELD is Professor of Political Science at The Massachusetts Institute of Technology and Co-Director of the European Security Project at the Center for International Studies. Dr. Bloomfield has served on the Presidential Commission on the United Nations and is currently a consultant to the Department of State and the U.S. Arms Control and Disarmament Agency. He is the author of *Controlling Small Wars: A Strategy for the Seventies* (co-author, 1969), *The Power to Keep Peace* (1971), and other works.

DONALD G. BRENNAN is a Staff Member and Past President of the Hudson Institute. A consultant to several research organizations and government agencies, Dr. Brennan is the editor of *Arms Control, Disarmament and National Security* (1961) and has contributed to numerous books and journals dealing with arms control and other aspects of national security.

SAMUEL T. COHEN is a Senior Staff Member of The RAND Corporation. He has written several articles on nuclear weapons, including "Tactical Nuclear Weapons and U.S. Military Strategy," which appeared in *Orbis* (Spring 1971). Mr. Cohen is currently a consultant to the Office of the Secretary of Defense and to the Los Alamos Scientific Laboratory, University of California.

WALDO H. DUBBERSTEIN is Director of International Studies at the American Enterprise Institute for Public Policy Research, Washington, D.C. Dr. Dubberstein has served as Visiting Professor of International Affairs at the National War College and is currently a consultant to the Center for International Business, Los Angeles, and to several government agencies.

RICHARD B. FOSTER is the founder and Director of the Strategic Studies Center at the Stanford Research Institute, Washington, D.C. His professional works include studies on the U.S. and Soviet ABM and ICBM programs and on U.S. security interests. He is the author of "The SAFEGUARD Ballistic Missile Defense Proposal and Arms Control Prospects for the 1970's," in *SAFEGUARD: Why the ABM Makes Sense* (1969).

MARC GENESTE, a retired French Army Colonel, is currently associated with the French Atomic Energy Commission. He has served on the faculty of the Ecole Supérieure de Guerre, Paris, and the U.S. Army Command and General Staff College, Leavenworth, Kansas. M. Geneste has contributed to *Modern Guerrilla Warfare* (1962) and *Arms Control for the Late Sixties* (1967) as well as to leading military and strategic journals in Europe and the United States.

WILLIAM E. GRIFFITH is Professor of Political Science and Director of the research project on communism, revisionism, and revolution at the Center for International Studies, The Massachusetts Institute of Technology. He is also currently Adjunct Professor of Soviet Diplomacy at The Fletcher School of Law and Diplomacy, Tufts University. Dr. Griffith is the author of several books on Sino-Soviet relations, including *Albania and the Sino-Soviet Rift* (1963) and *Cold War and Coexistence: Russia, China and the United States* (1971), in addition to numerous articles in the field of Communist affairs.

EDMUND A. GULLION has been Dean of The Fletcher School of Law and Diplomacy, Tufts University, since 1964, when he retired from the Foreign Service. Mr. Gullion's twenty-seven-year foreign service career included assignments in Marseilles, London, Algiers, Helsinki, Stockholm, Salonika, and Saigon. His last post was from August 1961 to February 1964, when he served as Ambassador to the Republic of the Congo (Leopoldville). He writes and speaks extensively on such subjects as the U.S. aid program, the formation of U.S. foreign policy, and U.S. diplomacy.

PIERRE HASSNER is Senior Research Associate at the Centre d'Etudes des Relations Internationales of the Fondation Nationale des Sciences Politiques, Paris, and Professor of Politics at The Johns Hopkins University European Center, Bologna. M. Hassner is co-author of *Europe and the Superpowers* (1971) and has contributed articles to many prominent journals in Europe and the United States.

MORTON A. KAPLAN is Chairman of the Committee on International Relations and Professor of Political Science at the University of Chicago. He has been a consultant to the Hudson Institute, a staff member of The Brookings Institution, and a lecturer at the Army War College. Dr. Kaplan's many works include *Macropolitics: Essays on the Philosophy and Science of Politics* (1968), *New Approaches to International Relations* (editor, 1968), *Dissent and the State in Peace and War* (1970), and *On Historical and Political Knowing* (1971).

AMROM KATZ is a consultant to several U.S. government agencies, to industry, and to several research institutions. Mr. Katz's career has included fifteen years with the Air Force's reconnaissance laboratory and sixteen years as a member of the Senior Staff of The RAND Corporation. He is the author of numerous papers on astronautics, observation satellites, inspection, disarmament, arms control, reconnaissance, strategy, and counterinsurgency.

EVGENY G. KUTOVOJ is Special Assistant to the Under Secretary General and Chief of the Unit for Coordination, Office of the Under Secretary General, Office of Political and Security Council Affairs, in the United Nations Secretariat.

CHARLES BURTON MARSHALL is Professor of International Politics at the School of Advanced International Studies, The Johns Hopkins University, and Research Associate of the Washington Center of Foreign Policy Research. He is the author of *The Limits of Foreign Policy* (1954, enlarged edition, 1968), *The Exercise of Sovereignty* (1965), *The Cold War: A Concise History* (1966), and *Crisis Over Rhodesia: A Skeptical View* (1967).

ANDREW J. PIERRE is a Research Fellow at the Council on Foreign Relations. Formerly a staff member of The Brookings Institution and the Hudson Institute, he has also taught at Columbia University. From 1962 to 1964 he served as a Foreign Service Officer, first in Washington and later at the American Embassy in London. Dr. Pierre is the author of *Nuclear Politics: The British Experience with an Independent Strategic Force, 1939–1970* (1972) and numerous articles in leading journals.

URI RA'ANAN is Professor of International Politics at The Fletcher School of Law and Diplomacy, Tufts University; an Affiliate of the Center of International Studies, The Massachusetts Institute of Technology; and an Associate of the Russian Research Center, Harvard University. He has taught courses in political science and government at The Massachusetts Institute of Technology, Columbia University, and the City University of New York. Professor Ra'anan is the author of *The USSR Arms the Third World: Case Studies in Soviet Foreign Policy* (1969), *Politics of the Coup D'etat: Five Case Studies* (co-author, 1969), and many other works.

GEORGE W. RATHJENS is Professor of Political Science at The Massachusetts Institute of Technology. He has held several positions in the U.S. government, including Deputy Director, Advanced Research Projects Agency, U.S. Department of Defense, and Special Assistant to the Director, U.S. Arms Control and Disarmament Agency. Dr. Rathjens is the author of *The Future of the Strategic Arms Race: Options for the 1970's* (1969) and "The Dynamics of the Arms Race," *Scientific American* (April 1969), and has contributed to several volumes, including *American Militarism 1970* (1969) and *Nuclear Proliferation: Prospects for Control* (1970).

ROBERT C. RICHARDSON III is President of the Encabulator Corporation and a Washington policy consultant. A retired Brigadier General in the U.S. Air Force, General Richardson writes and lectures frequently on issues related to NATO, defense policy, and technology.

SEYMOUR WEISS is a Senior Member of the Secretary of State's Planning and Coordination Staff, and as such he specializes in politico-military affairs, including the SALT negotiations.

YUAN-LI WU is Professor of Economics at the University of San Francisco and a consultant to both the Hoover Institution on War, Revolution, and Peace and the Stanford Research Institute. Dr. Wu is the author of *Economy of Communist China: An Introduction* (1966), *As Peking Sees Us: People's War in the United States and Communist China's American Policy* (1969), and *Organization and Support of Scientific Research and Development in Mainland China* (co-author, 1970), and the editor of *People's Republic of China: A Handbook* (1971).

Index

Action-reaction syndrome: in Soviet-American relationships, 103, 138

Adams, Benson: on technological considerations of SALT, 107, 108

Agnew, Harold: on implications of technological dynamism for SALT, 118

Agreement to Reduce the Risk of Accidental Outbreak of Nuclear War, 342

Airborne Warning and Control System (AWACS), 80–81

Alekseyev, Colonel General N. N.: as part of Soviet SALT delegation, 36

Antiballistic missile (ABM), xxiii, 83–85, 98, 100, 122, 124, 130, 133, 135–36, 208–09, 211–14, 222–25, 230–31, 254, 256, 268–69, 271, 300, 305, 317, 320, 323, 325, 327, 354, 356–58, 373, 386, 390, 393, 395–97, 399, 401–03; as perceived by aerospace industry, 82–83; American proposal for limitation of, 87; as limited by SALT, 157. See also Galosh; Safeguard

Antiballistic Treaty, 385–86, 396, 403

Antisubmarine warfare (ASW): developments in, xxiii, 114–16, 206, 209, 212–13, 218, 230–31, 323; Soviet capability as threat to Western European, 202; European force, 221, 228; Soviet force, 210

Arab-Israeli conflict: impact of, on proliferation, 245, 246–47, 248, 253. See also Middle East

Arbatov, G. A.: influence of, on Kosygin's policy, 32; role of, in Soviet policy, 32, 324, 325

Arms control, 19n3, 63, 97, 116, 160, 255, 316, 324, 325, 326; strategic rationale for, 3–5; Soviet interests in, 3–18, 21–54, 61; U.S. rationale for, 3–18, 64–70; technological considerations of, 4–5, 17; as means to reduce chance of accidental war, 7; used to prevent dissemination to allies, 8; used by superpowers to prevent third parties from acquisition, 8; in multipolar world, 9; Soviet proposal for five-power negotiations, 10; creates environment conducive to broader negotiations, 13; political rationale for, 13–14; economic rationale for, 14–17; Soviet economic consideration, 15; as affected by nature of international system, 18; Soviets perceive U.S. weary of nuclear race, 42; to allay mutual destructiveness of nuclear weapons, 42; U.S. interests in, 55–94; qualitative limitations on, 79, 319, 325; dynamism of, 89; within context of international system, 96; U.S. favors, 102; Chinese initiative and, 190; Chinese pledge no first-use, 190; requirement of regional approaches for, 190–91; theory of, 381. See also Disarmament; Strategic arms limitation talks

Arms control agreements, 128, 351, 375; as limiting the linkage between strategic deterrent and defense of allies, 11; impact of, on international system, 11; effects of, on Europe, 12; Chinese interest in, 12; as link to solution of other political problems, 14, 16, 18; U.S. considerations for, 15; Soviet considerations for, 16–17; advocated in U.S., 17; implications of, for international system, 18; in Soviet political system, 192

Arms control negotiations, 161–62,

439